THE CRAFT APPRENTICE

The Craft Apprentice

FROM FRANKLIN TO THE MACHINE AGE IN AMERICA

W. J. Rorabaugh

OXFORD UNIVERSITY PRESS
New York   Oxford

Oxford University Press

Oxford   New York   Toronto
Delhi   Bombay   Calcutta   Madras   Karachi
Petaling Jaya   Singapore   Hong Kong   Tokyo
Nairobi   Dar es Salaam   Cape Town
Melbourne   Auckland

and associated companies in
Beirut   Berlin   Ibadan   Nicosia

Library of Congress Cataloging in Publication Data
Rorabaugh, W. J.
The craft apprentice.
Includes index.
1. Apprentices—United States—History.
2. United States—Social life and customs—1783–1865.
I. Title.   HD4885.U5R67   1986   331.5'5'0973   85-8779
ISBN 0-19-503647-6
ISBN 0-19-50189-0 (PPBK.)

4   6   8   10   9   7   5
Printed in the United States of America

For Charles Sellers,
my brother Jim,
and the two Marys

❧ PREFACE ❧

This book tells what it was like to be a craft apprentice in America before, during, and after the early Industrial Revolution. The story begins in colonial America, when apprenticeship served several important functions. It was a system of education and job training by which important practical information was passed from one generation to the next; it was a mechanism by which youths could model themselves on socially approved adults; it was an institution devised to insure proper moral development through the master's fatherly responsibility for the behavior of his apprentice; and it was a means of social control imposed upon potentially disruptive male adolescents. Like other institutions with multiple functions, it often failed to meet all of its objectives and frequently expressed conflicts among its multiple purposes in internal contradiction rather than in external conflict with other institutions. In that sense apprenticeship was complex, diverse, and amorphous. These qualities explain both why it is difficult to understand apprenticeship in all its subtlety and why it survived as an institution for many generations. In its many functions, some boldly stated and some, even now, hidden from view, it provided a safe passage from childhood to adulthood in psychological, social, and economic ways for a large number of people over a long period of time.

Eventually, however, apprenticeship entered a period of decline. From the Revolution to the Civil War, amid the growth of cities, factories, and immigration, the craft apprentice gradually disappeared. Like a glacier, the institution receded year by year, imperceptibly at first and more rapidly later. It first lost its traditional economic and social functions, then for a time remained an empty facade caricaturing its former self, and by 1865 was, except for odd semisurvivals, moribund. This book tells the story both of that transformation and of how American youths who participated in this declining institution behaved, thought, felt, and responded along the way. To consider significant regional variations, the entire country has been surveyed; to consider how the emerging money economy, market system, and Industrial Revolution affected apprentices differently situated, the period from the Revolution to the Civil War has been examined; and to compare and contrast the impact of changing economic conditions upon different crafts at different times, all skilled crafts have been included. When I began, it was my hope to be able to say something about apprentices of both sexes, but I quickly learned that apprenticeship was a male institution. Occasionally, a woman practiced a craft that she had learned from her husband or father, but in all the first-person accounts I read and documents I examined, I never encountered a female craft apprentice. Poor girls were "apprenticed" to housewifery or sewing, but that sort of apprenticeship provided only legal guardianship and training in traditional female work rather than the learning of a craft.[1]

This study draws heavily upon personal accounts—particularly the diaries, letters, and autobiographies of apprentices. Through these accounts apprentices have told their own stories, which give a flavor of apprenticeship that can be derived only from the words of participants and which also enable the reader to ponder these words. These biographical materials reveal a wide range of attitudes, beliefs, and behaviors both in and out of the workplace. It is the complexity of these experiences that is perhaps most important, for it warns against the historian's tendency to arrange the variety of human experiences into neat and ultimately false stereotypical categories. This use of literary sources goes against the grain of much recent social history, which has focused on cold, objective data. Unfortunately, in many cases the data have been so limited as to reveal little that was new about average people and almost nothing about their thoughts or feelings. Even when statistical information is combined with occasional first-person accounts, the paucity of such accounts for a particular locale makes it difficult for the historian who focuses on one community to find enough accounts to express richness or diversity— much less offer historical explanation of thoughts or feelings. This study has been able to overcome that problem by using many accounts covering numerous crafts, all sections of the country, and an extended period of time.

Some will worry that this extant material is not representative, to which I reply: it is the only material we have for ascertaining the thoughts and feelings of apprentices, and a careful examination of the social backgrounds of the authors shows that they were little different from those of other apprentices. It is true that the Northeast, Quakers, and the craft of printing are overrepresented—indeed, not a single illiterate apprentice left behind an account. But this problem should not be exaggerated. Although printing attracted boys who had some fascination for the written word, such apprentices came from the same sorts of backgrounds as other apprentices and entered a craft that stood socially and economically on a par with or only modestly above other crafts. The descriptions of family

backgrounds in the first-person accounts are similar to the statistical find-
ings in the many excellent social-mobility studies, and an examination of
the 1850 manuscript census for those apprentices who left behind records
shows that their situations were, almost without exception, similar to
those of other artisan youths in the same census. In only one respect are
the apprentices who left behind first-person accounts truly different. Many
were unusually talented and subsequently became famous. But, as their
accounts make clear, when they were apprentices, they were far more like
their youthful fellows than like the famous men they became. Furthermore, we have to learn what we can, where we can. An articulate Sam
Clemens is more revealing of the apprentice state of mind than the apprentice tanner whose diary merely noted "work" after each daily entry.
That sort of diary may be more typical, but it is far less useful. I do not,
of course, suggest that this book was written only from apprentices' accounts, and in addition to a wide variety of primary sources that I consulted, I am grateful for the numerous excellent secondary studies that
have provided valuable statistics and insights.[2]

My original plan for investigating apprentices was somewhat different.
Since apprentices were supposed to be bound to masters with indentures,
I expected to compile data from lists of indented apprentices. Two fine
studies of colonial Boston and Philadelphia, by Lawrence Towner and
Ian Quimby respectively, showed how local indenture records could be
used to study apprenticeship. David Ruddel's study of nineteenth-century
Quebec City offered interesting comparisons from French Canada. These
three studies depended upon scrupulous records, and, alas, except for
French Canada, there were no such records in the nineteenth century.
The common law did not require registration of indentures, few localities
or states ever required registration, and those that had such requirements
did not enforce them. In addition, as the firsthand accounts make clear,
the decline of apprenticeship was accompanied by a growing proportion
of youths who served informally rather than being indented. While this
dwindling proportion of indentures would make registation lists useless,
even if we had a usable list, it would yield only a few statistics and reveal
nothing about the apprentices' states of mind.[3]

The rich variety exhibited in the first-person accounts present a dilemma for the historian, who seeks to extrapolate a cohesive story of a
group from the particular experiences of individuals. It is the tension
between the particular and the general that gives history its ever changing
shape. The particulars never change, but how they are arranged to form
new general patterns does change. The present study can be summarized
as simply the chronicling of the long-term decline of apprenticeship under
the onslaught of the Industrial Revolution. But to summarize such long-

term historical forces in such a simple way is to miss the rich variety of experiences that individuals had along the way. For some people, personal experience was nothing more than a microcosm of the larger, general picture; for others, personal experience went in a contrary, opposite direction. Still others had experiences that neither fitted nor defied any pattern yet described. Taken together, the first-person accounts remind us how varied life is and how every generalization must be narrowed, qualified, and made subject to exception. To suggest that conclusion is somewhat heretical, since it calls into question the essence of history: the sense of certainty, the identification of mainline trends and themes. But here is a truth that explains why most history is not art, and why all art transcends the mere telling of history. In this work I do not always analyze but sometimes leave the material for the contemplation of the reader, who may find in it new meanings both of the apprentices' experiences and of the generalizing tendencies.

The apparent shapelessness of much of the material does not represent an unwillingness on my part to impose my own ordered structure upon the material; rather, it shows a firm conviction on my part that the truth about these apprentices is best served by presenting their stories in as holistic a fashion as possible, with little interruption for historical hindsight and without shredding the evidence into documentation for my own preconceived notions. I want, more than anything else, to convey what it was like to be an apprentice, how that experience felt, the way it was shaped, and how over time the nature of the experience changed. But I also want to show that each apprentice had a different experience and that what was happening to the institution of apprenticeship as a whole often had little to do with a particular individual's experience. I have not, of course, given the entire range of apprentice experience; to do so would have required the replication of the entirety of history. Rather, I have sampled the range of apprentice experience so that the reader can sense the degree of variation from what might be termed the mainline trend of decline. It is in the subtlety of variation that the essence of history lies. A rose may be only a rose, but the gardener knows the traits that separate one variety from another. So it is with these experiences. In the aggregate they often look alike, but a careful reading will reveal the subtle changes that were taking place over several generations in the way young Americans worked, played, learned, thought, and felt. While there are many ways to measure such changes, we can sometimes gain more simply by stepping back, pausing a bit, and pondering. The apprentices, through their first-hand accounts, have enabled us to do just that.

I am grateful to many people and organizations for supporting this study. Research began with successive summer grants from the Newberry

Library, Chicago, and the Henry E. Huntington Library, San Marino, California. The bulk of archival research was undertaken with a six-month fellowship from the National Endowment for the Humanities. In my travels I learned much from many archivists, including Diane Frese at the Maryland Hall of Records, Betty-Bright Low at the Hagley Museum and Library, Peter Parker at the Historical Society of Pennsylvania, Stone Miller at Louisiana State University, and the exceptionally able staffs at the Massachusetts Historical Society and at the American Antiquarian Society. Part of the manuscript was written with a summer grant from the University of Washington Graduate School Research Fund, and its completion was hastened by a year's fellowship at the National Humanities Center, Research Triangle Park, North Carolina. The Center's secretaries typed much of one draft, Alan Tuttle and Rebecca Sutton cheerfully handled numerous library requests, and Wayne Pend never ceased asking provocative and probing questions. In addition, several scholars read part or all of the manuscript or heard ideas presented over lunch. I would like to thank particularly Shaul Bakhash, T. H. Breen, Vincent Carretta, Jack and Jane Censer, A. W. Coats, Robert Hill, Kurt and Gladys Lang, Anthony LaVopa, John Seelye, Stephen Vincent, Harry Watson, and Harold Woodman.

Early on I benefited from correspondence with Stanley Engerman, Sean Wilentz, and Alfred Young as well as from conversations with David Brion Davis, Gary Kornblith, Jonathan Prude, Ian Quimby, and John Rumm. More recently the manuscript was read in whole or in part by Joseph Corn, William Gienapp, Elizabeth Rosenfield, Carlos Schwantes, Charles Sellers, William Youngs, and the University of Washington History Research Group. I am particularly grateful to Richard R. Johnson, Otis Pease, and Charles Royster, whose contributions to this project are numerous and varied, stretching over many years. Also helpful were Karen Blair, Jeffry and Barbara Diefendorf, Lee and Cheryle Drago, Robert Glen, Keith Howard, Anthony Martin, Mark Nackman, Steven and Sheila Novak, Martin Ridge, Michael and Lisa Shapiro, Thelma Valenstein, Roy and Wendy Weatherup, Hugh and Rosalie West, Kent Wood and Terri Lukas, and all the Rorabaughs. For permission to quote manuscripts I thank the American Antiquarian Society; the American Philosophical Society; Columbia University; the Connecticut Historical Society; East Carolina University; Emory University; the Hagley Museum and Library; the Historical Society of Delaware; the Historical Society of Pennsylvania; Louisiana State University; the Maryland Historical Society; the Massachusetts Historical Society; the New Hampshire Historical Society; the New-York Historical Society; the Rhode Island Historical Society; the Southern Historical Collection, University of North

Carolina, Chapel Hill; Tulane University; University of Illinois Archives; and the Virginia Historical Society. Finally, I am grateful to Sheldon Meyer, Otto Sonntag, Leona Capeless, and everyone at Oxford University Press.

W.J.R.

Seattle
February 22, 1985

✍ CONTENTS ✍

PREFACE, vii

PROLOGUE: *Benjamin Franklin's Legacy,* 3

CHAPTER ONE *Chaos,* 16

CHAPTER TWO *The Master's Authority,* 32

CHAPTER THREE *A Cash Wage,* 57

CHAPTER FOUR *The Crisis in Printing,* 76

CHAPTER FIVE *Personal Relations,* 97

CHAPTER SIX *The Limits of Reform,* 113

CHAPTER SEVEN *The Machine Age,* 131

CHAPTER EIGHT *A Way Out?,* 157

CHAPTER NINE *Lingering Traditions,* 176

EPILOGUE: *Civil War,* 198

STATISTICAL APPENDIX, 211

NOTES, 213

INDEX, 255

THE CRAFT APPRENTICE

Benjamin Franklin's Legacy

The most famous American apprentice was Benjamin Franklin. Born in 1706 in Boston, he was the son of Josiah Franklin, a poor candle- and soapmaker. The boy grew up surrounded by a large family, an enduring Puritan tradition, and the ships and sailors of a seaport. Because Ben was a precocious reader, his father decided to make a minister of him, and at eight the boy was sent to a grammar school. But Ben's father was not prosperous, the family was large, and after a year or so Josiah concluded that it would be too expensive to fit Ben for college. So Ben was withdrawn from the grammar school and sent to a practical school that stressed writing and arithmetic, skills more appropriate for an artisan than Latin or Greek. At ten Ben left school to return home to learn his father's trade of candle- and soapmaking, but he did not find it a very agreeable trade, and he expressed a desire to go to sea. This desire of Ben's chagrined Josiah Franklin, who quickly resolved to apprentice him to some other trade. Ben's father followed the common practice, for in colonial America a boy of twelve or fourteen began to learn how to make a living either from his father or through an apprenticeship to a master craftsman. Practically everyone followed this pattern except the rich, who sometimes educated their sons to be gentlemen of leisure, and the poor, who had no trades to teach their sons. Even a poor boy, however, sometimes managed to learn a trade through an apprenticeship. Among the middling majority the son of a farmer naturally became a farmer, and the son of a craftsman often followed his father's trade. But a craftsman with several sons might not be able to teach them all, or, as in Ben's case, a son might be disinclined toward his father's trade, and thus many sons of craftsmen were apprenticed to masters in other trades.[1]

When Ben was twelve, his father took him around Boston, which then had about 12,000 people, and showed him various artisans at work. It was a common way for a boy to pick a trade and a master. While exploring the town with his father, Ben had time to muse on the ancient nature of the institution of apprenticeship. Since the Middle Ages apprenticeship had been a traditional phase in the life cycle, and it was widely sanctioned by both custom and law. Under the English Statute of Artificers (1563), parents, unless they could demonstrate the means to educate their sons for business or the professions, were required to bind them either to a trade or to agriculture. Apprentices were to serve seven years, with a term for males that ended sometime between twenty-one and twenty-four. The seven-year term, considerably longer than the three- to five-year apprenticeships that prevailed in Germany and France, was designed to ensure English supremacy in handmade manufactures and to discourage the wandering and strolling that had characterized earlier periods of English life. Another important English statute was the Poor Law (1601), which required local authorities to bind children whose parents were unable or unwilling to apprentice their children. While both the Statute of Artificers and the Poor Law applied to the American colonies, local conditions discouraged enforcement, with the result that colonial apprenticeship was considerably less vigorous than its English counterpart.

In England the statutes regulating apprenticeship were enforced by craftsmen through their guilds. In the Middle Ages artisans of each craft had organized guilds composed of both masters and journeymen to protect the interests of all members of the craft. Since the Statute of Artificers prohibited the practice of numerous trades without completion of an apprenticeship, and since each guild controlled the admission of apprentices, this combination created a closed labor market that kept craft wages high. At the same time, guilds enjoyed the power of discipline over both apprentices and masters. The quality of work was monitored, and the quality of apprentice training was controlled. Before an English apprentice could be admitted formally to guild membership as a journeyman, he had to produce a masterpiece, that is, a work in the trade worthy of a master craftsman.[2]

Like so many other English institutions, guilds failed to develop in the American colonies. Vast distances, shortages of skilled labor, a largely agricultural population, and a poorly developed legal system all contributed to this result. Since the American colonies had no guilds, the interlocking regulatory system that prevailed in England really did not exist in the colonies. In America anyone could call himself a master artisan, and any such artisan could take an apprentice. If he took an apprentice, and if the apprentice was legally bound, then English law governed the terms. But there was no guild to guarantee that the apprentice was trained in the trade, the apprentice produced no masterpiece, and the journeyman had no guild to join. One consequence was shoddy workmanship. "All my clothes are miserably spoiled by the Bunglars here," complained Savannah's James Habersham, who took to having his clothes imported from London. Furthermore, since there were no guilds, there was no restriction on the number of apprentices a master could take, and American masters took as many apprentices as they pleased. There was one other important difference. If an English apprentice ran away from his master, guild jurisdiction was so strong that the runaway would probably find it impossible to take up the trade anywhere in the country. But in the American colonies a clever and knowledgeable boy, like Benjamin Franklin, could simply move to a different colony and pass himself as a journeyman. Legal penalties for running away did not extend beyond the boundaries of a particular colony, and a high demand for skilled labor gave the runaway a good chance of being hired.[3]

Even before Ben went on the tour of Boston with his father, the boy must have noticed that not all Bostonians were of equal status. Indeed, there existed a distinct socioeconomic hierarchy. Women and children, by both custom and law, derived their status from the adult males to whom they were attached by blood or marriage. At the bottom of the hierarchy were slaves, indentured servants, hired servants, apprentices, and unskilled laborers. These workers were paid either in kind, receiving only clothes, room, and board, or such low wages that, combined with the sporadic nature of unskilled labor, they always hovered on the edge of poverty. In this group only apprentices had any expectation of improving their lot after they had learned their trades. In towns like Boston, artisans, mostly self-employed, constituted the middle ranks of society. Above the artisans were a small number of doctors, lawyers, ministers, teachers, and government officials, who enjoyed high prestige even when incomes sometimes fell below that of some artisans. At the top were the wealthy merchants, who controlled the economy and also exercised a great deal of political authority. In Boston, as in the other seaports, wealth was distributed quite unevenly: the bottom half owned virtually no real estate, and the wealthiest tenth owned perhaps two-fifths of all the property. During Ben's boyhood the percentage of Bostonians who owned real estate was declining, inequality in the distribution of wealth was increasing, the local economy was stagnant, and real wages of artisans were falling—perhaps cut in half in the generation after 1712. Although Ben did not realize it at the time, there were better opportunities in New York and, especially, in Philadelphia, which was then in the midst of a major economic boom. Nevertheless, even in these more prosperous seaports wealth was becoming more concentrated, and many artisans found themselves in declining circumstances.[4]

Ben also knew that not all craftsmen were equal. At the bottom were such trades as tailoring, shoemaking, and his father's craft of candle-making, in the middle were trades like blacksmithing and carpentry, and at the top elite trades such as silversmithing. These rankings, based on a calculation of a particular craft's earning power, were in turn based on the ease or difficulty of becoming a master craftsman. An apprentice tailor, for example, did not need to be either literate or muscular to learn the craft. The skills of that trade were readily passed from master to apprentice, and when the apprentice had finished his training, it was easy for him to open a shop. All he needed was a needle, some thread, and a tape measure. Shoemakers were only slightly higher in the craft hierarchy. Although modest capital requirements did force men to work for wages as journeymen in order to save money to acquire tools, eventually they became masters, and since there were so many master shoemakers, the rewards for making shoes were necessarily low. It is not surprising that Ben showed no inclination to become either a tailor or a shoemaker. Carpentry was somewhat more skilled, dangerous, and seasonal, with high wages and sporadic employment. Opportunities were offset by risks. Compared to carpenters, master blacksmiths did about as well in income and faced less risk. That craft required great strength, and since few had the capacity, those who did could command more for their labor. Ben did not have the build of a blacksmith. At the top of the craft hierarchy were silversmiths. They had to be careful workmen, and it helped to have a sense of fashion and taste. But the most important barriers to entry into this craft were fine tools and expensive raw materials. Silversmiths did little rough work, took few apprentices, and profited from lack of competition. It is not likely that Ben's father would have been able to place his son in a silversmith's shop.[5]

In any event Ben was placed with a cutler, his cousin Samuel Franklin. Placing an apprentice with a master who was related was a well-established custom that reinforced the parental nature of apprenticeship. It was expected that an apprentice would be bound formally by contract, but it was customary to have a trial period of up to six months to see whether the boy and the master got along. After a few days' trial in Samuel's shop Josiah and Samuel quarreled over whether Ben's father would have to pay a fee for this apprenticeship, and Ben was taken home. At that time in England a fee was customary, but in America there was no fee except for apprenticeship in high-status crafts or the professions. Ben's love of books led his father to decide to make a printer of him, although Josiah hesitated for a time because an older son, James, had already learned that trade. Artisans preferred to apprentice their sons to different trades to increase the possibility of family barter and to decrease family hardship should a particular trade succumb to hard times. Josiah also may have worried that he would be unable to assist Ben in setting up as a master printer upon completion of his apprenticeship. Printing was nearly as elite a trade as silversmithing, and it required a relatively large amount of capital to buy a press and types in order to open a shop. Still, the craft was lucrative. A growing population and increased literacy, as well as increased commerce and political controversy, gave the colonial printer a growing market.[6]

Ben's older brother James was one of the few printers in Boston. Born in 1696, he had set up in Boston in 1717 with a press and types obtained on a trip to England. Although Ben thought he would like printing better than candlemaking, he still talked of going to sea, and finally his father insisted that Ben, although only twelve, sign indentures binding himself as an apprentice to his brother. The documents were called indentures because of their indented edges. The agreement was written in duplicate on a single sheet of paper, each part was signed and witnessed, and then the sheet was torn into copies to be retained by each party to the agreement. The master got one copy, and the apprentice's parents or guardian got the other. If either party became dissatisfied, the issue could be settled by taking the indentures into court. Because the matching indentations on the two copies proved each to be genuine and thus protected against fraud, apprenticeships in England and the American colonies, except for those involving orphans, were generally not recorded with any government authority. In rural areas a small fee was sometimes paid to register the agreement with a justice of the peace or other local official, but such registration was not common. Only in the large seaports of Boston, New York, and Philadelphia did local officials copy indentures into a record book. That precaution discouraged an unscrupulous master from luring an apprentice from a lawful master, and it made it impossible for a runaway to get work as a journeyman in his hometown. But such limited local registration did not prevent apprentices from moving from one locale to another. When the apprenticeship was finished, or if both parties mutually agreed to void the agreement, the indentures were canceled by an exchange of copies, by a destruction of both copies, or by a cancellation signed and witnessed on the back of each copy.[7]

Although a parent and master might bargain over specific terms for a particular apprentice, indentures followed a standard format. Ben Franklin's indentures no doubt provided that James was to feed, clothe, house, and otherwise maintain his brother during the term of service. Because Ben already had been to school, there would have been no provision for education. Since James was unmarried, the Franklin brothers and James's other apprentices were to live in a boardinghouse at James's expense. James was to teach Ben the art and mystery of printing. The followers of each craft liked to believe that their trade both required special skill ("art") and special knowledge ("mystery"). In return for these benefits, Ben was to work loyally for James, to do his bidding in all lawful things, to live wherever he directed, and to remain with him until Ben turned twenty-one. Ben presumably also promised not to marry, to fornicate, to gamble, to give away the secrets of James's family or business, or to buy or sell on his own account without his master's permission. At the conclusion of the contract Ben was to be paid his freedom dues—consisting, as was traditional at the time, of one new suit of clothes plus the clothes Ben was wearing at the time of his freedom. The contract did contain two unusual features that might have been included either because James was Ben's brother or, more likely, because Josiah Franklin insisted upon these conditions. First, unlike most printers in the early 1700s, James did not charge his father a fee for taking Ben as an apprentice; second, the contract specified that Ben was to receive journeyman's wages during his last year of service. In colonial America such cash payments were rare.[8]

The new apprentice might well have pondered what he was getting into. Just as, in theory, colonial society formed an orderly hierarchy with various crafts having a certain position in society, so each craft had its own internal hierarchy. The new apprentice was stepping onto the lowest rung of the ladder of craftsmanship. Thus, an apprentice sought to learn his trade well so that he might be hired as a journeyman, save some money, and then set up as a master. A journeyman, as the word suggests, would move willingly around the country in search of the best pay in order to hasten the day when he could set up his own shop. And a master would seek to increase his profits by substituting the unpaid labor of apprentices for the paid labor of journeymen. This policy seemed particularly to be a problem in the fledgling American printing trade, which, unlike silversmithing, could usefully employ numerous apprentices. The policy created its own irony. When a master substituted apprentices for journeymen, he increased eventually the number of journeymen in the labor market. That glut drove down journeymen's wages, which temporarily delighted the master, but so long as it took little capital to open a shop, most journeymen eventually became masters. Then instead of a glut of journeymen, there was a glut of masters. It was this problem that had led European artisans to organize guilds that limited the number of apprentices and thus forced the master to hire journeymen. The demand for journeymen kept journeymen's wages high and enabled journeymen to set up for themselves more easily, but in the long run even the masters benefited because the reduced number of apprentices meant less competition within the trade. The losers were youths barred from pursuing a trade and consumers charged more for a product made under guild restrictions than would otherwise have been the case.

Franklin was a New Englander, and that fact was also important to his apprenticeship. In both the middle and southern colonies the practice of importing indentured servants weakened apprenticeship. In those colonies, where a land owner or master artisan could take either an untrained local boy who might not be suited for the trade or an already trained immigrant adult, the need for immediate skilled labor created a preference for the indentured servant. Indeed, the practice of importing indentured servants into the middle and southern colonies may explain why native artisan skills were less developed in those colonies than in New England, where the lack of indentured servants forced the development of local artisan skills. Of course, the converse was also true: a plentiful supply of local apprentices discouraged the importation of indentured servants. And in the southernmost colonies widespread use of slave craftsmen led to a different system. Many white southerners considered artisanship degrading and resisted the apprenticing of whites to skilled trades. Slave labor, of course, was governed by its own laws and customs, and it was neither necessary nor desirable to indent a slave to teach him a craft. Nevertheless, artisan skills were passed from generation to generation within the slave community as if formal apprenticeship had existed.[9]

In rural New England skilled crafts developed along with agriculture. Abundant land and a relative scarcity of agricultural labor drove up the price of labor, which in turn forced up the price of skilled labor. While high wages made local artisan goods expensive, often more expensive than English imports, remoteness from England, plentiful local resources, and lack of ready cash encouraged home production. In New England a long winter without farm chores led farmers to pursue crafts during that season. For example, five generations of the Lane family of New Hampshire were engaged in a combination of farming, tanning, and shoemaking. Samuel Lane, born in 1718, began at age nine to learn to make shoes, just as his father and grandfather had done. At fifteen his father taught him the more difficult art of tanning, at twenty-one he was given £20 worth of leather and free board for a year as a start in life, and two years later he bought land, raised a house, opened a tannery, and married. Like other farmer-craftsmen, Lane trained his own sons and also took apprentices from the neighborhood. Another New Hampshire family, the Dunlaps, made furniture. Like other farmer-craftsmen, they were often paid in corn, cloth, or other barter, or their customers felled trees, hauled wood, or sawed boards in return for furniture. Since family members knew only this one, rather esoteric craft, they found it necessary to dis-perse in order to market their product. On New England–settled Long Island, New York, the remarkable Dominy family remained under one roof by carrying on several crafts simultaneously. Along with farming, four generations made jewelry, cabinets, and clock cases, repaired clocks and watches, operated a forge, practiced carpentry, and tinkered. While various family members specialized, each Dominy was trained in vir-tually every craft. The Dominys never attained more than middling wealth, although barter enabled them to live well in terms of local products.[10]

The rural artisan tradition, with its mixture of agriculture and part-time craftsmanship, its low level of skills, and its lack of capital, left little opportunity for apprentices from outside the family. A graphic, painful description has been left by John Fitch. Born in Windsor, Connecticut, in 1744, he was the son of a poor farmer. The boy had little education, found farm work hard because of his small size, and at seventeen appren-ticed himself to a farmer-clockmaker named Benjamin Cheney. After a six-week trial, three-year indentures were signed in 1762 providing that John would farm five months a year and learn clockmaking the other seven months each year until a few months past his twenty-first birthday. The agreement provided that John furnish his own clothes, and when the boy consulted with his parents, they flatly refused to provide any. Finally, an older sister, wife of a poor weaver, gave him clothes. When this had been settled, John's father insisted upon his common law right to John's labor for three weeks each year at harvest, and Cheney was forced to concede the point.

John Fitch soon discovered that he was trapped in a bad apprentice-ship. Cheney kept him busy with farm chores, and after two years the youth calculated that he had used all the time allotted for farm work in the indentures. He also found the food "very coarse and hard." Mrs. Cheney was lazy, a bad housekeeper, and drunk whenever she could get the liquor. She quarreled with milkmaids, and they left in anger, so John had to milk the cows. "Nay Sir," he later confessed, "I did there demean myself to the washing of dishes. . . ." One time Mrs. Cheney boiled a mutton-and-bean broth. For several days John ate it heartily. "But when it came to be about one week old I began to grow tired of it eating it constant twice a day and frequently three times and began to complain of its being too salt," he wrote. "To which she found an immediate rem-edy by adding water. I stuck to it until it was nine days old without com-plaining but finding no one eat it but myself and that it rather increased upon my hands I got almost dishartned and on the tenth day eat but very little and on the eleventh day eat none but a piece of dry bread only. And unfortunately on the twelve day after many complaints that no one would eat such fine broth and expanating on the loss of its being thrown away it was finally condemned to the hogwash. Which sacrifice I thought but just nor ever did I think that the gods was offended at it."[11]

Some time after these memorable meals Cheney proposed giving John to his brother, who made both wooden and brass clocks and repaired watches. Timothy Cheney agreed to take the youth for one year, new indentures were executed, and John's spirits were raised until he discovered that his new master intended to keep him at making small brass pieces without teaching him any other part of the trade. John would sometimes try to stand near Cheney to watch him work; Cheney always ordered him away. The youth reported, "It was but seldom that I could get to see any of his tooles for watchwork as he had a drawer where he was particularly cairful always to lock them up as if he was affraid I should know their use and by that means gain some information of the business." Finally, a few days after John turned twenty-one, he asked Cheney directly to be put to watchmaking. Cheney refused and threatened to strike John, but the young man reminded him that he was no longer an underage apprentice. After this quarrel, life became unbearable, and Cheney offered to let John go four months before the expiration of the indentures for £8. Two of John's brothers paid, and John was free. Free, £20 in debt, with worn-out clothes, and without the knowledge of his trade. On the way home he "cryed the whole distance."[12]

Fitch's grotesque experiences were only an exaggerated version of the exploitation many colonial apprentices faced. Twelve-year-old Ben Franklin found himself performing the usual menial chores—sweeping out his brother's office, rising early to build a fire, fetching water, and so on. An apprentice was expected to spend his first year or two as a household drudge rather than to begin learning the trade right away. Like many apprentices, Ben quickly became bored and frustrated. He resented James's authoritarian pronouncements, his older-brother bossiness, and his angry blows, and frequently the brothers referred their disputes to Josiah Franklin, who often found reason to side with Ben, which only increased the boy's resentment. James, like all masters, had an incentive to delay Ben's training as long as possible. Not only did a master get valuable help this way, but an apprentice who did not begin to learn the trade until late in his apprenticeship could not master the trade until near the end of his time—and no apprentice would dare run away until he had mastered his trade.

An office like James Franklin's had only a few pieces of equipment, most notably typecases and a press. Printers arranged their types in a case according to a standard system, and the case was then placed on a high

APPRENTICE PRINTER

sloping stand, so that a printer stood in front of the case. With his left hand the printer held his composing stick, and with his right hand he selected without looking into the case the proper letters one after another. He read handwritten copy kept in front of him, and he tried to set sentences from memory. Working at case required some knowledge, nimble fingers, and no strength. It was a job an apprentice could soon learn to do. Early on Ben got the chance to set type. He became proficient at stick and case, as typesetting was called. After a printer or his apprentice had composed several lines in his stick, he set them aside to make room for more composing. These blocks of composition were gathered together by the shop foreman, who worked at the imposing stone, a medium-size table covered with a slab of stone or tin. Here the foreman fitted the already set type into a heavy metal form, which was capable of containing the type for several small pages. When the form was filled, the foreman locked it tight, so that the type would not fall out, and then he carried it to the press.

The wooden press was the most valuable piece of equipment in the shop, and its operation was complex and exhausting, even though it was worked by two men or, more commonly, by one man and an older apprentice. The man's job—estimated to require a man weighing at least 160 pounds—was to pull a lever that made an impression on each sheet of paper that was to be printed. To ensure that the impression was good, two pulls were required for each sheet. A good pressman could make up to five hundred pulls an hour, but the result of this heavy labor was that the pressman's muscles became overdeveloped on his right side, particularly in the shoulder, and his body became permanently distorted. A pressman advertised his occupation by the way he walked. While the pressman pulled, the apprentice assistant had to feed each sheet of paper onto the form, remove it after it was printed, and between impressions ink the form by beating it with two inked leather balls held on long wooden sticks. This could be hard work, and it explains why apprentices were allowed to work at press only after they had learned to set type. The press was the last part of the trade that an apprentice learned, and pulling press required so much strength that some boys never could do it and remained just typesetters, with little prospect of ever having their own shops.[13]

After the form was printed, it was cleaned, then the foreman unlocked it, and an apprentice broke the lines of type apart and distributed the type into a case. This job was one of an apprentice's first tasks in the office, because it enabled him to learn the position of the letters in the type case. Another apprentice duty was to make the balls used to beat the form. The wooden handles were reused, but the balls wore out rapidly because of their constant beating. The apprentice took pieces of soft leather, or goat's skin, which was preferred but harder to get, and after scraping off the hair, soaked the skin in a jar of urine for a fortnight. To soften the material further, the apprentice every day had to remove the leather from the jar and stamp on it. This was a smelly and obnoxious job. Finally, the apprentice had to sew the leather covering over the tightly wadded rags that were used for the interior of the balls. Another task for an apprentice was to make ink. In order to get ink perfect for a particular press, the printer preferred to make his own ink by boiling lampblack and other ingredients for up to twenty-four hours. During the boiling the apprentice watched and stirred the vat. Printers had a mystical relationship with ink, perhaps because they were so often covered with it, and it was not unheard of for an apprentice to boil bread dough in the ink vat and serve up the black-encrusted crullers to all in the shop. Eating something that had been boiled in ink was said to ward off the devil.[14]

A couple of years after Ben Franklin became an apprentice, his older brother began to publish a newspaper called the *New-England Courant*. Ben helped set type, print the sheets, and deliver the paper. While setting type, he grew interested in the stories that he set, and soon he wanted to write as well as to set type. But he knew that James, who had few literary ambitions, would have greeted his literary efforts with abuse and ridicule and would have refused to print them. So late at night Ben wrote his contributions and then placed them on the front doorstep of the printshop, where James found them in the morning. The older Franklin recognized talent in these anonymous manuscripts and, without suspecting their origin, printed them. Then James quarreled with government officials, and he was jailed for a month. When James was released, it was upon the condition that he discontinue his offensive newspaper. James and his friends, looking for a legal way around the order, put Ben in charge of the newspaper, but to do so they found it necessary legally to end Ben's apprenticeship. To prove to the authorities that Ben was free, his old indentures were canceled, and to make sure that Ben understood that he was not truly free, new indentures were drawn up in secret. The canceled indentures later served Ben well, for they were accepted as proof that he was not a runaway apprentice. Jail had not improved James's disposition, and the hot-tempered brother continued to treat Ben with a combination of contempt and blows.[15]

At age seventeen Ben was a fully trained and knowledgeable printer. He was expert both at setting type and at pulling copies from the press, knew his value as a journeyman, and was not being paid a cent by his brother James. To improve his fortune, therefore, or to practice a little free enterprise on his own behalf, Ben resolved to break his apprentice indentures, to renege on his contract, to violate his solemn obligation— in short, to run away. Forgoing his freedom suit, his receipt of a journeyman's wage during the last year of his apprenticeship, the respect of the people of Boston, and even leaving his family in ignorance, Ben sailed on a ship out of Boston harbor. Years later, Ben formally apologized to James and asked his mother her forgiveness for so rash an act. But it is difficult to believe that deep down Ben Franklin ever much regretted having left either Boston, then a stagnant seaport cramped in style and circumstance, or his brother, as mercurial and domineering as Boston was dowdy. Ben sailed first to New York, where he sought work without success, and then went on to Philadelphia. He arrived with little money and a large appetite, bought three huge rolls, and carried them down the street conscious of his own ridiculous appearance. His future wife spotted the absurd figure and laughed at him. Soon he found work as a journeyman printer, took a partner, and set up for himself; but discovering that his partner was not reliable, he bought out the partner. He became the most famous printer and publisher in Philadelphia, got into politics, experimented with science, ran the post office, and by the age of forty-two had amassed a fortune sufficient for him to retire.[16]

Thus did the poor candlemaker's son from Boston make good in Philadelphia. Thus did the abused brother of James Franklin triumph in the eyes of the world. Thus did Benjamin Franklin conquer. And generations of Americans, as a result in part of Franklin's own self-promotion in his newspaper, almanacs, and autobiography, have become aware of the full measure of his success. However, behind that success in the beginning lurked what Franklin himself called "one of the first errata of my life"—running away. To any unhappy apprentice, running away had always been an option, a hope, a last desperate measure to thwart boredom or frustration, and an act that seemed to promise little for the future. But here was Franklin, a runaway apprentice who made good. Franklin's life, despite his words of regret, showed that running away could be the beginning of a new, profitable way of life. His autobiography, published in fifty-five editions between 1794 and 1833, led several generations of American apprentices to ponder running away. English custom and law, the Puritan regard for contractual obligations, and the respect that an apprentice was supposed to have for a master's authority could be flouted; an apprentice could escape from the tyranny of a bad master, from miserable working conditions, from the many restrictions imposed by the terms of an apprenticeship; he might avoid painful consequences and benefit himself in the long run. Franklin had achieved his spectacular success in violation of custom and contract, by defying his brother, by leaving home, by running away. An example of wrongdoing richly rewarded was the legacy that Benjamin Franklin left to later generations of apprentices. And in leaving this legacy, Franklin did more than any other American to put the age-old institution of apprenticeship on the road to extinction.[17]

✑ CHAPTER ONE ✑

Chaos

If apprenticeship was an entrenched though anemic institution on the eve of the American Revolution, it became both less entrenched and more anemic as a result of wartime turmoil and fluctuating economic conditions during the last quarter of the century. The war produced massive dislocations. For part of the war the British army occupied Boston, New York, and Philadelphia, and many people fled either when the British arrived or when they departed. Such upheaval affected many apprentices. For example, Stephen Allen was apprenticed to a Tory sailmaker during the British occupation of New York. When the redcoats evacuated the city, Stephen's master sailed for Nova Scotia, and the fifteen-year-old boy was "turned loose upon the world to seek [his] fortune, with nothing to commence but a good constitution, and a scanty wardrobe." During the war the British effectively blockaded much of the American coast and cut off foreign trade. The demand for American-made substitutes for traditional British imports soared, just at the time that the Continental army itself demanded clothes, food, wagons, and armaments. Demand was further increased by the policy of financing the war with paper currency. The huge and sudden demand for consumer goods and war materiel could not be met, because of an acute labor shortage due to the enlistment of so many men in the army. The consequence was a critical demand for labor that led to soaring wages and soaring prices. Such conditions created tension between master and apprentice. In the Moravian community at Salem, North Carolina, for example, apprentices staged a protest strike. A boy who had learned his trade was unwilling, amid so much opportunity, to remain as an unpaid skilled laborer. He demanded to be hired as a journeyman, and if his demands were not met, he threatened to join the army.[1]

For American boys the chaos of the war was wonderfully exciting. On the morning of April 19, 1775, Benjamin Russell, the fourteen-year-old son of the Boston stonemason John Russell, rose from bed, breakfasted, and left home to go to school. As Ben walked to school, he noticed an air of excitement, fear, and apprehension. The British troops that had occupied Boston since 1768 were astir, and rumor had it that the troops were assembling to march inland. When Ben got to school, he found the other boys and the master caught up by the excitement. The school proceeded as usual until the master could contain neither himself nor the pupils any longer. He asked several older boys to leave the school, to reconnoiter the situation, and to report back. The master, Ben Russell, and the other pupils waited, and the school became nervous with anticipation. Finally, the scouts returned with the news that the British had killed American militiamen at Lexington. Master Carter said, "Boys, war has begun—the school is broken up." The boys gave three cheers and raced out to look. Several boys, including young Russell, followed the redcoats through the Neck to Roxbury, where British sentries allowed them to pass through the lines, and they made their way to Cambridge.[2]

At Cambridge they found chaos. Harvard College had been all but broken up, and its halls had been used by the American minutemen. The Cambridge Common had served as a parade ground for the ill-equipped and ill-trained militia companies, and a house near the Common had been the militia headquarters. When the British troops had marched through Cambridge toward Concord in the morning, the local militia companies had fled. Cambridge was deserted, and the Boston boys spent the afternoon playing on the Common until sunset, when they watched the British troops, under fire, retreat through Cambridge back toward the safety of Boston. Afterward the boys wandered around and found a sympathetic farmer, who gave them supper. The American militia companies returned, and the boys were told they could spend the night in one of the college halls. By this time Ben and his friends realized that Boston was under siege and that they could not get through the British lines to return home. They settled down to what must have been a sense of exhaustion mingled with exhilaration.[3]

In Boston, Ben's parents became alarmed when their son did not return home. For weeks after the boy's disappearance the family tried frantically to discover his whereabouts. Ben's friends had reported that he was last seen heading for the Boston Neck, and the family surmised that he had made his way out of the city. But what had happened to him then? Had he been killed in the chaos of the first battles of the war? Or had he fallen into British hands? That could be dangerous. Young Peter Edes, a teenage son of a Boston printer, had been held hostage by British authorities under a possible death sentence in order to curtail his father's political activities. While the Russell family worried, the son was oblivious to their fears. Like other boys, Ben was caught up in the war and the spirit of war. He had attached himself to the American soldiers encamped at Cambridge. They expected him to assist them in return for the "quarters" and "rations" he got at Harvard College. Ben became a company clerk. It was, no doubt, the greatest responsibility that the schoolboy Ben Russell had had in his life.[4]

One day in August two strangers wandered into the camp, and one of them spotted Ben and was suddenly overjoyed. It was Ben's father, whose joy quickly turned to anger and who seized his wayward son and started to shake him. As Ben struggled to free himself, a soldier rushed over and said, "Don't shake that boy, Sir, he is our clerk." This explanation did not impress John Russell, who escorted his son to the tent of Gen. Israel Putnam, where the general agreed that Ben was too young to enlist and that his father could remove him immediately from the camp. Russell put Ben in a chaise, and they drove away. The father swore that Ben was never, ever to see the army again. It was no place for a boy.[5]

The pair could not return to Boston, which was sealed off to Americans. As father and son drove along, Ben was forced to admit that not once had he tried to contact his parents. He knew that if he had, and if somehow the message had gotten through, his father would have found a way to remove him from the patriot's camp at Cambridge. Now he had to confess his fault to his father. They drove on. John Russell explained that Ben's continued absence had finally led him to make his own dangerous, nighttime escape from Boston. Now Russell intended to remove his family to some part of Massachusetts safe from British troops. But he did not intend to take Ben with the family. Ben was too grown up now, too cocksure of himself, and not easily controlled. It was no time to go to school, and Ben was too young to be a soldier. This, reasoned the elder Russell, was an excellent time for Ben to become an apprentice. Indeed, as they drove from Cambridge and turned the horses west, away from Boston, John Russell informed his son what was to be done. Russell had contacted Isaiah Thomas, an old family friend and Boston printer who only a few months before had fled the British army in Boston to reestablish himself forty miles west in Worcester. Thomas, like other master craftsmen, was having difficulty getting or keeping help because of the war. When Thomas learned that Russell was eager to have his son made an apprentice, Thomas had jumped at the chance. Thus, they were now on their way to Worcester, where Russell and Thomas would sign indentures binding young Ben to Thomas as his apprentice until age twenty-one. Ben, as the dutiful son molded and shaped by his father, was expected to obey this parental command. His consent was not sought.

After a day's drive the Russells arrived in Worcester, a sleepy town of nineteen hundred people that was temporarily prospering from the British occupation of Boston. When Thomas fled Boston, he had been lucky enough to bring his printing press with him. He had thus brought to the provinces one of the most up-to-date and modern presses in the country. And while the presses of Boston were choked by British censorship and intimidation, Thomas in Worcester was free to print the ardently anti-British propaganda pieces that had gotten him in trouble with British authorities in the first place. It was ironic that a man who was regarded as such a cantankerous rebel and who was known for his quick temper and his demand for perfect work from his journeymen and apprentices would in later life be revered as a kind old gentleman, an establishment figure, indeed, the father of American printing. But that was all years later. The Thomas whom Ben Russell met in 1775 was only twenty-six years old, a vigorous and often impatient young man who drove himself as hard as he drove those around him. Already a master printer with several employees, Thomas had known bitter poverty, and, like Benjamin Franklin, he believed in the efficacy of hard work to overcome it.[6]

Ben Russell's life as the son of a Boston stonemason had been comfortable compared with Isaiah Thomas's boyhood. At the age of seven Isaiah had suffered the humiliation of being bound as an apprentice by the Boston Overseers of the Poor. Although family connections prevented Isaiah from being sent to a farm, a common fate for poor boys, his extreme youth had made it impossible to place him in a truly advantageous apprenticeship. Masters could get little work out of a mere boy and naturally shunned boys for apprentices. Isaiah's master was Zechariah Fowle, an undistinguished and eccentric printer of street ballads. At seven the boy, who had never been to school, found himself standing on a wooden box setting his first type—for a bawdy ballad. Thomas later recalled, "I set the types . . . in two days, tho' I then knew only the letters, but had never been taught to put them together and spell." Miraculously, he did not confuse his *p*'s and *q*'s. As the years passed, Isaiah grew to resent his master. The youth was not sent to school as was promised in his indentures, was fed scarcely from the meager Fowle stores, and could not truly learn the printer's trade, since Fowle had only a modest sort of type and lacked the kind of press used for book or newspaper printing. Eventually, Isaiah ran away, but after an unhappy sojourn as a makeshift journeyman in Nova Scotia, he had returned to Boston and made peace with his master. Soon he was a newspaper publisher, embroiled in politics, and an active Son of Liberty. After receiving death threats, and just prior to the opening salvo in the Revolution, Thomas wisely had his press smuggled out of Boston to Worcester in the middle of the night.[7]

Isaiah Thomas and Ben Russell were too much alike. They were an odd couple—the passionate young patriot printer and his apprentice boy. In the beginning they shared poverty. The sudden move to Worcester had cost Thomas his Tory wife, half his type, and more than 90 percent of the circulation of his newspaper, the *Massachusetts Spy*. Thomas, Ben, and one other apprentice lived in the office on bread and an occasional penny's worth of milk, while the two apprentices slept in the garret on rags collected for the papermaker. At first the relationship was mutually beneficial, and although there must have been quarrels—Thomas had a fierce temper, and Ben was a noted prankster—each learned to respect the other's abilities. Thomas was a first-rate printer, perhaps at that time technically the finest printer in America. He was one of the first printers to reproduce satisfactory woodcuts, many of which he cut himself, and, unlike many printers, he took particular pains to get good rag paper. There was much that Ben could learn from Thomas. And he did. Within two years Ben was almost certainly doing the work of a journeyman. That suited Thomas, but as the war dragged on, and as labor shortages continued, Ben surely noticed that he was not paid so much as a Continental dollar—just room and board, provided by the second Mrs. Thomas. Ben's recognition of his own competence must have brought increasing frustration. All around him journeymen demanded and got high wages, quit to set up their own shops, or collected large bounties to enlist in the Continental army. Ben turned seventeen, even eighteen, and he was only a printer boy. It was "Yes, Mr. Thomas," and "No, Mr. Thomas." Others made their way in the world while he marked time. From time to time his thoughts drifted to the war and the army.[8]

From the beginning of the Revolutionary War one of the gravest dangers to apprenticeship had come from the heavy demand for military recruits. The traditional private-property rights of the master to the labor services of his apprentice clashed with a public need for soldiers. Both private rights and public need were so strong that politicians were unwilling to give a complete victory to either claim, and public policy concerning the enlistment of apprentices was inconsistent. Early on, in 1775, Rhode Island allowed apprentices to enlist and gave them the right to keep the enlistment bounty, but insisted that a master was entitled to half the apprentice's military pay. Since the bounties were large compared with the pay, the effect was to encourage such enlistments. By 1776 the enlistment of apprentices, particularly from the middle states, had led masters to protest to the Continental Congress. The Congress agreed that no apprentice from New Jersey, Pennsylvania, Delaware, or Maryland was to be allowed to enlist without his master's written consent. Furthermore, any apprentice who already had enlisted would be discharged at the master's request. Some masters would consent to an enlistment only if the apprentice formally agreed to turn over a portion of his military pay, but the Continental army resisted giving military pay to masters. In 1777 Congress barred such payments and postponed consideration of whether Congress or the states would reimburse masters for the time lost by apprentices who enlisted. While Congress did not wish to overturn traditional property rights of the master, it also recognized that the enlistment of apprentices might be the only way some states could fill their military quotas. As masters came to realize they would get no compensation, they greeted each new apprentice suspiciously.[9]

Some masters were anxious to employ apprentices as substitutes for their own military service. In 1779, when the Massachusetts militia ordered John Bosson to duty in New York, the Boston barber and wigmaker was distressed. He could afford neither to hire a substitute nor to lose money from closing his shop. He thus paced the shop sharpening razors that already were sharp, glared at his two apprentices, and finally said, "Hard times—don't need two apprentices any more than a toad needs a tail." He added, "If either of you had the spunk of a louse, you would offer to go for me." Bosson then left the shop. The apprentice Ebenezer Fox found the monotony of the shop irritating, the spirit of adventure called, and the other, older apprentice, who feared that Bosson would coerce him into volunteering, encouraged Ebenezer to go as Bosson's substitute. So the youth consented, a relieved master generously outfitted his apprentice with clothes and arms, and shortly before his sixteenth birthday Ebenezer Fox made his militia debut parading on Boston Common. He marched to New York and back, served two months, and swore he would never be a substitute again.[10]

Late in the war Ebenezer joined the navy. Bosson's business had fallen off so much that he was willing to consent to Ebenezer's departure, provided the youth agreed to split with Bosson any sea wages or prize money he earned. Ebenezer listened to a naval recruiter, who stood in the street and sang:

> *All you that have bad masters,*
> *And cannot get your due;*
> *Come, come, my brave boys,*
> *And join with our ship's crew.*

So he enlisted. At the end of the war Ebenezer returned to Boston to his master. The youth showed his master $80 in prize money, and Bosson, despite his earlier promise, seized it. Since Ebenezer was an underage apprentice, he had no legal right to the money. The youth, however, had kept $30 from an earlier voyage that Bosson did not know about. Ebenezer lost that money by lending it to a friend, and Bosson lost the rest in paper currency that turned out to be worthless.[11]

Some youths used apprenticeship to escape military service. One North Carolinian sent his son to be apprenticed to a Moravian craftsman in order to avoid a military draft. Not that American service was the only worry for an apprentice. In British-occupied New York press-gangs operated vigorously. Especially eager to catch seasoned sailors, they sought youths wearing naval canvas trousers and short jackets. Frequently, one or another of the apprentices at James Leonard's sail loft would be taken and held overnight, but the victim was always released in the morning when the Tory master, a British contractor, appeared to claim his apprentice. On one occasion a member of a press-gang chased Stephen Allen into his mother's bedroom, where the two Allens clung to each other so tightly that the pressman, realizing he would have to take both of them, left. The press-gangs turned at least some of Leonard's apprentices into patriots.[12]

The war touched Ben Russell, too. When news of the Declaration of Independence reached Worcester, the populace had adjourned to a tavern to celebrate. The next morning about a dozen celebrants, including Ben, were surprised to learn that amid the festivities they had enlisted in the Continental army. Isaiah Thomas was furious, because he could not continue his business without Ben's help, and the master began to agitate for the release of his apprentice. Thomas went before a justice of the peace to have the enlistment set aside; he presented several arguments but emphasized that Ben at the time was under sixteen and therefore could not be enlisted. The justice called Ben to testify, swore him in, and asked him if he was sixteen. Although Ben was willing to leave printing for the glory of military life, he did not wish to lie under oath, so he evaded the justice's question by stating that he could not swear to his age, since he had no distinct recollection of the circumstances surrounding his birth. This clever speech did not impress the justice, who voided the enlistment.[13]

Four years later Thomas was informed that he had been drafted. This was bad news. He had a wife and seven children to support, his business would fail if he were not there to manage it, and, besides, he did not see himself as a soldier. He was a patriot, an ardent, even zealous patriot, and no one could deny the daring risks he had taken when in Boston. But he was a printer and not a soldier. He could do more for the cause with his press than with a musket. Still, the government demanded his services—or those of a substitute. Ben watched the gloom cross Thomas's face. Here was his chance. He offered to be Thomas's substitute. Normally, Thomas would have had to pay a substitute considerable money, and since the war had not been good for Thomas's business, he was in no position to make a generous offer. That did not bother Ben. The draft laws provided that an apprentice could go in place of his master. Ben went. He served in the army only a few months and never saw a battle. He was discharged and returned to Worcester, where, at age twenty, he demanded that his master yield up his indentures as a fair compensation for his having risked his life on Thomas's behalf. Although the master was reluctant to give up his apprentice, he recognized that Ben's claim to freedom was, in the court of public opinion, overwhelming.[14]

The chaos of the war created both opportunity and adversity that led some apprentices to premature success and others to premature death. Like a lottery, the war dished up winners and losers willy-nilly. Some apprentices begged and cajoled their masters for permission to enlist, signed up for a lucrative bounty, and died of camp fever with their new riches unspent. Other apprentices stayed home, worked, married the master's daughter, inherited a shop, and prospered. Still others enlisted, survived the war, and returned home to take up the old trade again, sometimes with success, sometimes without. We have seen some of the various possibilities in the lives of Stephen Allen, Ebenezer Fox, and Ben Russell. This wide range of possible outcomes reveals a pattern of uncertainty that was antithetical to apprenticeship, which, as an institution, depended upon predictability and rationality in its everyday operations. Master and apprentice had entered into contractual obligations, and as in all contracts, the presumption of both parties was that the world was politically, socially, and economically stable, governed by custom and law, and, in short, predictable. The chaos of the Revolution called those assumptions into doubt and left both master and apprentice questioning more closely what benefits each could derive from an apprenticeship. In colonial America tradition itself had been a major force for the maintenance of apprenticeship, but the war raised questions about tradition and forced Americans to put matters on a new footing.

The Revolution had also brought about other changes that would affect apprenticeship. What was one to make of a world in which a breeches maker named Timothy Dexter had speculated so successfully that he was able to take over the mansion of a bankrupt Salem merchant? Or what was one to make of heroes like Roger Sherman, a onetime farmer-shoemaker; Paul Revere, silversmith; Gen. Henry Knox, bookseller; Gen. Nathanael Greene, blacksmith? What is important about such men is that they rose from artisan origins into the ranks of a political and military elite long dominated by men from mercantile, planter, or professional backgrounds. Their rise did not mean that artisans would govern the new country, but it did mean that men who had been artisans could help govern it. That was a far cry from the days when a carpenter's son had been taught to treat the wealthy "as beings of a superior order." The class structure of colonial America had, at the level of ideology and by wartime heroes, been blown apart. In a world perceived to be more fluid—and perception here counts for more than reality—artisan parents were bound to develop different priorities for their children. One radical break with tradition was in the naming of sons. Before the Revolution about three-fifths of all firstborn sons had been named for fathers; by 1790 only one-quarter were. And whereas an artisan father who named a son after himself might expect that son to carry on his own craft, who can say what aspirations a father now had? It was no longer enough for an artisan father to train his sons or to apprentice them to other craftsmen. Now he wanted to give them the chance to develop their potential in a free society.[15]

And yet this new world was profoundly disturbing. Liberty and equality, while exhilarating, were accompanied by a loss of position and place. In traditional society common people lacked power, but at least they knew where authority was lodged, what their relation to it was, and, by extension, what their relation to everyone else was. Now everything was in disarray. If the people were no longer subordinate to kings, if church congregations did without bishops, if skilled journeymen could become master craftsmen overnight, as many did during the war, if a mere breeches maker could get rich through speculation, and if children were no longer subordinate to fathers, then what was the point of being an apprentice? Indeed, in a society in which upheaval was everywhere and respect for tradition had waned, apprenticeship was seen not as a stepping stone to an honored niche in society but as an irksome burden that permitted exploitation and prevented a talented youth from rising by his own natural abilities. Benjamin Franklin's legacy loomed large. Conservatives grappled with this new social reality. The Reverend Devereux Jarrett of Virginia scorned "high *republican times*." A more thoughtful Robert Coram argued for free public education to inculcate virtue and morality in the masses. In addition, he favored new laws requiring youths to be bound to trades as apprentices. "A good trade," he concluded, "seems to be the only sheet anchor on which we may firmly rely for safety in the general storms of human adversity." Perhaps. But this conservative defense of apprenticeship only generated more suspicions on the part of restless libertarians—especially young ones.[16]

The chaos of the war was followed by the chaos of chronic economic fluctuation. The frantic, inflationary wartime boom ended in a postwar depression in which master craftsmen went bankrupt, journeymen lost jobs, and returning soldiers could not find work. The currency was worthless, capital was short, and the British, seeking to punish the former colonies, cut off the lucrative West Indies trade and quarantined the United States outside the imperial trade system. During the mid-1780s masters did not clamor to take apprentices. Indeed, negotiations for an apprenticeship could be protracted, as in the case of fourteen-year-old Joseph Belknap, who was sent by his father in 1783 from New England to Philadelphia to learn printing from Robert Aitken. In the late 1780s the economy began to improve, and it was soon aided by the financial policies of Alexander Hamilton and by a series of European wars that enabled Americans to produce successfully for the home market and to capture an unprecedented proportion of world trade. As it turned out, the 1790s would be a major boom decade. Suddenly, master craftsmen who had not had enough business to employ journeymen or apprentices were clamoring for help. Boys found it easy to get apprenticeships, and trained workmen found it easy to open their own shops. Among those who prospered during at least part of the decade were the printers Robert Aitken, the newly set-up Joseph Belknap, and Benjamin Franklin Bache. The latter, a favorite grandson of Franklin, had been trained in printing by his grandfather at Passy, France, during the 1780s. "I have determin'd to give him a trade," wrote Franklin, "that he may have something to depend on, and not be oblig'd to ask Favours or Offices of anybody." Bache's apprenticeship, in keeping with his grandfather's connections, included time with François-Ambroise Didot, then the most renowned printer in the world.[17]

While the boom of the 1790s benefited many master craftsmen, it clearly helped most those who were already well established and able to take advantage of the opportunity offered by an expanding economy. And certain trades did better than others. Craftsmen who made goods used in foreign trade or as a substitute for imports subject to tariffs did well, as did those craftsmen in the building trades or in furniture making, which underwent major expansion, thanks to purchases by newly successful merchants. In New York City, for example, from 1790 to 1794 the number of households doubled, and each new home had to be furnished. Federal-style furniture, today exhibited with pride by major American museums, was one indication of prosperity. By the mid-1790s the cabinetmaker Duncan Phyfe, a Scots immigrant who had served his apprenticeship in Albany, had established a shop in New York that specialized in fine, expensive furniture. Other craftsmen who catered to the wealthy, such as clockmakers and silversmiths, also prospered. Not

all craftsmen enjoyed success, however, and those who made goods for ordinary use, such as shoes or clothes, found somewhat less success, although
some of them benefited from the general prosperity of the times. From
the depressed 1780s to the 1790s real wages of Philadelphia shoemakers
doubled to regain the levels of the late colonial period. This newfound
prosperity was due both to a tariff that partially protected shoemakers
from cheap British imports and to a growing foreign market for American shoes. Philadelphia tailors, on the other hand, were not able to regain the standard of living they had enjoyed before the Revolution.[18]

Perhaps no trade prospered more than printing, which was the bene-
ficiary of increasing literacy, a rising tide of newspapers and periodicals,
and the displacement of imported books by American-made ones. Of all
titles printed in America before 1800, half were printed in the sixteen
years following the close of the Revolution; and from the 1780s to the
1790s the annual rate of publication grew by nearly 50 percent. Perhaps
no master printer profited from this boom so handsomely as Isaiah
Thomas. During the 1790s he operated seven presses in Worcester, and
he maintained with his onetime apprentice turned partner Ebenezer T.
Andrews in Boston another shop with five presses. When the Boston firm
was dissolved in 1804, the property was valued at $200,000. Thomas's in-
fluence was widespread through his well-placed former apprentices, such
as the Boston daily *Centinel* publisher Benjamin Russell, who remained
a close friend. Whenever an apprentice to Thomas completed his service,
he was offered a chance to open his own shop with Thomas as partner at
some remote location. Through this system, patterned after earlier fran-
chising practices innovated by Benjamin Franklin, Thomas and his former apprentices became a powerful influence in the printing trade
throughout the country. While Russell succeeded in Boston, and nephew
Ebenezer Smith Thomas prospered first at Charleston, South Carolina,
and later in Cincinnati, Thomas also had disappointments. Leonard
Worcester, one of his most gifted and trusted apprentices, left the business to become a minister; and David Carlisle, Jr., set up in Walpole,
New Hampshire, went bankrupt, and in 1808 fled to Canada to avoid
debtor's prison.[19]

Thomas's success and willingness to assist former apprentices encouraged parents to place their sons with him. The master printer found himself with a glut of applicants, and the terms of apprenticeship began to
shift in Thomas's favor. Thomas's own indentures in 1756 had provided
him with lodging, board, washing, all his clothes, and two freedom suits.
In 1771, when Thomas was new in the business, he had taken as an
apprentice Anthony Haswell, an English-born fifteen-year-old who was
bound, like Thomas, by the Overseers of the Poor. The conditions in

Anthony's indentures were identical to those in Thomas's fifteen years earlier. In 1785, during the depression that put would-be apprentices at a disadvantage in bargaining, Thomas promised to furnish the apprentice James Reed Hutchins with lodging, board, and "part of his wearing apparel to wit with good hats shoes & close bodied coats, his other cloathing to be provided by his said guardian." When Hutchins became free, he was to get neither cash nor a traditional freedom suit.[20]

By the 1790s parents were writing Thomas letters begging him to take their sons. Stephen Sewall boasted that his thirteen-year-old son, "a boy of good capacity" with "no vicious propensities," was doing well "in one of the best Schools in the Country." Sewall hoped his son could continue in school one more year, but he was so eager to have him placed with Thomas that he was willing to remove him from school immediately, if that was necessary to obtain a position. Joseph Reynolds wrote with a somewhat different proposal. His son, aged seventeen, had been bound to a bookbinder, who had just died. "He has got a Considerable Inste [i.e, Insight] into the Buisness," wrote Reynolds, "—and wishes to get the Buisness perfect—there is none of that profession here which Is able to Instruct him." Archibald McElroy sent his son in person to see Thomas. The boy carried a letter explaining that he had finished an apprenticeship in a small printing office. The father hoped that work in Thomas's office would furnish "improvement." While Thomas considered such begging letters carefully, he was most inclined, like other craftsmen, to take apprentices from among his relatives. Alexander Thomas, Jr., became a clerk in one of the family bookstores, and Ebenezer Smith Thomas learned printing in his Uncle Isaiah's Worcester shop. Smith, finding the work dreary and "very severe," eventually left his uncle's shop. To seek his fortune, he sailed for Charleston—carrying along a copy of Franklin's autobiography.[21]

Among Thomas's postwar apprentices was Elisha H. Waldo. In the fall of 1785 Dr. Albigance Waldo of Pomfret arranged for Thomas to take his son the following spring. Shortly after the thirteen-year-old boy arrived at Worcester, his father wrote him a letter of advice. It expresses well the hopes and fears of fathers during those times. The father wrote, "Nothing will gain you the love & esteem of your worthy Master, his family, and of all your acquaintance but your constant endeavours to conduct yourself peaceably, faithfully, and honestly—let not the strongest temptation; let not the most powerfull persuasations, ever occation you to injure the interests or Character of any One or lead you into a quarrel with your companion.—Be always as faithful in the absence of your Master, as if he were present; and never suffer any falshood to come from your mouth; nor Ever be guilty of relating any thing which you hear that may give trouble to others; [un]less your Masters interest is very much concerned, in such a Case [and in?] such a Case only, you may be allowed to give information." Elisha was sent for a trial period. After he had been with Thomas two years, indentures were signed. This two-year trial, considerably longer than the more traditional six months, illustrates the way in which the length of time fixed in the indentures provides an erroneous impression concerning the length of an apprenticeship.[22]

Elisha's letters to his father show his state of mind and how he changed, developed, and matured during his apprenticeship. The first letter is the work of an amiable, pliable, malleable boy. He wrote, "Dear Dada. . . . My kind Dada. I shall endeavour to follow the good examples which you have Laid before me.—as I know that I am young and now growing up in the world, and such practices as I use myself to now in youth, shall, undoubtedly, be [   ] to follow the Remainder of my Days, whether good or bad.—I hope I live that I shall be able to reward you for your kind and tender affections to me.—I shall strive to Conduct myself as well to my Master and Mistress as I am Capable of,—also to my Brother printers and for that Matter to the whole world—knowing that as I Conduct myself in this world, so shall I expect to receive my Reward from the Supreme Governour of the Univ[erse] who gave me existance. . . ." He liked his trade "exceedingly well" and found the Thomases "very kind." He asked his parents to send summer clothes and a pair of shoes. A letter seven months later, following a brief visit to his parents, reported his safe arrival "home" in Worcester. The apprenticeship was performing one of its traditional functions of weaning Elisha from an emotional attachment to his family. His future was with his master and his trade and not with his father and boyhood dreams. A few days later Elisha wrote again begging his father, now "my *Worthy Sir*," to come for a visit. The visitor, of course, might bear gifts. Thirteen-year-old Elisha wanted a pair of ice skates.[23]

The next letter, written the following spring, informed the "Kind Parent" that the son needed "a little money" and that he must have "a new coat" for his was "not fit to ware." Six months later "Dear Dady" was told of a need for winter clothes, stockings, and gloves. More than a year later, in January 1789, Elisha had been sent temporarily by Thomas to his branch office at Woodstock. His clothes—obviously to be supplied by his father according to the indentures—were again a problem. He complained, "I have not a rag of any kind to wear to Meeting, and scarcely any for to wear to work in." Dr. Waldo had told Thomas to supply the clothes and bill him, but Thomas, ever the shrewd businessman, was not about to incur a debt that might not be repaid, so he had declined, and Elisha found himself shivering while two stiff-necked adults stubbornly refused to give him any new clothes. In 1790, back in Worcester, Elisha expressed filial devotion to "the dearest" of all his relatives "in the whole world." He wrote, "Oh! may that time come when I can dwell near my beloved Father, when I can never see him want, so that he may be my constant guide, and I may be his protector, God grant it!!" More soberly, he commented on the early years of his apprenticeship. "When I first came to Worcester," he wrote, "I knowed nothing how I was going to live, or how I should get along, but since I have got more knowledge of the world, I begin to think for myself, I look on forward what I expect will come by and bye." The son proposed that, when he visited home that summer, his father give him $100 in lieu of the clothes he was obligated to supply for the next four years, until his indentures expired at twenty-one. The apprenticeship was becoming a burden, and visits to his father were rarer, for Elisha was a valuable worker, which made Thomas reluctant to give him time off. On at least one occasion Elisha had to pay Thomas for the time he spent visiting his relatives. In 1794 Elisha Waldo finished his apprenticeship, and Thomas helped Waldo open his own shop in partnership.[24]

In the 1790s some master printers, like Thomas, prospered, but not all did. Eventually, Robert Aitken and Joseph Belknap failed, as did the naïve and simple Elisha Waldo. The problem, as identified by the apprentice Leonard Worcester, was that masters took too many apprentices and preferred their cheap labor to that of journeymen. When journeymen could find jobs, it was at such low wages that they lacked the ability to save the money to go into business for themselves. Worcester decided to leave printing for the ministry. David Chambers, on trial to Benjamin Franklin Bache in 1796, came to a similar conclusion. "All the The [*sic*] Journay men tell that I had not better learn the printing," he wrote. "They say They would give any thing if they had not. They say if they had money to set up independently they could make a fortune but without it, it is but a poor business." David extracted from his father the promise that he could forgo the trade, if he still felt disenchanted at the end of the trial period. When the trial ended, David did not bind himself to Bache, but, while Bache was away on business, the boy left suddenly to join his father in clearing a wilderness farm. Miffed by the sudden departure, Bache wrote the elder Chambers to defend his trade as respectable and "lucrative." But the Chamberses, like Leonard Worcester, had a different view. By the 1790s the capital required to open a successful printing office was substantial, and only those like Bache or Thomas, with family money or a network of political patrons, could thrive.[25]

During the prosperous 1790s the real wages of American workers rose rapidly, and the wages of skilled workers rose faster than those of the unskilled. But there is no evidence that apprentices benefited from high wages. Indeed, to the extent that the boom led master craftsmen to take more apprentices than they usually employed, within a few years a glut of journeymen developed. That trend was nowhere more striking than in printing, where the nature of the business led to the use of cheap, unskilled labor for many tasks. By the late 1790s the first journeymen's organizations were demanding restrictions on the numbers of apprentices. In the years between 1800 and 1815, real wages for both skilled and unskilled workers remained static. By then the economy had slowed, masters no longer clamored for more journeymen, newly trained journeymen like Andrew Henkel found it difficult to get work, and the labor of apprentices had ceased to be the valuable commodity that it had been during the boom. A study of New York City newspaper advertising for 1800 through 1804 shows a marked increase in the number of cases where a master offered only a token reward for the return of a runaway apprentice. In a glutted labor market, the master did not want the apprentice back, since a replacement with a possibly better disposition might be obtained easily. Some statistics from Boston bear upon this point. In the 1770s and 1780s the Boston Overseers of the Poor bound 40 percent of all poor boys to craftsmen; most of the remainder were treated less favorably by being indented to farmers. During the 1790s the proportion bound to craftsmen rose to 45 percent; between 1800 and 1805 it fell to 14 percent. And whereas in the 1780s 11 percent of these poor children had been bound to masters in Boston, in the 1790s that proportion rose to 18 percent, and from 1800 to 1806 it fell to a mere 10 percent.[26]

The period between the embargo of 1808 and the panic of 1819 was one of economic fluctuation. The embargo caused a severe curtailment of trade that drove numerous merchants into bankruptcy and made survivors less likely to buy houses, furniture, or other craft products. At the same time, the cutting off of imports created a demand for American-made substitutes. Then, between 1810 and 1812, merchants again made money in the European trade, craftsmen linked to those merchants prospered, and craftsmen who faced competition from imports suffered. The War of 1812 brought three years of reversal that partially reestablished the patterns prevalent during the embargo, but this time the federal government made large military procurements that bolstered some crafts, and the pouring of men into the army temporarily created labor shortages. When the war ended in 1815, cheap British imports drove out of business many craftsmen who had entered business during the war. Among the victims was the hatmaker David G. Bright, who in 1817 let go three apprentices when orders for new hats ceased. The establishment of the Second Bank of the United States in 1816 enabled a nearly bankrupt government to refinance its war debts, but the resultant flood of paper currency created further distortions in the economy, and after a brief inflationary boom, the bank reduced the money supply and created the financial panic of 1819. That year Hiram Hill had hoped to start an apprenticeship in his father's trade of carpentry, but "no one seemed to want any more boys at that time." Caleb Foote made a similar discovery and nearly became a cabin boy on an Arctic-bound sealing ship before good luck made him an apprentice printer. Between 1815 and 1825, real-wage rates rose, primarily because of a decline in living costs, but shorter work weeks during the depression of 1819 may have kept real income from increasing.[27]

The gyrations in economic activity that occurred in the decade before 1819, combined with the fact that different crafts were vulnerable to specific economic changes in different ways, created chaos in the relationship between master and apprentice. Fluctuating economic conditions meant that masters were reluctant to commit themselves to the fixed, long-term labor supply that traditional apprenticeship implied. In the new environment, no master craftsman could predict the needs of his shop, and he did not wish to feed, clothe, and train an apprentice only to discover, like David G. Bright, that he needed no help. And the apprentice had a similar concern. He had no desire to be exploited to learn a trade that could not be practiced profitably after it was learned. That was why youths like Leonard Worcester or David Chambers changed occupations, and why apprentices like Joseph Belknap felt free to move around to look for better opportunities. In this new environment running away, as Benjamin Franklin earlier demonstrated, might be a rational economic calculation. Because fluctuating economic conditions made masters as well as apprentices reluctant to engage in long term contracts, the consequence was that both came to prefer either short-term indentures or more informal arrangements. For example, in wartime New York neither Stephen Allen nor his master cared particularly that the youth had not been indented. The arrangement was, at least for the moment, mutually convenient. A generation of violent economic fluctuation coming on top of the disruptions of the Revolutionary War undermined apprenticeship economically, socially, politically, and intellectually. Never again would Americans accept tradition merely because it was tradition.[28]

CHAPTER TWO

The Master's Authority

In the decades following the Revolution, the authority of master crafts-men to manage their apprentices came under increasing challenge. In part, the war and the fluctuating economy had produced uncertainty that clashed with a master's authority. Since that authority rested largely on the primacy of tradition, any uncertainty was bound to undermine that authority. At the same time, the master's superior knowledge was called into question by the rise of alternative sources of knowledge about crafts-manship. And as if these threats were not enough, the master had to con-tend with a generation of apprentices who, having absorbed Revolution-ary rhetoric, spouted claims to liberty and equality. Republican ideology did not square very well with absolute supremacy of the master over his apprentices. Even the religious revivals of the day sometimes proved to be disruptive to the master's authority. A youth who had just had a con-version experience, especially when he contrasted his newfound religion with the often guilt-ridden irreligion of his master, had found in God an authority figure beside which his master did not compare. For a variety of reasons apprentices increasingly challenged masters, and masters, com-ing from older generations that venerated authority, saw the challenges as signs of insolence and impudence that needed to be crushed. So ordi-nances were passed to punish rowdy youths, to hush up their demands to be heard, and to restore the decorum of the past. Apprentices, for their part, decided that if they could not get what they considered to be just treatment, then they would simply leave. The evidence points to an in-crease in the number of runaway apprentices. Masters responded to this problem as one might expect, by lobbying for and getting tough new laws for the regulation of apprenticeship. In the end, it seemed that the master's authority could be maintained only through the courts.

One of the most important changes was in the way in which knowledge and technical skills were passed from generation to generation. Traditionally, skilled crafts were passed either from father to son or from master to apprentice. While the transmission of knowledge was important, it was perhaps less important than the withholding of knowledge from outsiders. Secret family recipes, passed from generation to generation orally, enabled a family to gain a reputation and to retain an exclusive control of production that was better than any patent. One has only to ponder the reputation of the violin maker Antonio Stradivari, whose family died out taking their secrets to the grave. Apprenticeship formally recognized the passage of skilled-craft techniques by specifying, in the indentures, that the master was to reveal his "mystery" to the apprentice, and, in return, the apprentice pledged to keep these techniques secret.

By the late eighteenth century craft secrets had begun to lose their "mystery." Craftsmen were increasingly willing to reveal their secrets to those who were neither sons nor apprentices. The trend was accelerated by the rise of science and technology, whereby outsiders often developed new techniques that destroyed the value of secrets customarily passed from generation to generation. For example, the innovation of using coal tar to help prevent rot in wooden sailing ships superseded less effective methods long used by ship carpenters. Technological advancement also made it more important for craftsmen to acquire the new techniques than to maintain old secrets. A weaver might thus choose to sell his secrets in order to raise capital to buy textile machinery. The decline of secrecy was also encouraged by rising literacy among craftsmen, a wider dissemination of information in books, pamphlets, and newspapers, and the ability, for the first time, of a craftsman to make money by selling craft secrets to the public through the press. In the United States the dissemination of craft secrets was launched by various how-to books. Early examples were George Fisher's *The Instructor* (1786) and *One Thousand Valuable Secrets* (1795). The latter volume included material on engraving, ironmongering, varnishes, mastics, cements, sealing wax, glass, paint, gilding, dyeing wood, casting in molds, and ink. Sometimes trade secrets appeared in popular agricultural manuals or encyclopedias, such as the one published by Dr. Rees. All these volumes, however, presented fairly general information about a variety of crafts, and it soon became clear that what the public prized was a book in which a craftsman told all his own craft's secrets.[1]

In 1792 John Hargrove published detailed information about weaving. In his preface he boasted, "I am the first Mechanic, who has ever favored the American Weaver and Manufacturer, with a public Assistant of this kind. Long! too long! has the Weaving trade remained a mystery (at least in the figured line) to hundreds, and thousands, who have served a regular Apprenticeship to that business, & followed it afterwards for many years: Selfish motives have prevented those, who *were* capable of giving Instructions, from revealing the art, least it might operate against their own personal interest (having no desire to promote the Prosperity of their Country at the risk of their own) but the secret has (in a good measure) lately fallen into the hands of one, who is willing that all concerned should share the benefit." Hargrove's work was followed by others, sometimes offered at extravagant prices. In 1795 Oliver Evans, a onetime apprentice wheelwright turned engineer and inventor, published a guide for the building of a mill. Some of the new works were American imprints of English editions. For example, in 1800 Batty Langley's architectural pattern book for carpenters first appeared in the United States. It helped revolutionize the building industry by giving carpenters easy rules for creating popular architectural styles. The American edition contained one hundred plates, a tribute to the changing art of engraving. Indeed, the increased cheapness and rising popularity of engraving made craft books possible for the first time.[2]

The new century brought more volumes of this type, and they tended to be more detailed, more complete, more carefully written, and more useful. In the 1820s Amanda Jones revealed the secrets of tailoring. She claimed, "In a few hours, a person may acquire such a knowledge of the art, as will enable him to cut all sizes and fashions, with the greatest accuracy." If one could learn tailoring in a few hours, who needed to be apprenticed to a tailor? Other tailor's books were soon in print. J. D. Yates took pains to sign every copy of his book to discourage pirated editions, while Joseph Watts wrote his own testimonial: "The author of the following work served a regular apprenticeship at the Tailoring business in England, and received the best instruction that could be obtained from the most intelligent and skillful workmen of that country." In 1817 Bronson and Bronson published a guide to home weaving and dyeing that so impressed the president of the Berkshire Agricultural Society in Massachusetts that he urged every householder to purchase a copy of the book. In 1826 the dyeing section was reprinted, and the entire book is still in print for modern use. A few years later William Tucker, author of yet another home-dyeing book, defended the dissemination of knowledge, even at the expense of revealing trade secrets. "The world cannot long be kept in darkness," he wrote, "and if there be any business or profession, affording larger profits than those of tradesmen in general, this, like every thing else, will eventually find its level." In 1833 Cornelius Molony sought to postpone such an eventuality by charging $10 a copy for his book revealing professional dyeing secrets.[3]

Such publications had a profound effect upon apprenticeship. Widespread dissemination of traditional craft secrets, particularly in such popular outlets as encyclopedias, devalued apprenticeship. If a youth wanted to learn a craft, he needed only a book and not a master. One day in 1787 twelve-year-old Alexander Anderson found in a friend's encyclopedia an article on engraving, and he decided to try learning this art. He obtained a few copper pennies, visited a friendly silversmith, and had the smith flatten the pennies in his mill. Using a graver made from the back spring of an old pocketknife, Sandy, as the boy was called, etched a head on a flattened copper. Then he built a crude rolling press and printed copies of his engraving in red oil paint. Later he persuaded a blacksmith to make some engraving tools. Engraving on copper, pewter, or soft type metal, Sandy found that small ships cut into type metal could be sold to the newspapers for use in advertising. Although Anderson later was apprenticed to a surgeon, he was so obsessed with engraving that he abandoned a medical practice to pursue his self-taught trade and eventually took a number of apprentices. He produced more than ten thousand engravings—not bad for a career that began with the perusal of an encyclopedia article.[4]

The new books also subverted the master's authority. A technical book often presented more knowledge of the craft than the master had, and an honest master might admit this fact by instructing his apprentice to read a book. Simon Newcomb, apprenticed to a medical practitioner in Nova Scotia, was at first surprised, even mortified, by his master's telling him to read a medical book. In time, however, Simon came to see that the author of the book was considerably more knowledgeable than his ignorant master. That discovery reduced the apprentice's opinion of his master and, by implication, threatened the master's status and authority. If the master had less information to offer the apprentice, the apprentice had less inclination to look to the master for training and education in his trade. At the same time science and technology had begun to generate innovations that in many crafts displaced traditional processes. These new techniques had to be learned from the books, pamphlets, and newspapers that announced the innovations, and the master was no more an expert than was his apprentice. Indeed, since youth is always more open to experimentation, the apprentice might more readily adopt new ways that the master, bound to tradition, simply could not bring himself to try. Under those circumstances, a master who knew and revered craft secrets was to his apprentice not an asset but a burden. Traditionally, the master's authority had rested on his technical expertise and on an aura of mystery, captured in the language of the indentures, that surrounded that expertise. The boyish apprentice was to be in awe of his master both because he knew so much and, perhaps more important, because of the seeming magic by which the knowledgeable master turned raw leather into shoes, wood into barrels, or paper, type, and ink into books. To an untrained youth, the myriad processes, the little rituals invoked at each step, and the repetitions that always produced the same result were a form of magic. The craft books stripped away that magic, and if a youth could read, he could discover the processes of his craft on the sterile printed page. The master ceased to be a magician and became only one of a thousand followers of a routine.[5]

In addition to the loss of craft secrets, the master's authority suffered from the power of republican ideology. A people who could suddenly overthrow centuries of tradition to agree that "Common Sense" required their dispensing with monarchy could overthrow almost any tradition. Indeed, the more an institution resembled kingship, the more easily it could be challenged. The Revolution that rejected the authority of George III was not long in spawning a host of religious sects that rejected the authority of bishops and other church leaders. And it was republican ideology, more than anything else, that led to an assault upon slavery, successfully in the North, with only partial success in the South. The evil of slavery, like the evil of monarchy, was the concentration of power and authority in a single, unchecked hand. The Revolution, of course, was incomplete. Not only did slavery survive, but women gained no liberty from fathers or husbands, and apprentices did not gain freedom from their masters, at least not officially. Yet boys could not help breathing what was in the air. There was "a loss of subordination in society" that led boys to "assume the airs of full-grown coxcombs," as Charles Janson put it. "I, and other boys situated similarly to myself," recalled Ebenezer Fox, "thought we had wrongs to be redressed; rights to be maintained; and, as no one appeared disposed to act the part of a redresser, it was our duty and our privilege to assert our own rights. We made a direct application of the doctrines we daily heard, in relation to the oppression of the mother country, to our own circumstances; and thought that we were more oppressed than our fathers were. I thought that I was doing myself great injustice by remaining in bondage, when I ought to go free; and that the time was come, when I should liberate myself from the thraldom of others, and set up a government of my own; or, in other words, do what was right in the sight of my own eyes."[6]

Such sentiments expressed the prevailing views of the day. It became an age of republican manners, and children naturally espoused the new fashion of frank and open expression. "They seem to be taught in the cradle," said Grenville Mellen, "that there is freedom of mind. . . ." He added, in keeping with the new spirit, "and 'tis well they think so. . . ."

These independent children did not always endear themselves to their more restrained, traditional, and conservative parents. For example, when the apprentice printer Simeon Ide's masters dissolved their partnership and closed their shop, the eighteen-year-old did not hesitate to find another position without parental consent. Simeon apprenticed himself to the publisher of the *Washingtonian,* a staunch Federalist newspaper. Because the youth was a strong Jeffersonian, he agreed to take the position only if he could do book and job work and not have to print the politically offensive paper. Although the new master acceded to this request, Simeon's Republican father was outraged. He wrote, "I . . . am sorry to learn you are in that dirty business and place; . . . I had not supposed that I had a child that would . . . tarnish true Republicanism, by touching that unclean thing. The Mosaic rules, I fear, will not cleanse the man that touches that loathsome Press, the *Washingtonian.*" The father commanded, "I must insist on your coming home immediately." To this old-fashioned letter asserting parental authority, the impertinent Simeon replied, "Sir—You yourself cannot have a greater antipathy for the *Washingtonian* and the cause its editor is engaged in, than I have." He added, without any promise of filial obedience, that he was currently engaged setting type for the Constitution and Washington's Farewell Address and not for the newspaper. In the new order of things, a father was not to command his son.[7]

Conservatives were horrified. They sought to maintain social order and hierarchy, especially within the family. These ideas paralleled developments in the political realm, where the new Constitution also created both order and hierarchy. And as Simeon Baldwin suggested in 1788, one reason for adopting the Constitution was "to lop off the libertinism of juvenile independence." In 1792 *A Parent's Advice for His Family* took a conservative, insistent, and constructive line. "It pleases divine Providence," this advice book bluntly stated, "to dispose of persons into various stations and relations in this world. As it is the duty of parents conscienciously to endeavour to bring up their children in the nurture and admonition of the Lord, so it is the duty of children to endeavour to hearken to, obey, and follow their parents instructions and counsels. . . ." In 1794 William Arthur expressed a similar view. "Society is a chain of many links," he wrote. "With tender care, the parents rear up the children; and the children, when pious example and education are blessed, as the means of softening, and forming their hearts, are a comfort to the parents." Then he asked, "Are not husbands and wives, parents and children, masters and servants culpable, very culpable for neglecting the duties of their respective stations?" Arthur concluded by admonishing masters to be responsible for the religious instruction and behavior of their servants. Guardians of virtue looked for support in the restoration and maintenance of order wherever they could find it. One address urged godparents to watch that the godchild was placed with a master who held daily family religious exercises. This policy would ensure that the youth would not fall away from religion because of an irreligious master.[8]

Conservative hopes were swept away, ironically, by a tide of religion. It was, however, religion with a difference. In the 1790s revivals that began on the frontier and then spread to the cities offered a religion in which man had a personal and direct relationship with God. This evangelical faith found a vast popular audience in a series of revivals that swept and reswept the country between 1800 and 1830. Called the Second Great Awakening, to distinguish it from an earlier era of revivals in the 1740s, the movement had many local variations but a common theme of religious renewal through direct, personal experience. The greatest appeal was to youths. As early as 1798 the revival reached New England, and from Hartford came the report, "Young people of both sexes flock by hundreds, and the prospect is flattering in the extreme." Youths wrote each other religious letters, and hundreds in Hartford became excited and interested in religion for the first time. In Shaftsbury, Vermont, a minister reported that more than seventy youths and children came to a religious meeting at his house, and in Litchfield, Maine, there was "a wonderful out-pouring of God's Spirit . . . especially among the youth. As many as twenty-five have joined this church this winter, who are not more than twenty years old; and one lad who was but nine." In Dorchester, Massachusetts, just outside Boston, Thaddeus M. Harris organized a religious society of youths. Religious enthusiasm continued well into the new century. In 1822 the Reverend Nathan Perkins commented, "Now, when I look round on the congregation, with pleasure, I see many, many youths, professors of the divine religion of *Jesus,* and on sacramental sabbaths, are found taking their seat at his table." To Perkins the contrast with 1772 was striking; at that time, not a single youth had taken communion.[9]

Evangelical religion, with its emphasis upon personal responsibility, put family government, with its emphasis upon parental authority, on the defensive. In 1802 Martin Tullar, while lamenting the fact, also offered a concise explanation. He wrote, "The support of family government, a due subordination among children, which has, in time past, been thought essential to good order, and the peace of community; and which has been injoined as a parental duty of divine appointment, is now, more generally, rejected, as a species of rigid sovereignty unbecoming the spirit and genius of a free, independant people; and as calculated to stupify the senses, and destroy the spirit of laudable ambation, in children." Tullar, and other conservatives who wrote after 1800, increasingly had to take into account new social realities, and while conservatives did not openly concede any virtues to the looser child-rearing practices that prevailed, their very admission that traditional family government was threatened showed the weakness of their position and the trends of the time. The declining emphasis on the righteousness of hierarchy and authority was accompanied by a growing emphasis on the spirit of religion. The revivals sought to transcend the matter by stressing a religion of love— man's love for God, a parent's love for the child, and the child's love for the parent. Family relations, as Luther Gleson suggested in 1805, were to be more reciprocal than hierarchical. Children still were expected to obey parents, because children were after all children, but there was less distance between child and parent, and both were awash in Christian love. While this concept had appeal within the family, it could not be applied easily to the positions of master and apprentice. In one sense, the relationship was too distant, for the apprentice always was an untutored, ignorant learner of a craft, and no religious concept could bring closer the work relations of master and apprentice. In another sense, the relationship was too close, for an apprentice might be nearly as old as his master, an adult in size and strength, and the closeness between master and apprentice implied by the decline of the hierarchical tradition left the two uncomfortably close—so close that they quarreled, that the master's moral authority was swept away, and that the apprentice ran away with little or no guilt.[10]

The triumph of evangelicalism heralded the waning of traditional society. That society had functioned on the basis of hierarchy, subordination to authority, and the use of rich rituals by which subordinates continually gave evidence of their loyalty to authority. Ritual, of course, was traditional and largely static. Its significance was less in the content of the ritual than in the act of a subordinating relationship that occurred whenever ritual was performed. Consider, for example, the matter of family government. The father or master as head of the family was responsible for the behavior of all the members of the family, including apprentices, and other family members were to respect this hierarchical arrangement. In this kind of family fathers were held in fear and awe. But the source of the father's power was the willing subordination of the other family members to the father's authority. The father could be good or bad, and it mattered little, since the source of his authority was prescribed not by his behavior but by the social role that he filled and the relationship of others to that role. Ritual provided a means for the constant invocation of the correctness of the relationships and the just authority of the father. Perhaps nowhere was this more certain than in the matter of family religious exercises. The importance of family devotions in the morning and evening, and before and after each meal, was not so much to maintain a religious sensibility in the family as to reaffirm the father's role as head of the family. Indeed, the father had the sole responsibility for each of these religious exercises precisely as a way to remind each family member who was in charge. The symbolic significance of this role was paramount, for it was a matter of controversy whether, in the temporary absence of the father, the family should forgo family devotion, follow the mother's lead, or act under the authority of the eldest son. Traditional religious authorities did not agree on the solution, but they did agree that none of these was a truly satisfactory substitute for the father leading family worship.[11]

Another example of rich ritual concerns the religious instruction of children. In traditional society a child was instructed in religion by being told to memorize a catechism of questions and answers. The child often was asked to memorize such a catechism at the age of four or five, when he could not understand the concepts discussed in the dialogue. Moreover, children were not the only ones without comprehension, as the apprentice Isaiah Thomas discovered. The boy's master, teaching the catechism, once asked, "What are the Decrees of God?" Isaiah replied he did not know and asked his master to tell him. When the master read the answer from the catechism book, Isaiah became convinced that his master understood as little of the answer as he himself did. In a society where content was less important than form, where ritual was respected and admired, it was less worrisome to a parent or master if a child did not understand what he had memorized than if he had not been able to memorize at all. The father, holding the position of authority, commanded the memorization, and the child, as the dutiful subordinate, obeyed and thus confirmed the father's authority.[12]

After 1800 religious instruction was given on a new basis. There were religious pamphlets and books specifically written for children four to six years old, either to be read by the children or to be read to the children by a parent, quite possibly the mother rather than the father. These tracts were not to be memorized; rather, they used the vehicle of telling stories to instill moral virtues. Children were trained in what was right or wrong not by the presence of external authority figures who ordered subordinates to behave in correct ways but by the inculcation of moral values in the mind of the child. At the same time Sunday schools began to be organized for children. In other words, the father ceased to be the sole source of religious instruction and now shared that role with Sunday school teachers. While these teachers encouraged children to memorize the catechism, it was no longer the central feature of religious instruction. Teachers sought to motivate their pupils, through the use of such prizes as religious pamphlets and books, to memorize Bible verses. And after a child recited a particular verse, the teacher would ask the class to discuss its meaning and significance. Again, content replaced form. And now, for the first time, the child was molded and shaped in morals by the institution of the Sunday school rather than by parental command.[13]

Because evangelicals stressed salvation through a personal experience consistent with a ripening maturity, youths living in an evangelical atmosphere underwent severe pressure to have a religious experience and conversion. As an eighteen-year-old clerk in a Philadelphia bookstore, James Barton Longacre kept a diary that largely expressed his religious anxieties. He upbraided himself for worldliness, negligence in prayer, and lack of religious spirit. A year later James indented himself to an engraver, but this apprenticeship did not alleviate his anxieties. "I want to know and feel more of the love of God," he wrote a friend. "I want to possess it strong enough to lift me above the world, and the fear of Death—Do you love me? pray for me—O! may our God keep you my brother—and tho' seperated in body, may we be united in heart and united in his heavenly kingdom." There is no evidence Longacre ever had the religious experience he so desperately craved.[14]

Perhaps Henry Clarke Wright was more fortunate. Brought up in a strict Calvinist family, Henry was at seventeen apprenticed to a nonreligious hatmaker. The youth, at first relieved to be free from religious duties, soon became friends with an older religious woman. Mrs. Snow did not talk to him as a Calvinist invoking duty, but she sought out his religious sentiment, answered his questions, and showed him that faith could be based on feelings. To Mrs. Snow, the proof of God's existence was her faith that it was so. At twenty Henry, along with fifty other mostly young people, was converted in a revival. His conversion began while he was sitting on his bed reading and thinking. Suddenly, brooding gave way to a great joy and a sense of deliverance. This event was so important that he sat down and wrote his father a letter, the first one he had ever written. In it Henry revealed how fear of ridicule from his companions at work had kept him from religion. Now he was reconciled to death—and salvation. He noted, "This day has been more happy to me than ten thousand times ten thousand days of mirth." When Henry left his apprenticeship, the youth's master was in tears over his own lack of faith.[15]

Henry Wright's conversion freed him from psychological dependence upon his master. His greater duty now, he knew, was to spiritual authority that called from heaven and not to earthly authority that called from the shop. And when an apprentice's religious experience was not matched by any similar experience by the master, the master's ability to govern the apprentice was threatened by the apprentice's newly gained religion and the sincere and serene self-confidence that usually accompanied it. It is not surprising to learn that master craftsmen were often among the first converted in a revival and that their journeymen and apprentices tended to follow in the master's footsteps. Heman Bangs, for example, was apprenticed to his brother John, a blacksmith soon converted into a zealous Methodist. "John now became very strict," recalled Heman, "and wished to make us all Christians—if not by Gospel-suasion, by Law-compulsion." These heavy-handed practices produced a good number of quarrels, but in the end Heman was converted. To a master, the mass conversion of his help in a revival offered the possibility for a decline in drinking, gaming, swearing, and shop pranks that disrupted business, a reduction in employee theft of raw materials, and the development of group morale that would lead to better cooperation and higher output. Yet evangelical religion was not without its price for the master, since the emphasis on personal salvation undercut the hierarchical tradition that had long prevailed in the shop. The new religion, then, weakened the old authority of the master.[16]

On the whole, apprentices were becoming not religious but insolent and saucy. Generations of unhappy apprentices, such as John Fitch or Stephen Allen, had behaved meekly; they were now superseded by a generation of republican apprentices devoted to an assertion of their rights, even at the cost of displeasing their masters. For example, the apprentices in Thomas Adams's Boston printing shop were offended by the food. John Prentiss recalled, "Our breakfast was usually a bowl of *thin* chocolate, with brown bread. With often a poor cook, the bread was *doughy* and sometimes too old. On one occasion we talked *out loud loud* about it, and this brought forward the mistress of the house, indignant at our expressed satisfaction. The other boys did not defend, but I, the youngest took a coarse piece of our bread and brake it in her presense, making the mouldy strings very visible, and she said no more!" But this encounter did not end the moldy bread. Sometime later the apprentices were given another bad half-loaf, and Bill Cowan resolved to humiliate the Adamses by tossing the loaf over a high fence into a neighbor's yard. Unfortunately for Bill, someone in the Adams house watching from an upper window saw what had been done, and the neighbor was asked to send the bread home. Adams considered the incident a high misdemeanor, and he called in each apprentice in turn for an interview. Cowan did not deny what he had done, and he so justified his conduct—refusing to apologize—that he left either of his own account or at Adams's request. This lack of humility deeply offended members of the older generation, who saw it, correctly, as an attack upon their authority. The other apprentices were allowed to remain, but Prentiss felt guilty and ashamed and had no answer to Adams's question, "What would [your] father say to be informed of such conduct?"[17]

Bill Cowan was not the only apprentice who neglected to show a proper respect for authority. Another defiant youth, fourteen-year-old Millard Fillmore, found that his apprenticeship at cloth dressing had turned into perpetual woodchopping to keep the charcoal pit going. One evening after a day of chopping, Millard came into the shop and was ordered to chop wood for the shop fireplace. The boy lifted his axe, told his master he had not come to the shop merely to chop wood, and, before his master could reply, darted outside and began to chop. The master followed and asked Millard if he felt abused because he had to chop wood. The youth said he did and added he was not disposed to submit. The master insisted on obedience to his orders. Millard bridled, "Yes, if they are right; otherwise I will not; and I have submitted to this injustice long enough." The master said, "I will chastise you for your disobedience." As the master stepped closer, the apprentice raised his axe and said, "You will not chastise me. If you approach me I will split you down." The master wisely walked away.[18]

Joseph Belknap, apprenticed to the Philadelphia printer Robert Aitken, was in constant trouble. Aitken charged Jo with neglecting business and keeping the company of "*bad* boys." Whatever the truth of this charge, there is no doubt that the streets of Philadelphia could be remarkably fascinating to a youth who had grown up in rural New Hampshire. Jo's father wrote a frank letter to a friend concerning his son and Aitken. "I find the breach is grown so wide," wrote the Reverend Jeremy Belknap, "that they *both* desire a seperation. A., by *his own* account, has made a very free use of 'the fist' and the 'knotted cord,' both very bad instruments of reformation in the hands of a perfervid Caledonian." The master complained that the boy had skipped Sunday services—a right apprentices were likely to assert under the new doctrine of personal liberty—and Jo justified his absence to his father by saying it was due to an eye blackened by his master at Sunday dinner. One senses that more was at stake here than the clash of two strong-willed individuals. Aitken, a Scots immigrant, expected his apprentices to be subservient to his authority, and Jo Belknap, infected with the new republican ideology prevalent in postwar Philadelphia, detested the very notion of subservience. Aitken's blows were given not so much to cow the apprentice as to show his own rage for not being given the respect he deemed proper for his station. The senior Belknap and Aitken called in arbitrators, who saw no chance for reconciliation, and the indentures were canceled. The Reverend Belknap recognized the danger in this outcome, for his eighteen-year-old son had been allowed to triumph over his master and escape from all authority.[19]

The Reverend Belknap next indented his son to William Mycall of Newburyport. This master printer, like Aitken, found his modern apprentices too spirited, outspoken, and lacking in respect for his authority. One morning Mycall's three apprentices were scolded. At the time they prudently said little, but half an hour later at breakfast they reflected upon what they perceived to be their ill treatment. The oldest said, "All my comfort is that it is only one year more I have got to live in this situation." The youngest of the trio added that "though he had more than *one*, yet *he* had only two years to stay and that was not quite so much as seven which he once had." Jo then observed that he had only fifteen months left. At this point Mycall, who had eavesdropped, flew into the room in a rage. The master, reportedly looking like "a mad boar," said that "he did not wish any body to live with him who was not contented" and that the youths "might all go as soon as [they] pleased." The apprentices boasted they could do better elsewhere, and the master offered to tear up their indentures. But, given the weak economy, the apprentices did not leave.[20]

What was to become of this younger generation of saucy and insolent boys? Everywhere there were lamentations. Thus, in 1783 Samuel Mather of Boston called that city's youths "corrupt and vicious" with a "disorderly, loose, profane and vicious manner of speaking and acting." Careless, neglectful parents failed to govern their children, and the result was children who grew up to be ungovernable youths who showed no respect for authority. In 1784 Joseph Huntington told the Connecticut legislature the country was overrun with idleness, luxury, profanity, Sabbath breaking, intemperance, lasciviousness, wantonness, pride, and extravagance. The worst vice of the day, however, was a "raging spirit of jealousy pointed against all in power." This popular spirit made men "rebellious, obstinate and heady." Behind this spirit, Huntington and Mather agreed, was the decline of Calvinism. People who no longer recognized themselves as lowly sinners before an all-powerful God were natural victims of vice and social disorder. The following year Jeremy Belknap, addressing the New Hampshire General Court, lamented, "How melancholy to think that a great part of the rising generation is likely to be ignorant & unprincipled!" He, too, no doubt in part influenced by his troubles with his son, feared the popular contempt for authority.[21]

The fear of a corrupted rising generation existed outside New England, and in 1795 Matthew Clarkson discussed the matter with reference to the large and growing city of Philadelphia. Clarkson, the city recorder, was alarmed by throngs of youths who collected together on the street corners in the evenings. These crowds of youths had become gangs that attacked small children, innocent youths who passed through the gangs, and each other. They taunted passersby with obscenities and occasionally attacked older persons, particularly strangers. They frightened citizens by burning dangerous bonfires in the streets, they exhibited effigies of persons they disliked, and they broke windows and threw stones, sticks, dirt, and snowballs. These youths thieved, violated the Sabbath, disturbed worshipers with noise, blocked carriages in the streets, and played such tricks as knocking on doors and then running away. Clarkson warned that Philadelphia's reputation was becoming so bad that reputable people would not move to the city to raise families in such an environment. Clarkson, an extraordinarily shrewd observer, noted that the passage of time brought acts that were more and more outrageous, as youths dared each other to commit an act that went beyond any previously committed. He feared the long-range consequences of this pattern of escalation. Criminal tendencies, he warned, began in the home, beyond the view of the police, and they had to be crushed there by authority—by a combination of ministers, teachers, and, especially, heads of families, both fathers and master craftsmen.

About masters and apprentices Clarkson had a great deal to say. Masters and apprentices alike brought complaints into court, and in many cases the court found it necessary to admonish both parties to carry out the duties that each station required. Apprentices most commonly became vicious and disobedient only after a want of regular attention and proper family government. The master carelessly threw away his responsibility for moral training, and then he faced the dilemma of dealing with an insolent apprentice either by bearing the insult or by using extreme severity; neither response was entirely satisfactory. A master could prevent this kind of situation from developing by governing "at *all times*" with "a strict and steady hand in exercising authority." Clarkson showed little sympathy for apprentices. Their time belonged entirely to the master, and they had no right to the company of other apprentices, to loiter in the streets, or to spend their evenings in idle amusement. The master's permission was necessary in all cases, and it was Clarkson's view that a master should require his apprentices to remain in the master's house in the evening. Furthermore, an apprentice who was insolent, idle, or disobedient was subject to being corrected—that is, beaten—by the master, who neglected his duty if he did not correct the youth. "There are, at present," he stated, "loud and general complaints of the insubordination of apprentice youth, as well as servants of other descriptions, and of the difficulties and inconvenience produced in families by their unreasonable expectations and demands. To check these, therefore, as far as law and duty will permit, is peculiarly incumbent on the magistrates. Parents who have bound their children as apprentices are too apt to listen to their unjust complaints, and to apply to the magistrate in their behalf and against their masters. This practice ought to be pointedly discouraged." While neighbors, schools, and government officials all had a role to play, in the long run Clarkson traced all youthful vice to the want of family government, example, and instruction.[22]

Clarkson, like others of his generation, ignored the republican ideology that youths imbibed. Yet he raised an important question: where did fierce republican pride end and mere rowdyism begin? It was not always easy to tell. At seventeen William Otter was apprenticed to Kenwith King, a New York plasterer. Although King had preferred that the boy serve a trial period, William's father insisted upon the immediate signing of indentures, because the boy already had quit three other trades during trials. As it turned out, King was a good master, but he could not keep the independent-minded William from making trouble for himself. About a year after the signing of the indentures, the youth's mother died, and about eight months later, his father died. The son, on the basis of his father's deathbed testimony, expected a small inheritance, but the will had been drawn by Thomas Mills, who had married William's sister, and the will left everything to Mills. The boy boiled, and after a time he threatened Mills, who promptly complained to King, and the master exerted his authority to exact a promise from his apprentice that he would stay away from Mills. Privately, however, William swore to break this promise and obtain vengeance.[23]

Young Otter discussed his problem with a friend, the apprentice baker John Lane, who advised Otter to give Mills a "genteel and good walloping." Otter pointed out that if he did that he would lose his apprenticeship. Lane then revealed that he was planning to leave New York for Philadelphia. Otter could come along. The two swore a secret pact and became fast friends. On Christmas Eve they went to a dance together, joined a mob rioting at a Catholic church, and wound up at an Irish grogshop ordering rum. The tavern keeper refused to serve them and called them rascals. So they beat him and his two assistants, and when the tavern keeper's wife fled to the cellar, they locked her in. Then they took over the shop and refreshed themselves. A mob came in and smashed everything. By the time Otter got home, he had two gashes on his head and a black eye. His master, wise enough not to try to control his young republican apprentice, merely said it was a wonder his brains weren't knocked out. About four days later Lane and Otter went to a notorious dance hall and raised a row for which the police nearly caught them. After Christmas, King sent Otter to night school, but about half the time the youth cut classes and went to dances instead. Once Otter started a fight in order to sneak into a dance without paying; he became part of a gang that smashed an oyster shop because the owner was saucy; he hit a grocer with a slingshot to avenge an earlier beating when the grocer had been a bouncer. In March the pair laid plans to leave town. Otter borrowed $10 from his sister and saved another $10 from his overtime earnings as a plasterer. With trip money in hand, Otter joined Lane in a final brawl, leading a gang of fifty through a dance hall. Afterward, Otter waylaid Mills and beat him. Then the two fled to Philadelphia. "The city of New York," said Otter, "lost two very fine boys."[24]

In Philadelphia Lane already had a journeyman baker's job lined up, and his new boss arranged for Otter's temporary board while the two youths combed the city looking for a journeyman's situation for Otter. Otter had a job interview with Timothy Currans, a master plasterer.

Currans asked, "Where did you learn the trade?"

"New York," replied Otter.

"Who with?"

"With Mr. King."

"You look too young to be a journeyman," observed Currans.

"I bought my time," lied Otter.

"Do you call yourself a master workman?"

"Any kind of plain work."

"How much a day do you want?"

"What is the going rate?"

"$1.25-2.00 a day; I would give $2 a day, if you could cornish."

"I can't cornish. Do you ever board hands?"

"Never."

"If you board me, I will come on two weeks trial."

"Do you have tools?"

"No."

"Buy them at Rose's factory, the cheapest and best place."[25]

For two weeks Otter worked for Currans on trial, and then Currans offered the youth work at $8 a week for the summer season. After bargaining over some details, the two signed an agreement. A month later both Otter and Lane felt rich—after expenses, primarily board, each had earned about $25. Otter wrote a friend in New York to boast of his success and to find out how Mills was doing. A reply stated that both Mills and King were hunting for Otter, and so was the owner of the smashed dance hall, who wanted $25 to repair damages. The boys sent the man some money. For three months Otter worked steadily, and then King wrote from New York asking him to return. His old master now offered him $1 a day plus a promise to help clear up Otter's difficulties with

Mills. King's generous offer shows an important shift taking place in the institution of apprenticeship. The master did not assert a customary right to control his apprentice, whom he treated much more as an equal than as a lowly subordinate who should be compelled to submit to the master's authority. Otter replied that he would be back in New York in two months, but both lads agreed he was better off in Philadelphia. Young Otter earned money fast and spent it on clothes and entertainment. With this sense of independence the former apprentice's penchant for rowdy violence came to an end.[26]

If an independent-minded republican apprentice did not like his master, his trade, or his surroundings, he could always invoke the high ideal of liberty and run away. Increasingly, perhaps influenced by the example of Benjamin Franklin, apprentices deserted. At age seventeen Robert Bailey might have pondered that in eight years he had tried four trades—tanning, masonry, carpentry, and milling—and that he had learned none of them. While economic fluctuation had eliminated his chances to learn tanning and carpentry, personal disgruntlement had led the youth to abandon masonry and milling by running away. It is doubtful he had any regrets, however, since learning a trade was less important to him than the maintenance of his own fierce republican pride. In 1815, when the seventeen-year-old apprentice printer Ellis Lewis confided his unhappiness to his brother, the youth was told in the old-fashioned way to reconcile himself to his fate. Ellis bridled. "I am not reconciled at all," he wrote, adding that certain members of his master's household were obnoxious, that he feared getting consumption, and that the business did not agree with him at all. He continued in the Harrisburg, Pennsylvania, office for a time, visited relatives at Christmas, returned to the office, and then vanished.[27]

Ellis's master was not amused, and his newspaper carried a rather long advertisement offering $20 for the boy's return. The master described his runaway: "He was decently clad when he went away, but as it is pretty well ascertained that he was encouraged and enticed to his desertion by those whose sense of moral obligations is equal to his own, it is probable he will be provided with funds to exchange his apparel." As the master composed these lines, his anger must have grown, for he added, "All persons are forbidden harboring him at their peril. And the young man himself may rest assured, that however he may hug himself on his dexterity at running away, *justice*, sooner or later, will overtake him, to his cost." Ellis laid low, slipped away to New York, and sought to gain a livelihood as a journeyman under an assumed name. Eight months later Ellis wrote his brother. He seemed to seek sympathy when he noted, "Here I am—behold me at the age of eighteen, alone and unprotected, cast on a tem-

pestuous and unfeeling world, to do and act for myself. In a city where
the most shocking immoralities . . . have full sway—where every allure-
ment is offered to seduce youth from morality and rectitude, it is scarcely
to be expected that I should remain free and uncontaminated amid this
chaos of immoralities;—but I believe I am as well, and perhaps better,
than many others in similar situations with myself." Lonesome yet proud
of his newly acquired independence, he remained in New York for two
years because of his old master's refusal to discuss settling their differences.[28]

In these years runaways were so common that the public was on the
lookout. When thirteen-year-old Sol Smith was sent from Cortland
County, New York, to Boston to work in his brothers' store, he had to
walk. On his second day from home he was picked up by a man who
thought he was a runaway apprentice and accordingly turned the carriage around and drove back three miles. Sol was so astonished that it
took him that long to remember the pass his father had written for him
to avoid such an incident. Once Sol showed his pass, the man turned
around and took Sol five miles in the right direction and gave him
twenty-five cents. Sol clerked for his brothers for three years, until he
quarreled and left for the West. In Louisville, Kentucky, he apprenticed
himself to a newspaper office, but the work was too hard, so he quit and
again drifted west. In Vincennes, Indiana, he apprenticed himself to
Elihu Stout, publisher of the *Western Sun*. Although Sol's master was
sweet-tempered, Mrs. Stout, who had grown up in a slaveholder's household in Kentucky, treated the apprentices like slaves. For a time that fact
was overshadowed by a drama society organized by Sol, his master, and
the other apprentices. Its collapse left Sol restless, and when he heard
about a theater in Nashville, he plotted with another apprentice to run
away. They carefully planned their escape and resolved not to be taken
alive by any fifty men. Mainly, however, they were afraid of Mrs. Stout.
In the middle of the night they crept away and ran fifteen miles to avoid
being overtaken. Later Sol returned to Vincennes to work as a journeyman, and Mrs. Stout told him that she liked him better for having had
the spirit to run away.[29]

When a master advertised a runaway, he sometimes provoked an an-
swering advertisement. One master's offer of a $10 reward for the return
of his apprentice brought an indignant reply from the boy's brother
claiming mistreatment and an illegal binding. In this case the master ran
a second advertisement, accusing the brother of falsehood and warning
against "taking the said runaway for an apprentice without consulting
[the master] first on the occasion." A blacksmith's apprentice stated he
left only after being "abused in the grossest manner" not only by his

master but also by another apprentice and "nay even Negroes." A master shipwright drew from his apprentice the complaint that the advertisement describing him was incomplete. "I think in describing my features," stated Alexander Phillips, "you omitted the number of marks and blood you made with a Cow Skin." Another apprentice explained his departure in somewhat different terms. The master's conduct had made the apprentice "ashamed to be seen in his house any longer." This apprentice had a point, for his master had been accused of hiding a suspected murderer in the house. Another boy had been left in rags. The master, complained the apprentice's father, was "indifferent whether he perished or lived." Sometimes a master learned that his apprentice had left because he had turned twenty-one. After the shipwright John Jarvis read that claim from Samuel Davis's father, Jarvis inserted a second advertisement to demand proof of the youth's age. "I took him as an Apprentice when he was an expence to his father," complained Jarvis, "and after raising him and learning him to work, then, says Mr. Davis, son you can earn something for yourself; you may go away and work for yourself: you never was bound, you cannot be compelled to stay any longer." Jarvis seems to have had trouble keeping straight the ages of his apprentices, for a few years later he had a similar dispute with another apprentice.[30]

When the master's authority had begun to come under attack, whether from the chaos of the Revolution, economic fluctuations, the loss of craft secrecy, republican ideology rampant among the young, or increased rowdyism and violence, masters had tried to supplement traditional authority with new laws. After 1790 increasing violence and disorder in American towns and cities led to the enactment of new municipal ordinances, many of which dealt specifically with apprentices. In 1791, for example, Albany, New York, passed legislation "to suppress improper diversions in the streets and lanes." Gaming, making noise in the streets, and playing so as to attract a crowd were prohibited. Offenders were to pay fines, and masters were responsible for the fines of their apprentices. If a master refused, his apprentice was to be sent to jail. A special provision applied to swearing. If the convicted oath maker was under sixteen, the parent or master had to pay a fine; but if he was sixteen or older, he had to pay his own fine or stand in the stocks for one hour. In 1795 Georgetown, Maryland, prohibited apprentices from obtaining liquor. If an apprentice did so, his master was to be fined $5, or the apprentice was to be given up to thirty-nine stripes or imprisoned twenty days, as determined by the court. Two years later Newburyport, Massachusetts, passed a series of similar ordinances, and, again, the master was expected to pay for the misbehavior of his apprentice. In 1799 the New York Common Council ordered two thousand handbills warning citizens to stay away from nightly gatherings of "Crowds of Apprentices and other disorderly Persons who have assembled in a tumultuous Manner." Masters were admonished to restrain their apprentices.[31]

Increased municipal regulation was accompanied by increased state regulation. Between 1783 and 1799 an unprecedented twelve states passed new statutes concerning apprenticeship. The only states that did not— North Carolina, Georgia, Tennessee, and Vermont—were overwhelmingly rural and had few apprentices. These new state laws codified practices inherited from the English common law, modified those practices in the light of post-Revolutionary American experience, and dealt with problems that first arose during the economic boom of the 1790s. One way in which these laws bowed to republican ideology was in breaking with English precedent to prohibit a youth from being indented past the age of twenty-one. At that age all males, except slaves, were to be free to pursue whatever business they wanted. The laws also specified more clearly the conditions under which an apprentice might bring charges against a master for cruelty or neglect and how such a suit was to be handled. The greater ease with which an apprentice could lodge a complaint against his master was another sign of the erosion of the master's authority. The laws, however, concentrated on the problem of runaways. In most states new, efficient procedures were established for the return of runaways, and several states imposed stiff fines for anyone enticing an apprentice to run away or harboring a runaway. In New York a runaway who was caught was required to serve double the time lost, while in New Jersey the master of a runaway could sue the runaway anytime within six years of the runaway's attaining twenty-one. Such provisions were a sign of a growing social problem related to the decline of the master's authority.[32]

While new laws were shoring up the master's authority, he continued to bear a heavy responsibility for his apprentice. Several examples from New York City illustrate the point. One master, whose insane apprentice had been confined in the city hospital at the master's expense, sought relief from the Common Council for this heavy burden. The common law held that the master had a parental duty to nurture his apprentice, and this duty extended to illness. In another case, an apprentice took ill and left his master to go home to his father. The master specifically instructed the father not to call a physician, but the father did so anyway. Unfortunately, the boy died, the master refused to reimburse the father for the physician, and the father sued the master. A jury, upheld on appeal, found that the master had the obligation to provide medical care and ordered reimbursement for medical costs. A less tragic case involved Joseph O. Bogart, a master fined $100 for an offense committed by his apprentice. In appealing to the Common Council for remission of the heavy fine, Bogart persuaded two aldermen to testify that the apprentice was "not the best inclined." The officials added, "Mr. Bogart has endeavoured to get rid of him by giving up his indentures but his parents refused to take them. His master has offered to give said boy his time but he would not accept that." The Common Council remitted Bogart's fine and ordered the city attorney to prosecute the apprentice in a criminal action.[33]

The problem of the master's authority lurked throughout the court cases of the period. In the 1790s the courts seldom sided with complaining apprentices. An apprentice who sought to prove that he had been beaten severely by his master had little chance of having his indentures revoked; and if he did, the court would insist upon an immediate court-approved binding to a new master. Nor were the courts speedy. When the apprentice Benjamin Johnson complained to the Richmond Hustings Court, the case was continued for six months. During that time the apprentice had to continue to live with his master. The courts also had to grapple with contradictions between the common law and the new statutes regulating apprenticeship. For example, did indentures obliging a master to pay a father for the loss of his minor son's services violate laws requiring that all money be paid for the benefit of the apprentice? Pennsylvania's Chief Justice Edward Shippen, clearly puzzled, decided, "Any binding, however, of this kind, must evidently appear to be for the benefit of the children themselves, and not put Money into the pockets of the parents." Even the rules under which justices of the peace operated were muddled. Traditionally justices, before whom most disputes involving apprentices were tried, had depended upon rules and models set forth in the *Conductor Generalis,* a legal guide based on the English common law first published in the colonies in 1711. By the time of the tenth American edition in 1792, the *Conductor Generalis* had been modified somewhat to take the new statutes into account. Yet this guide continued to be based on English practices that were increasingly divorced from American circumstances, and not surprisingly the 1801 edition was the last.[34]

After 1800, when apprentices were less valuable economically to masters, the courts began to side more often with complaining apprentices. For example, in 1803 a Connecticut apprentice drove his master to such exasperation that the master sent a note to the apprentice's legal guardian. In part it read, "I was in hopes you would continue to keep him, when he come home; but I tell you plainly, that I do not intend to keep him no longer. If you will come and take him away, very well; but if not, I will turn him out o' doors very soon; for I will not have so saucy a boy in my house." When the guardian, following the instructions in this note, tried to remove the boy, the master objected. The youth departed anyway, and the master sued the guardian for enticing his apprentice. The master, having abrogated his responsibility with the letter, failed in his suit. In 1806 a Massachusetts appeals court disallowed a suit brought by a master against the guardian of a runaway apprentice. The court did so despite a warning from the master's attorney that "every apprentice in the commonwealth, as soon as he has become master of the trade which he is to learn, may leave his master's service, and the master is without remedy." The courts, however, were less concerned with a master's loss than with the good of society, and the balance of power shifted away from the master.[35]

This gradual erosion of the master's lawful authority, predictably, provoked a backlash. The reaction came in a most interesting case tried before the New York Mayor's Court. In 1820 William P. Connelly was an apprentice to the chairmaker John G. Bartholf. The two did not get along, and eventually Bartholf had his apprentice charged with a criminal assault before the Mayor's Court. The master testified that Connelly was "very disobedient and neglectful of his work." He thought the youth could mat four chairs a day, but he gave him only three to do, and yet the apprentice only finished about one and a half chairs a day. Connelly "was sometimes out all night," and recently "he had absented himself four days." When Bartholf had reprimanded his wayward apprentice for the absence, the youth "sneered at him and was very insulting." The master warned the apprentice that if he continued his ill behavior "he must go to his guardian and get the indentures, and they should be cancelled." After this warning, the youth left the shop. The following day the master spotted his apprentice coming out of a shop in another part of town, and he ordered him to go home to work. When the master returned home, he found the apprentice at work, but shortly afterward young Connelly started to leave the shop by the back door. Bartholf asked where he was going, and Connelly replied that "he was going out to get his dinner—that the other boys had ate, and he wanted to eat too." Bartholf ordered the youth to take his dinner upstairs, and Connelly refused. The master grabbed the youth by the arm, and the youth seized his master's throat and tried to choke him. A scuffle followed, the master called for help, and the apprentice was tied, taken to the police, and committed to jail for several weeks until trial.[36]

Joel Freeman, who happened to be in the shop during the scuffle, gave a different version of what had happened. He testified that the incident began when the master refused to allow his apprentice to go to dinner. Bartholf had struck the youth severely, and blood had run down the apprentice's face. Then the two clenched each other, the master called for assistance, and the apprentice cried murder. Two of Bartholf's apprentices testified that their master was a passionate man, that he swore at his apprentices bitterly, and that he was stingy in providing food. After hearing the testimony, Mayor Cadwallader Colden charged the jury with a long, philosophical defense of the institution of apprenticeship. To the mayor, apprenticeship was one of the foundations of urban society and culture, the very basis of morals for much of the population, and nothing that interfered with or weakened a master's authority could be tolerated without damage to the moral fabric of society. "It is the duty of the apprentice," he said, "to submit in all things to his master, even when he is chastised by him, if such chastisement be not outrageously immoderate." The apprentice was bound to submit; he was not the fit and proper person to judge whether a master's correction transcended propriety. That discretion, said the mayor, had to be left in the hands of the master. Even the court should not interfere with the master, who was the only person who understood the entirety of the situation. Furthermore, added the mayor, even if the master in the present instance had committed immoderate correction, the apprentice had no right to commit an assault. If the apprentice was ill treated, he had the right to go to the authorities and have his indentures canceled. This charge to the jury resulted in a verdict of guilty, and the entire trial was published in a pamphlet so that apprentices might ponder its lesson.[37]

While Mayor Colden intended for his well-publicized decision to scare apprentices into silent, efficient obedience, the decision had a second result. Masters concluded that the law would back them in all cases where apprentices challenged authority. Only three years later another case came before the New York Mayor's Court, where it was tried by the recorder—a man whose views were considerably different from those of Cadwallader Colden. After an apprentice had been saucy to a shop foreman, his master came in and decided to flog the boy. The apprentice, however, resisted, whereupon the master asked the foreman to get a rope, and the boy's hands were tied behind his back. The master then beat the apprentice with a riding whip so severely that marks were visible for several days. Both the master and the foreman were charged with an assault. While the court acknowledged the right of the master to chastise his apprentice, it held that that right had been breached by the assistance of the foreman, who had no right to touch the apprentice or to assist the master in administering chastisement. In one sense, the court said a master's right to chastise was limited by personal capacity. But in a larger sense, the court had overturned Colden's doctrine of the master's absolute supremacy in order to curb the master's authority. This decision, taken in conjunction with the one three years earlier, signaled a legal muddle from which escape became impossible. Courts increasingly disagreed, with conservatives seeking almost desperately to shore up the master's waning authority and with liberals showing increasing sympathy with the plight of poor, abused apprentices. The consequence, as might be predicted, was a flurry of court cases. Of all the significant court cases pertaining to apprentices between 1791 and 1867, more than half were concentrated in the quarter century after 1810. The institution began to break down under the pressure of legal controversy.[38]

One sign of erosion was the decline in the practice of indenting apprentices. Youths like Isaac Hill were not indented; Isaac got along with his master in part because the master never insisted upon subservience, and the apprentice responded by acceding to his master's reasonable demands. In 1814, when Hill was conducting his own business, he hired one apprentice with an informal agreement in lieu of indentures. Hill promised a widow to "take her son, and instruct him in the art of printing, finding him food and clothing for his services; that, as he is left without a father, he will, as far as is in his power, endeavor to supply the place of a father, and interest himself in her son's favor whenever his aid can be of service or advantage." In return, the apprentice was to render "faithful services." That such informal practices were becoming common is clear from evidence for Frederick County, Maryland. In that largely rural area from the 1790s to 1810 about one-fifth of all white males aged fifteen through twenty had been indented; by 1820 the proportion indented had fallen to one-tenth. Another sign of erosion concerns the fate of *A Present for an Apprentice,* a mid-eighteenth-century advice book written by a lord mayor of London. Between 1747 and 1804 this volume, which stressed the master's authority, went through eight American editions; it then lost its appeal, presumably for masters as well as apprentices, and a last edition was published in 1822 by the conservative Quakers who ran the Philadelphia Apprentices Library. While this volume was fading into obscurity, Benjamin Franklin's autobiography, with a distinctly more modern appeal, continued to hold the attention of its apprentice audience.[39]

In the end, the law could not save the master's authority, because society did not want that authority to be saved. Economic fluctuations and republican ideology had brought forth new conditions under which the traditional authority of the master could not flourish. For a generation or more the saucy and brash style of republican youths had proved sufficiently offensive to bring an attempted clampdown, but in the end the new style prevailed. Americans got used to the idea of strong-willed, independent youths, and by the time Alexis de Tocqueville visited in 1831 such children were the pride of their parents. Meanwhile, evangelical religion had meshed with the values of youth to produce an independence that replaced rowdy violence with enthusiasm and intensity of purpose.

At the same time, masters tried harder to understand their apprentices, and rather than dismissing their frank and open remarks as impertinent and impudent outbursts, masters were more inclined to sift through the remarks to find out what apprentices were thinking. All the kindness and understanding in the world, of course, did not prevent some apprentices from running away, and masters became rather philosophical about that common bad habit. The modern master, like the modern apprentice, had little use for indentures, and both agreed that the apprentice should stay only so long as he wanted. In that way the desires of youths were met, and the needs of masters were maintained, although something important had clearly been lost in the transition. No longer was the master totally responsible for his apprentice, and no longer did the apprentice owe the master an absolute fidelity until he turned twenty-one. In the new order of things both master and apprentice would be free from embarrassing entanglements, and in being free, each had to stand alone. The apprentice did not always find it easy, but it was what he most wanted.[40]

∞ CHAPTER THREE ∞

A Cash Wage

From the mid-1820s to the depression of 1837 Americans were an optimistic people. And there was room for optimism. Steamboats, canals, and banks promised to generate both western settlement and new wealth. There were problems, such as low wages for Philadelphia seamstresses, but the American System, said Henry Clay and his supporters, through high tariffs would keep out English imports, break the economic bondage of the United States to that country, produce jobs for craftsmen in America's cities, and enable farmers to sell food to the ever growing urban population. Clay's carefully calculated plan drew frowns from the Democrats, who saw in it a scheme to line the pockets of bankers, speculators, and manufacturers. They were probably not wrong. But the Democrats, still wedded to Jeffersonian ideals of minimal government, offered only a curious counterpoint to Clay's plan. They wanted to extend the republic of hardy subsistence farmers forever westward, from sea to sea, and they saw no reason to exclude Canada, Texas, Mexico, and Cuba. One supposes that many Americans agreed with both Clay and the Democrats. There was nothing wrong with a transcontinental agricultural republic, but there was also nothing wrong with cutting English ties, encouraging American manufactures, and enriching craftsmen.

America was a land where everyone could be rich. And in the twenties and thirties that idea seemed to be not just fantasy but attainable reality. Innovations in technology, the construction of textile mills, and improved transportation were correctly perceived as heralding the introduction of a new age. Equally important to the optimism of the age, moreover, was evangelical Christianity—with its emphasis on regeneration and reform, and, hence, an acceptance of change as a positive good—the rise of education, and the increased publication of books, pamphlets, and newspapers. All of these changes mingled in myriad ways to suggest the emergence of a new and more vibrant America. During these years, for the first time, Americans began to be envious of the kind of life their children might enjoy. Before 1820, younger Americans had trembled with regret that they had missed the great event in American life—the Revolution. Now, once celebrated as the semicentennial, the Revolution was put behind, and Americans of the late 1820s chose to celebrate the idea of progress.[1]

Progress was a curious, new idea. No longer would tradition dictate how life was lived or business conducted. Now everything under the sun was open to challenge—to improvement. Nothing could or would be done because it always had been done that way. Now it could or would be done according to the needs of the day. During the boom youthful Americans, in particular, had unbounded optimism, belief in progress, self-confidence, and ambition. On his nineteenth birthday James Jesse Strang wrote, "I ought to have been a member of Assembly or a Brigadier General before this time if I am ever to rival Cesar or Napoleon which I have sworn to." Strang's ambition conjured up various fantasies. One day he wrote, "I have spent the day in trying to contrive some plan of obtaining in marriage the heir to the English Crown. It is a difficult business for me, but I shall try if there is the least chance." The equally ambitious eighteen-year-old Sam Colt hatched a more practical scheme for making his fortune. The boy, adding a hint of mystery to his name by calling himself "Doctor Coult," toured the country presenting a show in which he experimented with laughing gas. Admission to the show included the right to be gassed, and soon young Colt made a large number of people laugh. For three years he traveled, learned a lot about Americans, and made a modest fortune. Sam's father, proud of the success, wrote, "It gratifies me much to see the efforts you air making to git forward in life by your own talents & industry. . . ."[2]

The base for optimism in what Col. David Crockett had called a "go-ahead" country was a revolution in the economic system. Improved transportation, financial stability, and technological innovation had led to a radical change in the way many goods were produced and distributed. The concentration of raw materials, capital, and labor in a strategically advantageous locale made it possible to produce superior goods at lower costs that could be sold throughout the country. Local production for local use gave way to concentrated production for nationwide use, in what became a national market. Among the affected trades were distilling, which became concentrated in the midwestern corn belt; tanning, centered in upstate New York on the main trade route to the hide

THE SHOEMAKER

market in New York City; and shoemaking, which developed intensively in Lynn, Massachusetts. Farmer-shoemakers, traveling shoemakers who roved the countryside, and city shoemakers who made shoes to order faced severe competition from Lynn, where the most important innovation was the subdivision of labor. The traditional shoemaker had few tools, lacked practice at repeating any particular step, and could not hope to be expert at each step in making a shoe. In Lynn work was divided so that experts, according to talent, sorted leather, cut it, sewed, or polished. In time master shoemakers hired women and children at low wages to displace journeymen. Cheap Lynn shoes, financed by credit, flooded the country, and by the 1830s profits enabled Lynn master shoemakers to invest in the first machinery that further reduced skill levels and, thus, further cut labor costs. This new system for shoe production, which was in place twenty years before the first shoe factory opened, affected youths more than journeymen shoemakers. A shrinking number of journeymen could, for a time, prosper from the introduction of machinery; after 1840, however, apprentices were no longer taken in the Lynn shoe industry.

While boys were hired to tend machines, no one learned how to make an entire shoe. And with millions and millions of shoes pouring out of Lynn, there were few apprentice shoemakers anywhere in the country.[3]

Although the market revolution devastated shoemaking and some other crafts, it did not touch all crafts. During this period of prosperity a construction boom greatly benefited the building trades, which were not susceptible to concentrated production for a national market. Youths found an apprenticeship in carpentry a quick route to becoming a master carpenter or building contractor. If, like John Milton Cargill or James E. English, they were levelheaded and avoided real estate speculation, and if they were old enough to become well established before the depression of 1837, then their early success enabled them to ride out the economic storms of the late thirties and early forties—and indeed, in some cases, even to continue to prosper amid general hard times. Others, like William G. Brownlow and Solon Robinson, practiced carpentry during the building boom to purchase an education that enabled them to enter the professions. Still others benefited specifically from construction associated with the new textile industry. It took much timber and thousands of bricks to build the mills at Lowell, Massachusetts, and Calvin Goodspeed, among others, profited from the needs of the mills. Goodspeed, who had started as an apprentice brickmaker, ended as a mill construction foreman, a position with considerably more responsibility and more secure wages than a journeyman brickmaker had. His apprenticeship, his timing, and his close proximity to Lowell were all ingredients in his success. Opportunity was also seized by Ezra Cornell, a house carpenter who discovered more lucrative employment repairing textile mills. His reputation for fine craftsmanship led a prominent mill owner to retain him as permanent agent, and that position led Cornell into telegraphy and the challenge of building telegraph lines, which was how he made his fortune.[4]

What is striking is how only a few years' difference in age could affect a youth's prospects. Although Cargill, English, Goodspeed, and Cornell came of age during the boom and were able to extract sufficient financial rewards before 1837 to enable them to prosper even in the 1840s, others were not so fortunate. In 1837, when George W. Swartz's employer went bankrupt, the twenty-year-old journeyman carpenter got papers certifying he was not a pauper. "We are obliged to send men off destitute of funds," apologized the company. Armed with his begging papers, Swartz made his way to a brother's home. Like so many other youths who came of age in the late thirties, he never achieved financial independence. Young Nathaniel P. Banks, who might have followed his father into carpentry, was instead driven by the poor economic climate for construction to become a textile machinist. As a career choice, it meant that Banks would never have the chance for independence and wealth that the building trades had offered during the boom. And Joseph Dwinnell, an apprentice brick-maker during the depression could take little comfort in the fact that he was learning a trade dominated increasingly by highly capitalized busi-nessmen and entrepreneurs like his master. Twenty years earlier an ambi-tious youth might have dreamed of buying a clay pit to manufacture bricks, but by the 1840s the manufacture of bricks had become a science, and expensive kilns and storage sheds, not to mention marketing, formed significant barriers to entry into the business. Unlike a carpenter, who could become a master builder, a brickmaker, unless he had the luck of a Calvin Goodspeed, could aspire at most to becoming foreman in a large brick factory.[5]

One of the key businesses in the new market economy was textile manufacturing, where water-powered spinning machinery was used prof-itably to challenge both imported English cloth and domestic homespun traditionally made by farm wives. Among the most successful manufac-turers was Samuel Slater, who had immigrated from England in 1789 immediately after finishing an apprenticeship to a water-powered cotton spinner. Neglecting even to inform his mother of his plans, young Slater had disguised himself as a common sailor and set out for America in vio-lation of the English laws prohibiting the emigration of mechanics. He carried with him the secrets for the new spinning machinery, cleverness in using his hands at perfecting that technology, and a burning convic-tion that water-powered spinning was only the threshold of a revolution in the manufacture of textiles. Slater went to Rhode Island and, after lo-cating important local capital, erected a water-powered spinning mill. His mill became part of a new industry that grew up in Rhode Island, in the Philadelphia area, and near Boston. In the Delaware Valley the small-scale, individually owned, water-powered spinning mills turned out specialty yarns for immigrant weavers who did fancy work. At Waltham, Lowell, and Manchester large-scale, corporate-owned mills early adopted the water-powered weaving of cheap, rough cloth and burlap. Slater, and other mills in his vicinity, followed a midway course. Within all the mills much of the work was simple, light, and repetitive, and since it could be performed by low-paid women and children, few youths were hired.[6]

Although the early spinning mills increased the demand for weavers, power loom weaving soon reversed the craft's prospects, and what had been a well-paying and somewhat elite craft was by the 1830s in the dol-drums. As weaving declined, the textile mills prospered, and many par-ents sought to place their sons in mills so that, like Slater, they could learn a new technology and make their fortunes. There was something bewitching about mill machinery. Years later John Fritz, who had seen his first spinning mill at eleven, recalled that encounter as the most astonishing event of his life. The lure of the mills drew Benjamin Franklin Peale, who was sent to Delaware to learn the machinist's trade in preparation for setting up a small family-financed mill or mill repair service. When Franklin finished his apprenticeship, he worked in a Wilmington cotton mill. "After having gone through the machine making bussiness and made preparations for commencing bussiness for myself," Franklin wrote a brother, "I have entered into one of the cotton factories to become acquainted with the use of them—and shall be established in bussiness for myself in the course of two months from date." The barely trained Peale—his two months in the cotton mill is in striking contrast with Slater's seven years—did establish his mill, but after 1815 severe competition from English imports, partly the result of advanced technology in English power weaving, destroyed American homespun and left the small, poorly capitalized American mills, particularly those near Philadelphia, tottering on the brink of bankruptcy. The census of manufactures for 1820 tells the gloomy story—everywhere mills were "uncertain," "much injured," and "not proffitable." Peale's mill did not survive.[7]

Early American textile manufacturing suffered from the primitive nature of American machine shops. In a leading Philadelphia shop, no one had heard of draftsmen, and plans for machine castings were customarily drawn in chalk by blacksmiths or founders. One day, when Escol Sellers was a boy, he met a man who had made scale drawings, and Escol was so impressed that he persuaded his father, the machine shop owner, to buy drafting tools and taught himself, with the help of the draftsman he had met, to make scale drawings. The Sellers family shop, which specialized in making fire engines, had only hand tools; more to the point, many of the better tools had been imported from England. There were no safety precautions. One day Escol's grandfather, who often sat in the shop, suddenly screamed, and the boy looked up to see a workman with his necktie caught in a lathe. Escol quickly turned the belt off the lathe and then backed the lathe by hand. As the tie came off the lathe, the workman slumped to the floor, and it was some time before he revived. In those days knowledge of machinery was poor, and much that was learned was accomplished by trial and error. Once a retired sea captain, a friend of the Sellers family, invented a new type of toggle, a device used to prevent a rope from slipping. Although Coleman Sellers saw from the design that the device would not work, because it was misgeared, he could make no satisfactory explanation of the defect to the stubborn captain. So the toggle was made, and all in the shop gathered to watch a demonstration of its use. The captain stepped forward to operate the toggle and lift a weight off the ground. But when the captain gave a tug, the weight did not move, and the reversed action from the misgearing hurled the captain to the floor.[8]

The Sellers shop, like others, did not have a foreman, and it was part of a lackadaisical system that prevailed in Philadelphia. Each machine shop specialized in casting, gearing, filing, boring, or fitting parts. Thus, the manufacture of a new tool or machine part had to pass through several shops before its completion. Because so many different craftsmen handled an item, much time was lost, and the opportunity for constructing new and complex tools was minimal. Still, the Sellers shop was the sort of place where innovation occurred. It offered Escol a fine mechanical education, at least in part because of one wandering journeyman. Henrie Mogeme, an English-speaking German who had been trained thoroughly in a German polytechnic school, taught Escol many useful things. For example, one day Mogeme told the boy that a journeyman blacksmith named Jack was taking shortcuts in making welds. Because Escol's father was away on business, the youth went to the smith's fire and immediately recognized that Mogeme was correct. The boy had words with Jack, and when the stubborn journeyman refused to change his welding technique, Escol replied he would report the matter to his father. Jack boiled, swore, announced he would not be bossed by a boy, threw off his apron, and began to talk to the other men in the shop, in the hope of provoking a strike. Mogeme advised Escol to say nothing but perform the weld properly and thus set an example. And so it was that fifteen-year-old Escol Sellers made his first weld, Jack saw the point, and the smith apologized and resumed work.[9]

The best way to learn about machinery, unless one was the son of a machine shop owner, was to spend time traveling around the country picking up information from all the little machine shops where innovations were taking place. A traditional apprenticeship, as Franklin Peale had discovered to his sorrow, was of little value. Other youths tried to follow the model provided by Henrie Mogeme. In 1830 Thomas C. Servoss, son of a merchant, left New York City, against his father's wishes, to become an apprentice machinist in a small shop at the textile mill at Matteawan, New York. Almost immediately, the mechanically inclined youth declared himself "delighted with his situation," despite a workday that ran from 4:30 A.M. to 7:30 P.M. Although this apprentice had agreed to serve four years, after two and a half years his employer sent him to Virginia as superintendent of a cotton mill. At Matteawan one of young Servoss's fellow apprentices had been Morton Poole, an eighteen-year-old from Delaware. When Morton arrived, business was "not verry brisk," and the youth was not even allowed to work on textile machinery. Given the dull times, it is not surprising that the manufacture of power textile machinery caused controversy. "There was also two woollen mules built for the Glenham Company under the direction of an Englishman who had just arrived but who has since met with a serious misfortune from two of their hands who by his comeing had been thrown out of employ," wrote the youth. "They cought him one night and beat and abused him most unmercifully breaking three of his ribs and for a while he could not see owing to their kicking him in the face."[10]

Two years later Morton was still at Matteawan, and the machine business was booming. In those days, just as it is today, the machine tool industry was undergoing an exaggerated business cycle. In 1832 anyone who walked in and asked for a job was hired immediately. One day a man from Connecticut called to order some castings, and while in the shop he tried to hire away several workmen. The boss "shewed him the door" and refused to sell him any castings. A year later Morton had left Matteawan to work for a company that specialized in setting up textile machinery at the numerous new, small mills springing up all over the Northeast. Morton had persuaded his new boss to let him travel to set up the machinery rather than work in the shop constructing it. "There is," he noted, "so much more to be learned in that way." Three years later Poole was in Providence hoping to be able to go to Lowell and work long enough to learn its secrets. He was restless to return to Delaware, where he envisioned opening his own machine shop. He had considered a shop in Providence, but the price of labor was very high. "Common loafers about the wharves," he wrote in disbelief, "are getting 1.50 per day for nine hours work." Such high wages, and his own lack of capital, discouraged him from trying to open a shop in New England, where highly capitalized machine shops were already well established.[11]

By the 1830s machine shops had lost the primitive innocence of Escol Sellers's boyhood to become appendages to the American textile industry. The textile machinery industry, ironically, was in large part created by the refusal of the English, until the 1840s, to permit the export of their textile machinery. Among the important early works were the Whitin Works at Northbridge, Massachusetts, and the Saco-Lowell shops connected with the Lowell mills. Each eventually became one of the largest textile machinery works in the country. In the 1820s the Saco-Lowell shops took apprentice machinists for three-year terms. Apprentices were bound not to the company but to individual machinists within the shops. As early as 1827 these apprentices earned cash wages: $25 the first year, $50 the second, and $75 the third. Despite the cash, a sense of paternalism prevailed. When a Mrs. Stuart wrote Superintendent Paul Moody inquiring whether her son could be taken as an apprentice, Moody replied favorably, stated the cash-wage terms, and added, "Proper care will be taken that the money which he earns as above be not expended by him unwisely." The machinists at Saco-Lowell, part of a labor aristocracy, hired their own apprentices, set the conditions for apprentice labor, and contracted individually with the company for specific jobs within the shops. In 1825 these highly skilled craftsmen formed the Middlesex Mechanics Association, a trade guild whose principal object was to discourage members from stealing each other's trained apprentices. The company, however, naturally was suspicious of such an organization, and by 1834 it was under company control.[12]

The textile machine industry was not the only one where machinists and metal workers prospered. In Taunton, Massachusetts, Isaac Babbitt and William W. Crossman, both trained as jewelers, began in 1824 to make Britannia ware, a type of brittle pewter poured into molds rather than pounded into shape. In a few years higher tariffs stimulated sales dramatically, but the company had to be reorganized into a corporation capitalized at $40,000 to obtain a water-powered site for a new factory. The entire business was conducted on a cash basis, even though the firm had to pay its workers in heavily discounted notes. In 1831 the company paid the keeper of a boardinghouse $126 to board nine apprentices for three months. One of the apprentice machinists, William Wood, began work in the low-skilled polishing department at $6 a month; a year later he earned $12 a month. In 1837 Henry Reed and Charles Barton, who had invented a superior casting metal, bought the firm. Both new owners worked in the shop and lived in a company-owned two-family house among their workers. Reed, a bit old-fashioned, never felt fully at ease paying his apprentices cash wages, but competition forced the firm to pay, and in fact it paid handsomely through a generous use of overtime. As a result, the work force was stable, and working for the company became a family tradition. In 1858 five of the eight apprentices were sons of employees. A three-year apprenticeship with a cash wage followed by the promise of a steady job with overtime was attractive.[13]

Cash wages were also important to the development of the federal armories at Harpers Ferry, Virginia, and Springfield, Massachusetts. These armories had been established in the 1790s by the new federal government as a result of difficulties in procuring arms during the Revolution. When the government had needed to buy arms in large quantities, it had discovered that it could not depend upon scattered individual craftsmen. Nor had attempts to use private contractors such as Eli Whitney or Simeon North worked very well. Suppliers sometimes produced shoddy products, went bankrupt and produced nothing, fell far behind in filling orders, or overcharged and profited at the expense of the tax-payer. To solve some of these problems, the federal government had opened its two armories, where costs of production could be monitored and compared with those of private suppliers who still sold to the government. Records from the Springfield Armory show a radical decline in gunsmithing as a craft. Between 1800 and 1820 skill levels fell as craftsmen specialized in turning barrels, making locks, or assembling rifles. Then between 1820 and 1840 new machinery, often steam-powered, led skilled craftsmen, except at the highest level, to be replaced by semiskilled machine tenders. For example, Thomas Blanchard's stocking machine, patented in 1820, required only an attendant to watch the machine follow a pattern to carve gun stocks from blocks of wood.[14]

The Springfield Armory, like the Saco-Lowell shops, was not a single large factory under a single management. While the work was done under one roof for the sake of convenience, many craftsmen within the armory had the privilege of contracting with management for various jobs. These contract armorers hired their own journeymen, worked themselves, and supervised their workers. The armory in turn supplied the contract armorers with materials, space to work, machinery, fires, and sometimes even working tools. Each contract armorer specialized in a particular phase of production. Contracts were normally made for one month at a time. Some skilled workers, however, were not hired in this competitive manner. Machinists, toolmakers, pattern makers, and shop tenders were simply hired by the management to do specific jobs. These skilled craftsmen enjoyed high wages and a ten-hour day, and, since government policy was to maintain a large work force even when military orders were low, the workers often had free time to care for their nearby garden plots. Sometimes, Congress neglected to appropriate funds in a timely fashion, and workers went for months without pay, but in the end they always were paid. It was a cash-wage job paid in good money. If workers had to be laid off, the government helped them obtain work in private armories. Working in the Springfield Armory was so good that, until 1833, workers who left were allowed the privilege of selling their spaces, which were usually worth about $100 each. Gradually, the government introduced piece rates, and as mechanization drove down skill levels, the use of piece rates soared. Even so, real wages for armory workers tripled between 1802 and 1830.[15]

When the armory had been projected in 1794, the government planned to employ seventy journeymen and thirty apprentices. This high proportion of apprentices was designed both to save money and to increase the number of skilled armorers in the country. Even in the early years apprentices were provided with board and some cash, including a $20 an-

GRINDING AT THE SPRINGFIELD ARMORY

nual clothing allowance. These cash payments, and the clothing allowance, are an early example of the way in which money would erode the traditional terms of apprenticeship. Apprentices were also promised access to a basic education. By 1806, when arms production was low, the armory no longer accepted apprentices, although contractors within the armory were free to take apprentices. Sons of workers continued to be admitted to work in the armory at early ages. In 1825, when William Riddell asked Superintendent Roswell Lee whether his son should become an apprentice armorer, Lee advised against it. He noted that few youths in the armory were able to learn all the branches of the trade and that, as a consequence, the youth would be forced to remain a mere journeyman. Lee suggested the youth become a carpenter, a cabinetmaker, or a blacksmith or whitesmith. Springfield journeymen continued to use apprentices in conjunction with the system of inside contracting until the depression year 1838, when the apprenticeship of youths as armorers was abolished. In the 1840s the Harpers Ferry Armory began to use unskilled youths as machine tenders—a far cry from apprenticeship. A decade later at Springfield the only apprentices left were machinists.[16]

What the armories, firms like Reed & Barton, and the textile mills had in common is that they were large-scale entities that paid cash wages. Neither in organization nor in production methods were they factories, and yet, like the factory, they produced goods for sale in the market, generated cash proceeds and profits, and employed workers for cash. Their emergence and growth, not the industrialization of a later period, heralded the beginning of modern, moneyed society. Today we are apt to forget that there was a time when people lived without cash through a system of barter involving both agricultural and mechanical products. In rural areas, except for some cash-crop regions in the plantation South, barter had been the nearly universal way in which business had been conducted; indeed, it had been the government's demand for cash tax payments that in 1794 had led cash-poor western Pennsylvania farmers to stage the Whiskey Rebellion. Even in the seaports much business was traditionally conducted by barter, with debts and credits entered into record books but never settled in cash, and with private notes of debt that circulated throughout the community. Only among the commercial classes engaged in overseas trade, land speculation, or other large-scale business activities did gold, silver, or banknotes play a role in the transactions. And yet people not involved in the commercial world hungered for the opportunities to buy and to sell that the tiny cash-rich minority enjoyed. The masses, even while they continued to subsist and barter, clamored for cash, whenever they could get it. In the 1790s Alexander Hamilton's financial system generated new commercial opportunities. Men like Hamilton expected the new government's banking system both to encourage trade favored by traditional commercial interests and to open new opportunities for manufacturing. This new system of manufacturing products did not necessarily mean the use of machinery; it did mean the concentration of capital, available for the first time through the new financial system, under the leadership of selected master craftsmen in order to use skilled labor more efficiently. The journeyman was to be lured to work for these enterprises with a cash wage.[17]

An economy based on cash-wage jobs threatened apprenticeship. In a society without much money a youth sacrificed little in lost wages by becoming an apprentice. The free room and board that the apprentice received in return for learning a trade was compensation enough. In that kind of society no true alternative existed. Of course, such an apprentice sacrificed earnings to some extent, since an itinerant farmhand could earn a modest cash wage if he labored in an area where farmers grew a cash crop. But the farmhand could seldom earn enough money from his relatively unskilled work to buy either land or the animals and implements necessary to start a farm. Thus, the apprentice craftsman sacrificed only a small immediate advantage in exchange for a lifelong security as a skilled craftsman. It was a sacrifice that many youths were willing, even eager, to make. The possibility of earning some kind of cash wage in a textile mill, or later, in some kind of factory, altered the situation. If a youth could find a mill job that both paid a wage and offered a chance to learn a trade, then a mill job was clearly preferable to a traditional apprenticeship. Even if the work in the mill did not guarantee his learning a skilled craft, the wage might be a sufficient lure for a boy to choose mill work. Family necessity could force that decision. While mills never employed large numbers of youths, the opportunities for work clearly enticed some away from traditional apprenticeships.

As the entire economy was infused with cash, it became clear that a master craftsman had to pay cash wages to keep his apprentices. By the 1830s a majority of apprentices in Philadelphia were working for wages. In part this was a response to mills luring youths into mill jobs, and in part it was an attempt, in a world now awash with cash, by any given master to hold valuable labor in his own shop. The practice spread beyond the mill towns and larger cities to the entire country. In 1833 the Moravians at Salem, North Carolina, were alarmed when a master craftsman began to pay his seventeen-year-old apprentice journeyman's wages. That same year apprentices in a Hartford, Connecticut, bindery began to work a fixed eleven-hour day with six cents an hour paid for overtime. Like all major changes, this one was not adopted without protest, and it was more than a year before the boys wholeheartedly embraced the new system. In a cash economy, where money commanded immediate results in the labor market, the value of labor was more volatile and, hence, more sensitive to immediate needs, to changed conditions, or even to personal attributes. A reliable and highly productive youth could be lured easily from one master to another by the offer of a higher wage. Nor could a master simply refuse to pay a wage. No one would enter an apprenticeship on those terms.[18]

Not surprisingly, apprentices haggled and bargained over wages just like adults. Diamond Ingalls, with his father's written permission, renegotiated the financial terms of his service with his nearly bankrupt master, and Philetus Sawyer, who desperately wanted to be independent from his chronically indebted father, borrowed $100 from an older brother and paid his father for the remainder of his time. Then the seventeen-year-old went to work in a sawmill for a cash wage and repaid his brother before he reached his majority. Millard Fillmore, apprenticed to two cloth dressers at fifteen, made a verbal agreement. Since the trade was seasonal, lasting from June through mid-December, the youth had to work only during those months. He was to serve each season until he reached twenty, to be taught the trade, and to receive board plus $55 a year, except during his final year, when he would be paid more. This cash was to be used to buy clothes and provide spending money. The time out of season, and any money earned during that time, was to belong to Millard's father. As it turned out, Millard did not finish this apprenticeship. While he was not legally bound, he felt such a strong moral obligation to keep his word that he bought his time for $30, a cash wage that he earned by teaching a winter school.[19]

The cash wage did not immediately destroy all traditional practices, as was shown by young Fillmore's sense of moral obligation or Sawyer's payment to his father. During these years runaway apprentices provoked a curious, mixed response. Whereas old-time masters had captured runaways, brought them home, punished them, and made them serve out their time, in the developing cash-wage society masters ignored runaways and hired replacements. There were many cases like the apprentice saddler Kit Carson, whose Missouri master offered only a one-cent reward for Kit's return. Not that the youth's return was likely, for Kit fled to Taos, New Mexico. Interestingly enough, despite the published newspaper advertisement, Kit never admitted to having run away. Such an admission was, in his generation, still an embarrassment. The confusion of the times could have bizarre consequences. When the apprentice tailors Andy and Bill Johnson got into a scrape and fled, their Raleigh, North Carolina, master inserted a rather long newspaper advertisement seeking their return. This search was serious, as was evidenced by a complete physical description, a full account of their clothes, and a $10 reward. The runaways went to Laurens County, South Carolina, where they opened a tailor's shop beyond the reach of North Carolina sheriffs. More than a year later Andy returned to Raleigh to make peace with his master, but that mean and vindictive man would neither take Andy back nor give him a legal release from his indentures. As a practical matter this meant that Andy could not work as a journeyman tailor, since the penalties for hiring a runaway apprentice were severe. Unable to work at his trade, Andy's only recourse, if he remained in North Carolina, was to become a casual day laborer. He soon left for Tennessee.[20]

It is instructive that the first item dropped as part of the master's obligation to his apprentice was clothing. Clothes were no longer spun, woven, and made by the master's wife; they were now purchased for cash in a shop and probably made from milled cloth, either foreign or domestic. Since clothes had to be bought, the master decided to pay the apprentice money with which he could clothe himself. For one thing, if the clothes fell apart, as sometimes happened, the master could not be blamed. Of course, an apprentice who bought his own clothes also had more respect for those clothes than for ones merely given to him. He appreciated their value more, since he had had to work hard to earn the money to buy them. Furthermore, a master could, during good times, persuade an apprentice to work overtime in order to earn extra money,

SADDLER'S SHOP

which the apprentice might choose to spend on clothes. And he did. The high price of being well dressed, however, did not escape the apprentice's notice. When one of the apprentice cabinetmaker Jenner Carpenter's fellows received a trunk of clothes from a dying uncle, Jenner lamented, "I wish somebody would send me such a lot, but my sick relation are all in the poor house."[21]

American parents had traditionally neglected the dress of their children, and that became all the more reason for a youth with money in his pocket to tell the world with visual display of his hard-earned, newfound wealth. It was during the 1830s that New York City was overrun for the first time with dandies—those ostentatious young men, often apprentices, flaunting their newly spent cash wages before the world. To one foreign observer, the result was only slightly short of ridiculous: "he dresses in a style that would be deemed the very height of extravagance anywhere else, London and Paris, perhaps, excepted." And if there was not enough money for a showy suit of new clothes, then limited funds could be spent

on fancy shoes and hats. Not everyone approved of such sartorial splen-
dor; William E. Channing lamented that the money, time, and energy
spent on fashionable dress were part of the deficiency in education that
kept the working class from rising in stature. Channing's lamentations
would hold more appeal after 1837, when the decline of overtime income
deprived the next generation of apprentices of the opportunity for showy
dress.[22]

Traditionally, masters had boarded their apprentices with little out-
of-pocket expense. Farmer-craftsmen often raised much of the food that
appeared on the family table, but even masters who did not grow crops
fed their apprentices with the truck customers used in lieu of cash. The
addition of one or two apprentices to a master's family, commonly including a wife, five or six children, and one live-in servant, made little
difference—at least to the master. His wife probably kept her reservations
to herself. But when the new economic conditions led some masters to a
larger amount of business that brought eight or ten apprentices into the
household, as happened in the 1790s, then the boarding of apprentices
became a major problem. There were some wives, like the second Mrs.
Isaiah Thomas, who thrived on operating what was in effect a small res-
taurant and hotel. Indeed, Mrs. William Williams was so adept at running a large-scale boardinghouse that most of her husband's apprentices
recalled her with deep affection. This intensely religious woman used her
influence to bring about conversions, and she was proud that two sons
and four apprentices eventually became ministers. But women like Mrs.
Thomas and Mrs. Williams were never common, and if a master's business was prosperous enough to warrant large numbers of apprentices, the
chances were good that the business was generating a large cash income.
That cash could be used to board the apprentices in private families,
often with widows who needed the income, or in public boardinghouses.
At times snobbery played a role in the decision to board out an apprentice. David Clapp's master came from a wealthy family that did not wish
to degrade itself by boarding an apprentice, and so arrangements were
made for David to board in a mechanic's family. In the end, however,
David's master never paid the board bill, went bankrupt, and left the
apprentice in the awkward position of having consumed board that no
one could pay.[23]

When an apprentice lived in his master's family, he usually avoided
the worst abuses, since the master could not treat the apprentice too differently from the way other family members were treated without raising
eyebrows or provoking quarrels. Furthermore, there was a subtle corre-
lation between the way an apprentice was treated in the household and
the way the apprentice might choose to behave at work in the shop.

When a master arranged for an apprentice's board elsewhere, that bond was broken, and the apprentice faced the possibility that the master, more eager to save money than to provide for the just needs of his apprentice, would place the youth in a cheap boardinghouse with bad accommodations and scanty, poor food. David Clapp's embarrassment suggests another reason why an apprentice did not favor having the master arrange his board. For the apprentice, it was better if the master paid him a cash wage, and the apprentice then found his own board. That way an apprentice who wanted to save money might choose to live in cheap accommodations; one who did not care about savings might prefer to live better. In any case, the apprentice who was given cash to find his own board could no longer complain to the master about his boardinghouse. The apprentice became more responsible for himself. By 1834 apprentices in Rochester, New York, were rarely living in the households of their masters, and there is every reason to believe that this new pattern prevailed wherever the cash wage had replaced a barter economy.[24]

Because textile mills were the first places to offer cash wages, they were also the first ones where an apprentice could get pay rather than just board for his work. In 1828, when David Carroll became an apprentice to a machinist in a Maryland textile mill, the boy took the unusual step of recording the agreement in his account book. His apprenticeship was to last three years. During the first he would be paid $104, the second $154, and the final year $204. David had to find his own room, board, clothes, and laundry. His board bill was $8 a month, which meant that during his first year he had little spending money, unless he could earn some extra money through overtime. David also kept track of the days that he lost from work while sick or traveling. Between April 1830 and January 1831 he lost twelve days, mostly because of one- or two-day outings that were most likely family visits. Unless he made up the time through overtime, the lost days were subtracted from his stated annual wage. The apprentice carefully recorded his expenditures. Clothes, a large portion of his expenses, included such luxuries as "crape for hat" (23¢) and "one umbrellen" (87½¢). He also bought a trunk ($3), a slate (12½¢), shaving glass (12½¢), snuff box (12½¢), pocket book (37½¢), a pair of brass candlesticks (87½¢), and a mirror (37½¢) and had his watch repaired ($1.87). After he had completed his apprenticeship, young Carroll worked for his former master at $7 a week.[25]

What is most striking about David Carroll's cash wage is the degree to which it made him independent. In the old days, when an apprentice was expected merely to do his master's bidding, all apprentices were kept on a par, and an ambitious apprentice, unless he could make a special arrangement with his master, was constrained within a system that lacked incentives. The use of overtime, along with the cash wage, changed the prospect for apprentices, who suddenly found that it paid to calculate. Under the old system all of an apprentice's time was his master's until the contract was complete, but under the new system an apprentice's time was somewhat more flexible. He might increase his wages by over-work, or he might decrease his wages by sacrificing work for leisure. That sort of flexibility, always subject to negotiation with the master, encour-aged the apprentice to keep a record of his work. Otherwise, he risked that an unscrupulous master might try to cheat him of his just wages. Perhaps even more important was the fact that the cash wage gave the apprentice some flexibility in determining how his money was spent. While few apprentices were as meticulous in their record keeping as David Carroll, even sketchy records were helpful to an apprentice who later wanted to figure out where all his hard-earned cash had gone. The cash wage increased his experience in handling money, developed his sense of responsibility, and gave him an awesome freedom to save or spend—and the freedom to decide how he would spend the money. Never before had apprenticed youths enjoyed so much autonomy, and that au-tonomy perhaps explains the lure of wages and the sharp decline in tra-ditional apprenticeship.

The cash nexus weakened the master's moral authority, and the ap-prentice had both the right and the obligation to make his own decisions concerning clothes, board, and recreation. Indeed, if the youth chose poorly—and many inexperienced apprentices naturally did so—the mas-ter could absolve himself of any blame. During this period we begin to hear of the notion of individual responsibility, of the need for a person, even a young person, to be responsible for himself. The cash nexus made that change inevitable. At the same time, apprenticeship was undermined by the emergence of the mill and factory. The new factory system con-fused many Americans, who accepted uncritically the belief that what-ever was called an apprenticeship must in fact be one. Factory owners discovered that they could lure naïve and unsuspecting parents into bind-ing youths, or even children, to factory work. For example, Thomas Dyott indented hundreds of boys as young as eight years old to his glass-works outside Philadelphia. To the factory owner, the temptation to use "apprenticeship" to get low-paid, easily exploited, guaranteed, bound la-bor was enormous. Yet thoughtful observers early noticed that appren-ticeship in a factory frequently led not to the learning of a trade but to mere exploitation as a factory drudge. Dyott, among others, was forced to modify his practices. Immigrants particularly, perhaps often as a result of desperation, fell into this trap. American-born skilled craftsmen were under no such illusions, and they refused to apprentice their sons to factories. But with traditional craftsmen paying apprentices cash wages, and with factory owners competing for the same youths with similar wages and their own so-called apprenticeships, it was perhaps not always easy to tell the difference between a true apprenticeship and a false one.[26]

CHAPTER FOUR

The Crisis in Printing

The craft of printing offers an instructive example of how partial technological innovation could create a crisis within a trade. While some crafts, including the important building trades, continued traditional practices, other crafts, such as weaving, shoemaking, and gunsmithing, were transformed as the national market and technological innovation led semiskilled machine tenders to displace skilled journeymen. As older workers in those trades muttered about the destruction of their age-old crafts, younger skilled workers took up other kinds of work, and apprentices ceased to exist. The total destruction of a craft, it turned out, provoked surprisingly few reactions. Printing, in contrast, occupied a peculiar middle ground. For hundreds of years printing had been divided into two branches, typesetting and presswork, and though no significant innovations took place in typesetting until late in the nineteenth century, new technology was destroying the old branch of presswork as early as the 1820s. The first innovation was the replacement of the leather balls used to beat ink onto the type with an ink roller made of molasses boiled with glue. Since a mere boy could use the new roller, master printers replaced journeymen with roller boys. Unless these journeymen were nimble typesetters, they simply were out of work. While skilled craftsmen were eliminated from one branch of the trade, they continued to be needed in the other branch. It was the survival of typesetters rather than the destruction of pressmen that explains why there was a crisis in the craft of printing. The crisis affected both journeymen and apprentices, and though apprenticeship did not cease to exist, the innovations that did take place created much wrangling about apprentices and their proper role in the rapidly changing trade.[1]

The most important innovation that exacerbated the plight of journeymen was the introduction of the steam-powered press. By the 1830s steam presses were used in many of the largest printing shops in the country. Their advantages included faster and more even printing, and, unlike journeymen pressmen, they never grumbled, complained, or got drunk. A boy tended the machine, feeding in the paper and pulling off the printed sheets that came out. Except for specialized work, pressmen were superfluous in the larger shops, including those where the new high-circulation mass-market newspapers were printed. At the very moment when the steam press forced pressmen to seek jobs as typesetters, which devalued the labor of typesetters, all the extra roller boys graduated into the ranks of journeymen. Suddenly, in the early 1830s, the printing craft was awash in a glut of skilled labor just as technology within the craft called for labor that was less skilled. In 1834 twenty-year-old Brown Thurston, a newly minted journeyman, went to New York, where he was able to find only sporadic part-time work. Finally, forced to seek some new line of employment, he sailed on a whaler out of Nantucket. Unemployment for printers would have been higher, except that general prosperity, combined with greater literacy, more leisure, and lower printing costs as a result of cheaper paper, lower wages, the use of apprentices, and machinery, led to a greater production of books, pamphlets, and especially newspapers.[2]

Because it was expensive to buy and set up a steam press, the dream of many journeymen to save money to buy equipment and open their own shops was dashed. It was still possible to buy a used handpress and open a shop in some remote place, probably in the West, but the chance of turning such a venture into a profitable business was limited, because the handpress could not compete with the steam press. During these years the printing trade rapidly became divided between handpress shops in the small towns and power press shops in the cities. Even that division hurt journeymen, because a journeyman in the city could not become a journeyman in a small town, since the poor competitive position of the small shops forced masters to depend upon boys. In the Ohio Valley some shops operated with five apprentices and only a single journeyman. Then, like a swarm of locusts, these apprentices from the small towns flew to the cities in search of sustenance. There youths like Brown Thurston glutted the labor market and worsened the problems of the local journeymen.[3]

As capital became more crucial in the establishment of a successful printing shop, the craft of printing became more and more separated from both publishing and editing. By the 1830s well-connected political operators, often not practical printers, used connections to launch political propaganda organs. The publisher Duff Green, for example, had been born into the southern planter aristocracy, and it was profits from slavery rather than craftsmanship that had enabled him to buy his first newspaper. Sometimes even the men who were hired to run newspapers were chosen for editorial skills rather than for a knowledge of printing. Although the recruitment of college-educated editors was largely in the future, a journeyman printer could no longer assume that his editor would come from the ranks of printers. For bright young journeymen like Horace Greeley leaving printing for an editorship presented the easiest route to influence, status, and success, but ordinary journeymen knew they would have to spend their lives working for a firm owned by financiers and politicians and operated increasingly by gifted writers. To many journeymen the prospect was gloomy, because it heralded a decline in the status of their craft. The separation of printing from publishing and editing led some journeymen to boast about the nobility of their craft, and by the 1850s these printers emphasized their pride in printing as an art. But the more common responses were embittered resentment, tiresome complaints, and heavy drinking. The end of the dream of becoming a master printer who published and edited his own work, coincided with a growing reputation of urban journeymen as unreliable, unsteady souses.[4]

Horace Greeley's journey from apprentice printer to the most famous journalist of his day was not straight and easy. Born in New Hampshire, Horace was the son of a poor subsistence farmer who lost his land in the depressed early 1820s. The Greeleys went west to Vermont, rented a poor farm in the middle of a lumber region, and sank into "genuine poverty"; all their possessions, including clothes, were worth perhaps $200. After a boyhood of dreary unskilled labor, Horace sought to escape, and in 1826 he spotted an advertisement for an apprentice printer in a new rural newspaper. So Horace walked to East Poultney and found the proprietor, Amos Bliss, planting potatoes. The fifteen-year-old boy appeared in Bliss's potato patch wearing short, baggy trousers, no stockings, very worn shoes, and a small, ill-fitting hat. When this thin and slump-shouldered rustic showed up, the proprietor nearly laughed. Horace asked, "Don't you want a boy to learn the trade?" Replied Bliss, "Well, we have been thinking of it. Do *you* want to learn to print?"

"I've had some notion of it."

There was a pause before Bliss spoke. "Well, my boy—but, you know, it takes considerable learning to be a printer. Have you been to school much?"

"No, I haven't had much chance at school. I've read some."

"What have you read?"

"Well, I've read some history, and some travels, and a little of most everything."

"Where do you live?"

"At Westhaven."

"How did you come over?"

"I came on foot."

"What's your name?"

"Horace Greeley."[5]

Bliss, a school board inspector, examined Horace, and to Bliss's surprise, the youth answered all his questions, including those usually put to prospective teachers at job interviews. The precocious boy was sent to talk to the foreman of the printing office. As Horace entered the office, the apprentices snickered at his rough appearance, and after a ten-minute interview with the foreman, Horace was sent back to Bliss in the potato patch with a note that read, "Guess we'd better try him." Horace was told he could have the apprenticeship, if his father would consent to indentures. While the boy walked home to tell his father what he had done, the printing office was astir. One apprentice asked, "You're not going to hire that tow-head, Mr. Bliss, are you?" Bliss replied, "I am, and if you boys are expecting to get any fun out of him, you'd better get it quick, or you'll be too late. There's something *in* that tow-head, as you'll find out before you're a week older."[6]

Horace and his father visited Bliss to negotiate the terms of the apprenticeship. After Bliss, following local custom, proposed that Horace be bound for five years and get board plus $20 a year for clothes, Horace's father turned hostile. He objected to the principle of binding, thought five years too long, and found the pay too low. An apprehensive Horace worried that his stubborn father would fail to reach an agreement. When Bliss issued an ultimatum, the elder Greeley turned to walk out, but Horace refused to leave, so the negotiations had to be continued. In the end, Horace got the right to a kind of trial period, which was explained in a curious and unusual handwritten agreement.[7]

Terms of Horace Greeley's Apprenticeship

Mr. Greeley says his boy may stay as an apprentice to Dewey & Bliss in the printing business till he is twenty years of age: That he may stay one year, and he will clothe him, and then determine whether he may stay another year. He means that the boy shall stay till twenty years old, and that he will not take him away for any thing except ill usage. If the boy stays till he is twenty years old he is to have $40 a year in clothing after the first six months, and have his board. The boy is to be faithful and serve with the best of his ability in the office under the direction of the foreman. He is to be allowed reasonable time to go home to see his friends, occasionally and as other apprentices do. The boys name is Horace Greeley.—A. Bliss. Poultney, April 18, 1826.

With this remarkable, peculiar, and legally dubious document, Horace Greeley entered into his apprenticeship. The terms, in contrast with those of indentures from early in the century, included no references to Horace's moral character, and the agreement's failure to require either education or training in the trade raised questions about its validity. However, one should not make too much of the peculiar form of the agreement, since Vermont was one of a handful of states that did not require apprentices to be bound by indentures, and by 1826 indentures had become so rare that the once popular standard printed forms no longer were in widespread use.[8]

After the agreement was reached, Horace went home to bid family and friends farewell. Some relatives suggested he give up the apprenticeship, and if his mother had asked him, he would have, but she remained silent. Like so many other youths leaving home for the first time, Horace found his twelve-mile walk to East Poultney slow, sad, and thoughtful. While East Poultney, a village of a few hundred people, was an excellent place for a rural youth to serve an apprenticeship, the printing office, like so many others strewn across the countryside, was more doubtful. First came Horace's initiation. At the end of the first day the other apprentices threw type at him, and Horace ignored it. The next day they talked saucily, and he also ignored that. On the third day the oldest apprentice, finding Horace's blond hair too light-colored, dabbed him four times with the black-inked balls. Horace said nothing. After the inking, there were no more trials, Horace made rapid progress at typesetting, and all in the shop became friends. Often left alone in the shop, the apprentices played chess, whist, or poker. In moral New England, just having a pack of cards in the office produced the pleasure of secret, sinful delights. Of more importance was the fact that the village lacked the population to support the newspaper, which was sold several times. Indeed, Horace sometimes had two or three masters at once. While the office was lax and lacked formal instruction, Horace found "perfect liberty to learn whatever he could." Within a year he was able to practice all aspects of the craft, although he really did not have the strength to pull the old handpress without injuring his back.[9]

Village life meant fascinating after-dinner conversations with passing travelers at the public tavern where Horace boarded and the excitement of a debating society where the apprentice was treated like an adult. No doubt Horace would have liked his life to continue in this pleasant vein, but in late 1829 he faced the sobering reality that, after several changes of ownership, the newspaper was losing $1,000 a year. A year later the newspaper collapsed, and nineteen-year-old Greeley found himself unemployed. The forces of the market made no provision for the continuity of an apprenticeship. Greeley's friend Thurlow Weed also had been abandoned, when his master quarreled with political sponsors, walked out of the office through the back garden, and never returned. Although Greeley was confident that he knew how to run a printing office, he lacked any capital to go into business on his own and was too young to persuade anyone to back him. So he left Vermont to visit his parents, who had moved to a frontier farm in Pennsylvania. On his last day in East Poultney, as he sat on the tavern porch waiting for the stage, two friends in the bar inside noticed that Horace did not have a proper over-coat for his journey. So one of them donated an old coat as a farewell present. As he accepted the coat, young Greeley might have reflected that he came away from his apprenticeship with a knowledge of his trade, a wide reading in the local public library, a few clothes, $20 in cash, and a sore leg. It was not the most auspicious beginning for an underage journeyman printer.[10]

Greeley, like other apprentices trained in undercapitalized rural print-ing offices that went bankrupt, now found himself looking for work. After visiting his parents, he worked for six weeks as a journeyman in Catta-raugus County for $11 a month, but that job came to an end, no new job appeared, and he returned to his father's farm to chop wood. Then he went to Erie, where he sought work at the *Erie Gazette*. The youth ar-rived at the office, found the proprietor out, and sat down to read the ex-change newspapers. Finally, Joseph M. Sterrett, the proprietor, came into the office, picked up his composing stick, and began to set type. The shy, nervous Greeley, who had never asked for a job in his life, continued reading about twenty minutes, until he finally screwed up the courage to ask Sterrett if he needed any help. The astonished proprietor blurted out, "Why did *you* ever work at the trade?" Greeley, startled and cowed by the incredulity lurking in the question, limply replied, "Yes, I worked *some* at it in an office in Vermont, and I should be willing to work under instruction, if you could give me a job." Sterrett found this reply so modest he concluded that Greeley was a runaway apprentice. So he told Greeley he did not need any help, and the discouraged youth returned to his father's farm.[11]

A couple of weeks later, when a friend told Sterrett about a journey-man from New England who needed work, the proprietor immediately recognized that it was Greeley who was being recommended to him. The two corresponded, Greeley went back to Erie, and Sterrett hired him. Greeley got the Erie journeyman's rate of $12 a month plus board, and like all who worked in the shop, he boarded with Sterrett. The other printers were Samuel Nelson, a rather dull twenty-year-old, who had been brought up in the office; John W. Hunter, about the same age and a "dashing blade" who dressed ostentatiously, wearing gold breast pins; and Fred Fluck, a seventeen-year-old German apprentice. The youthful printers who worked in this office were typical of those who worked in many small offices. Both Hunter and Nelson were hostile to Greeley, the former worrying that Greeley would obtain his position and the latter fearing that if Hunter was replaced by the partially lame Greeley, the burden of press work would fall on him. A few days after Greeley's arrival, a master printer called and asked Sterrett to lend him a hand temporarily. When Sterrett volunteered Hunter, that mortified youth swore he would quit and stomped out of the office. A few days later he was seen working in another Erie printing office. Although Greeley found his work tolerable, he did not have kind words for Mrs. Sterrett. "Among my troubles," he complained to his friend Obadiah A. Bowe, "the good lady of the house, a *Dutch*ess, who weighs about two cwt [i.e., 200 lbs.] gross, not one ounce of which is politeness or any thing akin to it, has entertained a violent dislike to me, ever since I came here, which I labor in vain to remove."[12]

At this time both Greeley and Bowe, like other youthful printers, yearned for independence and the chance to become their own masters. Wrote Greeley, "I suppose we shall both have to keep starvation at a proper distance, till some new turn of madam Fortune's wheel, by shuffling & dealing other folks's type—and that is a confounded hard way of doing it. I shall do it no longer than dire necessity compels." One of the best ways for a young journeyman without capital to open his own shop was to become a willing agent for a political interest that needed a newspaper. If Bowe could find someone who wanted to finance a Whig newspaper, Greeley was only too happy to propose himself as Bowe's junior partner. A month later Greeley wrote, "I hold myself ready to embark with you in any such adventure as you speak of, whenever and wherever you may think proper." He added, "*Adventure* did I say? Faith, if I did, I spoke without reflecting: for I have nothing to risk but my carcase, which will not probably be placed in any imminent peril, by accepting your proposal. Let that be as it may, if you want to see an ill behaved, ill looking, and worse dressed chap, with only about fifteen or twenty dollars in money, and as cross as the———, in the village of Cortlandville, about the 25th of next month, or such other time as you may choose to direct, why you have only to say so." Greeley's eagerness was overcome by lack of capital, and in the end he could not form a partnership with Bowe. Greeley had no capital, and Bowe had only $400, which was not enough to stock a decent country printing office. Furthermore, such a small printing office had no way of generating internal capital for expansion from its earnings. Greeley and Bowe, like other young journeymen, discovered that they lacked the means to become master printers. Dreams of independence were in doubt, and both risked becoming the lifelong employees of other men.[13]

Although Greeley was a practicing journeyman, he was under twenty-one and thus legally obligated to provide services to his father. The common law held clearly that the earnings of a minor belonged to the father. As a practical matter, this meant that Greeley had to ask his father's permission before accepting any kind of employment. When the partnership with Bowe had been a possibility, Horace had written his father, and he received a reply from a brother with a stern warning "from the old man." The warning angered Greeley, who wrote Bowe, "Father says that he understands that I intend going to C [i.e., Cortlandville] and declares that he disapproves of the whole scheme, and insists upon my foreswearing it immediately as he wishes me to render him some pecuniary assistance this summer to enable him to put up some buildings, and concludes with this injunction 'Fail not of hearing to me.' " The father's message, written in the spirit of old-school authority, had irritated Greeley sufficiently that he prepared to break with his father, but Bowe's project collapsed, and the youthful journeyman was left in Erie.[14]

And more restless than ever. He was tired of being criticized for his shabby clothes, when the fact was he had no money to buy clothes because he sent virtually all his money home. Tired of "living on sour looks, solitude and salt pork," he grew to dislike his boss. "Sterrett never says a word to his hands except—'Do this'—and that very seldom," he complained. "His second in command is a heartless, brainless coxcomb; and he has added moroseness to his qualifications—having been [the] subject of a great revival, with which Erie has been blessed since I came here." One day a journeyman who once had worked for Sterrett returned after recovering from an illness, and Greeley was out of a job. After failing to get a job in Wilkes-Barre, Greeley returned to his father's farm and struck a bargain. In return for his Erie earnings, Horace was to be free from further obligations to his parents.[15]

In August 1831 Horace Greeley went to New York City. Like so many other youths brought up in country printing offices who could find no permanent work in the small country shops, he had migrated to the city. This twenty-year-old, arriving with $10 in his pocket and $10 worth of clothes on his back, was amazed by New York, with miles and miles of "mainly brick or stone houses" and "furlongs of masts and yards." On Saturday, the day after his arrival, Horace looked for work, but he found that he had arrived in the middle of the midsummer slack season, had only a modest grasp of his trade, was a rustic, and had no friend to counsel him or write a letter of introduction within two hundred miles.

To succeed in the city was no easy task for a youth brought up in the country. The city's anonymity and hurly-burly ensured that only a person who stood out from the crowd would be noticed and hired. The urban environment put a premium upon widespread personal contacts, dogged persistence, and even an exaggerated self-confidence necessary to compete successfully for scarce jobs. When Horace called at the *Journal of Commerce,* the editor David Hale did not hesitate to tell the "tall, slender, pale, and plain" youth that he was a runaway. Saturday evening the demoralized Greeley resolved to leave the city on Monday morning.[16]

On Sunday an Irish immigrant visiting Greeley's boardinghouse gave the youth directions to a printing office, and on Monday morning Greeley went to the office and was hired. The work at John T. West's was available because no one wanted it. Greeley's job was to set type for a New Testament, double columned in small type, with a column of notes in between in tiny type. The text was larded with Greek words and numerals to the notes, and prefatory remarks to each book were set in tiny type but paid as if they were larger type. The task was so tedious that it was necessary to do two sets of correcting proofs, and sometimes Greeley had to wait for pages to be printed to get more letters to set the next pages. The work was as disagreeable as West, a "martinet." According to Greeley, his boss was "not satisfied with merely having his work well done" but insisted "upon having it done according to the nicest rules of art." The journeyman added, "He quarrels with and discharges more hands than any other printer in the city, though some employ ten times as many. I work for him because his office is but a few rods from my boarding house and he is sure to pay, which you must know is not the case with all the printers here. He hires me because he knows I can set any manuscript, however abominable, and make a cleaner proof than almost anybody else: besides, I can humor his taste exactly. You would have been amused to see how he managed with me, when I first worked for him. He somehow got it into his head that I was a green Yankee, just catched, and that it was his business to make a printer and a man of me. Accordingly he went about it, by finding fault with every thing I did or neglected to do. If there was any noise or loud talking in the case-room, if there were any errors in the form or the imposition, &c. I was sure of a lecture. In fact I was the 'whipping boy' of the office." Greeley managed to endure the torment. "We have never quarreled," noted Greeley, "because he has never been able to extract a word of sauce from me." When West lectured him, Greeley smiled.[17]

Smiling at West was about all that Greeley could afford, although, in truth, he had little to smile about. In the first few weeks on this job, he earned barely enough to cover his board bill. During a good week, working fourteen hours a day, he could make $6. While he was setting type, he had time to reflect upon the fact that fifteen years earlier, when his friend Thurlow Weed had also been a young journeyman printer, Weed had earned $12 a week. The contrast was a powerful comment on the declining value of the skills of journeymen printers. As Greeley plodded on, other compositors came into the shop, tried setting type, cursed, and left; few lasted more than a couple of days. Eventually the Bible was finished, and Greeley found himself unemployed for two weeks. Then, after working for a magazine, which folded without paying him, he went back to West's and set a religious commentary that was only a little easier than the Bible. Winter came, business was dull, and Greeley, along with many other journeymen, was unemployed. Around New Year's William T. Porter and James Howe started the *Spirit of the Times,* and Greeley worked on that newspaper, until the cholera struck, people fled the city, the newspaper's circulation dropped, and Greeley had trouble getting his pay. Unemployed again, Greeley visited relatives in New England and then returned to New York to work. He saved some money, and with the help of Francis V. Story he used $200 and borrowed type in 1833 to publish the *Morning Post.* His newspaper lasted one week before exhaustion of capital forced suspension. A year later a weekly newspaper, the *New Yorker,* proved more successful, but, after the depression of 1837 threw Greeley into debt, he never enjoyed complete financial independence. In 1841, when the *New York Tribune* was founded, Greeley owned only a tiny portion of stock. Although he became the most famous editor in the country, he never achieved control of a printing office.[18]

While Greeley struggled to gain a toehold in New York, he had ample opportunity to compare his situation with that of the book publisher James Harper, who was seventeen years older. Both Harper and Greeley were brilliant, hardworking men, but Harper amassed a fortune while Greeley achieved mainly fame. Perhaps Harper was more ambitious for wealth, and he certainly used both his family and the Methodist Church to promote his business interests, but the crucial difference in the lives of these two men appears to be timing. Although each finished apprenticeships and became journeymen, each found the state of the craft quite different. In 1816, when James Harper had finished his apprenticeship, before the vast changes that produced the journeymen's glut of two decades later, young Harper was hired as a pressman at $12 a week. His press mate on the old handpress was a youthful Thurlow Weed. The two went to the office before first light and sometimes did a half day's work before breakfast. After finishing a normal day's work, James would say, "Now, Thurlow, let's break the back of another token,—just break its back." A token was 250 impressions. Thurlow would agree reluctantly, and then James through coaxing and good humor would push on till the token was completed. The overtime enabled each young printer to save nearly $50 a month. In 1817 James's brother John finished his apprenticeship as a printer, and the two brothers used $500 they had saved plus a little money borrowed from their father to buy two old handpresses and open a printing office. Soon James and John took two younger brothers, also trained as printers, into the firm, and the Harper Brothers began to publish books under their own imprint. They specialized in school textbooks, Methodist tracts, and pirated English novels. Because English authors could not copyright their works in the United States, American publishers found it profitable to rush out editions of new English novels. Generally, the first American publisher to offer an edition gained the advantage, and the Harpers became expert at being first. By 1825 the firm, which operated ten presses in a four-story building, printed more books than anyone else in New York City.[19]

The decade after 1824, the last year the brothers regularly worked at press, was crucial to the triumph of this publishing house. In 1825 the energetic nineteen-year-old Fletcher Harper paid $500 for a share in the firm; by 1869 his share was worth $312,500. Much of the success of the firm was due to the ability and willingness of the progressive brothers to innovate. For example, they issued the first American clothbound book; previously, books had been bound by bookstores or owners. Outside readers evaluated manuscripts submitted for publication, and later the firm hired the first American in-house manuscript reader. By the 1830s the firm routinely stereotyped its works. This process saved money and space by eliminating the practice of holding type for a new edition. The most important changes, however, were technological. In 1828 horse-powered presses were installed, and five years later the horses were retired to the family farm on Long Island and replaced with steam presses. The new presses transformed the trade, because their speed made large-scale production practical for the first time. Whereas James Harper and Thurlow Weed had exhausted themselves hand pulling 250 impressions an hour, by the 1830s Adams steam presses made 1,000 impressions an hour, and later in the decade the Napier steam press did 3,000 an hour. Boys and girls operated the new steam presses, and journeymen were relegated to typesetting, where they competed with apprentices—or women. When rumor swept the trade in 1832 that a Philadelphia master printer planned to employ low-paid female compositors, journeymen denounced the scheme. By the 1830s the Harpers were turning out more than one million volumes a year, half the production of all New York City publishers. Their business was built on large sales, low prices, and low profits per volume.[20]

When large-scale, highly capitalized, and mechanized firms like the Harpers destroyed the dream of journeymen to become master printers, the journeymen organized labor unions to protect themselves. To understand the labor organizations of the 1830s, it is necessary to begin with the numerous craft organizations that became important, for the first time, in the 1790s. These early craft organizations came in a variety of forms. Some, modeled on age-old guilds, admitted both masters and journeymen to membership and sought to regulate wages and working conditions for the craft throughout the community. Others were masters' organizations that sought to impose wage ceilings upon journeymen at a time when rising living costs and increased demand for skilled labor encouraged journeymen to play one master against another. Still others were journeymen's organizations that sought to extract higher wages from masters by fixing minimum wages for journeymen. In the 1790s, under both the common law and English precedent, the latter groups faced the threat of being charged with conspiracy to form an illegal combination, and journeymen sometimes disguised the true purpose of their societies by claiming they were charitable organizations to pay sickness and burial benefits. Sometimes care was taken to keep the business of a craft society secret. For example, heavy fines or even expulsion might be levied upon a member who showed outsiders the list of the society's prices. Secrecy was not always successful, as was evidenced by three highly publicized conspiracy trials against New York, Philadelphia, and Baltimore journeymen shoemakers. Few of these early craft organizations showed much interest in the subject of apprenticeship, which was barely mentioned in the various charters, constitutions, by laws, and regulations. Growing clashes between masters and journeymen took place in an environment where apprenticeship seldom was an issue.[21]

By the 1820s craft organizations that included both masters and journeymen had withered, and self-interest encouraged masters and journeymen to maintain separate organizations. Yet the twenties were more notable for the intellectual confusion that prevailed within the ranks of skilled labor. The depressed economy following the panic of 1819 brought a cacophony of complaints and demands. Some clamored for higher tariffs with the conviction that a reduction in imports would revive American production. Others railed against the banking system, which they perceived as a scheme to make the rich even richer while the rest suffered. Still others followed Henry Clay in advocating a combination of banks, high tariffs, and federal aid for internal improvements. The more reform-minded, like Robert Owen and Frances Wright, wondered whether the new industrial system could not be fostered on a cooperative rather than a capitalist basis. Others followed Adam Smith and adopted the labor theory of value, which held that all wealth was created by producers who labored. What was most striking about the twenties was the lack of any orchestration of the various themes and ideas that floated in the air. And the lack of intellectual cohesion had its effect upon journeymen and their organizations, which continued during the decade to be concerned mainly with narrowly traditional issues such as increased wages for journeymen. Only at the end of the decade did labor leaders like William Heighton begin to suggest that journeymen should organize into modern labor unions that would cooperate across traditional craft barriers in an attempt to obtain a larger share of the economic wealth of the country for all skilled labor. And it was only after that idea had been expressed that journeymen could begin to ponder what the status of apprentices was and how apprentices in the new, emerging industrial economy could function both as strikebreakers and as cheap, exploited child labor used by employers in lieu of the more expensive labor of journeymen. By the end of the 1820s such issues were ripe for consideration.[22]

Among skilled craftsmen the 1830s brought a growing interest in broad economic questions. Speech after speech addressed the issue of the origin of wealth, and mechanics almost universally held that all wealth was created by labor. According to this theory, farmers and mechanics were the producers of wealth, while merchants, attorneys, absentee owners, and others were mere parasitic drones. They were consumers of wealth who had cleverly transferred into their own pockets wealth created by others. This theory was made more palatable by the new working conditions that prevailed in such trades as printing. It was easier for a journeyman to resent his boss when the boss had ceased to be a fellow laborer in the shop, and it was perhaps even easier to grow suspicious when the owner turned out to be a man who had never studied the craft at all. By the thirties many journeymen felt victimized, and though they had no single plan of action for dealing with their declining status, they used every opportunity in their power to remind themselves and anyone who would listen of what had been happening. This sense of being cheated by an unfair economic system led not to direct attacks upon master craftsmen, who were considered to be naïve rather than vicious beneficiaries, but to a desire by journeymen to extract more money from the system. While journeymen might hope that in the long run the labor theory of value would become the basis for a restructuring of the social order through cooperatives or other mechanisms of association, in the here-and-now capitalist world in which they lived and worked, the feeling of unfairness led journeymen to seek to organize labor unions in order to extract financial concessions from the rich and powerful nonproducing owners of the means of production.[23]

During the early 1830s better economic conditions led to shortages of craftsmen in many trades, and, in turn, craftsmen gained both higher wages and shorter hours. In the nation's most populous industrial centers, the workday was reduced to ten hours. When that idea had first been suggested at a large public meeting in New York, the 900 mechanics in the audience had laughed. They considered the ten-hour day ten times more remote than the millennium. In time mechanics reconsidered, and one day the journeymen in the New York shipyards called a strike. As the journeymen put down their tools and milled around the yard, one apprentice was confused. When the apprentice asked what was happening, the journeyman he worked with told him that they were going to "strike" the bosses, and the alarmed boy, who had always admired the master ship carpenters, grabbed his adze to defend the bosses from the workers' blows. Only then did the apprentice learn what a strike was. In some yards apprentices joined the journeymen on strike, but in others the apprentices continued to work while the journeymen walked out. To whom did an apprentice owe his loyalty? Custom offered no answer in this unprecedented situation. As successful strikes encouraged journeymen to raise demands, masters responded, as one might expect, by seeking to reduce labor costs by replacing expensive journeymen with cheap apprentices. In at least one case apprentices were used as strikebreakers. Suddenly, the traditions that had held the world of artisans together through the centuries had shattered. It turned out that masters, journeymen, and apprentices had distinct interests. If journeymen grew restless, masters would use apprentices as a form of discipline, and the new industrial world of semiskilled labor made that threat credible. For journeymen, apprentices became a curse both to the present, as strikebreakers, and to the future, as prospective journeymen whose presence would drive down wages in what had become a perpetual battle with masters.[24]

The old relations were beyond repair. Among the first formalities to disappear were indentures, which in a cash-wage market economy threatened to bankrupt masters during downturns in the business cycle and to tie youths to below-market wages during boom times. Moravian officials in Salem, North Carolina, were surprised and irritated when a widow who had been given permission to settle in the town on condition that she bind out her sons neglected to indent her oldest son to a craftsman. The tradition-minded officials proposed a specific master and hinted that, if the matter was neglected, the boy would be turned over to the local court for binding as a poor boy. A year later Salem authorities approved the hiring of two youths, each "partly as journeyman, partly as apprentice." This curious designation was scarcely more peculiar than an incident that took place at a Hartford, Connecticut, bindery. When a runaway apprentice had returned voluntarily, the foreman had threatened to dismiss the youth, and the apprentice asked for his indentures. Since a boom was under way and help was scarce, the foreman refused and ordered the apprentice to return to work. During good times masters feared a shortage of apprentices and a bidding war that could ruin masters. In 1830 the Masters Association in Concord, New Hampshire, met to set standards to hold down the cost of apprentices. The association, in a break with tradition, declined to fix an absolute penalty for enticing an apprentice away from a member of the organization. Masters were urged to pay no medical bills, to take apprentices for four or five years, to give a standard amount of schooling calculated according to the age of the apprentice, and to board apprentices either in their own houses or in private boardinghouses where morals could be protected. Such standards, the association no doubt hoped, would restore some of the stability of the past. But the hope was futile.[25]

Strained relations among the craft ranks did not sit well with older craftsmen, who had nostalgic memories of the days when craft camaraderie had united the practitioners of a particular art. Sometimes these craftsmen of the old school sought to restore the old relationship, or at least to lessen the frictions of the new one. Much artisan activity during this period consisted of Fourth of July parades, city mechanics fairs, and technical lecture series that were designed to draw attention away from the increasing differences that separated apprentices, journeymen, and masters and to accentuate the common needs, aspirations, and abilities that continued to unite mechanical endeavors. No mechanic expressed the point more frankly than James L. Homer. In 1836 this master mechanic urged the Massachusetts Charitable Mechanic Association to construct a building for social and educational purposes. "It would," he said, "bring master workmen, journeymen and apprentices together—not under the cold forms, discipline, distance and austerity of the workshop—but upon a footing of courtesy, kindness, and respect, and afford the best opportunity of promoting a good understanding, personal friendship, and reciprocal interest in each other, which would remove unjust prejudices, explain all unfortunate misunderstandings, and cure those jealousies and hostilities which, sometimes, untoward events, bad companions and bad advice, disorganizing conspiracies, and a blind zeal, stir up between those who ought to live together in harmony and benevolence."[26]

During the 1830s perhaps no trade saw journeymen so concerned about losing their places to apprentices as printing. In 1832 the Baltimore journeymen typographers association proposed to expel any member who took boys to do presswork at low rates of pay in those offices where journeymen pressmen hired their own roller boys. This organization also threatened to expel any member who worked either in an office that employed nonindented youths at reduced rates of pay or in one where journeymen were paid less than union scale. The following year the New York journeymen printers union made similar complaints and blamed recent hard times for journeymen upon the practice of employing runaway or dismissed apprentices at low wages. "These were called *two-thirds men*," said the union, "and have always proved a great pest to the profession." In addition, the journeymen lamented the new machinery that was becoming common in the trade; it enabled a few, such as the Harpers, to grow rich, while journeymen and apprentices suffered. "Many who had spent from five to seven years of the flower of their lives in acquiring a knowledge of their profession," said the union report, "were left either without employment, or were obliged to resort to some business with which they were unacquainted, and thus constrained to serve a sort of second apprenticeship."[27]

Into this scene of discontent stepped Duff Green with a daring, innovative, and radical proposal for the alteration of the printing trade. Green, a descendant of slaveholding planters who had grown up in the rough world of frontier business and politics, had moved to Washington, D.C., where he owned and edited the *U.S. Telegraph*. At first a promoter of Andrew Jackson, after 1830 he followed Calhoun into the anti-Jackson, antitariff, proslavery camp. During the early thirties he was both a potent political force and an influential Washington businessman. At the time the powerful Washington printers union, the Columbia Typographical Society, had succeeded in obtaining the highest wage rates for printers in the country. This outcome had been brought about by the peculiar nature of Washington's government-based printing industry. Government printing was assigned through patronage rather than by competitive bidding, and the master printer who obtained a lucrative contract did not particularly mind having to share a portion of the lucre with his workmen. Furthermore, the chances for a Washington journeyman to open a successful printing office in competition with politically influential printers were slim, so a Washington journeyman could regard extra earnings as compensation for giving up the hope of becoming a master. But the most important reason for the strength of the union and the resultant high wages was the seasonal nature of the work, which oscillated between prodigious quantities of congressional reports, laws, pamphlet propaganda, and newspapers issued while Congress was in session and very little the rest of the year. High wages were needed both to attract out-of-town journeymen during the busy season and to enable local journeymen to get through unemployment during slack times. In that situation the union acted as a kind of stabilizing force.[28]

On January 1, 1834, Duff Green proposed a radical change in the Washington printing industry. He suggested that local citizens donate money to build an orphan asylum to be called the Washington Institute. Thus far the proposal appeared merely to imitate other asylums then being constructed. But Green apparently also had followed the manual-labor-school movement, and he proposed an innovation in this orphanage. The asylum would take up to two hundred boys aged eleven to fourteen, and it would board them, lodge them, clothe them, and even provide a nurse and doctor for them. The boys would attain a good common-school education by attending school five hours a day. Naturally, providing these services would be very costly, and Green proposed that the expenses be met by the establishment of a printing office on the premises. The boys would serve as apprentice printers for eight hours a day. After the first year, each boy would earn from $1 to $3 a week, depending upon his skill. This money was to be held for the boy until he graduated from the orphanage at twenty-one. By that time, Green estimated, a youth would have accumulated at least $725 in his account. The funds would then be lent to the youth, who could go west and open a printing office of his own.[29]

The reaction to Green's proposal was immediate and hostile. Other master printers bitterly opposed a scheme that would enable Green, through his exclusive use of orphanage apprentices, to undercut them by employing apprentices in lieu of expensive union journeymen. Furthermore, the plan to withhold the apprentices' cash wages until they turned twenty-one meant that for several years Green would have to pay out nothing. And it was well known that youths frequently ran away from orphanages. How many of Green's apprentices in the orphanage would stay long enough to collect any of the money promised to them? But the hostility of master printers was nothing compared with the vituperation heaped upon the proposed institute by the Columbia Typographical Society. The union accused Green of "personal aggrandizement." Labor's hatred of Green, it should be noted, did not start with the institute plan. In 1828, when the House of Representatives had elected Green its official printer, he had paid the union wage scale. Within a year, however, Green had tried to reduce journeymen's wages from $10 to $8 a week. Although the journeymen successfully resisted this attempted reduction, a year later Green managed to reduce the night overtime rate from 20 cents an hour to 16⅔ cents an hour. The journeymen acquiesced in this nonstandard rate primarily because the union work rules did not specifically cover night overtime rates. Some time later Green brought forty to fifty boys into his printing office. To the union, the Washington Institute was nothing more than a new attempt by a greedy Green to extract more money from the printing business at the expense of the workmen. The master printer publicly estimated that the use of boys in place of journeymen would save $15,600 a year in labor costs.[30]

The journeymen attacked the plan on numerous fronts. Outraged at the scheme to hold apprentices' earnings until they reached twenty-one and then to lend the money to them to set up for themselves, the journeymen noted, "We venture to say, that there is scarcely a practical printer now living, who cannot remember the feeling of delight with which, when a boy, he received from the hands of his employer the amount of his weekly 'over-work.' " Green, never having been a practical printer, missed the psychological importance of such payments. The proposal also called for sick boys to be dismissed from the institute and supported by parents or guardians; this break with the tradition that a master was responsible for the medical care of apprentices struck the journeymen as "inhuman." Green, claiming to be a modern innovator, stated that the institute would punish wrongdoing by "solitary confinement" rather than by "corporal punishment." The journeymen were amazed that confinement might be considered a means of moral reformation for youths, but they were even more astonished at the assumption that corporal punishment was inflicted upon apprentices in any printing office. "Flagellation," they wrote, "has almost entirely ceased in all well regulated offices in this country." Union printers also questioned whether the true reason for lending money to graduates was not the wish to create a nationwide system of Green-controlled partisan newspapers orchestrated from Washington. And if this master printer succeeded in establishing such a system, other Washington printers would be forced to undertake a similar scheme. For journeymen, the consequences would be terrible. "If the principles upon which it is founded," they warned, "should obtain throughout the country, the very name of a journeyman printer would be unknown, or known only as a title of reproach and degradation; and a large body of men, who now depend upon their labor as journeymen, for the support of themselves and their families, must seek new channels for the prosecution of labor, or be exposed to all the miseries which attend the want of employment."[31]

Present journeymen would be displaced or degraded, and the future graduates of the Washington Institute would join an ever increasing horde of wandering journeymen or small-time would-be masters seeking places to set up. The graduates would never succeed in wiping out their debts. What would be the condition of a graduate? "What has he gained by the labors and studies of his boyhood?" asked the journeymen. "The money which he possessed, and for which he is amenable to the law, is gone! He cannot enter his business as an employer, and there are now no journeymen printers—the baneful school which generated him having destroyed their occupation. The business which he has learned is now, to all practical purposes, altogether useless to him; and he now finds, too late for any efficient remedy, that, if he wishes to be numbered among the honorable of the land, he must begin the business of life anew!" These printers thought the plan so unfair that they were confident few parents or guardians would enter their children into such an institution. But more than fairness was at stake. To a journeyman, his craft was his only property. It was as valuable to him as real estate or stock certificates were to a rich man. Just as the government protected the property of the rich, so too did the government have an obligation to protect the labor property rights of the journeyman craftsman. Yet this was not the case with this plan. A youth who spent years learning his craft would find that others who had acquired the trade through Green's institute had destroyed the value of his training. The journeymen printers of Washington sensed, correctly, a deadly threat, and they appealed to their fellows throughout the country: "Boys will usurp your places, and our honorable occupation will be numbered among the things that are gone! Can you, will you, submit to this humiliating condition?"[32]

The combative editor saw the matter differently. The principal purpose of the institute, he wrote, was to teach discipline and "a lofty spirit of independence." The schooling at the institute would be classical, and servants would do all the menial chores. The graduates would become a new generation of well-educated printers who would both enhance the craft of printing and step into other careers. Printing, said Green, was an intellectual occupation, and many printers could become editors, publishers, attorneys, book dealers, or other businessmen, if only they were educated better. The institute was presented as a means to upward social mobility. "The moral of such a school," wrote Green, "is, that he, who, in his infancy, has fed, clothed and educated himself, and especially if in his minority he has provided a capital wherewith to commence business for himself, will necessarily have too much character to become a dependant upon other men. He will have the spirit and feeling of a freeman; and will act as becomes an American citizen."[33]

Such high-minded rhetoric did not ease the union's concern that the orphanage would train more journeymen than the craft needed. The journeymen asked, "Does it comport with the true principle of philanthropy, to educate men for a profession which they can never follow? to overburden the business to which they must look for support? to hold up to the inexperienced eye of youth the pleasing picture of an honorable career, and certain prosperity, which, when he comes to grasp it, vanishes like the ignis fatuus, and leaves him in darkness and disappointment." To this objection, Green had an answer. He argued slyly that the union misunderstood the purpose of his scheme. "Without meaning any disparagement to those who are now journeymen printers," he wrote, "I respectfully suggest, that there are very few who would labor at the press or case if they were fully qualified by education for more lucrative and agreeable pursuits." He denied that the institute was "to educate a class of *superior* journeymen who are to supercede the old *jours*. Not so. It is to be a school in which the sons of printers and of reputable poor parents may be fitted for a competition with the sons of the rich, in the pursuit of those honors which are held up by our glorious institutions as the reward of merit and of talent." Green added that no group of journeymen had the right to control the number of apprentices that an employer chose to take on. The union doggedly stuck to its main point. The use of large numbers of apprentices by Green would lead to a glut of journeymen that would depress wages and cause the craft of printing to decline markedly. While the journeymen doubted Green's claim that most of the apprentices would end up in the professions, they thought that if that were true then it would be patently unfair for the single trade of printing to bear the burden of preparing youths for a variety of other occupations. This debate continued, Green defied the union and opened the institute, the union struck Green's office, and the following year the institute closed. Continued union hostility to the *U.S. Telegraph,* along with declining political fortunes, led Green to give up the newspaper in 1837. The Columbia Typographical Society had won its battle against an orphanage for apprentice printers.[34]

The controversy over the Washington Institute had lasting reverberations. It led almost immediately to the first national convention of journeymen printers, held in Washington in 1836. At that meeting journeymen discussed particularly the problem of apprentices supplanting journeymen with the new machinery that was then coming into use. While unable to agree upon any national plan of action, the convention did recommend that local unions impose uniform local standards concerning apprenticeship. Locals were urged to adopt rules requiring apprentices to be bound, not to be taken over sixteen, and to be obliged to serve till they turned twenty-one. No runaways were to be hired either as apprentices or as journeymen. After 1839 no union member was to work in an office where apprentices were taken for less than five years, and after 1844 no person would be admitted to the union without proof of having served a five-year apprenticeship. These two rules were to go into effect after ratification by two-thirds of the local unions. The following year the depression struck, and ratification never took place. Plans for a national union disappeared, and it was more than a decade before journeymen printers again met in a national convention to consider a national union.[35]

The depression threw journeymen printers out of work as the production of books, pamphlets, and newspapers declined. A number of major publishing houses, built on credit and badly overextended, collapsed, and even the largest firm in the country, Harper Brothers, found it difficult to pay cash advances to authors for new works. For several months the Harpers printed only English works, on which they paid no royalties. Among journeymen the high hopes of the national convention gave way to gloom, and during the remainder of the decade no local union ever succeeded in enacting a rule limiting the ratio of apprentices to journeymen. In New Orleans journeymen in 1839 did succeed in persuading the publishers of the morning newspapers to dispense with apprentices. But that was a small victory. Perhaps the only cheery thought for journeymen amid the depression was that youths no longer clamored to become apprentice printers, and master craftsmen offered few youths positions. The decline in business that kept large numbers of new youths from entering the craft in time caused the number of journeymen to stabilize. Despite this trend, there was no doubt that the depression had hurt journeymen. The disarray of their union organizations, the destruction of their hope for a national organization, massive layoffs, and the continued use of boys in offices left journeymen printers with less hope and more despair than ever before. The crisis in printing was beginning to assume an ominously permanent form.[36]

✑ CHAPTER FIVE ✑

Personal Relations

As the decline of the master's authority, the rise of the cash wage, and a growing tendency for apprentices to assert their independence eroded the traditional structure of apprenticeship, it became necessary for apprentices to find new ways to define their status within the institution. The collapse of formal relationships based upon tradition, ritual, well-defined status positions, or lines of authority led to an increased importance for personal relations. No longer did an apprentice play a role opposite his master's in which the cake of custom circumscribed the performances of each party. Now the apprentice was free to develop a more personal relationship with his parents, his master, his master's wife, his shop mates, his fellow apprentices, and young ladies of the community. The rising importance of personal relations, as we shall see, had both advantages and dangers, for they could lead either to unprecedented bonds of mutual emotional support or to equally unprecedented neglect, contempt, and loathing. It is significant that during this period apprentices increasingly report a wide range of experiences.

Ties between parents and children are among the strongest of all ties, and the most solemn aspect of apprenticeship always was the breaking of those bonds and the substitution of a master for a father and of a master's household for a family. The severity of the break explains why many men who recalled apprenticeships late in life had little to say about their trades or masters but a great deal about the day they left home to begin the apprenticeship. Sometimes the parting brought maternal admonition, as when James Harper's devout mother advised, "Don't forget your home or your religious duties, James, and always remember that you have good blood in you." Or paternal concern, as when Henry Clarke Wright's

stern, cold father developed a tear in his eye. The parting was so trau-
matic for Horace Greeley that he nearly gave up his apprenticeship.[1]

No youth has left a better record of his feelings at parting than David
Clapp, Jr. A sister took this sixteen-year-old apprentice printer from Dorchester to Boston, where he was to board in a private family. "It being
the first night I ever slept in Boston," recorded David, "and the whole
family entire strangers to me, I was rather inclined to wakefulness through
the night, though less disturbed than I anticipated." The next morning,
as he walked through the streets to the printing office, he grew appre-
hensive. "But the character of the inhabitants is what I am most fearful
about," he confided in his diary. "Anticipation about being despised on
account of coming from the country, and my naturally reserved disposition and ignorance of the world being treated with ridicule and contempt, and other circumstances, are the reasons of my approaching the
office with trembling heart and faltering steps." He knew the importance
of the apprenticeship he was about to begin. The printing office would be
"the scene of my labours—of my industry or laziness for years to come;
where I shall form new connections, new habits and desires, and where
perhaps the die will be cast for my future character in life; so that in a
great measure my prospects depend upon my good or bad behaviour in
this office, as youth is the time we are most susceptible of impressions, and
impressions formed in youth generally have an influence over our conduct through life."[2]

Family ties produced a steady flow of advice from the family to boys
contemplating their livelihoods. Some parents, like Christopher Colt,
were lavishly broad-minded. "It matters but little what employ you embark in," he wrote his son Sam, "if it is but an honest one and well followed up, with a determination to excel in whatever you undertake. This
will enable you to obtain a good living, and to command respect." Other
parents, rooted in artisan tradition, insisted that learning a trade was the
only way to guarantee a respectable, happy station in life. Neal Dow's
parents, hostile to his desire either to go to college or to enter a law office,
insisted that he work in the family tannery. Like many Quakers, the
Dows feared that higher education and the professions undermined religion. Some youths received mixed advice from different family members.
While William S. Robinson's father opposed a college education, a brother
favored the idea. Pushed and pulled by these conflicting opinions, young
Robinson concluded, "I think I shall learn a trade, though I have not
determined what one." A parent, of course, did not know whether his
advice would be taken. Charles Willson Peale worried a great deal about
his sons Franklin and Linn. "I have my fears about him as well as yourself," the father confessed to Franklin. "My only consolation is, that I

have given the best advice and done what I could to serve him in the duty of a Parent." Sometimes advice came to a youth not from his parents but from an older brother. "As the time is near at hand that thou art to leave School and go to some trade and take thy chance in the world with others," wrote the apprentice printer Joseph S. Wall to his brother Caleb, "it ought to be a subject of serious consideration to thee." Joseph's concern may have influenced Caleb's decision to take up printing. Beginning an apprenticeship, however, did not necessarily mean that a youth had decided upon his life's work. "I do not intend to trouble myself much about what business I follow, for a livelihood," Alexander J. Davis, an apprentice printer, wrote his aunt, "—but jog along through the world without cares, and at my ease. It's the best way!!!"[3]

Many youths learned trades from their fathers, from relatives who lived nearby, or from neighbors. In some ways these were the most satisfactory apprenticeships, because a youth could maintain a degree of contact with his family while learning to become more independent. Morton Poole tried to persuade his sister to send him her son. "Don't you want to make a machine maker of him?" he asked. "We want an apprentice now," he offered, "if you want to bind him out till he is twenty-one. Here is two of the verry best masters in the country who are willing to take him and make a man of him. Had you not better accept the chance? You will never get an other so good. He shall share as just we do. Eat at the same table, that is crackers and cheese eaten on the vice bench, and sleep in the same bed, that is a mahoganny board and the carpenters bench and shall have a share of my old cloak for a coverlid. I won't promise you that there shall be no *covers* on his hips, but the soft side of an ash or mahogany plank *arnt* so hard as you might think, for I understand he looks quite like his uncle Morton. What a confounded good looking fellow he must be. Has he got a blue scar on his right cheek? If not, how would it do to mark him in this form? Then he would look some thing like." When Poole hinted that family ties would compensate for the crude surroundings found in most apprenticeships, he stated a view that led many parents to send their sons to work for nearby relatives.[4]

Such apprenticeships, however, not only limited the opportunity of a youth to choose a suitable trade but also prevented any escape from a stagnant, isolated locale. Joel Munsell's father, a poor farmer and wagonmaker in the sleepy village of Northfield, Massachusetts, bitterly opposed his son's plan to go to the bustling county seat at Greenfield and become an apprentice printer. Undeterred by parental opposition, Joel went to the *Franklin Post,* applied for the apprenticeship, and got it. "I immediately returned elated with joy inexpressible at the prospect that lay before me," recalled Munsell. "At sunset I had reached home. My father was the first one whom I met, & I shall always recollect the look he gave me as I passed him." Suddenly, everyone in Northfield became interested in Joel—and in his departure. To heighten the sense of mystery, the youth refused to disclose where he was going or what he was going to do. "It afforded me infinite gratification," wrote Munsell, "to tell each inquisitor a different story, reserving the truth for time to develope." Many of the locals considered the departure of this youth, who had been the terror of the village, to be "good riddance of bad rubbage." Some of the prophets predicted that it would prove impossible for Joel to live away from his family, and the village speculated on how long it would be before he returned.[5]

While some parents discouraged their sons from leaving home, other parents were willing to sacrifice close family ties in order to assure a son of a good apprenticeship in a distant location. In 1808 William Lloyd Garrison's father abandoned his family, and Fanny Garrison was left with three children, the oldest of whom was seven. While Mrs. Garrison went to work as a nurse, the children were dispersed to live with different families in Newburyport, Massachusetts. James, the oldest son, learned shoemaking, and as the mother's health began to fail, she decided that it was important to place Lloyd at a trade. The nine-year-old boy was sent to Lynn and apprenticed to a Quaker shoemaker, but the apprenticeship failed because the slightly built Lloyd lacked sufficient strength to work with a lapstone. In late 1815, when a Lynn shoe manufacturer decided to take several workmen with him to open a business in the thriving seaport of Baltimore, Mrs. Garrison and her two sons accompanied the party. In the end the shoe factory failed, the shoe manufacturer returned to Lynn, James ran away to sea, and Fanny decided to remain in Baltimore as a nurse. Homesick Lloyd was returned to Newburyport to live with friends and attend school. In the depressed year of 1817 Mrs. Garrison could find no apprenticeship for this twelve-year-old in either Baltimore or Newburyport. Finally, however, she was able to apprentice Lloyd to a Haverhill, Massachusetts, cabinetmaker. Although the boy was treated kindly, he was unhappy and homesick, and one day he tried to run away. The master overtook Lloyd on the road, and when the boy confessed his homesickness, he was released from the apprenticeship and sent back to friends in Newburyport.[6]

In 1818, after a short trial, Lloyd was indented for seven years as an apprentice to Ephraim W. Allen, the publisher and editor of the semiweekly Newburyport Herald. Although the thirteen-year-old found the trade challenging and his master kind, he was pained by the separation from his mother. It did not seem likely that he would see her for a long time. Fanny could support herself in Baltimore, and she was unwilling to risk leaving that certainty for the chance of something in Newburyport. Since Lloyd was indented in Newburyport, there was little prospect that he could visit Baltimore before his time was out. When Lloyd complained to his mother that her letters were infrequent, she explained that neither of them could afford to pay the twenty-five-cent postage very often. Meanwhile, Fanny's health declined, Lloyd worried about her, and the lonesome mother finally had her daughter Elizabeth sent to Baltimore to be with her. In 1822, when Lloyd wrote a piece for the newspaper signed "An Old Bachelor," he concealed his authorship from everyone except his mother. In a rare letter, she puckishly advised, "You must write me one of your pieces so that I can read [it] on one side of your letter, and I will give you my opinion whether you are an old bachelor, or whether you are A.O.B., as A may stand for Ass, and O for Oaf, and B for Blockhead." Just as the apprentice began to develop his literary talent, his sister died in Baltimore, and Fanny's health became desperate. In March 1823 she wrote Lloyd urging him to get permission from Allen to visit before her own death. Allen's reluctance led Lloyd to advise his mother to write Allen begging permission for the visit. The son concluded, "O may Heaven grant that I shall clasp you again to my throbbing breast."[7]

Fanny wrote Allen a pathetic appeal that worked its magic, and at the same time she sent Lloyd some advice concerning a career as an author. "You have no doubt read and heard the fate of such characters," she noted, "that they generally starve to death in some garret or place that no one inhabits; so you may see what fortune and luck belong to you if you are of that class of people. Secondly, you think your time was wisely spent while you was writing political pieces. I cannot join with you there, for had you been searching the scriptures for truth, and praying for direction of the holy spirit to lead your mind into the path of holiness, your time would have been more wisely spent, and your advance to the heavenly world more rapid. But instead of that you have taken the Hydra by the head, and now beware of his mouth; but as it is done, I suppose you think you had better go on and seek the applause of mortals. But, my dear L., lose not the favour of God; have an eye single to his glory, and you will not lose your reward." Soon after receiving this letter, Lloyd sailed from Boston to Baltimore, and in July, while visiting his dying mother, he wrote Allen describing his shock at seeing this emaciated, feeble woman, whom he had not seen for seven years. The visit had to be a short one, and Lloyd was already back in Allen's office in September when Fanny Garrison died.[8]

Parting from the family could be eased by a good relationship between the apprentice and his master. Both Lloyd Garrison and Henry Wright were grateful for the kind and considerate treatment they received, and

Henry's master even rewarded the bookish apprentice by supplying him with books. John Frazee, an apprentice bricklayer, recalled his master fondly. "William Lawrence was the man who first inspired me to think philosophically," remembered Frazee. "When he had all his boys at home and seated around his winter evenings' fire, we constituted a sort of debating club. . . ." Such close relationships were less likely when the apprentice did not board with the master, and surely some of David Clapp's anxiety upon first leaving home was due to his having to adjust to two new environments—both the family home where he boarded and the shop where he worked. Horace Greeley, apprentice in a printing office frequently bought and sold and resident in a public tavern, never identified with any master printer and instead—perhaps out of desperation—became familial with the entire village. As changing economic conditions led masters to board out apprentices or encouraged apprentices to demand the right to board themselves, the link between work and everyday life that had existed in apprenticeship was broken. The new-style master was apt to demand proficiency and efficiency without much interest in an apprentice's personal welfare, and the apprentice was free to do as he pleased outside of working hours. The tendencies of the times were to destroy what had been a personal relation just at the moment when confusion about roles and status made the apprentice yearn for personal relations with an increased longing.[9]

When an apprentice did live in his master's house, the relations between the apprentice and the master's wife were important. Simon Newcomb ran away largely because of the sharp tongue of his mistress, and Greeley as an underage journeyman was driven to exasperation by Mrs. Sterrett. Other apprentices were more fortunate. Mrs. David Bright and Mrs. William Williams created home environments, showed affection for their husbands' apprentices, and became effective surrogate mothers offering advice concerning both the minor crises of ordinary life and the larger questions of ethics, morals, and religion. Perhaps no one had more influence than James Harper's mother, who encouraged one Irish immigrant apprentice in her household to renounce Catholicism and become a Presbyterian minister. While not every master craftsman's wife encouraged and coddled her husband's apprentices, a wise mistress knew that a tranquil household helped keep the shop running smoothly. And a wise master knew the importance of having a wise mistress. When two bachelor iron molders, John Gage and William Smith, opened a foundry, they quickly hired an apprentice who brought along his mother and three sisters to keep house and make a family. Eventually, Gage married one of the daughters. When an apprentice boarded out, the boardinghouse keeper lacked both the incentive of the master's wife and the intimate knowledge of the master and his shop necessary to keep the apprentice happy. The consequence, in many cases, was that the apprentice's freedom from the mistress's control after working hours was purchased by a weakening of personal relations.[10]

The new fashion of having the apprentice board outside the master's house did not always work. For David Clapp, there were several difficulties. In the first place, his master neglected to pay the board bill owed to the blacksmith's family with which he lived. As the bill grew larger and larger, rising to more than $20, David became so embarrassed that he could scarcely look the Bartholomew family in the eye. Second, although David was fond of the family, especially the kind Mrs. Bartholomew, he found it hard to get along with thirteen-year-old Truman Bartholomew, with whom he shared a bed. "He was a most confounded noisy, troublesome fellow," wrote Clapp, "and none of the family had the least control over him except his father, the lashes of whose rod he feared, and very frequently felt." While Clapp did not mind leaving the Bartholomews, he dreaded his master's decision to have the apprentice board with the master's family. "This proposal," he wrote, "struck a chill through me at once. It was what I had been expecting, and very much dreading. I had always been very bashful in going among strangers; but in this instance I felt an unusual backwardness and a great disinclination to remove. I feared I should have to be the youngest apprentice at the house, do all the choirs [sic], and be made a complete servant of. Besides, it was a family that I knew nothing about, but I knew they were rich, and probably grand, and the very idea of being a menial in a gentleman's family preyed upon my spirits. . . ."[11]

Like other apprentices, David Clapp had little choice concerning his domestic arrangements, and he moved into the house of his master's father. Instructed to go to Cotton's home for dinner, at 2 P.M. he hesitantly rang the front doorbell. David was shown inside, past the dining room to the kitchen, where he was seated next to Edward Hall, another apprentice printer who boarded with the Cottons. Outraged at not being allowed to eat in the dining room, and furious when served the leavings from the family table, Clapp resolved to look for another apprenticeship. But as it turned out, the dinner was quite tasty, and Edward was an amiable, sociable fellow. That night at 8 P.M., when David came home from the office, he found the family in the parlor enjoying a fire. He found himself in the cold, dark kitchen with only the choice of building a fire for himself or going to bed. Crawling into bed, the apprentice discovered it to be the worst he had ever slept in; and it had only a scanty cover. Sometime after eleven Edward appeared and announced that he never came home any earlier. It was then that Clapp learned that in the morning he was to rise to make the kitchen fire, boil water, and make coffee for the family. Edward was profane, the family ignored him, and David's only cheery thought was that with business at the printing office so slack, his stay in this house was apt to be short. It promised to be a bleak—and cold—winter. Edward came to dinner regularly but never appeared at supper and was out every evening. Clapp grew depressed each night in his cold bed. He took to leaving Boston on Saturday evening to spend the weekend at his father's house in Dorchester, and he returned to the city only on Monday morning to go to work. Not only was it more pleasant, but he cleverly had hit upon a scheme that made it impossible for him to light a fire on either Sunday or Monday morning.[12]

In many shops an apprentice found a better friend in a journeyman than in his master. Early in his apprenticeship Lloyd Garrison fell under the influence of the sweet-tempered Tobias H. Miller, who later became a minister and city missionary. Miller taught, by example, the virtues of duty, patience, self-control, good cheer, generosity, and sympathy. This journeyman's watchwords were picked up by the apprentice, who remembered such lines as "Patience and perseverance!" "Tisn't as bad as it would be if it were worse!" and "Never mind! 'Twill be all the same a thousand years hence!" For an apprentice, meeting a journeyman who shared a similar interest and temperament could be intoxicating. When fifteen-year-old Rufus Griswold, who had been raised in a strict, sober New England farm family, discovered romantic poetry, the apprentice printer ran away to live with a poetry-loving journeyman, George G. Foster. Two years later, after Griswold had fled, Foster wrote, "Griswold, my own Griswold—. . . . I have loved often and deeply. My heart has burned itself almost to a charred cinder by the flames of passion which have glowed within it—and yet I have never felt towards any human being—man or woman—so strong and absorbing an affection as I bear you. . . . I enjoin you by our friendship, and by those Gods of the pure and the bright whom we both worship to come to me. I scarcely know what else to add—except that which you do or should already know— that my love, my *devotion,* (we may both I trust use the word,) is unaltered and unalterable.—Farewell—farewell—come to me if you love me—G. G. Foster." One scarcely knows how to interpret such sentiments, but they illustrate perfectly the way in which the more formal, restrained relations of the past were eroding under a rising tide of personal feelings.[13]

Not every apprentice was enchanted by the journeymen in his shop. When the owner of the Howell Iron Works forced his journeymen to teach John Roach the trade, the molders demanded that the new apprentice follow custom and provide a footing—that is, one day's supply of liquor to all the molders in the foundry. After John, broke and a teetotaler, declined, the journeymen used persuasion. Roach recalled, "I remember very well how they laid me face down over a barrel and rolled me back and forth while a big Englishman spanked me with a board until I agreed to give them whiskey enough to pay my footing." These journeymen were a raucous, hard-drinking bunch, but other apprentices, like Horace Greeley or David Clapp, worked in shops that frequently had only a single journeyman. When Clapp first went to work in the printing office of John Cotton, Jr., he found the master an absentee owner and took instruction from a journeyman foreman named Peck, who had to endure pranks played by three apprentices. Peck expected the senior apprentice John Fisher to assist at press, but when that youth claimed to have a sore finger, the inexperienced Clapp had to take his place. In half an hour Clapp's hands were so blistered he had to quit the press, and Peck had to work the press alone. Later Clapp learned that Fisher had feigned the sore finger. On another occasion Peck and Clapp worked off more than a hundred copies of one side of a magazine when they discovered that the "points" used to register the paper so that the obverse could be printed with correct placement had been removed. After Peck accused Fisher of sabotage, that insolent youth dared to suggest that Peck's failure to notice the missing points proved that he was not a good workman. Fisher, as usual, had the last word. On a shutter next to a front window he scrawled, "Mr Peck, foreman of this office, worked off five quires on the news form without any points; what a foreman!"[14]

Poor Peck was not paid his wages and left the shop. John Cotton, the owner, continued to stay away from the office, which was now run by his apprentice John Fisher. "I had no one to teach me the trade," wrote David Clapp, "but an apprentice who was younger than I was, and who was very wild, and sometimes inattentive to his business." Amid rumors that Cotton had been seen visiting the local houses of prostitution, creditors arrived with constables. The owner went bankrupt, Cotton's father took over the office, business dwindled, and the remaining apprentices were dismissed. Young Clapp, still an apprentice, was the only employee, and since the elder Cotton was not a printer, he had neither anyone to talk to nor anyone to teach him the trade. When the office suddenly landed a contract to print a hymnal as a rush order, a dissipated journeyman named Fowles was hired for the project. Fowles and Charles Crocker, author of the hymnal, pulled press, while Clapp set up the forms. The apprentice discovered that he could learn quite a bit about his trade from the itinerant Crocker. Two months later Peck returned to the office to print a medical journal. Peck, however, had a problem with liquor; when he was drunk, he had no desire to work; and when he was not drunk, his hands shook so much that he could not work. After the medical journal fell behind schedule, the elder Cotton bought the right to print it and bestowed the work upon Clapp. The youth, who continued nominally as an apprentice but was in reality a self-trained master printer, always felt sympathy for the younger Cotton and admiration and respect for the elder Cotton, who had arranged matters so that Clapp could continue to learn the craft. On finishing the apprenticeship, Clapp continued to work for Cotton, who later helped him set up his own shop. In appreciation, Clapp's first son was named for John Cotton, Sr. Clapp, it turned out, had better relations with his master's father than either with his master or with any of the journeymen who had passed through the office.[15]

Apprentices, like other youths, were fond of companions and hated to be alone. Masters sometimes obliged these feelings by having two apprentices share a bed in the shop. The shop gained security, and bed sharing made sleep less uncomfortable on a cold winter's night. The apprentice cabinetmaker Jenner Carpenter usually shared his bed with another apprentice, but sometimes that youth visited relatives, and Jenner was left alone. Whenever that happened, Jenner tried to find a friend—most often, an apprentice in another craft—to spend the night with him. Once he wrote, "I must go and get somebody to sleep with me tonight for it is rather lonesome to sleep alone." A parade of friends warmed Jenner's bed, and at least once Jenner reciprocated to become the bedfellow of a friend. Occasionally, things could be even cosier, as when Jenner noted, "Jo. Moore staid with Dexter & I last night. We slept three in a bed. He brought up his accordian & we had some music before we went to bed." Few of Jenner's guests ever returned for a second visit. There was a reason. Wrote the apprentice, "The bed bugs have got so thick here that we cant sleep here."[16]

Relations among apprentices in a shop were often strained by competition for status, youthful jealousy and rivalry, and peer pressure common among all adolescents. In principle, the pecking order among apprentices was determined by the age and length of service of the apprentices. Had all apprentices begun their service at the same age, such rankings might have been easy to fix. Of course, there was still the problem that some apprentices had more talent than others, and it was only natural for a master craftsman or his foreman to favor apprentices who were more skilled or productive. When David Clapp first became an apprentice, for example, he set as his goal learning the trade faster than Abraham Treadwell, another apprentice who had arrived in the shop only a few days earlier. David found his goal easy to attain, because Abraham was younger and not conscientious at learning the craft. The result was a rising tension within the shop. Usually, an apprentice's rank was dated from his entrance into the shop, but some allowance had to be made for a newly hired youth who had served part of an apprenticeship elsewhere. A week or two after Joel Munsell began his apprenticeship, a second apprentice was hired. Because Franz had had some knowledge of printing, he claimed seniority over Joel. It was only natural that Joel felt a certain amount of resentment, and his ill feeling was increased when he discovered that the new apprentice was stupid, overbearing, conceited, and a poor workman. The two frequently clashed. "This mortification at seeing me so much better liked in the office than himself somewhat humbled him," noted Munsell, "although it no ways served to lessen our wrangling." Joel was so disgusted that he decided to drive Franz from the office, and the opportunity arrived when a new foreman had frequent disputes with Franz. As if difficulties in the office were not discouraging enough, poor Franz also failed to woo a young lady, and he was so humiliated he left town.[17]

The rivalries sometimes got out of hand. When David Clapp entered John Cotton's office, he was the youngest apprentice. The new devil, who had to do all the menial chores, was not impressed with James Freeman ("appears to be nearly a fool"), John Fisher ("very smart, active . . . very profane"), or Abraham Treadwell ("rather lazy"), who had been in the office only a few days. It took some time for Clapp to learn that Freeman, who he had thought was the oldest apprentice, was in fact not an apprentice at all. Freeman, a lazy and stupid nineteen-year-old casual laborer, was paid only $2 a week. Fisher and Treadwell could not resist tormenting Freeman by "stuffing his hat full of paper, putting things in his coat pocket, as his coat hangs up, when he is at work, which only makes him scold and threaten most excessively." After Peck had left the office, and Fisher was in charge, Fisher and Treadwell had teased Freeman so much he could not work. Sometimes he would stupidly scuffle with them, and the duo always bested him. And then they laughed at him. Matters got worse whenever Treadwell's idle, dissipated brother came to the office, and the two Treadwells and Fisher attacked Freeman. There were other incidents. Fisher and Treadwell hit upon a scheme for saving money. Instead of boarding with Treadwell's father, they planned to live in the office and buy cheap meals from a hotel across the street. Treadwell's mother made her son live at home, but for several weeks Fisher lived in the office, until one day the younger Cotton discovered Fisher's dirty plates hidden under the stairwell. Fisher was fired, and soon afterward Freeman, who had spent most of his time reading newspapers, was dismissed. Treadwell continued in the office until he quarreled with Cotton and left. At first Clapp was sorry to see Treadwell go, because he feared having to do all the menial chores, but as it turned out, Clapp was left to run the office however he chose.[18]

Rivalries were sometimes expressed through practical jokes. One time the apprentice tailor Isaac T. Hopper and a fellow apprentice went to the cellar to steal a pitcher of cider from a barrel. Isaac pulled the spile and hid it while his victim drew the cider. When the pitcher was full, Isaac pretended to look for the spile, declared he could not find it, and told his companion to put his finger in the hole while he went to get another spile. The boy waited an hour, but Isaac never returned. Finally, the apprentice yelled, and the yells brought not Isaac but the mistress, who scolded him. Petty quarrels among apprentices became magnified when an older, stronger youth took on the role of bully and picked on the other boys. As Isaac Hopper watched such a bully knock about the younger boys, he had a desire to fight, but he knew that his master would be outraged if the apprentices fought. Once fights broke out among the apprentices, they could lead to the kind of chaos that had engulfed David Clapp's shop. Besides, in this instance, Isaac was smaller than the bully. One day, the bully knocked Isaac down, and Isaac said, "If you ever do that again, I'll kill you. Mind what I say. I tell you I'll kill you." The next day the bully knocked Isaac down, and Isaac got up quietly, found a heavy window bar, and waited behind a door for the bully to go to breakfast. When the bully appeared, Isaac sprang forth and smote the tyrant, who slumped to the floor. Isaac left him there and went to breakfast, where the master asked, "Where is Samson?" Isaac replied, "I've killed him." His startled master asked, "Killed him? What do you mean?" Answered Isaac, "I told him I would kill him if he ever knocked me down again, and I *have* killed him." All rushed from the table, a physician was summoned, and the bully revived, but he looked so "pale and helpless" that a sorry Isaac resolved to control his temper. The bully never struck another apprentice.[19]

Peer pressure could be merciless, for an apprentice who was different in any way from his fellows drew their scorn and ridicule. While the bookish Henry Wright had found this a heavy burden to endure in David Bright's hat shop, another apprentice in that shop had had worse problems. Henry Folsom, who began with the handicap of being older than the other apprentices, had been the rather spoiled only son of a widow, and he tended to become angry at practical jokes. His anger delighted the other apprentices, who picked on Folsom. The sensitive youth retaliated as best he could, but his torment continued, and finally he appealed tearfully to Wright to help him procure relief. Wright urged the other apprentices to desist, and for a few days Folsom would have peace, but then the awkward youth would bungle some process, spoil a pound of wool, or otherwise draw attention to himself, and again he would be ridiculed. After a year he had to be sent home to his mother. Folsom had less grit than

James Harper, who had arrived at his apprenticeship in New York City wearing homespun and rough country boots. James's countrified appearance immediately set him apart from the other apprentices, who were city bred and well dressed. For months James endured ridicule about his appearance, until one day a fellow apprentice looked at James's bedraggled trousers and sarcastically asked for the calling card of the tailor. "That's my card," said James, as he kicked the apprentice in the seat of his pants. "Take good care of it! When I am out of my time, and set up for myself, and you need employment, as you will, come to me, bring the card, and I will give you work."[20]

The divisions that beset the ranks of apprentices threatened to isolate a youth, and the one sure way to avoid such isolation was to join with other apprentices against a common enemy—such as the master. Joel Munsell, foreman in a small printing office at eighteen, worked with two other apprentices, named Whitcomb and Mitchell. The three became friends, and one Saturday night they stayed up late printing an item for their own amusement. As a result the three overslept on Sunday morning, until awakened at nine by the village church bell. The apprentices rushed to the kitchen in hopes of a tardy breakfast and found the dishes cleared away. The master showed up, berated them for being late, and ordered the servant not to feed them. The "astonished" apprentices left in a hurry and swore a pact never to enter that house again. The master, reconsidering his hasty action, attempted a reconcilation, but it failed when the stubborn Whitcomb insisted that the trio stay away from the master's house and buy crackers and butter from a store. Although the apprentices were specifically invited to dinner, which they later learned had been a particularly rich one, they did not go. On Monday the newspaper editor begged the three to resume work, but they declined to do so without talking to the paper's owner. In the end the dispute was not settled, and each apprentice went his own way. Whitcomb gave up printing, Munsell went to work for a rival newspaper, and Mitchell returned to his position. The temporary alliances of youth were apt to be broken by the compelling need for work and the acquisition of skills. In a larger sense, apprentices were competitors for the skills that enabled a man to earn a living, and the essential nature of that competition perpetually stirred up rivalries and discouraged close friendships inside a shop.[21]

While relations within the shop were important, so were relations outside the shop, where young men met young women. The age during which a youth was an apprentice was, to use a nineteenth-century phrase, a time ripe for discovering the charms of the female sex. Like youths in other times and places, the apprentices expended much time, energy, and effort upon the subject. Occasionally, apprentices who had been friends and then parted compared the girls in different locales. After Tom Mc-Kellar finished his apprenticeship in New York to become a journeyman in Philadelphia, he reported on the relative merits of the females in the two cities. Philadelphia girls, though pretty, lacked the sophisticated style of New York girls, and they promenaded the streets at night without their beaux. In Philadelphia the sexes appeared to be more separated, and the young men were "exceedingly ungallant." He expressed a popular sentiment of the times, when he added, "Young people of both sexes must mix together, or the manners of the males will be without that refining touch which intercourse with 'female women' can alone effect." A homesick and lonely Tom, more than a little in need of that "refining touch," later received a letter from New York announcing the "matrimonial probabilities and statistics of all [his] friends." He called himself "Tom—that poor, doomed-to-be-a-bachelor animal." Not long after that remark Tom reported he had just been jilted. "I am not one of those who can content themselves with an occasional sprinkle of affection," wrote the melancholy swain. "She must be mine *wholly*." A year later Tom's cousin, a journeyman quill maker, moved to Philadelphia and reported six girls working in his shop, but, alas, they were "the homeliest set of girls" he had seen there. In general, however, the Philadelphia girls were "good looking."[22]

For an apprentice looking was about all that was allowed. While society approved of groups of young people gathering for balls, sleigh rides, singing clubs, or work parties at the harvest, almost the only proper purpose for a young man to be alone with a young woman was that of escorting her to or from church. No wonder religious services were so popular. One should not underestimate the peril a youth placed himself in if he chose to ignore conventions and customs. When Joel Munsell's arch-rival, Franz, vainly sought acceptance into the most polished circles of the village where he worked, he refused to recognize his failure. One evening Franz passed the house of the village's reigning belle, and although a stranger, he called on the young lady, entered her parlor, and asked her to take a walk with him. The indignant miss said she did not walk with strangers. Franz persisted, until finally the woman got up, announced that her candle wanted snuffing, snuffed it, and retired from the parlor—leaving Franz in the dark. He sat in the room quite some time before realizing that he had been rebuffed and then went home cursing the village, its dullards, and its manners. Soon the entire village learned the story, and boys who passed Franz in the street greeted him with the phrase "take a short walk." Franz was so humiliated he left his apprenticeship.[23]

The belle's seeming cruelty in refusing to take a walk must be put into the context of village life. For a couple to promenade up and down the main street of a village several evenings was as good as announcing their engagement, and such a courtship implied a commitment that could bring a breach-of-promise suit if no marriage took place. Complained John Rogers, "A young man cannot be seen with a girl without having the most outrageous stories told about him." He got even with the village gossips by sending each of them an invitation to join "The Cochituate Gossiping Club." This invitation had produced a great sensation, and a gleeful Rogers crowed, "If it don't make some of the old women wrathy I am mistaken." For further amusement, Rogers dressed as a girl and paraded arm in arm with another youth; the couple were disappointed because only one person saw them. The local gossips had good reason to keep an eye on Rogers. To his sister, he boasted, "I find that I have got to be quite a hand amongst the girls & I suppose that you will be surprised to hear that I have just had a kiss from one of the prettiest girls that you can find any where round. O—h! but didn't it taste good. But that is only one from an innumerable number which have been accumulating from the prettiest girls round. I have been out sailing or walking on moonlight evenings most every night with them & go home about 12 or one o'clock."[24]

Not all youths were so bold. Indentures customarily pledged the apprentice neither to commit fornication nor to marry, and even after the decline of indentures, it was understood that an apprentice could not marry. The penalty for an apprentice who got a girl pregnant was severe. Not only did the apprentice ruin the reputation of the girl, which was an act of humiliation for the male in that age of romantic gallantry, but the penniless apprentice faced the prospect of court-ordered child support for the bastard he had fathered. Paying child support or the alternative, an early marriage, meant the end of apprenticeship, the loss of a half-learned craft, and perpetual poverty as an unskilled laborer. Henry Wilson bitterly recalled the way in which his own birth had pushed his parents into the lowest ranks of society. The only time a pregnancy benefited an apprentice was when he had taken up with the master's daughter and planned a marriage that would enable him to inherit the business. No wonder many masters wanted apprentices to board outside their houses. On the other hand, the master's daughter—sometimes with parental encouragement—might choose an apprentice for herself, as Mathias Kuglar discovered. "He was sent to the Barn to Frail out Grain with the imployers Daughter," recalled a later employee, "& they got mixt up amongst the Grain & Couglar Had to Marry hur." Years later, when this journeyman papermaker worked for and boarded with Kuglar, one of the master's daughters, copying her mother, stole into the journeyman's room late at night and jumped into his bed. He must not have coveted the family papermill, for he pretended to be asleep, until she left.[25]

While parents naturally took steps to discourage sons from becoming involved with girls too seriously at too early an age, youths themselves had the most compelling reasons to avoid entanglements that could ruin their prospects. Nathaniel P. Willis, the son of a master printer, feared female entrapment, and he left behind a letter describing the perils of being nineteen. "I have been in danger of seduction," he wrote, ". . . from a lascivious though handsome girl who is nursery maid in the house opposite—she had seen me, I found out, for several hot nights strip naked & walk my room to get cool—and being pleased I suppose with the view of my inexpressibles she began a conversation with me across from house to house, in which she was pleased to introduce many and various hints with regard to subjects too delicate to be touched upon by the chastity of my good quill—She sat there reading a book one night when I went to bed, and I asked her what it was—I anticipated the answer, for she said *Fanny Hill.*—She then remarked that the pictures were beautiful—and that she would like to practice on them, but *she had no one to practice with her*—Phew!!"[26]

CHAPTER SIX

The Limits of Reform

While traditional patterns of life were crumbling, a spirit of reform was helping to create new patterns. No examination of the two decades after 1815 can ignore the numerous ways in which reformers influenced American life. Perhaps no reform was more important to the long-term development of the United States than the creation of a public school system, which began to evolve into its modern form during the first half of the nineteenth century. While public schools fulfilled widespread egalitarian and democratic aspirations, they also emerged as a means by which the dominant social, economic, and political groups in American society sought to inculcate the masses with the values of cleanliness, order, and discipline. These moral values were designed to lead the masses both to accept the dominance of the emerging middle class and its mores and to adopt habits of life and ways of thinking that would supply the new industrial system with a disciplined, motivated work force. It was no accident that the public schools emerged first in precisely those areas, such as Massachusetts, where the new industrial system was also emerging and that the most enthusiastic supporters of the schools included industrialists who could see advantages for themselves in mass education. But we would miss an important point if we ignored the fact that the public schools were created largely as a result of intense public demand. As is so often the case, the elite educational reformers led the public where it already wanted to go. The interesting question, then, is why Americans in general, and an older generation of not very well educated Americans in particular, sought to create public schools for their children and future generations. The answer to that question will take us beyond both the rhetoric of democratic idealism and the notion that public schools were imposed from the top down.[1]

As early as the 1780s thoughtful men like Benjamin Rush advocated an improved system of education to sustain the new republic. To the Revolutionary generation, widespread public education was to be one of the main guarantors against tyranny. Early action to provide more accessible education included the provision for school lands in the new western territories, the Connecticut plan for a permanent school fund, and various funding schemes in other states. Yet little was accomplished outside New England, where public education always had been strongest, and in large cities such as New York the operators of free charity schools discovered that middle-class parents, including artisans, who could not afford private school fees, would keep their children home rather than send them to free charity schools. The southern states had few sources for school revenues, little enthusiasm for education, and a widely dispersed population that made difficult the organization of public schools. Throughout the country there were shortages of qualified teachers, schoolhouses, and books. Around the turn of the century progress was slight, although a greater publication of schoolbooks does suggest some improvement. Then in 1804 Joseph Lancaster's plan for public schools was brought from England to the United States. Under this scheme a school could be organized in any large meeting hall, and a single teacher could teach hundreds of pupils at little cost through the device of appointing more advanced pupils to teach the beginners. For about twenty years Lancasterian schools were popular in America's largest cities, and they enabled many American children to acquire basic literacy and elementary arithmetic. Lancaster was sufficiently enthusiastic that he came to the United States and set up model schools in Baltimore. But the scheme was never as successful as its advocates hoped, and by the 1820s critics pointed out that Lancasterian pupils failed to gain an education beyond the most rudimentary level.[2]

During the 1820s educational innovation continued. Experimental schools, such as Round Hill, were opened to serve the children of the wealthy. These schools, borrowing heavily from the ideas of the Italian educational reformer Pestalozzi, replaced traditional rote memorizing with analysis and creative thinking. A few itinerant schoolmasters, such as Bronson Alcott, became interested in experimentation and sought to apply new techniques to the public schools. Alcott discovered that success with the pupils did not always bring success with the parents, and in one case the school committee closed his school after parents complained that it was too radical. Among Alcott's controversial innovations were his efforts to use individual seats in place of common benches, to arrange the classroom with the teacher in the center and the pupils forming a U around the teacher, to teach reading with picture cards, to establish a school library, and to perform calisthenics in the classroom. Alcott gave up fighting tradition-minded parents and opened a private school, which enjoyed great success. While innovation was strongest in private education, it often seeped into the public schools through teachers who were graduates of the experimental private schools. The 1820s also brought the use of new textbooks. The age-old New England primer, with its staunch Calvinist bent, either was replaced with more modern and secular readers or appeared with the old title but subdued content. *A* was no longer for "Adams Fall" but now stood for "Ape." And *F* no longer stood for "The Idle Fool Is Whipt at School." Another innovation was the construction of better school buildings, as many towns used public money to build permanent brick buildings for the first time. These buildings were not elaborate, often containing only one large room, but they represented a permanent commitment to public education. Yet another innovation was the creation of infant schools for children under age six. Often church-sponsored, these schools inculcated religious values in young children, through whom they reached parents.[3]

In the 1820s many people debated the proper role, if any, for corporal punishment in the schools. As early as the 1780s the reformer Benjamin Rush, in a pamphlet attacking this all-but-universal traditional practice, held that physical punishment produced only pain without any hope for reformation of character, and in a republic, he warned, a self-restraining morality was the basis of the state. Despite Rush's views, the issue remained largely dormant until the 1820s, when a number of reform-minded educators for the first time seriously proposed the elimination of what many pupils bitterly recalled as the main business of the schools: beating pupils. Educators, unlike Rush, did not merely offer theoretical reasoning in support of their opinions but actually conducted schools such as Round Hill without the proverbial rod and ferule. Shocked conservatives expressed outrage, cited biblical injunctions, and warned that the failure to punish, and to punish physically with severity, would lead to a generation of degenerate, insolent, mannerless youths bent upon defying parents and all legitimate authority. Fear, one stated, was the basis of authority, and no youth in his minority should fail to be cowed. Reformers ignored such traditional criticisms and conducted their experiment in the classroom, where, at least under certain conditions, they proved that a school could be conducted without the use of brute force. "A *forced, frightened, whip-driven* obedience," chided Samuel Nott, Jr., "is not the obedience of a Christian child." Removing terror from the schoolroom had a positive effect upon youthful morale, and it could lead to improved scholastic performance. Yet many schools continued to be conducted along old lines, and it was often difficult for a young and inexperienced teacher to adopt the new plan in a school where pupils expected blows to fall. Blows, however, did gradually become less common, and by the 1840s Horace Mann was able to recommend as state policy that teachers use corporal punishment only as a last resort. That Mann's quasi-reformist view became widely shared is in itself evidence for how much attitudes had changed since the turn of the century.[4]

Behind the decline in the use of corporal punishment lay new attitudes about the nature of children, the proper roles for children and master in a school, and the process of education itself. According to tradition, children were born with malevolent tendencies, and their nasty little wills had to be broken. Therefore, it was only logical to beat a bad child. But the newer view, widely held by the 1820s, was that children were innocent and their minds blank pages upon which a future script might be written. The machinist Morton Poole urged his sister to raise his nephew by cultivating "the liberties which are ecential to the formation of a free and independent spirit." Parents needed to use a "superior understanding" rather than invoke fear. The child, he argued, should be taught "to look up to its parents with awe as we might be supposed to look up to a God. Now a child that is afraid of its parents can never feel that confidence which is necessary to the receiving of information in conversations with its parents. It can never confide to them its little secrets. In fact there never can be that social intercourse that ought allways to exist." What would happen if a parent followed Poole's advice? Perhaps an "independent spirit" could get out of hand. Joel Munsell blamed his own wildness and truancy on such parental indulgence. "By the time I reached my twelfth year I had pretty much divested myself of parental authority," wrote Munsell. "I had been allowed to follow my own inclinations with little restraint, & now with none."[5]

Too much restraint as well as too little led to difficulties, and the solution was to understand the nature of the young better. Children, said Pestalozzi, were imitators, and they would imitate whatever was set in front of them. In this view corporal punishment taught children that violence was, under certain conditions, acceptable. Indeed, the principal requirement for its acceptability was apparently the ability of the larger party to work its will upon smaller beings. Might, in other words, made right. In the old way of thinking, children submitted themselves to the schoolmaster's authority, because it was in the nature of things for lesser beings to submit to greater beings. All authority was noble, virtuous, and good, and if children did not learn to submit to a schoolmaster, as youths they would not submit to their craft masters, and later as men they would fail to submit to almighty God. The outcome of this failure to submit to authority was damnation. In the new view, children learned, and the schoolmaster taught. The master was in charge, but children were to some extent responsible for their own learning. They should not be afraid of a master, because a master who achieved authority through terror could not teach effectively. Teachers discovered pragmatically that authority had little to do with teaching and often was destructive to learning. Finally, in the traditional view, education consisted of children memorizing and reciting what they had memorized to the master. Knowledge was a constant transmitted intact from one generation to the next, rigidly, without change, and with eternal verities in place. There was scarcely any room for innovation in this system. In the new view, children were encouraged to explore, to think, to analyze, to act creatively, to question, to express themselves. This kind of education would enable the child, on his own, to advance beyond the knowledge of the master and to acquire knowledge for his own needs in his own way. It was, in the true sense of the term, the beginning of progressive education.[6]

By 1830 public education of all children (except slaves) to the age of twelve or fourteen was widely heralded as an excellent goal. Although that goal was seldom achieved, each year brought greater efforts, including substantial increases in tax support, to strengthen public education. In 1834 Pennsylvania, after many years of opposition from the German-speaking minority, finally adopted a plan for statewide public schools. Meanwhile, New York had followed the New England states in encouraging the organization of local school districts. Even in New York City, which still depended upon privately operated charity schools, the trend was toward a greater role for the government, and at the end of the decade, under Gov. William Henry Seward, the city took over the operation of the free schools. In 1829 Baltimore started a public school system, which in four years enrolled 544 pupils and by the end of the decade 2,270. This rapid growth did not satisfy school officials, however, and they continued to urge expansion, since a large number of children in the city received no education. Eventually, Baltimore officials discovered that their schools could not be expanded without more trained teachers, and they found, amid the general boom in education in the thirties, that competent teachers were hard to find. School officials noted that public education came to an abrupt end at age fourteen and left many half-educated youths who wanted to become teachers but lacked the opportunity to do so. So Baltimore, as well as other cities, including originally Boston, organized public high schools for youths aged twelve or fourteen to sixteen or eighteen. One of the principal purposes of these schools, in the earlier years, was to turn out teachers for the expanding public grade schools.[7]

In the 1820s public high schools were rare, and even in the 1830s they were neither common nor popular. But a high school education, it was soon perceived, could lead to a variety of careers, particularly in new occupations created by economic change. As the market revolution's increased circulation of goods had created jobs in shipping, wholesaling, and retailing, merchants found that the more complicated business activities of the day could be handled better by youths trained in penmanship, grammar, arithmetic, and accounting than by the traditional untrained twelve-year-old apprentice clerks of the preceding generation. So merchants turned to the high schools for clerks, and the schools reciprocated by changing their curricula to emphasize practical mercantile subjects at the expense of such traditional scholarly subjects as Latin. Manufacturers also needed clerks, overseers, and other skilled assistants who could be recruited already educated in the basics rather than trained on the job. In both cases the employer also gained the advantage that the high school youth had been subjected to order, discipline, and a regimen that predicted a similar useful behavior in the shop or factory. Other high school graduates went into teaching, another burgeoning profession rising in status, or managed to go to college or to make a private arrangement to enter one of the traditional professions of law, medicine, or the church. In contrast, a youth who entered a traditional apprenticeship in a skilled craft faced the possibility that he would emerge years later with a narrow training and an unmarketable skill, since either temporary business fluctuations or permanent injury to his particular craft could make the apprenticeship all but useless. And such a youth lacked the flexibility to change occupations that the high-school-educated youth enjoyed. Yet in the 1830s far more nonfarm youths entered apprenticeships than attended high schools that would have fitted them for a wider variety of careers in those segments of the economy that were growing most rapidly.

There were several reasons why youths did not undertake the most advantageous path to success. For one thing, many were more inclined toward mechanical endeavors than toward book learning. Moreover, high schools were an innovation that lacked a pattern of tradition handed down from generation to generation. Adolescents are always great imitators, and a son of a skilled craftsman naturally wanted to follow his father, who had been an apprentice and not a high school graduate. Indeed, in the 1830s Americans maintained a mystical reverence for the kind of traditional training that youths received through apprenticeship. Practical experience gained in the shop of a craftsman, it was held, was worth far more than any amount of book learning. Through the ages there had been a certain folk wisdom in that notion, and what youth of fourteen would doubt it? But there was more to the decision to begin an apprenticeship than that. It was not a choice between two equal opportunities; indeed, it was no choice at all. By the 1830s master craftsmen knew that factories hired youths as unskilled laborers, and to compete craftsmen had to pay apprentices cash wages. While apprentices often made less money than factory laborers, they recognized that learning a craft would enhance their future earning power. Poor parents who desperately needed money sent children into factories and thereby condemned them to a life of low earnings as unskilled laborers, but middle-class parents, including those who were craftsmen, put their sons into craft apprenticeships in the hope of adding valuable skills to the modest immediate return from apprentice wages. However, in the 1830s it was a rare craftsman who was able or willing to place a son in a high school, where bright future prospects were offset by the lack of any current income.[8]

The rising public school system was linked to oscillations in the business cycle. During the 1830s public education expanded, particularly the primary schools, as a generally prosperous country pumped new funds into public schools, but there was less success for the new high schools, for the simple reason that prosperity created many economic opportunities that were not dependent upon education. In most trades apprentices looked forward to good wages as journeymen, and along the way abundant overtime as well as a basic cash wage bid up by labor shortages amid a growing economy led apprentices into unprecedented wealth. That was why all those gaudily dressed apprentices pranced through the streets showing off their new wealth. Then came the depression of 1837. Many masters went bankrupt, and others found that declining business barred them from taking new apprentices. Youths lucky enough to find positions discovered that their wages, like everyone else's, fell and that the prospect for overtime vanished. Gaudily dressed youths largely disappeared from the streets. For a boy of fourteen, the changed economy encouraged a revision in career plans. If the parents were poor, and after 1837 more were, then economic necessity might require a youth to enter a factory as an unskilled laborer, if such a job could be found. Poverty drove youths away from apprenticeship. On the other hand, if the parents were not poor, then economic opportunity might encourage a youth to go to high school rather than begin a poor-paying apprenticeship. The result of the depression, then, was a soaring enrollment in the new high schools. During the 1840s male enrollment in Baltimore rose from 63 to 260, and many of these pupils, destined to be middle-class clerks, teachers, and professionals, were the sons of craftsmen. The public high school, in the end, undermined the artisan tradition of passing crafts from generation to generation.[9]

Another kind of new institution had the same effect. As early as 1787, leading Methodists had proposed the establishment of a manual-labor boarding school. The school, serving pupils from age seven up, would provide an education, teach older boys crafts, and gain self-sufficiency by operating a woodworking shop and by gardening. Both the Methodists and the Baptists ultimately established such schools, and in th early 1800s these schools enabled poor but bright would-be ministers to attain an education at little cost. By the late 1820s the idea had spread, and such schools as the Oneida Institute, the Chittenango Polytechny, and the Shrewsbury Polytechnic Institute opened as places where orphans or the sons of farmers could gain an education as well as a skilled trade. Such schools appealed to many reformers, including Frances Wright, who saw several advantages. These schools would be easy to establish, since they required little tax support, thanks to their self-sufficiency. Each school could impose discipline that would mold the pupils into egalitarian democrats and wipe out class distinctions based on different educational backgrounds. And youths who could not enter the rapidly declining world of traditional apprenticeship would have an alternative to becoming an unskilled factory laborer. In the end the manual-trade schools enjoyed a modest success. They were never able to achieve the complete financial independence their advocates envisioned, and many suffered from mismanagement of the craft operations within the school. It was difficult to find a competent master craftsman who was willing to work for school profits rather than for himself. On the other hand, youths did gain an education and knowledge of a trade and went on to become successful skilled craftsmen, particularly in woodworking and carpentry.[10]

In the field of education, institutional change was profound, but one must not forget that the ripening of education was a consequence of changed attitudes on the part of the American people. The younger generation's hunger for education sometimes created hostility among their elders. In the 1830s, when the apprentice machinist Nathaniel P. Banks carried a book in his pocket, one village gossip disapproved. She complained, "Wall, it's no use arguing about it. Times are so diff'rent now from what they was when I was young, and peoples thinks so diff'rent, that it 'pears to me sometimes that the world is going to rack and ruin. We got along well 'nough fifty or sixty years ago without so much education. But folks are got to be so stylish now, and boys know so much more than their grandpas, that I railly don't know what'll come on us." Despite such complaints, the younger generation continued to read and to study. In 1828 eighteen-year-old Elihu Burritt, an apprentice blacksmith, began a program of self-education that had the approval of his pious and benevolent master. The youth discovered that he could study languages while tending his forge. He later recalled, "Still I carried my Greek grammar in my hat, and often found a moment, when I was heating some large iron, when I could place my book open before me against the chimney of my forge, and go through with *tupto, tupteis, tuptei*, unperceived by my fellow apprentices, and, to my confusion of face, sometimes with a detrimental effect to the charge in my fire." Elihu, encouraged in his studies by a college-educated brother, taught himself Greek with a dictionary and a copy of Homer. After he had completed his apprenticeship, he ruined his health as a journeyman, turned to store-keeping, failed in the depression, and wandered about looking for black-smith's work. In Worcester, Massachusetts, he found both a job at a forge and the American Antiquarian Society, where he began to study. At that venerable institution—founded by Isaiah Thomas—his unusual back-ground brought him to the attention of Edward Everett, who turned Burritt, billed as the "Learned Blacksmith," into a public celebrity and Lyceum lecturer.[11]

Although few apprentices had Burritt's gifts, many profited from read-ing and study, and reformers created numerous institutions to promote such self-improvement. Apprentices were invited to Lyceums, public lec-ture series, mechanics institutes that offered educational courses, and pub-lic exhibitions that honored inventions and superior craftsmanship with prizes. In Philadelphia, for example, the Franklin Institute, founded in 1824, sponsored scientific lectures, published a technical journal for me-chanics, and held an annual fair. While such institutions reached all mechanics, including apprentices, there was one institution created solely for apprentices. The panic of 1819 had left many apprentices idle, and idleness, thought the Boston merchant William Wood, required a cure. He had an idea. Gathering together several hundred books, mostly cast-offs donated by friends, Wood planned a library exclusively for appren-tices. By the time the library opened in early 1820, Wood was over-whelmed by the enthusiastic response. Donated books poured in, excited apprentices all but mobbed the opening ceremonies, the Boston library was written up in the newspapers, Wood crisscrossed the country to ex-plain the concept, and within a few years apprentice libraries were orga-nized in Portland, Salem, Providence, Albany, New York, Philadelphia, Baltimore, and Charleston. Reformers heralded the libraries as symbols of the rising progressive spirit of the age. At the opening of the Boston Apprentices' Library, Theodore Lyman, Jr., called the institution a logi-cal extension to Boston's public schools. At a similar opening in New York, Thomas R. Mercein, a baker and president of the General Society of Mechanics and Tradesmen, thought the library would provide a prac-tical knowledge of mechanical skills, encourage artisans to undertake greater civic responsibility, and create a bond between artisans and the educated middle class through exposure to the same books. In Albany,

Solomon Southwick, a self-made master printer, hoped the apprentice would "catch from the page of the philosopher and the poet, the light of science and the love of virtue."[12]

The apprentice libraries flourished, but they did not live up to the expectations of the founders and lure thousands of apprentices from the streets into the quiet of the library. Still, youths of fourteen or sixteen could be seen walking down the street carrying books to or from the library. After the initial novelty had worn off, the libraries settled down to serving 5 to 10 percent of the apprentices. While a few used the libraries to read serious books or learn technical skills, the records of the library associations suggest that most youths were looking for entertainment. In 1833 the Boston library received free copies of twenty newspapers from various New England publishers. About the same time the Philadelphia library, which had been founded by conservative Quakers influenced by Roberts Vaux, noted that eagerly read military biographies rapidly wore out and had to be replaced and that the multiple copies of *Robinson Crusoe* were always checked out. One reason that the latter work was so popular was that library's general policy banning novels. Among the banned books were H. H. Brackenridge's *Modern Chivalry*, Scott's *Waverley*, and *Don Quixote*. The prohibition of such works was not done without reason. In 1830 Job R. Tyson explained that novels, plays, and romantic poetry were not suited for the laboring mechanic. Such works produced "a morbid sensibility and false delicacy, vitiate[d] the intellectual appetite, and undermine[d] every manly trait of character." Apprentices, however, had a different view. The onetime apprentice Joseph Harrison later recalled, "I remember well how I longed for books that lightened the mind after hours of toil, rather than weighed it down, and regretted the rule that excluded almost entirely such works from the Apprentices Library." In the long run, perhaps spurred by the dime novel available outside the library, censorship eased, and the libraries stocked the books their readers most wanted. A comparison of the book catalogs for Boston for 1820 and 1838 shows a marked increase in biography, history, travels, and fiction.[13]

The Boston library began with enthusiasm and then sank into lethargy, from which it was rescued in 1828 when the apprentices gained the right to operate the library. That control, including the important question of what books were to be purchased, made the organization a lively one, and the book collection soon ran to Scott novels and adventure stories. As an apprentice-run organization, the library not only distributed books to members but also developed a series of public lectures, scientific demonstrations, and debates. In 1831, members inaugurated the custom of hearing an annual address delivered by one of their own members; at the time the notion of a mechanic giving a public speech was a "novelty." The following year, when Joseph M. Wightman gave a public lecture on steam engines with working models, the lecture hall was packed. Minutes from the meetings in these years show a dozen or so members who attended regularly and gained important practical experience making motions, giving committee reports, and so on. Such activities, in the words of one reflective observer, developed "a sober and manly self-reliance" on the part of the participating apprentices. And whereas earlier generations of mechanics had looked to educated, wealthy, and influential merchants and professionals for political, economic, and social leadership, by the 1830s many mechanics sought to act in their own behalf. Yet artisans lacked the kind of experience and education that made for effective participation in public life. The activities within the Boston library were an attempt by a small group of apprentice artisans to rehearse for larger roles they expected to undertake in later years. The apprentice instrument maker Frederic W. Lincoln, president of the association in 1835, eventually became the mayor of Boston. Perhaps, like the women's clubs of the late nineteenth century, organizations such as the Boston Apprentices' Library were a necessary first step to an artisan self-confidence that could be translated into active artisan participation in public life.[14]

It is worth examining in some detail the Boston library's debates, because they reveal much about the consciousness and concerns of young mechanics in the 1830s. After two long and lively evenings of debate, the association voted that mechanics and merchants with a common school education were as qualified to hold high public office as professional men who had received a literary or scientific education. While the outcome is not surprising, the fact that the matter was debatable suggests the large amount of artisan insecurity. On the question whether wealth or talent had more influence in the United States, these talented but poor youths voted that wealth had greater influence. Not surprisingly, two weeks later the group held that circumstances were more important than talent in making a great man. These two results show the way in which existing social conditions were producing frustration in the ranks of artisans. Perhaps that frustration led to restlessness that manifested itself in other progressive views. A series of debates led the association to favor labor unions and to oppose imprisonment for debt, capital punishment, and Negro inferiority. While these views were in advance of public opinion, they were not truly radical, and the group retreated to a more conservative stance when it condemned abolitionists. Throughout the debates content was perhaps less important than practice in public speaking. On that subject Francis Parsons, the association president in 1833, lamented the members' "improper bashfulness" and "timidity," urged "close attendance," and promised that public speaking would "improve the memory," make "judgment acute and powerful," and advance "intellectual cultivation." While members were struggling to acquire self-confidence and polish, it remained to be seen whether apprentice craftsmen could raise the stature of mechanics.[15]

The fears of young mechanics were only part of a larger pattern of urban disarray. The beginnings of the Industrial Revolution had led to increased commerce and trade that caused cities to grow in population, business activity, and sophistication of taste, and to a breakdown in traditional urban social structures and institutions, including the institution of apprenticeship. Numerous local studies show the beginnings of large-scale manufacturing, greater inequality in the distribution of wealth, and the development of neighborhoods based on socioeconomic rank. Sons of skilled craftsmen no longer had a sure and easy path to a lifetime career either by following in the steps of their fathers or by becoming apprentices to other craftsmen. The laments first heard among printers in the 1790s were now spreading to shoemaking, blacksmithing, and cabinetmaking, just to mention three trades. And orphans who might in earlier times have been bound out to a local craftsman by a familiar local judge or selectman now faced the probability of being sent to the countryside to become farm laborers without ever having the opportunity to join the ranks of skilled labor. Large cities became magnets for immigrants, for the unemployed, and for the socially marginal, who preferred the anonymity of the city to the more severe restraints that operated in small towns and rural areas. And many of these new arrivals to the cities brought children who wandered aimlessly through the streets. The ignorant parents, too poor to clothe their children properly to attend the new free public schools, seldom realized that in the emerging industrial society the failure of their children to acquire an education doomed them forever to the ranks of haphazardly employed unskilled labor. Worse, some parents exploited their children by sending them out to beg, and then the family lived off the earnings of the children. By the time a youth was twelve or fourteen and ready to enter a traditional apprenticeship, it was discovered that the lack of a basic education, as well as bad habits learned by living in the streets, made masters reluctant to take such a youth. In a society in which crafts were gradually being mechanized, the need for apprentices was low, and masters naturally preferred to take educated, disciplined children of the artisan classes rather than street waifs.[16]

Too old to beg and cast adrift by a system that no longer had any need for them, the uneducated, poor youths of the cities drifted aimlessly into lives of excitement, crime, and violence. The line between begging and stealing was sometimes difficult to distinguish, especially for a child or

STREET ARABS

youth who had never been educated in the difference. And parents who beat their children when they did not return with a daily quota of money or goods taught their children that it did not much matter how the quota was met. Moreover, hunger and cold should not be discounted as elements in the making of a criminal. What cold and hungry boy of twelve would leave the market empty-handed or fail to find firewood on the wharf, even if he had to go by moonlight to get it? It was not long before such a boy discovered others of like mind, and by pooling their limited resources and ingenuity, they could increase their profits. Two might create a diversion while the third stole, or one might stand watch while an entire gang walked off with a stack of firewood that could be sold door to door. Inevitably, the gang encountered other boys in another gang who wanted to control the same territory. Terrific street brawls followed, but in the days when pistols were rare, and even sharp knives uncommon, few homicides took place. While members of gangs quarreled among themselves, they united together to claim control of entire sections of the largest cities, which were universally irregularly policed. By the late 1820s a new social problem had been born, and Americans spoke in terror of juvenile delinquents, a new term coined to describe a new phenomenon. A decade later such places as New York's Five Points district were so notorious that respectable people dared not go there for fear of being robbed or murdered.[17]

Even reformers did not agree how to rid the nation's largest cities of marauding, criminal youths. Some blamed the problem on drunken parents, and there was a good deal of truth in the point. They thought that the closing of saloons and taverns would reduce drinking, make parents responsible, and keep youths in line. Others saw the problem as one of animal ignorance, for these wild youths were universally uneducated. In New York in 1823 it was reported that only one-eighth of the youths committed to prison were literate. If only more money were spent on public schools, went this argument, such youths could be saved as children, before they became hardened in street crime. But when more money was spent on the schools, the children of the poor did not attend with regularity. Still others blamed parents for allowing children to grow up wild and unregulated. Youths who came from those kinds of backgrounds had to be taken away from the parents and placed in foster homes, in reform schools, or in families in the country beyond the contamination of the city. But these policies required considerable public funds for the building of asylums and reform schools, and the money was never adequate for the job. Furthermore, parents generally resisted any attempt to take children away from them, and the age-old tradition that gave parents virtually total control of offspring until they turned twenty-one discouraged and restrained reformers who sought to operate against that tradition. Still others saw the problem beginning with little children begging from door to door, and they sought to take the profit to parents out of this seemingly innocent activity. Householders were advised not to give a child money or food, but to present a ticket from a central charity agency. The child could go to the agency, and the agency would send a welfare caseworker to visit the child's home and investigate the needs of the family. Relief might then be granted through the central office, which could coordinate matters to avoid duplication and the abuse of children by parents.[18]

What is ironic about this search for a solution to the problem of juvenile delinquency is that no one much noticed the decline in opportunities for apprenticeship. Society and the economy had changed, and the consequences for youths were profound. Yet no one—least of all, the reformers—commented on the change. No one could bring back the age of dutiful youths undertaking contracted apprenticeships that guaranteed social control. Yet the most successful attempts to deal with the new problem of juvenile delinquency were precisely those policies that established conditions surprisingly similar to those that had prevailed under the old order. Closing taverns did not reduce youthful crime and disorder, nor did spending money on schools. And reform schools quickly became notorious as schools for the training of criminals. But when youths were taken off the streets, cleaned up, given decent clothing, food, and housing, placed in a temporary shelter with a structured environment and an educational program, and then apprenticed to a trade a remarkable success took place. To make a clean break with the past, it was thought necessary to apprentice the youths out of town, and because cities were perceived to offer too much temptation, youths were sent either to farms or to small towns. Most poor youths recognized that a chance to learn a skilled craft offered them the only realistic opportunity they would ever have to rise out of the ranks of the poor and, possibly, into the middle class. They clamored for the chance, but the reformers who ran the programs had many more requests for farm laborers than for apprentice craftsmen, and records for the New York House of Refuge show that after 1837 a majority of youths were apprenticed to farmers. Even that, however, offered some promise for the future. The farmers who took the youths often agreed to an arrangement that enabled the youth to arrive at age twenty-one with some sort of financial stake, and a few farmers even adopted youths and made them their heirs.[19]

While a few youths left the refuge to become merchant clerks, and some went to sea, one-quarter to one-third were able to get highly sought-after apprenticeships in skilled crafts, although these positions seldom were in the most lucrative trades. A youth had the best chance to enter a skilled craft during the early 1830s or in the years around 1850, two periods during which the economy grew rapidly. In contrast, during the economic slowdowns that followed the financial crises of 1837 and 1857, opportunities for craft apprenticeships slumped. Although individual case histories suggest mixed results, officials apparently took more care in selecting masters than did parents or courts. An abused apprentice who complained to the refuge quickly would be placed with a different master. In contrast, privately arranged apprenticeships often continued under unfavorable conditions. Henry Wilson, whose impoverished parents had indented him to a farmer, recalled a life of dreary, cheerless, profitless work. On his twenty-first birthday Henry received both his freedom and his promised freedom dues of a yoke of oxen and six sheep. He sold the sheep immediately, but because he was unable to sell the oxen for two days, his former master charged him fifty cents for their feed over the weekend. That sort of cold reckoning was the fate of orphans or illegitimate children bound by the courts. Henry Harmon Spalding, who at fourteen months had been bound to a wife-beating farmer in Steuben County, New York, at seventeen was kicked out of the house and went to a neighbor's, crying he wished he were dead. Recognizing that his illegitimacy was a handicap locally, Spalding finally left to become a missionary in Oregon.[20]

House of Refuge placement was a makeshift solution, but it appeared to work. City toughs were sent to the farms and small towns, where a slower pace of life, fewer opportunities for mischief, and greater social control produced the kind of restraints that enabled most of these youths to lead stable, productive lives. At the same time restless youths from those same small towns and farms increasingly made their way to the cities to seek fame and fortune. Some, like Horace Greeley, found it, and others wound up in the streets. One of the most common themes in the popular literature of the period is that of a small-town youth who goes to the city to seek his fortune, falls in with evil companions, and dies a drunkard, usually after ruining his wife and child. The contrast between city and countryside was perhaps never so great as during these years. The city had already made the transition to modernity, and the collapse of apprenticeships as the usual mode for youths within the new urban environment was in striking contrast to the more traditional patterns that prevailed in the still largely subsistence and barter culture of the nation's rural areas. The contrast between the two parts of the nation also gave the countryside certain advantages. Small towns and rural areas offered a certain amount of stability at a time when institutional change in the city was at its greatest, and the ability of the countryside to absorb successfully numerous troubled urban youths is testimony to the staying power of the country. One must, however, emphasize the temporary nature of this solution, since the placement of urban youths into the countryside could work only so long as the nation was essentially rural. At the same time, rural stability made it easier for the cities to change more rapidly, for the social consequences of change could, in a sense, be exported. The rapidly changing cities became a source of hope and expectation to many rural youths, who contrasted the sleepiness of their own lives with the exciting changes taking place in the cities. Such youths were natural candidates for migration, and they gave the cities a bustling, self-confident air beyond what they would have had if no such migration had occurred.[21]

Among those lured to the city was John B. Gough, who at age twelve had been sent by his impoverished father from England to a farm in up-state New York. John's master, breaking his word to John's father, neither allowed the boy to attend school nor apprenticed him to a trade. Finally, the disgruntled fourteen-year-old sold his pocketknife to pay the postage on a letter asking his father for permission to leave the farm and go to New York City to learn a trade. The father replied that the youth was old enough to decide what to do for himself. Taking this advice as a form of permission, John left the farm for New York, where he became an apprentice bookbinder at the Methodist Book Concern, a large publishing house. His wage of $2.25 a week just about equaled the price of board. Two years later, when John was earning $3 a week, his mother and sister Mary arrived in New York. The father, who feared losing a small military pension, did not come. The three Goughs rented rooms and set up housekeeping with a few possessions, including three cups and saucers that Mrs. Gough had brought from England. They lived well for several months, until business slumped, and John and Mary, a straw bonnet maker, lost their jobs. They cut expenses by moving from two rooms at $1.25 a week into one small room at fifty cents a week. Matters got worse when winter came, and the Goughs could not afford firewood. For a while John worked as an errand boy in a bookstore and bindery, but his mother got sick, and food was short. On one occasion John pawned his overcoat to be able to make a mutton broth for his sick mother. Sometimes he went to the country and scavenged firewood, and once, standing in the street in tears over the lack of food, a stranger gave him a three-cent loaf of bread. When he brought it home, his mother insisted upon reading the Bible and asking a blessing. John was exasperated, because he could saw no wood without a saw and carry no coal without a shovel or basket. By spring, however, economic conditions had improved, both John and Mary found work, and John, now making $4.50 a week, was able to redeem his pawned coat.

Like others trapped in poverty, John found that prosperity was fickle. One hot July day John went swimming and came home to find his mother dead. All night he sat up with the body, held her hand, and became "half-delirious." There was no money for a funeral, and while the youth went for a walk, city officials entered the apartment and removed the body. He caught up with the cart on its way to the potter's field, where his mother was buried without a service, without a shroud, and with only John and Mary in attendance. For three days the youth could not eat, and he was unable to sleep in the room where his mother had died. So the two remaining Goughs moved to a boardinghouse for a week, until

Mary began to board with the family for which she worked, and John went to upstate New York to visit the farmer with whom he had once lived. Received with coldness, the youth quickly returned to New York and got a job in a printing office. He hid his inner bitterness with an outer gaiety that made him a favorite at his boardinghouse, where he sang and did funny imitations. Attaching himself to a giddy, dissipated set of friends, he frequented the theater, hungered to be an actor, played a few minor roles, plunged into debt, ignored his work, was fired, and took to heavy drinking. Gough, unlike Greeley, neither parlayed his apprenticeship into a brilliant career nor profited from his move to the city.[22]

The plight of youths such as John Gough shows the limits of reform. His needs were not met by public schools, apprentice libraries, reform schools, houses of refuge, or the placement of urban youths in the countryside. The fundamental problem that was not addressed—then as now—was the problem of what to do with youths in a modern urban environment. Apprenticeship had been a traditional solution to the problem of adolescence, and it had allowed youths to gain competency, self-respect, a useful trade for the future, and an education, while at the same time remaining under the control of an adult. Yet the master had known the apprentice intimately, and the two had a mutual obligation one to another, even though the master clearly was in charge. At the Methodist Book Concern, who knew John Gough intimately? To whom did he have a mutual obligation? Who was in charge? But the root function of apprenticeship had been an economic one, and in a society where craftsmanship was disappearing and factories were rising, apprenticeship no longer made economic sense. Some youths could go to school and obtain the kind of training necessary to become managers in the new economic system, and others fitted themselves into the factory system, with its emphasis upon punctuality, regularity, and discipline. But adolescence has never been an easy time of life, and for many youths the wisdom of the master was of more importance than the actual learning of a trade. Now that was gone. Youths were thrown on their own resources, and many stumbled and fell into bad company and bad habits with no mechanism to offer restraint. That was one of the basic deficiencies of the new social order. It simply did not recognize that youths had any such needs. Indeed, a capitalist ideology that stressed, in Horatio Alger fashion, the virtues of rugged individualism offered youths little practical advice on how to fit themselves into the ever changing social order. Some found answers for themselves, but a great many simply washed up on the shoals of experimentation, worn out as individualists more ragged than rugged.

✎ CHAPTER SEVEN ✎

The Machine Age

For many American craftsmen the depression of 1837 ushered in a period of chronic, long-term economic decline. While the overall economy was growing, with per capita income rising by 37 percent between 1840 and 1860, this increase in income was not shared equally. All the evidence, in fact, points to a mounting inequality in the distribution of income and wealth. In Cincinnati, for example, the wealthiest tenth increased its holdings from 55 percent of all the property in 1838 to 67 percent by 1860. Merchants, large-scale master craftsmen with access to capital, and commercial farmers prospered, while journeymen and unskilled laborers did not. Many craftsmen found themselves in the position of a journeyman ironworker in New Orleans. "I do not supose a days work could be obtained," he wrote. "I have enquired at every place I could see and no hands is wanted. Mechanichell Buiseness of all kinds is dull & 100^{ds} out of employ." In trade after trade the pressures of a national market and the introduction of machinery pushed craftsmen into unemployment. One laconic journeyman, who took a dangerous and disagreeable job that he did not want, wrote his wife, "I have only the option to throw up my employment and all starve together." The threat of unemployment caused wages to fall, until the skilled worker was little better off than the unskilled. And both groups now were at the mercy of machines and their owners. One ironworker gloomily wrote, "Baltimore is getting worse every year for the labouring Classes. So much so that in a few years they will have to be under as much subjugation as they are in most parts of Europe." In city after city, local studies show, machine processes devalued the skills of workers, and by 1850 shoemakers, weavers, silversmiths, potters, and cabinetmakers, among others, faced extinction as skilled craftsmen. They were to be replaced by unskilled machine tenders—boys hired as "apprentices." The transformation from craft to factory that had begun fifty years earlier with the first textile mills was now spreading throughout the artisan world.[1]

On the eve of this transformation, in 1842, Jenner Carpenter became an apprentice cabinetmaker in a small shop in Greenfield, Massachusetts. Miles and Lyons, the owners, worked in the shop along with one journeyman, two apprentices, and occasional extra help. The partners had sufficient capital for modern lathes and other tools, and they shrewdly specialized in what they produced. In 1844 Jenner noted, "I began another cheap Butternut Secratary this morning. It is Bureaus & Secratary all the time. I have worked on them about a year & I begin to think it is about time to learn to make something else." Six weeks later he complained, "I finished a Secratary today & begun another just like it, & I hope it is the last." But it was not. Despite this boring routine, the shop was not a factory, Jenner took his meals at Lyons's nearby house, and the youth chose to take off many evenings for lectures, games, or other entertainment. He was able to do this because he was paid piece rates. While still serving his apprenticeship, Jenner saw his traditional artisan world begin to dissolve. Once a journeyman cabinetmaker, laid off when his boss went bankrupt, passed through town looking for work. The man found none, and Jenner noted, "These times are hard times for Cabinet Journeymen." The fellow went to Chicago, where, no doubt, he found work in a furniture factory. A year later an improved economy with rising furniture sales led to the depletion of the Miles and Lyons inventory, and the partners bought out another cabinetmaker and merged the two shops. "It makes a pretty good shop full," noted Jenner, "four jours, two apprentices & two bosses, & they have advertised for another apprentice." The partners were prospering, and soon they subscribed to railroad stock issued for the construction of a line connecting Greenfield to the wider world. Such improved transportation to wider markets was necessary in order to gain the efficiencies of scale one required to stay in business. By the time Carpenter completed his apprenticeship, he lacked the capital needed to compete as a businessman in the emerging furniture industry. By 1850 furniture increasingly was made with unskilled labor in urban factories; one Chicago firm produced 18,000 bedsteads a year. A decade later most of those factories were steam powered; the average work force in the leading furniture-making city of Cincinnati had increased from eight to thirty-one. And in New York the average furniture worker earned about the same income as an unskilled hod carrier. Jenner Carpenter left the trade to open a newspaper agency in Vermont.[2]

As if mechanization had not been devastating enough, during the two decades after 1837 journeymen also faced competition from thousands of youthful Irish and German immigrants who flooded the cities as skilled or unskilled laborers. The immigrants glutted a labor market already overcrowded by the introduction of machinery. As the immigrants took craft jobs or moved into semiskilled machine tending, native-born Americans increasingly abandoned skilled crafts for white-collar mercantile and professional jobs. By the 1850s immigrants were a majority of the skilled carftsmen in most large cities; in New York, for example, they dominated thirty-two trades. Although real craft wages were lower than they had been in earlier years, immigrants seldom protested, since they earned more than in their native lands and perceived their chances for self-improvement to be better in the United States. Chronic unemployment, however, increased. In Boston, for example, where more than two thousand men had applied for work in 1843, about a third were directed to jobs, a third were persuaded to leave the city, and a third remained unemployed. Two years later massive immigration led twice as many applicants to seek work, and 90 percent of the applicants now were immigrants, but an improving economy enabled 70 percent to find jobs, although about half of those were sent outside the city. A decade later, with immigration outpacing the growth in jobs, it was possible to place only a quarter of the adult applicants.[3]

By the 1850s America's cities had a permanent underclass of chronically unemployed or underemployed residents. Who were these new urban poor? "As a general fact," stated the New York Association for Improving the Condition of the Poor, "steady, skilful mechanics, and sober, reliable workers, male and female, in ordinary times, find employment, and consequently are the last to suffer. It is the mechanics of inferior character and skill, and especially the lower grade of laborers of both sexes, and their families, chiefly foreigners, that contribute to swell, at all seasons, the number of the permanently dependent." The existence of such a permanent underclass had profound consequences for the next generation, for it meant that large numbers of children were growing up near starvation, uneducated, and on the streets. Reformers noted, "Our mechanics will not take them as apprentices; for, as soon as such lads get to be useful, wages are demanded for them by their parents, and they are taken to those who are not scrupulous as to their knowledge of their trade, so long as they can be had for low pay." Thus was the poverty of the parents transmitted to the children, whose numbers added to the ranks of the poor.[4]

As machines devalued the work that artisans had traditionally performed, artisan pride in craftsmanship was threatened. Pride of craft had been an important part of artisan culture. Mechanics had considered the utility of their work and their competence at performing it as a compensation for their lack of wealth, prestige, or status in the community. While others had more money, artisans had the consolation of performing useful work. Then, too, a craft that could be passed from generation to generation promised the maintenance of respectability if not gentility. While the sons of wealthy merchants often sank from grandeur into depravity, the sons of artisans maintained a steady course through the middle ranks of society. As machines threatened both the dignity of mechanical skill and the craftsman's ability to pass a respectable calling to the next generation, artisans at first became eloquent in their defenses of craftsmanship. In 1844, the *Awl*, the magazine of the Lynn journeymen shoemakers, published this song:

> *Our craft, you know, has been despised,*
> *By fools of every grade;*
> *Yet we can boast as noble men,*
> *As any other trade.*

This song suggests a nostalgia for the shoemaking craft, as it had existed in the days of yore, perhaps in those of Saint Crispin himself, and it also suggests the insecurity of the Lynn shoe workers, who defensively argued that they were as good as other craftsmen. At a time when new methods of organization and new machine processes were destroying skill levels in their own craft, these workers perhaps had good reason to claim parity with other crafts yet untouched by the Industrial Revolution.[5]

After machines had spread from craft to craft, it became impossible to maintain pride in craftsmanship. Artisan pride had traditionally compensated for social inferiority, but the eroding value of skills now made insecure artisans more willing to challenge widespread public assertions about artisan inferiority. Affronts were numerous. After all, what conclusion was young George Armstrong Custer to reach when he discovered that as the son of a blacksmith he could not be received socially in the household of Judge Bacon? Young Custer was in love with the judge's daughter, but not until he became a military hero did the judge assent to their marriage. In mid-nineteenth-century America there were still many who said, "Oh, he is only a mechanic!" Artisans bitterly denounced such attitudes. In a satirical poem in the *Voice of Industry*, for example, a Mr. Fop ridiculed "Dirty Mechanics" and suggested they walk in the middle of the street—that is, in the gutter—rather than on the sidewalks, sit in separate sections in church, and live "on a street by themselves, and associate there with each other." The bitterness of the denunciation shows the degree to which the machine age had stripped mechanics of their traditional psychological defenses and made them vulnerable to the assaults of modern society. Perhaps it was vulnerability that led to frequent public lectures on the virtues of mechanics. John Pendleton Kennedy declared the world to be "entering upon the Mechanical Epoch." He added, "That old proscriptive world which, for centuries, has turned its back upon the mechanic, now finds something in him for admiration and honor." While Kennedy spoke glowingly of the future and prudently dodged comment upon the present, the mechanics in his audience must have noticed the limits of the world's admiration.[6]

The early years of the new machine age left matters tangled and confused. Industrial practices had frequently outrun traditional language and become modern, leaving Americans with old words that imperfectly described the new conditions. Terminology from the past lingered, even after old meanings had disappeared. For example, a song in the *Awl* read:

> *O, the shoe jours, they are rising,*
> *O, the shoe jours, they are rising,*
> *O, the shoe jours, they are rising,*
> *In the old town of Lynn.*

The word "workers" had not yet displaced "jours," even though the journeymen shoemakers of Lynn no longer envisioned themselves as traditional journeymen on a way station to the position of master. Indeed, in this particular song the striking workers went on to attack the "bosses," using a modern word to replace "masters." The word "boss" was a new one, so new that when it appeared in a Rochester, New York, newspaper in 1829 the editor had felt obliged to define it. By 1834 the word was commonplace in the Rochester press. Old words described new functions, until the incongruity became so great that new words were coined. For a few years in the forties terminology was more confused than precise. Consider, for example, the mixture of old and new terms in the title of this advice book: *The Duties of Employers and Employed, Considered with Reference to Principals and Their Clerks or Apprentices* (1849). "Masters" have become "employers," and "apprentices" are in the process of becoming "employees." The emerging industrial economy had altered essential relationships and forced the development of a new terminology to describe those relationships.[7]

The decline of old-style apprenticeship was widely noticed by mechanics themselves. In 1845 Frederic W. Lincoln, speaking to the Massachusetts Charitable Mechanic Association, observed, "I suppose there is hardly a regular indented apprentice to any member of this Association, and it is becoming almost as equally rare that they live under the roof of the master, or that he feels any interest in them, excepting so far as relates to their mere mechanical duties." Lincoln worried that employers had no influence upon the formation of the character of their apprentices, failed to encourage feelings of self-respect, and thus did not prepare youths for manhood. He concluded, "Times have indeed changed; the paternal character of this connexion has become obsolete, but, still we are bound to act as guardians, and friends, and we cannot shake off the responsibility." Many masters, however, did wish to shake off the responsibility, and one of the easiest ways to do that was to give up indentures. Among the Moravians at Salem, North Carolina, the last indentures were executed in 1846. As informal work agreements became common, they sometimes were bizarre in content. One contract, for example, carried the stipulation that "in case of sickness or disenablement it is expected a fair thing to be done upon both Parties." The decline of indentures led to the disappearance of the printed forms that had formerly been used, so that even when an employer and a youth wanted to sign indentures, they found it difficult to draw up an agreement. The loosening tendencies of the times were so powerful that they even extended to the few formal indentures that were still being executed. During the 1850s the Talbott & Brother ironworks of Richmond, Virginia, used a standard printed form that included both a cash wage and a clause pledging that the youth would be taught the trade "in the department to which he may be assigned." A youth indented under that provision was not guaranteed training in any specific trade.[8]

During the forties the new ways and the old traditions sometimes commingled in a most curious fashion. For example, the Hartford printer Elihu Geer did not pay his apprentices a cash wage for the normal ten-hour day, but he had adopted a policy of paying them ten cents an hour for overtime either at night or on the nine to twelve holidays that were celebrated locally each year. On the other hand, Geer charged his apprentices that same ten cents an hour whenever they missed work on normal workdays, unless they were sick or agreed to make up the lost time by working nights or holidays. Wrote Geer, "If I pay boys for working on holidays they must pay me in the same ratio if they are absent at other times—it is optional with them whether they work on holidays—but all other days their time is mine." Geer believed that without his rule apprentices would come and go as they pleased on little vacations: "I should have fine times in my business!" The result would be "confusion and disarrangement." At no time did Geer argue that he was doing his apprentices a favor by encouraging steady work habits or building moral character. It was strictly a matter of economics, with the Hartford printer showing less a father's concern for his apprentices than a businessman's grasp of the balance sheet. Such attitudes, of course, did nothing to encourage old-style apprenticeship.[9]

A saucy boy, a broken tradition, and a boss with an eye on the bottom line led to all sorts of entanglements. Consider the complaint of William Z. Morton to his legal guardian. "I take the privilige of writing to you informing you where I am," wrote this apprentice. "I am now at work in yarmouth, having left the man i work with in Pertland as we could not agree. . . . There was no such thing as work in the shop for cross words an looks. The 4th of last September he was little croser than usual, with me. I asked him what i had done that he was sharp toward me. . . . As for working in hot water all the time, I could not do it, as i could not please him or myself either. I told him i was not satisfide with the usuage, and i had rather not work as i was then. He asked me what i meant by what i said. I then told i cam from home with the inte[n]tion of learng a trade, but i would leave off if he could not use me as a gentleman shloud an aprentice. Then he told me if i gave him him another word he would kick me out of the shop. Then i told as to work and qwarell all the time i would not do it. And i left him. Then i come Yarmouth and got 19 dollar and board for two month. Then Mr Safford sent a lawyers letter to Mr Grant, the man that i am to work for, to com an settle with him for my work. But he took no notice of it. The[n] i went to Boston to see my Uncles about it. . . . They told me if i could get at yarmouth for low wages and finish my trade, it was the best thing i could do, for Mr Safford could not ingure me no way as i was not bound to him. So I went to work for Mr Grant at 6 dollar a board for three month and then regular wages to the first of June. . . . Mr Safford has seen Mr Grant an forbid his paying me any thing as he can recover wages for my work, as I was lear[n]ing a trade of him. . . . As you are all the friend i have to look to, i have sent you some of the particulars and want you give me your advice. . . ."[10]

Quarrels and lawsuits were not new. What was new was the topsy-turvy way in which craftsmen opened and closed shops, changed locations, or bought and sold businesses. Entrepreneurial activity, stimulated by the rapidly changing nature of the economy, threw apprenticeship into chaos. Boys were hired or fired with such regularity that the changes caused little notice. In 1844 the apprentice cabinetmaker Jenner Carpenter reported, "I saw Ralph Carrier last night. He said he was going to Waltham about nine miles from Boston to work at his partly learned trade. He was turned off from J. P. Rust's." Whether the tailor Rust had dismissed his apprentice for lack of work or for misconduct was not noted, and young Carpenter expressed no surprise at the turn of events. Later Rust hired a replacement. The comings and goings of apprentices in Carpenter's diary are striking for their frequency. One Sunday, Jenner took a walk with a recently arrived apprentice. A week later the new boy was suddenly called home, and Jenner noted, "I am sorry for he was a first rate fellow." While apprentices bore much of the burden of frequent changes in business, the high turnover of youthful workers guaranteed both many employees and many jobs. This circulation of youths through the work force enabled many to gain the wide variety of experiences necessary to stimulate technological innovation. And the fragmented nature of apprenticeship kept youths from having to continue to work for employers they disliked. Moreover, in an environment in which shops came and went, masters could not hold apprentices to their own shifting fortunes. When one Greenfield, Massachusetts, partnership was dissolved, the firm's apprentice decided to move to Boston. The boy's ex-masters, noted Jenner Carpenter, had "tried to scare him to make him stay, they threatened to advertise him [as a runaway], but he knew enough to know that they could not hold him after they had dissolved."[11]

In the new environment, apprentices naturally imitated their money-grubbing employers. Henry C. Brokmeyer, a seventeen-year-old German who had immigrated to New York, indented himself for three years to become a currier. A rapid learner, he quickly mastered the trade, and one day the boss said, "I think, Jim, your Dutch cub is doing remarkably well. He is going to make a workman of himself some day, if he keeps on doing the way he is now." James Robertson, the journeyman for whom Harry worked, replied, "Make a workman—make a workman! He is no slouch of a hand now." The boss added, "That makes you feel pretty big, Harry, doesn't it?"

Harry replied, "No, I know when I am doing a man's work. But I do not know why I have to do a man's work for a boy's pay."

"You don't?" Said the boss, "You have forgotten then the articles of indenture which you signed, have you?"

"No, I have not. But I signed that paper under the belief that it would take me three years to learn the trade, as you told me."

"Well, it is too late to craw-fish now; a bargain is a bargain, Harry."

"With a boy? And that boy deceived in regard to the facts of the bargain?"

"Be careful there, Harry. I charge you 25¢ for every hole you cut in that skin!" He watched Harry make a hole in the skin he was working on.

"Is that all?" As Harry replied, he made a second hole.

"That is 50¢," said the boss.

Harry's eyes blazed. He cut more holes in the skin—ten.

The boss said, "That is ten holes—$2.50 for the skin."

"Is it?" Harry cut the ten holes into one large one. "There! and now it is 25¢—which you are welcome to deduct from my wages!"

By this point the boss had turned white. Harry took off his apron and headed for the door, but the boss got there first, blocked his exit, and said, "Young man, keep your apron on. Do the work of Mr. Robertson and you shall have the pay of Mr. Robertson."[12]

The boss was prepared to waive his legal rights to the apprentice's services in order to keep a good workman, because the boss knew that those claims could not be enforced. And the apprentice, for his part, knew that, unlike Andy Johnson and countless other youths who had run away in the middle of the night, he could make a bold exit in the boss's sight. He knew he could get hired as a journeyman in another shop—no questions asked. In one sense, both the employer and the employee were playing a game in which the rules had been changed by the developing market economy, the cash wage, and competition for partly trained, semiskilled labor in the labor market. The boss wanted to keep the apprentice not to teach him a trade but to exploit his labor, and the apprentice wanted to earn a journeyman's wage as soon as he could. But the boldness with which apprentices now asserted their right to decide matters for themselves and to walk out when they did not like the conditions of their work was something new. Although the change in attitude may have had its origins in the rise of an economic system that had destroyed the parental nature of apprenticeship, the forwardness of apprentices was itself another ingredient in the destruction of the institution. In theory, apprenticeship still existed, and the language and terminology of the past lingered, but Harry Brokmeyer's boss, like Elihu Geer, recognized that a profound upheaval was under way.

As the sons of artisans began to abandon the crafts of their forefathers, many advocated training in skilled crafts for blacks, orphans, and young petty criminals—the have-nots of society. If slaves performed degrading manual labor, argued Nathaniel Ware, then freedom would be "more dignified and valuable." In Philadelphia, Job R. Tyson lauded Girard College, an orphan asylum, for furnishing "paternal discipline" to youths, who would "form a class of candidates for the manual occupations of life, more numerous and better instructed, than any age or country has ever incorporated with its society." Perhaps no one was more enthusiastic about apprenticeship for the socially marginal than Charles Loring Brace. That New York reformer noted that most of the inmates in the city prison were unskilled laborers, who had been forced to rove from job to job. Sporadic work and long periods of idleness, in his view, led to crime. He particularly worried about ignorant, uneducated, unskilled youths in prison. "There is no doubt," he wrote, "that a lad with a trade feels a peculiar independence of the world, and is much less likely to take up dishonest means of living. . . ." A youth trained in a skilled craft would find demand for his labor, would have a sense of identity with his craft, could get union support when out of work, and would associate with respectable fellow crafts. Brace went on to criticize labor unions that restricted access to trades by limiting apprenticeships; he thought the long-range effect would be to force the importation of skilled craftsmen and to increase juvenile delinquency. The irony of Brace's recommendation is exceeded only by its pathos. Amid the destruction of traditional craft apprenticeship, with desertion by the sons of artisans and a loss of pride of craft by the semiskilled machine tenders who remained in many trades, apprenticeship now was recommended as the best employment for marginal members of society.[13]

Between 1837 and 1860, when opportunities for apprentices varied considerably from trade to trade, no craftsmen had greater opportunities than machinists. In 1838 John Fritz, the son of a farmer-mechanic, began an apprenticeship in a small, rural Pennsylvania machine shop. While this shop did the usual horseshoeing and repairing of carts and wagons common to blacksmiths, it also repaired threshing machines, new devices which were then coming into widespread usage, and cotton machinery, which was located at mills in the neighborhood. The surprisingly well supplied shop had four fires and anvils, three lathes, a crude drill press, and other tools, many of which were powered by a six-horse power steam engine that had been built by the shop owner. This master mechanic was a true all-around machinist—the only kind of machinist to be found in 1838. At first the new apprentice was ordered to pump bellows for a smith's fire and to hammer the sledge against hot metal being beaten into shape, but after a few days he gained the more interesting—and noisy—job of holding boilerplate while two workmen riveted it. After the boiler was completed, John was assigned as a helper to a journeyman smith. The apprentice was able to learn a lot because his boss, one of the best workmen, was given the most challenging jobs. One day the boss told John, "There is a very heavy wagon that must be ironed and it must be done soon, and I want you to do it." The boss had been ill and could do no physical labor, so he watched and instructed as the apprentice undertook the ordeal. At the time John was terrified. He had served only one year of his apprenticeship and had never worked on such a large and heavy job. The wagon's iron wheels were five inches wide and nearly three-quarters of an inch thick; the shop lacked the proper equipment for such heavy work. Nevertheless, the boss, his apprentice, and two helpers finished the job. When the journeyman praised young Fritz's work, the youth was proud. In this reaction we see how deftly applied mechanical skill could lead an artisan to feelings of deep satisfaction about his work, his life, and himself.[14]

Two decades later the kind of small country machine shop where Fritz had learned his trade had been superseded by larger, better-equipped shops conducted on modern principles. Thomas H. Savery, an apprentice machinist in Philadelphia, suffered from living in an impersonal boardinghouse and from a businesslike boss who criticized Tom for taking time off to attend a funeral. Still, the shop was a good place to learn the trade; after Tom had built a steam engine, he noted with satisfaction, "Sublime work! magnificent." About that same time John Rogers became an apprentice machinist at the Amoskeag textile mill. A bit homesick and somewhat lonesome, John found that the vastness of the shop discouraged workers from getting to know each other. At work he knew only the two other young men who worked at his bench and his foreman, who had personally shown the youth around town and placed him in a company-owned boardinghouse. Even the boardinghouse provided little company, since John was one of only three boarders. Life quickly fell into a routine:

4:30 a.m.	bells rung to get up
4:53 a.m.	second bells rung
	work commences
7:00 a.m.	breakfast
7:45 a.m.	back to work
12:30 p.m.	dinner
1:15 p.m.	back to work
7:00 p.m.	tea

After working this schedule, noted young Rogers, he was so tired he went right to bed. The bells, he said, reminded him of school. They were only one of the many ways in which education and the machine age went hand in hand in regimenting people's lives. Despite the shop's regimentation and the fact that many of the workmen were a "low sort," Rogers adjusted to the routine and felt that his wage of fifty cents a day made him "independent." While the new machine shops provided neither close contacts between master and apprentice nor the variety of experiences found in country shops, they did offer training that guaranteed work as a journeyman in one of the highest-paying crafts. Machinists were highly skilled, and far from being replaced by unskilled machine tenders, they profited from the introduction of machinery that proved so devastating to other craftsmen. One does not hear of machinists' unions or strikes, but one does hear of the difficulty a youth had in obtaining an apprenticeship in this trade.[15]

While machinists prospered, other ironworkers had mixed experiences. During the 1840s William H. Sylvis, son of a poor Pennsylvania wagon-maker, apprenticed himself for three or more years to a small, rural foundry to learn iron molding, but the youth never saw even his first year's wages, because the company failed. Young Sylvis wandered around Pennsylvania, finished his trade, became a journeyman, and rented a foundry with a friend for one year. This business failed, and Sylvis again wandered. As he did so, he might have pondered how small country forges were being displaced by large-scale foundries. In 1845, in striking contrast with Sylvis's experiences, one journeyman reported glowingly on conditions in Philadelphia. "I found many of my old friends here that was glad to see me," wrote William Turner, "and I had two or three jobs offered me as soon as I got here. . . . There seems to be more work for mechanick in philada then ever I seen before." The upsurge of the mid-forties was brought about by the construction of railroads, which then accounted for 10 percent of the total national capital formation. By the fifties railroads were using up to one-fifth of American pig iron, and rail-road locomotives were one-tenth of all machinery. Because railroads re-quired iron boilers strong enough to withstand pressure under steam and iron rails capable of carrying great weight, it was necessary to make rail-road iron in special furnaces, where skilled puddlers worked the impuri-ties out of the raw iron. These furnaces were expensive to construct, and they were the first indication that the industry was going to become capi-tal-intensive. After a ball of iron was removed from a furnace, it was hammered, and then a skilled workman rolled the ball. Most of the pud-dlers were English or Welsh immigrants, who played an important role in the transfer of technology across the Atlantic.[16]

The high demand for iron drove journeymen's wages to $4 a day, about four times the rate of a casual laborer, and high wages attracted both skilled English journeymen and American apprentices. At twenty-eight Harry Brokmeyer left his previously learned trades of currying, tanning, and shoemaking, all of which paid poorly, in order to become an appren-tice iron molder. He gave up trades that paid $10 to $12 a week in order to learn a trade paying $25 to $30 a week. Such a wage would enable Brokmeyer to save money, buy property, and enter business—although not as an iron founder. When he told his decision to a master currier, that friend, loyal to his trade, was aghast. Brokmeyer did not find the apprenticeship easy, and after his first day's work, he later noted in his diary, he had been so sore he could not write. After three days, however, he found that the heavy work had its pleasures and felt "supple as a cat." The next day he reported that "sense in the fingers, sure enough, and will in the muscles sums up the entire secret of all practical skill." Within a

PUDDLING

CUTTING AND TRIMMING STAVES

week he had made his first iron pot, but he had forgotten to put any "ears" on it, and his mistake provoked laughter throughout the shop. Harry had to drill holes in the pot so that a handle could be attached. The shop workers called it a "deaf pot" and said it could not "hear itself sing." One wag asked Harry when he would patent the idea. After Harry had been in the shop a week, he was voted the rights of an apprentice. The principal right was to treat the journeymen, and the shrewd Brokmeyer both bought a keg of beer and offered the men another one the following week in order to keep their goodwill.[17]

Among the journeymen in the shop was an Irishman named Mike, who asked Brokmeyer to join the union. Brokmeyer, who did not wish to be in the bad graces of any of his fellows, answered yes, but his diary shows that he was strongly suspicious of the union. Suspecting that the union had been started by whiskey-drinking journeymen who invoked group solidarity to encourage the better workers to join, Brokmeyer could see no reason why a good workman needed a union. Although the lure of a higher cash wage had led him to switch crafts and although Brokmeyer—already speculating in real estate—sought financial success as much as anyone, his strongly traditional sense of artisan pride clashed with the concept of a union that pitted workers against employers. Yet Brokmeyer was curious enough to ponder why Mike and Jake, the two most ardent union supporters, devoted all their intellectual energy to this cause. He concluded they did so because their craft was their entire life—it meant everything to them. He wrote, "Their craft is the source of their living, the one thing that does not fail them, the one thing that they have to look to, to trust, to rely upon, for their very means or existence." But both of these journeymen were extremely ignorant. He observed, "Of the relation of their craft to the productive industry of the world as a whole, they know nothing; of the reciprocal interdependence of that industry, each craft or function upon all, and all upon each, they know nothing." To Brokmeyer, such a limited vision of the world made a union an insignificant organization in the overall scheme of things. Far less interested in job protection than in technological innovation, he was confident that he would be able to advance himself and the industry in tandem. Soon Brokmeyer was promoted to pattern molder at $10 a day. He had become a labor aristocrat, but the limits of that position were perhaps not readily apparent to him.[18]

By the late 1850s the iron industry had undergone radical transformation from traditional to modern form. The small-scale foundries of the mid-forties that a man like William Sylvis might have hoped to own had been displaced by large-scale operations that only a wealthy capitalist could hope to buy or establish. Between 1830 and 1860 pig-iron produc-

INTERIOR OF BLAST FURNACE

tion quintupled. Changing technology, which Harry Brokmeyer and
John Fritz so much admired, was also a part of the changing industry. In
Sylvis's boyhood skilled journeymen had prided themselves on puddling
iron in the hot furnaces and pounding the iron balls that emerged from
the furnaces. But times had changed, and steam-powered crushers had
eliminated much of the skill in puddling, and the hammering was increasingly being performed by unskilled laborers operating mechanized
equipment. By the fifties the decline in skill levels in the largest foundries
meant that any vigorous and lusty youth with a taste for heat and noise
might step off the street and into a job in a foundry. Richard Croker,
later a gang leader and political boss, found an ironworks the perfect
place to develop his muscles by swinging forty-pound hammers. In the
less capitalized smaller foundries the displacement of journeymen had not
yet taken place, but the workers in those foundries had to face competition from large-scale works, and owners of small foundries were desperate
to reduce labor costs. In the larger works a few highly talented individuals, such as Harry Brokmeyer, could make as much as $10 a day de-
signing molds or doing other highly specialized work, but even these
skilled workers recognized that new processes and additional capital
would enable owners to displace more skilled artisans with unskilled
workers. Finally, one wonders whether labor militancy in the industry in

the 1850s was not related to the relatively high wages that the industry had paid throughout the forties. Wages had been high because the work was difficult, few could qualify, the industry was growing rapidly, and skilled workers were scarce. Many workers, like Brokmeyer and Sylvis, were attracted to the industry initially because of high wages. To these men, wages were important, and when Sylvis's employer tried to cut wages by one-quarter during the depression of 1857, the shop went on strike. Within two years Sylvis had helped organize a national union of iron molders.[19]

What made Sylvis a great labor leader was his understanding of all the subtleties and nuances of the situation. While fearlessly devoted to organizing and protecting skilled iron molders, he acted with caution and prudence to bring about a favorable result. Sylvis, more than other labor leaders of his day, recognized the tremendous power of capital and knew that it had to be offset by the only sort of power that journeymen could muster—unity. A union of journeymen within a single foundry was worthless, for the foundry itself was at the mercy of the market for its product. A union of journeymen within the foundries of a single city had no value either. Only when skilled journeymen throughout the country were brought together into a single union could the workers force the owners of all the foundries to treat the journeymen alike. The monopoly of capital that created giant foundries beyond the control and ownership of journeymen had to be met by a monopoly of skilled labor controlled, organized, and disciplined through a national trade union. Such a union could not only demand and obtain a single national standard of high wages that would prevent a few foundries from employing exploited workers to drive down the price of labor, but it could also obtain some voice in the way new technologies were introduced into the industry, control the number of unskilled workers allowed to work in any foundry, and, ultimately, control the number of apprentices taken and thus the future size of the skilled labor force that in turn would be related closely to the wages paid to that force. After taking a leading role in organizing a national union of skilled iron molders, Sylvis encouraged other skilled craftsmen to do likewise. By the time of his death, in 1869, he was the most prominent labor leader in the country.[20]

The transformation of iron molding from an age-old craft into an industry dominated by highly capitalized, large-scale firms was paralleled by a similar development in printing. While typesetting remained an occupation for skilled labor, presswork was increasingly transformed by automatically fed, steam-driven presses. The consequences for a would-be master printer were staggering. In the early 1840s an old-style handpress suitable for a country newspaper office could be bought for $150, but a

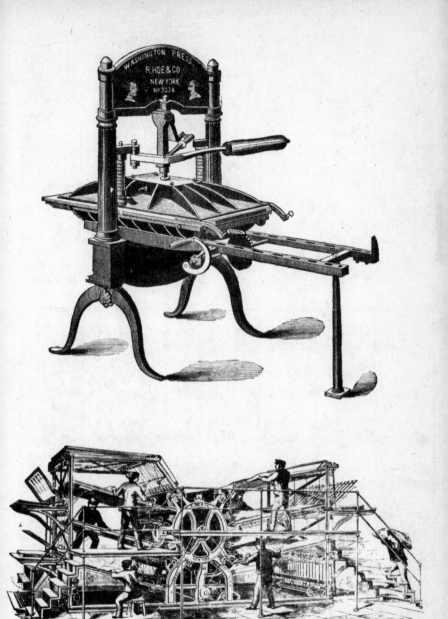

HOE HANDPRESS AND SIX-CYLINDER PRESS

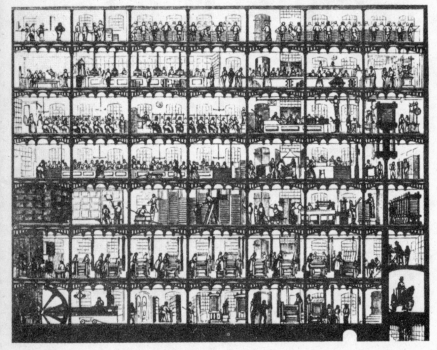

HARPER BROTHERS EXTERIOR, INTERIOR CUTAWAY, AND DETAIL OF THE HYDRAULIC PRESSES

double-cylinder rotary steam press capable of printing a daily newspaper cost $3,000. Few master printers could afford the latter, and many of those who purchased power presses came under the financial control of their suppliers. Others, like Nathan Geer, simply slid into bankruptcy. Geer had family ties, his brother's financial assistance, common sense, and a relish for hard work, but these ingredients had been insufficient for him to establish and maintain a daily newspaper in Chicago. The undercapitalized printer had been forced to the wall, retreated to Waukegan, Illinois, where $1,200 borrowed from political supporters had enabled him to operate for a time, and only a decade later achieved modest success with the Peoria *Daily Transcript*. What had handicapped Geer was the ever growing capital requirement for the establishment of a daily newspaper in a major city. Whereas in 1810 it had cost $20 a week to produce a leading Missouri weekly, in 1858 the St. Louis daily *Missouri Republican* cost $4,000 a week. Even a small-city daily required a surprising amount of capital. In 1847 Horatio King estimated that Seba Smith's Portland, Maine, *Daily Courier* office was worth $1,000. The types were worth $700 or $800, and the press $200 to $250. While a new handpress would cost $250, the difficulty in obtaining one increased the value of the old press. Some of the types were quite worn and had to be discounted, but the goodwill value of the newspaper also had to be considered.[21]

In major cities power presses had become necessary for daily newspapers, and such presses were not cheap. In 1850, for example, Richard Hoe & Company, New York press manufacturers, advertised one press at $1,650 with terms of half cash and the balance in six months. W. W. and L. A. Pratt, publishers of the Jersey City *Daily Sentinel and Advertiser*, wanted and needed Hoe's press but, like many other publishers, lacked ready cash. They were willing to buy a secondhand power press at discount, and they asked Hoe to give them a year's credit and to accept their old Hoe handpress in partial payment. While small publishers like the Pratts struggled to remain in business, Hoe was developing ever more elaborate and more expensive presses. In 1854 the company, now housed in a four-story factory, offered everything from a $165 handpress to an eight-cylinder revolving printing machine capable of making 20,000 impressions an hour for more than $10,000. This steam-driven revolving press automatically printed and stacked the finished sheets. Only eight boys were needed to feed the machine. "Thus," boasted the Hoe catalog, "effects a great saving of labor." By 1860 Hoe had introduced a ten-cylinder machine capable of making 25,000 impressions an hour and a color press capable of printing four colors at one time. In 1867 Hoe's ten-cylinder press sold for $52,500. The printing industry had been transformed, and the transformation had happened so rapidly that even informed observers could not always believe it. In 1859 Edward Everett wrote, "I suppose the statement . . . that 20,000 impressions are thrown off by the 'lightning presses' in an hour must be a misprint. . . . Twenty thousand in an hour would be 5½ in a second, which seems impossible." But it was true, and printing was changed forever. All the advice about presswork that Cornelius Van Winkle had written for the benefit of apprentices in his 1818 printer's manual was now useless; Thomas Lynch's 1859 manual contained new advice and added, "Within the last ten years there has been an entire revolution made in the printing-business by the application of machinery to the execution of all kinds of press-work."[22]

Perhaps no printing establishment illustrated the new order of things better than Harper & Brothers, which in the 1850s was the largest printing and publishing firm in the country. After a disastrous fire in 1853 the company had rebuilt an innovative fireproof iron-and-brick building covering two and a half acres and seven stories high. The firm's 500 workers and thirty power presses were able to produce 4.5 million volumes a year. In 1855 the children's author Jacob Abbott published a book about the new printing house. It was, explained Abbott, the scale of the operation that allowed a large number of books to be printed at low cost. "Hence," he added, "in the progress of society, manufactured articles will be brought within the means of all when all require them." The Harper Brothers facility was divided into two buildings, one a warehouse and the other a factory, connected by a walkway. On the factory's ground floor a giant steam engine provided all the power for the operation, and power from the engine was transferred throughout the building by pulleys, axles, and the like. In the basement paper was received, wetted, and prepared for printing. On the main floor twenty-eight girls fed each of the large steam-powered printing presses. That floor also contained the press foreman's office. On the third floor printed sheets were dried and pressed at machines tended by men. The fourth floor contained the folding room, where women folded the printed sheets at long tables. Engravings were also tipped into the sheets as they were folded. On the fifth floor two hydraulic presses pressed the already hand-folded sheets, and women at tables sewed sheets. The sixth floor contained the finishing room, where books were bound, trimmed, stamped, and gilded. In a separate section marbled covers were prepared. On the top floor was the composing room, where types were set by hand, and the electrotyping area, where men made facsimiles of original plates. Most Harper books were printed from electrotypes rather than from original types, which could not be used in high-speed power presses without the danger of the pages disintegrating. From one electrotype a million copies could be printed.[23]

To a visitor the power presses were awesome. Abbott declared the machinery "too complicated to be described in detail," but he did watch girls feeding damp paper into the presses, while printed sheets, automatically stacked, came out the other side. Watching that action, Abbott said, "There is something imposing and almost sublime in the calm and steady dignity with which the ponderous engines continue their ceaseless toil. There is, indeed, a real dignity and a real grace in the movements which they perform. The observer looks down the room from the elevated desk of the foreman, and surveys the scene with great interest and pleasure, wondering at the complicated massiveness of the constructions, and at the multitude of wheels, and pulleys, and bands that mingle and combine their motions with the revolutions of the machinery."[24]

The new printing machines entranced men like Abbott, but they left many master printers worried about capital, competition, and profits. Small-scale printers, unable to compete with the new machinery, found their trade growing less and less profitable. To prove the point, one publisher of a country weekly cited the prices that county officials had been willing to pay for job printing; from the 1820s to the 1840s the prices had dropped consistently. "Steam and competition," he said, "have made sad work upon high prices." While the country printer was able to survive with local jobs and his weekly newspaper, he lost bookwork, which could be printed cheaper and better on the new urban steam presses. One has only to look at book imprints to see the shift. The refusal of the city fathers of Charleston, South Carolina, for example, to allow any steam-driven machinery inside the city explains why even the laws of the sovereign state of South Carolina were by the 1850s being steam printed in New York or Philadelphia, where printing was cheaper, quicker, and better in quality. For master printers, the machine age was not always welcome. In 1847 Thurlow Weed spoke nostalgically of how machinery had robbed printing of its glory. "Rollers and Steam," he said, "do the work which FRANKLIN performed. Printers now learn but half the duties which pertained to our craft in other days." The long-range implication of what was happening was clear to anyone who chose to contemplate the situation. Joseph Griffin, a successful country printer in Maine, asked, "Is the business of newspaper printing, book-making, etc., aided by powerful and expensive machinery, destined eventually to pass ino the exclusive hands of great capitalists, by whom not only labor but mind may be controlled?" Griffin had discovered that his own shop could prosper only by the replacement of journeymen with apprentices, and he had found females to be preferable.[25]

During the 1840s, when the old-style printing office all but disappeared from the cities, journeymen increasingly recognized that they would never be able to acquire the capital to open a shop, and master printers faced intense, growing competition from within the industry. What had happened to John Miller, the owner of the *Providence Journal,* was not uncommon. The *Journal* had been a successful twice-weekly newspaper until 1829, when the inauguration of the *Providence Daily Advertiser* had forced the *Journal* to become a daily. Miller was undercapitalized, and in 1836 he was forced to sell the newspaper. Competition among master printers was intensified with the spread of the competitive bidding system. Publishing and printing became partially separated, and a publisher sometimes chose to have printing done outside rather than in-house. He took bids, and in a glutted industry master printers desperate for work undercut each other to get the contracts. By the late forties the practice of competitive bidding had spread to state governments, which no longer hired a state printer as part of a lucrative political deal. In state after state low bids were won by printing contractors determined to bring down costs no matter what the consequences. In Ohio contractors paid workers $2 to $3 a week less than the prevailing rates for journeymen; in Massachusetts the journeymen described the rates for state contract work as "ruinous." Unless the state adopted some sort of minimum price, warned the Boston journeymen, wages would be forced down. The New York contractors who had won the state printing at bargain rates hired youths at $3 a week to fill the order. More alarming to journeymen was the spread of competitive bidding throughout the industry. That is, anyone who wanted something printed took bids. Employers who obtained all their jobs through competitive bidding were forced to hire labor on a daily basis at a fluctuating rate. Wages were driven down to the point where excessive work yielded only a pittance. In New York it was estimated that the average journeyman earned only $7 a week, a meager wage that did not allow for any savings. It was suggested that some printers could earn more money, at less risk to their health, by digging canals.[26]

The glut of journeymen that drove down wages was made larger by the widespread use of apprentices in lieu of journeymen. To the employer, the advantage of hiring a youth for a fraction of the journeyman's wage was greater than the disadvantage of the youth's lack of skill. Moreover, the employer was not particularly interested in teaching an apprentice the craft of printing. In 1837, when B. W. Pearce was hired as an apprentice at Providence's leading firm, he was paid $3 a week to print lottery tickets on a small handpress. After six months Pearce complained that he had not been allowed to set any type, and the boss told him that the firm had no intention of teaching him anything. Neither did the journeymen, who had no interest in swelling their bloated ranks even further. Pearce quit, but his place was no doubt taken by another youth. Many were hired

APPRENTICE AT A JOB PRESS

off the street just for the novelty of learning how to set type. After six months the youth would become bored and disgruntled and run away, and nothing would prevent it, because he had never been bound legally. The runaway would find a shop where he could work at from half to two-thirds of the journeyman's rate; in time, he would be tossed aside in favor of another victim. All over the country journeymen had the same complaint: there were too many apprentices. In Detroit, when apprentices struck a newspaper office in 1846, the paper was closed for two days because there were not enough journeymen to do the work. In Boston it was estimated in 1848 that there were twice as many two-thirders as journeymen. And in New York in 1850 one of the largest printing shops contained twenty-three journeymen and twenty apprentices working as typesetters. If the youths served an average of five years and if the journeymen worked an average of twenty years, then during those two decades there would be eighty apprentices. The industry could not possibly absorb that many new journeymen. The overall statistics for New York were, to the journeymen, scarcely less alarming. The estimated employment in the printing industry was 150 foremen, 1,000 journeymen compositors, 200 pressmen, 600 boys at case, 100 boys at press, and 100 girls at press, for a total of 2,150. Two-fifths of the workers were underage apprentices.[27]

Although the printers' unions established during the 1830s had taken an interest in the glut of apprentices, the weak economy after 1837 had made it difficult for those unions to translate their interest into concrete policies. It was years before local unions acted, and even the discussion of rules could be dangerous; in 1845 members of the Washington, D.C., union who met to discuss the problem of too many apprentices were arrested for conspiracy. Gradually, local unions did adopt policies barring members from working in any office that employed runaway apprentices or journeymen paid below scale. Employers did not always resist these rules, since they promoted both stability and professional competence and placed all employers on an equal basis. The local unions, however, concluded that these measures were ineffective in solving the basic problem, and in 1847 the Baltimore local became the first in the nation to adopt a rule limiting the number of apprentices to one per three journeymen in a shop. The Baltimore rule, as it came to be called, was adopted in Albany and Cincinnati in 1848 and in Pittsburgh in 1851. As the economy improved in the late forties, journeymen became more militant. The local in Pittsburgh demanded that apprentices serve at least three years, and in 1849 a new union in New York, under the leadership of Horace Greeley, proposed a minimum piece-rate wage designed to improve the living standard of the worst-off journeymen. New York employers, perhaps influenced by Greeley's prestige, accepted the proposal, but the Philadelphia union organized in 1850 was not so fortunate. There the union's insistence on limiting the number of apprentices precipitated a strike that ended only when the local capitulated on that issue. Philadelphia employers believed that they needed cheap apprentice labor in order to compete in the New York–dominated national publishing market. Their point was not lost on the journeymen, who in 1850 concluded that their interests required a national union.[28]

In December 1850 eighteen journeymen printers from five states met in New York to organize a national coalition of local unions. Each local was to issue membership cards that could be transferred to any union shop in the country; thus, the tramping journeymen who were perpetually undermining established journeymen would be brought into the union system and regulated. A tramp who could not get work was entitled to financial assistance from any local union. Membership cards would also make it more difficult for irregularly trained or runaway apprentices to pass themselves off as journeymen, since a card would be issued only after an apprentice had completed a regular apprenticeship.

The delegates to this convention urged employers to indent apprentices for a minimum of five years and appealed to local unions to seek limits on the number of apprentices in each shop. At a second convention, held in Baltimore the next year, the subject of apprentices again arose, but the delegates took no action. The following year convention delegates in Cincinnati concluded that the loosely regulated convention system offered insufficient protection for journeymen printers and organized the National Typographical Union. That meeting also urged local unions to insist on five-year indentures for apprentices and to ban apprentices from daily newspapers. The latter policy was advocated because apprentices on daily papers frequently learned no skills and became incompetent workmen. Throughout the decade national union meetings urged similar measures.[29]

During the fifties a strong union movement and a more vigorous economy combined to raise the pay of journeymen printers. Washington journeymen who had earned $9 to $10 a week during the forties were making $14 a week by 1854. Such gains were possible because journeymen became more vigilant in controlling the industry's labor supply. For example, in 1854 the national union convention resolved to "not encourage" the employment of women typesetters. Females had been used as strikebreakers, and employers had generally paid them less than male workers. In 1857 the national convention insisted that traveling members had to apply for a job through the office foreman, who was usually sympathetic to the union. Locals became more militant about the issue of apprenticeship. In 1859 the Baton Rouge union demanded the immediate binding of an unbound apprentice. This demand proved impossible because one of the proprietors was out of town. One portion of the union then walked out of the shop and expelled the remaining members for not having left an office containing an unbound apprentice. It took action at the national level to resolve this quarrel. In late 1860, on the eve of the Civil War, the journeymen and proprietor of the Charleston *Evening News* disputed the use of apprentices in that shop. The journeymen demanded the right to control the flow of work within the shop, and when the proprietor came to the shop to explain his position, he found the workmen so unreasonable that he threatened to have them charged with "conspiracy." In reply, they hissed. That meeting ended in an impasse. Charleston journeymen recognized the importance of the national union and, after South Carolina's secession, voted not to dissolve their ties with the national organization.[30]

By 1860 the printing industry offered apprentices few opportunities to rise to positions of consequence within the industry. A talented handful made the transition to editorial work, but the majority of journeymen printers had to be content with long hours, hard work, and earnings sufficient for a modest standard of living without savings or luxuries. Those who could not be contented often took to tramping around the country looking for a pot of gold at the end of some rainbow. Few pots of gold were found, and the tramping journeymen tended to drift into a pattern of frenzied work alternating with equally frenzied drinking binges. Tramp printers were perhaps the first casualties of the new machine age. For machinists and ironworkers the situation was decidedly more mixed. In a growing industry it was possible for talented apprentices to learn the business and rise to positions of power, influence, and even ownership. While heavy capital requirements did not make such success stories common, the prosperity of the industry and its long-term high demand for skilled labor ensured that skilled workers would continue to be paid higher-than-average wages. Apprentice machinists could look forward to higher wages and higher prestige than other skilled workmen. But the contrast between printing and ironworking should not obscure the fundamental similarity of the two industries. By 1860 both industries, like so many others, were increasingly dominated by highly capitalized, large-scale enterprises in which labor was less important than capital and in which ownership was separated from a technical knowledge of the business. The days when an owner had been a master workman who had risen through the ranks were about over, and an apprentice's prospects of becoming more than a journeyman craftsman were slender. Whether the industry was iron, printing, furniture, or silverware mattered little in the overall scheme of things. The problem for apprentices in the machine age was to adjust to the new order of things.[31]

CHAPTER EIGHT

A Way Out?

Your great-grandfathers had been artisans, your grandfathers had been artisans, your father was an artisan, and your older brother or brothers were artisans. You had grown up in a family in which becoming an apprentice craftsman was a normal stage of life. Your whole childhood had been training for it, and your relatives, even if they had wished differently, would not have known how to guide you along any path except the familiar one. In 1844 you were a sixteen-year-old boy living in Philadelphia. What were your prospects? You could not become an apprentice shoemaker or weaver, because, as we have seen, machine-made products closed those trades forever to new craftsmen. You could become an apprentice hatter, but mechanization was beginning to destroy that trade, too, and if you did become an apprentice, you risked learning a declining trade and turning twenty-one with a skill of no value. Of course, a few trades were booming, particularly in iron, but you lacked the robust physique necessary to become an iron molder, and you lacked the mathematical skills necessary to become a machinist or draftsman. You knew there were opportunities for clerks, but merchants required a knowledge of bookkeeping and an elegant hand, and you had acquired neither with your common school education. Although you had received more schooling than any of your ancestors, it was not sufficient for you to join the ranks of aspiring young clerks. Your father was unable to spare the time or money for your further education, and even if he had been able, artisan pride made it unlikely that he would support your becoming a merchant's clerk. You could become an apprentice in the building trades or in a highly skilled trade like watchmaking, where machine-made goods were less threatening. But there you faced severe competition, both from other boys like yourself, whose range of opportunities was narrow, and from immigrants who came as skilled craftsmen willing to work for a pittance or who offered themselves as unskilled laborers and thereby enabled capitalists to open factories that displaced yet more craftsmen.

To such a youth the world of known values and certainties had disappeared. Neither parental example nor parental advice was of much help. One possibility was getting a job in a factory, and many did so, but the youth knew that in all likelihood such a position doomed him to a life of drudgery as someone else's wage slave. Perhaps it was necessary; certainly it was alienating. One could see it, said one observer, in the countenances of those who passed down the street. Merchants' clerks flaunted their wealth and status by dressing as effeminate coxcombs, while factory operatives were hollow-eyed and stupefied. Only young skilled craftsmen walked with lithe, bold steps of manly independence. It was an unpleasant prospect for a youth who either had become a factory operative or had taken an apprenticeship only to discover that it was a disguised label for learning the routinized processes of machine tending in a field where capital and machinery now foreclosed any prospects of becoming a master craftsman.[1]

How, then, might a youth respond to the industrial system? How might he find a way out? Although answers were varied and complex, the youth knew that this unprecedented situation called for new sources of advice. Between 1830 and 1860, youths and young men increasingly turned to professional advice books that offered moral admonitions as well as practical hints for adapting oneself to a changing world. While these books, often written by New England ministers, were most commonly addressed to upwardly mobile youths embarking upon mercantile life, they tried to appeal to all American youths, including apprentice craftsmen. What set these new books apart from more traditional volumes, such as Franklin's autobiography, were the larger number of their titles, their sheer massiveness, and the wide variety of topics they covered. Advice books became a veritable industry, and that industry, in the specifics of its advice, helped to shape the attitudes and behavior of the first generation of young men in the industrial cities. It is difficult to know how much advice was followed and how much ignored, but the multiplicity of books offering and reinforcing the same views makes it hard to conclude that the advice was entirely disregarded. Indeed, it seems likely that advice books that failed to tell their readers what they wanted to read were passed over in favor of ones that appealed to the already half-shaped sensibilities of youths.[2]

Whereas earlier advice books had emphasized tradition, obedience, and the maintenance of hierarchical order as the foundation of society, the new books played upon new themes, particularly how to succeed in business. Since youths no longer lived with their employers, the books were substitutes for a master's advice. Almost every book recommended early rising. A youth could do half a day's work before noon or use the early morning hours for study and self-improvement. Early rising did require some sacrifice. "People who are in the habit of making and attending parties which commence at nine or ten o'clock in the evening," wrote William A. Alcott, "can hardly be expected to rise with the sun." Such evening parties, moreover, were bad for one's health with their late suppers; besides, the candles used for staying up late at night wasted money. Success in business also meant an avoidance of gaming, drinking, smoking, horse racing, cockfighting, and theatergoing. These activities squandered time and money, destroyed precious opportunities for self-improvement, and risked a descent into debt, drunkenness, and licentiousness that would destroy a youth. For recreation Alcott suggested vigorous physical activities such as ice-skating or dancing. Or if a mechanic had a physically active occupation, then he should spend his spare time reading, studying, and attending Lyceum lectures. Another book equated success in business with diligence, self-denial, self-discipline, and respect for rules. It was learning how to conform to rules that at a later date qualified one to conduct one's own affairs. And it was a strict attention to business that made an apprenticeship successful. A main purpose of apprenticeship was to accustom the apprentice to the habit of work. It was easy to learn the rudiments of a craft; it was far more difficult to become habituated to working at the craft. For that reason it was practice that made a master craftsman.[3]

Since many youths became impatient with serving out their time, and some of them contemplated running away, the advice books took up this age-old problem. "It has not unfrequently occurred," warned the Reverend John C. Rudd, "that young men have urged the example of Franklin, as an excuse for deserting the employment of those to whom they are bound, as well by legal as moral obligation. But every runaway apprentice should consider in the first place, that faults committed by great men, are nevertheless, *faults*. The act of our Philosopher, in deserting the services of one lawfully entitled to his labour, can never be regarded in any other light than an offence against the good order of society and the law of the land. In the next place, apprentices who would excuse an elopement, by the conduct of this great man, would do well to remember, that such an act will by no means make them Franklins. Where one such occurrence ends as his did, hundreds have proved introductory to mortification, debasement, crime and misery. Again—let the apprentice bear in mind that this distinguished individual put down this particular in after life among his own errors. The restraints of apprenticeship are salutary, when limited by law and morality; if they are rendered oppressive, the sufferer, if faithful in the discharge of his duty, will always find redress in the protection which the law throws around him; and he had better, in this as in all other cases, 'suffer wrong, than do wrong,' by attempting to judge, and administer law in his own case." This passage offers a striking comment on the new attitudes emerging at mid-century. Running away is condemned, not because it is illegal, insults the master, or holds his authority in contempt, but because it threatens to ruin the apprentice's prospects for future happiness. The argument, in other words, appeals to the self-interest of the upwardly mobile youth reading the passage rather than to a fixed traditional moral point, and it uses reason to persuade the apprentice to remain on the job rather than threatening him with force. This style of argument shows how the advice books blended modern psychology with traditional morality.[4]

After a youth completed his apprenticeship, he naturally wanted to set up for himself. The advice books warned that despite the most stringent preparations, the odds for success were low. John Todd thought that only three out of a hundred young men who started on their own managed to succeed; a more optimistic T. S. Arthur estimated that one-third succeeded, but few of these were under twenty-five. Failure was common for many reasons. Young men, observed William A. Alcott, often lacked good advice and counsel. While peers were useless, because they tended to be enthusiastic and thoughtless, old men were too cautious and too set in their ways. And a young man frequently did not have access to a well-established middle-aged man. Too often a journeyman, only a year or two after his apprenticeship, would open a shop with a few hundred dollars and money advanced by a friend. Such shops usually failed, and the young man often ended up either ruined by drink or a suicide. The basic problem, thought Alcott, was that a youthful journeyman lacked true expertise in his craft. He advised journeymen to follow Christ's example and wait until they reached the age of thirty to set up shop. The problem, observed William Hague, was impatience in an era dominated by "a ruling passion for the quick acquisition of fortune." Alcott lamented that both journeymen and apprentices were impatient and that youths refused to serve the seven years common in England and thought three and a half years too long.[5]

As means to avoid failure in business, the advice books recommended study and self-improvement. A young journeyman mechanic, advised T. S. Arthur, had to recognize that without self-improvement he would remain a mechanic earning $6 to $10 a week for the rest of his life. If he wished to become a successful master mechanic, if that was possible in his trade without capital, or if he wished to change occupations, then he had

to expect to spend much of his time while an apprentice or young journeyman studying practical subjects. Arthur advised youths to acquire a
second marketable skill, such as bookkeeping. Two or three years of accounting and penmanship could lead to an advancement from a skilled
craft to a clerkship at higher pay. For example, one rather dull apprentice
learned bookkeeping and then enough mathematics to become a railroad
surveyor at $1,000 a year; in another year he headed the surveying team
at $2,500 a year; afterward he became a mathematics professor at a small
college. In another shop all the apprentices had followed the lead of one
or two who thirsted for knowledge. Studying became contagious, and that
shop eventually produced two ministers, two doctors, and an army surgeon. It was not enough for an apprentice to read. To succeed in business,
he had to direct the reading toward some goal. That was why novels were
so destructive. Novels, like the theater, made a young man an agreeable
companion in mixed company, but they did not prepare him for business.[6]

What did prepare a young man for business, in addition to self-improvement, was a reputation grounded in morality. Even to a youth
reputation was important, for no master mechanic wanted to apprentice
a youth whose bad reputation might corrupt the master's shop. "Have
you not found," asked the Reverend John C. Rudd, "that where one
unworthy and unprincipled youth has been introduced into an establishment, he has been the cause of continual trouble, as well to his companions as to his employer?" Yet many youths did not have a good character, because their parents had demanded little of them, and they grew
up like a "herd of leeches" destined "to drain the vitals of society of their
blood." Apprenticeship was the last chance for reform that would lead a
youth to the pursuit of virtue. If bad habits prevailed, warned Joel
Hawes, then the youth was on the road to hell. It was wiser to pursue
virtue. The private pursuit of virtue, said the Reverend Daniel C. Eddy,
made a man happy, and the collective pursuit of virtue by the community
made society possible. It was important, said John Todd, for individuals
to have "our influence combined and united with that of the millions
which compose our generation." A raindrop, he said, was insignificant
until it combined with other raindrops. The pursuit of virtue was therefore one of the principal duties of a young man. "The mission of the
young man in this age," wrote Eddy, "is, to meet these evils which have
crept in upon society, and with all his influence arrest if possible the tide
of sin which is sweeping over the world." Such a mission required moral
courage. While mere physical bravery was to be admired, it was more ad-
mirable when linked to the moral element. "The cardinal virtue in society," wrote T. S. Arthur, "is a determination to do right because it is

right, regardless of consequences. This is true courage." In 1861 many young Americans were prepared to follow Arthur's advice *"to do right, at any sacrifice, even of life itself."*[7]

Assertions about morality that encouraged militant behavior were rooted in the economic, social, and political turmoil of the times. In a society in which tradition was shattered, family hierarchy shaken, and masters no longer in control of apprentices, youths found themselves floundering. "Many of them are unsettled in their principles of conduct and have no fixed plan of life," wrote the Reverend William G. Eliot, Jr. "They are floating upon the surface of society, carried one way or the other by the currents of social influence, by the changing wind of good or ill success." This new and unsettling sense of drift permeated the lives of American youths, who became the first generation to find the tradition-minded advice of their elders to be not very useful. As a result, young men entered "upon the active duties of life with an imperfect education, and comparatively unformed in character." It was this incomplete state of moral development that led Americans, in the eyes of discerning observers, to act as if they were in a state of arrested adolescence, and it was this same state of imperfection that led American youths to hunger for advice books offering moral guidance.[8]

Authors of advice books invoked the popular ideology of the day to praise the revolutionary virtues of equality and liberty. "All are born equal," wrote Joel Hawes, "and are alike left to make their way in the world by their own exertions." Equality was perhaps easier to praise than liberty, which, advised the Reverend Edwin H. Chapin, consisted not in doing as you pleased but in obeying "the just laws of the majority." John Todd warned of the dangers of a freedom that could degenerate into profligacy and disorder. The corollary of freedom was restraint, and the only kind of restraint consistent with freedom was that imposed by a free person upon himself. The authors of advice books never missed the larger social context. The Reverend John C. Rudd stressed that youths, though the future ornaments of society, had an obligation to society. He cautioned, "There is perhaps no one feeling or sentiment more widely prevailing among young men, than that they are fully competent to judge for themselves, and that they have a perfect right to take just such courses as their fancy may point out." Such conduct was childish and immature. Each individual owed duties to society, and one of the most important was setting a good example for others to follow. "Young men," stated Chapin, "occupy such a position in society as to have an important bearing upon the taste and temper of the times. They are very apt to lead the fashion and give a tone to the morality of the sphere in which they move. The character of its young men weigh much in our judgment of the condition of a community." In part, Chapin was flattering his audience, but in part he was also making an important point: youths do set styles and fashions and readily adopt new theories, and to the extent that these theories and practices become identified with a particular generation, they in time become the dominant themes for society as a whole.[9]

One comes away from a survey of antebellum advice books with a sense of multiple ironies. In traditional society the behavior of youths had been prescribed by custom; in industrial society behavior was prescribed by the tyranny of public opinion as filtered through advice books. In traditional society custom had invoked the wisdom of the ages in fixing limits and defining opportunities in ways that benefited most youths; in industrial society newly articulated moral homilies that often were little more than clichés sought to perform that same function. They did not perform it very well. Moral homilies that failed as a guide for action in everyday life left youths floundering in a sea of uncertainty. But that very uncertainty itself generated a hunger for absolutes on the part of youths. Youths deprived of the standards of traditional society cried out for new standards, and their cries were met with the invocation of moral absolutes rooted not in experience but in the rhetoric of American political ideology and the theology of nineteenth-century evangelical Christianity. Yet the political ideals of liberty and equality had little to do with the realities of the lives of youths, and such an ideology offered little guidance to a youth facing everyday difficulties of adjustment, growth, and development into manhood. And the religion of the times, with its emphasis upon personal salvation, offered a solution to ordinary problems only in the sense that intense religiosity could sublimate or drown worldly concerns and cares. For most youths that kind of religion was too stultifying to be worth much attention or effort. On the religious level the advice books failed, and while they succeeded on the moral level, the advice to avoid stealing, cheating, or lying did not transcend the commonplace. As a guide to success in business, they stated mostly the obvious; as substitutes for the wisdom of the ages, they were wanting. The standards of behavior for youths in an industrial society, in the long run, could not be regulated through the moral idiom of nineteenth-century evangelical clergymen.

When a person is ripped out of a traditional social context, he usually responds by trying to establish a new social context. Most of all, he needs to belong to a group, and it is helpful if that group has traditions, lore, mystery, and significance. If he and others like him have to create a new group, then they must vest in the new group a sense of tradition, even where none exists. The two decades before the Civil War are sometimes called the Age of Reform because of the birth and robust development of so many organizations devoted to temperance, abolition, world peace, foreign missions, and other causes. While these movements were essentially for adults, youths played an active role, and sometimes, as in the case of the Sons of Temperance, the organizations were established specifically for youths. In addition, self-help societies, such as Lyceums, mechanics institutes, or apprentice library associations, offered youths a chance for self-improvement, another watchword of the times. Still other organizations, such as labor unions, sometimes permitted youths to affiliate even though full membership was reserved to those over twenty-one. But none of these specialized organizations quite provided the complete sense of identity that a youth needed. Reform societies were too ethereal and altruistic, self-help societies beyond the ambitions of most youths, and labor unions too radical and ideologically remote from the world of traditional artisan culture.[10]

The limitations of apprentice libraries form a case in point. By 1850 it was clear that the plan to use apprentice libraries as a means of social control, to regulate and elevate the behavior of apprentices, had largely failed. While such libraries were fine for the self-motivated youth who had already acquired a good basic education, many youths, particularly immigrants, were more in need of learning to read than of having a library open for their use. In Philadelphia an anonymous author advocated an evening school program. Such schools would both teach skills and discipline and remove some youths from the streets, where they collected on street corners and coalesced into gangs. The main function of the evening schools would be social control. "And, what is still more important," said the author, "the order maintained in every good school, the submission to authority exacted, the appeals successfully made to the reason and moral sense of the pupils, are so many precious lessons in practical morality, which must contribute greatly to the formation of good habits." An evening school did not so much "communicate knowledge" as lay "the foundation of self-restraint and self-improvement." Here we see an attempt to extend to a larger audience the kind of rational morality found in the advice books. While more able youths might be expected to find and read the books that would give them a moral foundation appropriate to the new social and economic conditions of industrial society, many others left drifting on the streets had to be lured or coaxed into the classroom where they too could be taught the virtues suited to the machine age.[11]

Evening schools would form a kind of juvenile police that would reverse the startling rise in juvenile crime that had taken place. Crime came about, noted this author, because many youths were factory operatives whose time out of the factory was totally their own, because parental authority had declined, and because masters no longer asserted any control over apprentices outside working hours. Youths congregated on the street corners, these groups formed into gangs on the basis of religious or geographical distinctions, the gangs created disorder, and the disorder went unpunished. Since youths were naturally "full of reckless courage and lust of adventure," it was hardly surprising that idleness led to evil. Some youths sought entertainment in bowling alleys, tippling shops, gaming houses, and theaters, and the desire to participate in such activities led youths who had no money to commit petty thefts in order to get the money for pursuing these amusements. There was a "want of proper places to which the young can resort, and in which they can find innocent recreation or useful employment, during their hours of leisure, and especially at night." The result was riotous behavior that brought "disgrace on the community, sacrificed many valuable lives, destroyed a vast amount of property, turned capital and enterprise from the city to locations less exposed to outrages and tumults, subjected multitudes to extreme terror, and often to great danger, and which, at this moment, may well fill the heart of every reflecting citizen with anxious foreboding." While the author was not so naïve as to suggest that evening schools would end all youthful vice, he did see a strong positive effect. Prosperity would increase with a more law-abiding, disciplined, and educated working class, riots that destroyed property would diminish, and Philadelphia employers would no longer hesitate to take local youths as apprentices out of fear of "disorder and insubordination."[12]

Such views were also expressed by apprentice craftsmen devoted to the culture of respectability. For example, in 1855 the apprentice Samuel S. Spear, in an address before the Boston Mechanic Apprentices' Library Association, praised education and learning. "The age in which we live," he said, "demands of every young man that he should know something, (it would be better if there were not such things as know-nothings,) and we must meet this demand. As apprentices, we have many obstacles to contend with, in the pursuit of knowledge, which are unknown to persons in other classes of society. We have not so easy an access to some founts of knowledge as others have; yet, if as our fathers sowed their seeds, and persevered in cultivating it with such means as they had, until they reaped a joyful harvest, we sow the seed of knowledge and truth in our hearts and minds, and persevere in cultivating them, by rightly improving the privileges we enjoy, in the summer and autumn of life we will reap a harvest which will not only make us happy in its possession, but render us useful to our fellow men, and enable us, when dying, to leave an example for others to follow in our steps." Spear's speech mirrored the views of those youths who saw in apprentice libraries a "safe retreat" from the world; the readers who frequented the libraries formed a "home-circle," as one of them put it. Herbert Gleason saw in these efforts a laboring class not only pulling itself up by its own bootstraps but rescuing the larger society as well:

> Despite these gloomy shadowings of fate,
> And the poor crew who hold the helm of state,
> The working classes through this wide spread land
> Could, if they wished, with their resistless hand,
> Rescue our banner from its foul disgrace,
> And guide our nation safely on its race.

The opportunity to put these words into practice would come six years later.[13]

One should not dwell too much either on advice books or on apprentice libraries, Lyceums, and educational courses. Although such books or institutions, and the ideas that kept them going, appealed to those apprentices devoted to respectability, they did not have much appeal for the majority of apprentices. What appealed to most youths were other sorts of group activities closer in tone and spirit to the rough-and-tumble world of traditional artisan culture. Rude initiation rites, parades by craftsmen, and the passing of a craft's lore from generation to generation had held great appeal. Industrial society had swept away many of these traditions, and others survived in twisted forms deprived of their ancient symbolic significance. But the need to belong to a group and to share activities with others remained, and industrial society had to evolve its own institutions. Much familiarity and camaraderie was cultivated in the emerging urban saloon. Tavern society offered chances to relax with others for a drink, to act grown-up, to borrow money, to learn about job openings, to participate in politics, and to visit prostitutes. Out of tavern culture emerged the street gang, which helped the saloonkeeper collect debts, maintain political control of his neighborhood, fend off rival gangs from other neighborhoods, or extort "protection" money from local businesses.[14]

Street gangs had names, identities, legends, and, most important, turf. In traditional artisan culture status was a function of age, and over time one's status changed, as a boy became an apprentice, then a journeyman, and finally a master. In the new industrial society status was a function of how much you were worth in dollars at a particular time. To be the son of a millionaire, or the father of one in the future, was of little value if you were broke in the present. The links of time were severed and replaced by geographical loyalties. It was the penniless young men of a given neighborhood who joined together to form a gang. The defense of turf was so important precisely because there was little to distinguish one such group of young men from another such group, and the members of each gang needed to create a sense of group identity in order to establish and maintain their own personal identities. Who they thought themselves to be depended upon the gang they chose to join. Turf faded in importance only when other differences came to the fore. Thus, two rival turf-defined gangs might join together as fellow Protestants in order to attack a Catholic gang or, indeed, even a Catholic church. In 1844, gangs came together as mobs and burned down two of Philadelphia's Catholic churches. And religion could be transcended by race as a necessary creator of identity. Thus, on several occasions, antiblack riots took place in Philadelphia, when gangs, almost certainly including both Protestants and Catholics, combined into mobs to attack blacks. But such racial or religious attacks always petered out after a time, much to the relief of the older population, because the turf-based gangs took to quarreling among themselves. In the final analysis, race and religion were insufficient creators of status, because they proscribed too few people and left the members of any particular gang threatened in their own status by the existence of other, similar gangs.[15]

One cannot discuss gangs, and the status they conferred upon youths deprived of status by industrial culture, without also mentioning fire companies. In the nineteenth century America's most populous cities had a large and growing number of private volunteer fire companies. In Philadelphia 90 percent of the companies operating in 1857 were organized after 1825. Artisans dominated the fire companies—which Benjamin Franklin claimed as his idea—in the beginning because so many master craftsmen were zealous to protect their property, and later because the companies became bastions of young artisans. One reason for the popularity of fire companies was the practice of allowing members to be exempt from militia duty. Another reason was the sense of tradition they evoked in a society in which tradition was everywhere being eroded. Some companies traced their origins to the eighteenth century, and firemen donned hats, badges, or uniforms that earlier generations had designed. Belonging to a fire company also enabled a youth to witness fires at close range and to participate in the excitement in a life that otherwise was dull and devoid of excitement. But perhaps most important was the fact that fire companies were useful social institutions that performed valuable public services. To an apprentice earning a marginal wage on the fringes of society without power and with minimal prospects for the future, the fire company offered a chance, at a fire, to become a hero, to be noticed in the newspapers, to be rewarded gratefully, and to show

RUNNING WITH FORTY

bravery. No wonder fire companies raced to fires to see which could put out the fire first. It was partly a matter of turf, but it was mostly a claim of utility. Nowhere else was a youth quite so much in demand.[16]

The popularity of fire companies contrasted markedly with the unpopularity of militia companies. In most American states from the time of the Revolution until around 1840 every male from eighteen to forty-five was required to turn out several times a year for a day of military drill. Although these musters were never popular, except in rural areas where they allowed farmers to come together for a day of drinking and gaming, by the 1830s, with the fear of foreign invasion at a minimum, they were widely hated. Urban craftsmen and their apprentices hated militia musters because of the class bias they presented. The laws provided that a man who did not appear for muster could pay a small fine instead, and from the beginning wealthy merchants and professionals had paid these fines rather than turn out with a weapon, pack, and uniform of sorts on muster day. Artisans had resented both the absence of wealthy men from this burden and their being pushed down socially into close proximity to the unskilled, but as time went on even master craftsmen began to pay fines rather than appear. With the rise of cash wages, journeymen in highly paid skilled crafts also paid fines. Soon the musters consisted only of unskilled laborers and apprentices too poor to pay fines. Apprentices had no more desire to associate with the common herd of society than did middle-class merchants, and many followed the example of Morton Poole, who vowed, "I shall join the fire company and so get clear of the scrape entirely."[17]

Other rituals became established. In Philadelphia, for example, it had long been the custom for local citizens to call upon each other on Christmas Eve or Day. As early as 1800, callers began to wear costumes and masks. Until the 1830s these practices, called mummery, were private and sporadic, but during that decade of giddy prosperity mobs of apprentices began to gather on Christmas Eve to celebrate what became known as the street Christmas. Dressing themselves in disguise, youths came in from the poorer artisan suburbs, such as Southwark, to parade through the streets of Philadelphia's most elegant merchant blocks blowing horns, banging on drums, and shooting pistols into the air. For many years the police were unable to do anything about it, and respectable people, despising the "street Christmas," stayed indoors behind locked front doors. Celebrants would enter a respectable tavern and demand a round of free drinks, and if the proprietor should be so unwise as to refuse, they would wreck the establishment. Or they might wreck the establishment in any case. Using disguises, and venturing beyond the normal boundaries of their own turf, gangs looked for rivals to rough up. The violence that lurked just beneath the surface of this merrymaking expressed a rage also found in the costumes of the celebrants. Some apprentices wore blackface; others dressed as girls. The two could be combined to produce an "Aunt Jane." The inversion of sex and race were significant, for they suggest the insecurity of these young white males. By the traditions and rights of the culture in which they had grown up, these artisan youths thought themselves the proper inheritors of the wealth, power, and mastery of the city. But they recognized that something fundamental had changed, and in the new industrial society they were no more powerful than the blacks and women they parodied. It was rage at the denial of their birthright that was expressed in these destructive mummer's parades. The most violent parades came in the late 1860s, during the last gasp of apprenticeship, and by 1900 city authorities had transformed the parade into a tame, city-sponsored New Year's event.[18]

One should also ponder the role of artisan youths in politics. In 1844 in Philadelphia and New York native-born artisans banded together in a wave of anti-Irish and anti-Catholic hysteria to elect local governments under the banner of the American Republican party. The movement quickly fizzled in New York, but in Philadelphia the more talented and more demagogic Lewis Levin kept the party alive for the remainder of the decade. Levin, a Jewish-born Methodist street preacher and temperance newspaper publisher, three times got himself elected to Congress from the artisan Southwark district. Evidence from Levin's rallies and nativist mobs suggests that apprentices were an important component of the movement. And perhaps it was the apprentices who compelled Levin and his associates to depend so heavily upon flag-waving and other sorts of symbolic patriotism—including the name "American Republican." Nativists also made symbolic use of Washington lore and celebrated February 22 as a holiday. George Washington was the father of his country, and nativists proclaimed themselves to be his sons. In part these gestures were an attempt to prove their patriotism, but, more important to youths and young men who as artisans had been stripped of social identity by industrial culture, patriotic symbols also gave historical legitimacy to a cause and reinforced their own sense of a historical origin. "No Popery here!" had long been a cry in Protestant countries; by rallying behind nativism, American-born youths reinvoked a sense of tradition and established themselves as legitimate heirs to at least a part of the nation's cultural heritage. If they could not be master mechanics, they could at least be good Catholic-haters.[19]

In the 1850s another burst of nativist sentiment would lead to a second American party, more popularly called the Know-Nothings. Recent investigation has established that virtually no Know-Nothing was past the age of thirty and that the party drew its greatest electoral support from among new voters just turned twenty-one. They were a party of artisan youths and young men. It was precisely among this age group that alienation, caused by changes in the economic system, ran highest. These were the sons of skilled craftsmen who had been forced to become mere semiskilled machine tenders. While their fathers had largely failed to realize earlier aspirations to become master craftsmen, these young men no longer had any such expectations. And they saw in Irish Catholic immigrants rivals who further drove down wages and threatened the cultural values of respectability that were their sole remaining claim to social status above that of unskilled laborers. It is perhaps not insignificant that they were called Know-Nothings. One should never ignore the labels of mass political parties, for they are symbols used to attract and hold followers. While Whigs and Democrats ridiculed the Know-Nothings with derisive repetitions of the name, it is interesting that the supporters of the fledgling American party wore the label as a kind of badge of honor. Why should one be proud to say, "I know nothing"? Psychologically, it was a cry of desperation by young men and youths totally alienated from society by the collapse of traditional artisan life. There was a sense in which every machine tender, in contrast with his more skilled artisan father, could claim to "know nothing." Youths are always insecure about their identity, and the decline of skilled trades that had provided

traditional artisan identity left young Americans uncertain about themselves. It is no accident that in 1856 the artisan-trained Millard Fillmore
was the Know-Nothing candidate for the presidency.[20]

While politics, like taverns, street gangs, and fire companies, had its
place in the lives of some apprentices, these sorts of group activities
offered only a limited adjustment to the realities of the new machine age.
Whereas advice books and reformers had advocated respectability through
self-improvement, urban culture had offered group membership through
group participation. The former held out only a slender hope that self-
improvement would lead to self-employment, and the latter guaranteed a
lifetime of journeyman's work with the consolation of the group. Neither
self-improvement nor group participation enabled a youth to become a
master craftsman. To become a master required capital, and some youths
chose not to desert their trades but to seek the capital to compete with
established masters. Late in 1848 gold was found in California. News of
the discovery swept across the country like a prairie fire, and between
1849 and the California census of 1852 almost 250,000 Americans, Euro-
peans, Mexicans, Chileans, and Chinese poured into California. More
than 90 percent were males. Half were between the ages of eighteen and
thirty, virtually all were single, and many were apprentices or young
journeymen looking for both adventure and a way to gain capital from
the goldfields. In 1850 the population of the United States was 23 million;
of that total about 5 million were adult white males; nearly 2 million
were men in their twenties. Probably half of those were married. Of
900,000 single young American males, about 10 percent went to California. This migration was one of the oddest and most striking in history;
nothing like it has ever taken place in the United States.[21]

One of those caught up in the gold frenzy was John Mohler Studebaker, who at nineteen left the family wagon works in South Bend,
Indiana, to spend five years in the California goldfields building wheel-
barrows. He returned home with $8,000 to open what eventually became
one of the most successful large-scale wagon factories in the country. Another gold seeker was Enos Christman, a twenty-year-old apprentice
printer, who persuaded his West Chester, Pennsylvania, master to waive
the last six months of his apprenticeship in return for half of Christman's
earnings during the youth's first two years in California. While on the
sea voyage around Cape Horn, young Christman kept a diary that revealed his ambivalent feelings about his quest. One day he wrote, "It will
be a long while before I forget that Monday is the day of all others in the
week for work in the old *Record* office. I suppose that tomorrow my old
comrades in arms will be dispatching business at a rapid rate, and perhaps my services would be acceptable for an hour or two. But I cannot

be here and there, too. Their memory cannot be forgotten and I hope I will not be. But I must not allow myself to get to musing in this way, as it might lead to disastrous results, and supper will soon be ready." Months later, still at sea, Christman turned twenty-one, and two days later he wrote, "On that day I was twenty-one years of age, the period I was anxiously looking forward to a short year ago while laboring at the case in the old *Record* office, as I then thought it would give me more unbounded liberty. But this wished-for liberty came some six months since, and my twenty-first birthday has been spent on the broad rolling Pacific where I have little desire to pass another." Christman eventually landed at San Francisco, and within a few months he was in Sonora, where he had purchased a half interest in the *Sonora Herald* and styled himself as its publisher. Boys grew up quickly in California. It was sixteen months from the time the restless apprentice left home to the time he became an instant master printer. Two years later Christman returned east and used his savings to open a printing office.[22]

Not every gold rush quest ended with a pot of gold. Henry George, son of a Philadelphia Custom House clerk, left school at thirteen to become a merchant's clerk at $2 a week. Bored and restless, at sixteen, with his father's consent, he sailed for India as a foremast boy. A year later, he was back in Philadelphia—unemployed. His parents opposed another sea voyage, and Henry's father finally found the youth an apprenticeship with a leading printing house. For nine months the boy set type willingly, until one afternoon he quarreled with the foreman and walked out. The bold, forthright youth of the mid-nineteenth century did not condescend to being ordered about by a foreman. Henry's father found his son a job in another printing office, although the pay was only $2.25 a week for the first year, and Henry would have to promise to stay until he turned twenty-one. Henry hesitated to accept this position, and instead he took an opening as a journeyman in an office that was on strike. Hired as a strikebreaker, he made $9.50 in one week. It was the most money he had ever earned; more important, he realized that he was capable of doing the work of a good journeyman. Unfortunately for Henry, the strike ended, and he was again out of work. He believed he could earn $5 a week if he could get hired as a journeyman—but he could not. He took a course in penmanship, as the advice books recommended, and he planned to take a course in bookkeeping, but Henry already felt that he was "Jack of three different trades, and . . . master of none." Frustrated with Philadelphia, he turned his attention to the Far West. "I *will* go out as soon as possible and in the best manner possible," he wrote a friend in Oregon, "even if I am obliged to work my way around the Horn—unless by a lucky windfall I shall get into some business." But this plan came to nothing, and he remained in Philadelphia.[23]

His life was aimless and pointless. He had no work to take pride in, and his self-esteem was low. He was, to use the modern word, alienated. One can see the drift in his diary entry for July 3, 1857: "Saw Jo Jeffreys in afternoon. In evening Bill Jones and I took Sallie Young and Amelia Reinhart to the Academy of Music. But Sallie Young deserted me there and went with Bill Jones. Curse these girls; they won't fool me so confoundedly again. After taking them home we adjourned to Stead's [cigar store], where Bill Horner was awaiting us. As we came down we stopped at Cook's and Bergner's [taverns]. Coming up again, we serenaded Charlie Walton with the national anthem, after which Bill left us. Horner and I again repaired to Stead's, where after a little while we were joined by Jo and a friend of his, John Owen, by name. They, together with Ebenezer Harrison, had been enjoying themselves in Owen's room, drinking punches and making speeches. At the corner of Sixth and Walnut Jo and I commenced to box, when Jo fell down and cut his head awfully. We raised him up, took him to Owen's, washed his wound and then set off to find a doctor. We dragged him around for about two hours before finding any person who could dress the wound. At length we took him to a German physician, who dressed the cut and charged a V for his trouble. We left him at Owen's and returned home about daybreak."[24]

About this time Henry and his friends—perhaps influenced by the advice books—founded the "Lawrence Literary Society." Although the society was created with the notion that its members would produce essays on topical subjects, it evolved into something quite different. The youths sat in a darkened hall and told ghost stories, or they brought boxing gloves and sparred. Or they tried fencing. Most of the exercises were "muscular rather than literary," and the true test of the society was "to drink Red Eye, sing good songs and smoke lots of cigars." Not surprisingly, the society was eventually evicted from its meeting hall. It had, however, served to help its members pass the time amid the unemployment of the depressed year 1857. Finally, having given up hope for a printing job, Henry sailed as a common seaman on a coastwise vessel carrying coal from Philadelphia to Boston. After this voyage, he returned home and found the economy even worse. "There are thousands of hardworking mechanics now out of employment in this city," he wrote in a letter dunning a friend during his own unemployment. He confessed, ". . . I am pretty hard up at present and haven't as much money as you could shake a stick at. Indeed, I would not have any hesitation in taking a situation on board a good canal boat for a short time, provided that it

would pay." Giving up on Philadelphia, he finally decided to try his luck
in California, but he lacked passage money. So he used his father's political connections to apply for an appointment as an able seaman on a
California-bound ship operated by the Light-House Bureau. To young
George's surprise, he was appointed ship's steward at $40 a month, al-
though he was required to sign papers promising one year's service. Three
days before Christmas 1857 he sailed for California.[25]

When his ship docked in San Francisco, the eighteen-year-old George,
like most of the other seamen aboard, jumped ship. Hearing of a gold
strike in Canada, he went to the Fraser River, but the rumored strike was
largely hype, and in a few months he was back in San Francisco—broke.
He got a job setting type at $16 a week and, despite a $9-a-week board
bill, followed his father's advice and saved money. Meanwhile, his mother
piously urged, "Look to Jesus, my dear child." George became frustrated
with his trade, because he watched journeymen earn $30 a week, but he
could not qualify for that rate until he turned twenty-one and got his
union card. At this time he wrote his sister Jennie an upbeat letter. "My
principal object now is to learn my trade well," wrote George, "and I am
pitching in with all my strength. So anxious am I now to get ahead and
make up for lost time that I never feel happier than when at work, and
that, so far from being irksome, is a pleasure. My heart just now is really
in my work. In another year I'll be twenty-one and I must be up and
doing. I have a pretty good prospect ahead and think that before many
months I shall get into something better where I can make good wages."
California had broken the gloom that Philadelphia had cast across
George's prospects, and instead of poverty and unemployment the youth
saw a future not unlike that envisioned by Horatio Alger. Infected with
enthusiasm for progress, self-improvement, and advancement, young
George bubbled with the self-confidence so typical of young Americans
of that day.[26]

In August, when George learned that his boyhood friend Jo Jeffreys
had died suddenly, the ties with the East snapped, and George began to
think less of home than of California. By 1860 he had decided to remain
in California as a printer for a year or two after his twenty-first birthday
in order to save some money; then he planned to return to Philadelphia
for a visit. He joined the Methodist church, which pleased his mother,
and on his twenty-first birthday became a journeyman member of the
Eureka Typographical Union of San Francisco. Soon thereafter he was
appointed a foreman at $30 a week, cast his first presidential vote (for
Abraham Lincoln), worked as a substitute on several newspapers, and
bought into the *Evening Journal*. When the Civil War broke out, and his
friends in Philadelphia enlisted, he remained in California. In a letter to

his sister Jennie, he wrote, "If I were home, and situated as they are, I would go, too." But he was not home, and he made no effort to go east, at least in part because he thought the war would not last long. Still, he confessed a desire to participate. "I have felt a great deal like enlisting, even here, and probably would have done so," he wrote, "had I not felt my duty to you all required me to remain, though I did not, and do not, think our volunteers are really needed or will do any fighting that will amount to anything; but I should like to place my willingness on record, and show that one of our family was willing to serve his country. We cannot tell. It may be my duty yet, though I sincerely hope not." George's newspaper failed, he eloped, and a year later the couple was living in poverty in Sacramento, with George again working as a journeyman.[27]

The contrast between young George's experience and that of earlier apprentice printers is striking. In 1817 James Harper had worked as a journeyman for one year, and as a result of his savings during that year, plus a little family assistance, he had been able to open his own printing office in partnership with his brother. By the time Horace Greeley went to New York in 1831, it was more difficult to become established as a printer. Greeley barely earned enough money to meet his board bills, but through skill, luck, and political connections the talented Greeley was within a decade able to found the *New York Tribune*. The capital required to establish the venture was enormous, and Greeley always was a tiny stockholder in the company, but friends owned the stock, and Greeley was able to project a powerful independent editorial voice. In 1857 Henry George faced a more dire situation. He could find no work at all, and living in a large family that was increasingly hard-pressed to support him along with younger siblings, he was driven to leave Philadelphia rather than to continue trying to find work there as a printer. Furthermore, even as a journeyman in California, George's wages were never high enough to enable him to save the kind of money necessary to open a successful shop. Eventually, he did set up his own shop, but it was undercapitalized and failed. In the long run, George would leave printing for journalism and political agitation. He would become a militant spokesman for those who saw declining opportunities as the major issue in post–Civil War America. One cannot help wondering whether George and others would have been so militant if they had been able to follow in the footsteps of a James Harper or a Horace Greeley.

CHAPTER NINE

Lingering Traditions

Although the machine age, particularly in the cities, had a profound effect upon apprentices, in rural America older handicraft traditions lingered on. In the 1850s there were still many youths like Will Howells, who learned the printing trade in his father's country printing office. By the time the boy was six, he had been brought into the shop to set type—even before he could read. Will's boyhood was a sequence of terrifying moves crisscrossing Ohio as his father grimly sought to establish a successful newspaper. In the end the *Ashtabula Sentinel* brought success, but only because Will's father was able to use the unpaid labor of his two sons. In a similar fashion Brick Pomeroy had learned the blacksmith's trade from an uncle with whom he lived. Ultimately, Brick had rejected this trade to take an old-fashioned apprenticeship in a small-scale country printing office. Although Brick was not indented, he agreed to terms scarcely different from those accepted by Horace Greeley a generation earlier. While Brick was pulling weeds in his master's garden, Arthur Richards had apprenticed himself to a small-time Ohio cabinetmaker. Despite competition from the capitalized, immigrant-worked furniture factories of Cincinnati, Richards's master survived. He thrived in the small town of Gallipolis thanks to a reputation for honesty, quality workmanship, and local customers. Arthur, who lived with his master, was allowed to use the shop tools to make items on his own time. This master and apprentice grew close to each other, and after the master asked young Richards to make each of his daughters a bureau, the youth swelled with pride. The apprentice knew that for forty years his master had saved special cherry burls to be used for the front panels. Although these examples show that the rural craft tradition did not die out, during the 1850s such craftsmen lost economic ground to other Americans.[1]

In no other section of the country was the rural craft tradition maintained in quite the way it was in the South, where craftsmanship was inexorably entangled with slavery. In those areas of the South where small-scale farmers predominated, and where there were few slaves, farmer-craftsmen carried on the same traditions practiced in the rural North; but in those areas of the South where large-scale planters predominated, and where there were many slaves, it was slaves who were craftsmen. A planter preferred to have craftwork done on the premises rather than to depend upon outside labor that might be remote, expensive, or not available at all. Rachel O'Connor, the manager of Evergreen Plantation, estimated that having blacksmithing done at a shop "would cost ten times as much as at home," where she could hire a slave craftsman from a neighbor. The planter therefore had an economic incentive to make craftsmen of some of his slaves. In addition, the slave system encouraged slave artisanship. In a racial caste system based on white supremacy, there had to be some role for talented blacks that did not threaten whites. Since whites preserved their racial supremacy by reserving for themselves all positions of power, influence, or high status, blacks could not be educated to become merchants or professionals. On the other hand, since the American elite had generally held mechanics in low regard, there was little difficulty in a black's becoming a mechanic. And the plantation system itself encouraged slave craftsmanship in another way. Most slaves on plantations were field hands worked in gangs, and that particular form of labor provided little opportunity for a talented slave to perform well. Indeed, an ambitious and talented slave could find no room for personal gain or increased status in being a field hand. A master found little profit in keeping an ambitious and talented slave in the field, when more might be gained by putting him to other work.[2]

The planter encouraged artisanship among his slaves because it increased their productivity, and hence his wealth, and because it made the slave more valuable. A slave with artisan skills was worth three times as much as a field hand. Slaves could learn crafts in one of three ways. Some were owned by master craftsmen, and they served apprenticeships, in effect, with their owners. Unlike a free laborer, such a slave was forced to remain as a permanent helper to his owner. A slave in this position did not have much incentive to learn his trade very well. A second way in which a slave could learn a trade was to be trained by another slave on a plantation. On large plantations it was common for artisan skills to be passed from generation to generation. Thus, the owner of a slave craftsman not only gained the benefit of that artisan's skills but also profited when the younger slaves on the plantation were trained in the craft and hence had higher skills, which both increased their value as slaves and generated more profits for the owner. The principal problem with such plantation-learned craft skills was that there was little cross-fertilization from passing journeymen. A slave who learned a craft on a plantation tended to replicate the methods and techniques of the fellow slave from whom he had learned his trade. It is this characteristic of plantation artisanship that explains why craftsmanship in the South seldom achieved the degree of artistry or skill that prevailed in the North. The third way for a slave to be trained as an artisan was to be hired out by the owner to a master craftsman. The master craftsman might be either a white or a slave on another plantation. Such hiring out was a form of apprenticeship, but because slaves did not enjoy full legal rights, no indentures were used, although a slave's owner sometimes signed a contract with a white master craftsman.[3]

Many planters considered mechanical labor fit only for blacks. Whites could be planters, overseers, small farmers, professionals, or merchants; blacks could be skilled craftsmen, household servants, or field hands. Sons of planters or small farmers, even when impoverished, did not become skilled craftsmen, because manual labor was not proper work for whites. But even in the most heavily black plantation districts of the South there were large numbers of small-scale white farmers. Such a farmer either owned no slaves or could not afford to turn one of his few field hands into a skilled craftsman; he lacked the capital to set up the slave in a shop, and he could not have furnished the slave with sufficient business to keep the shop profitable. Sometimes such small farmers turned to their large-scale planter neighbors for blacksmithing, carpentry, or shoemaking, the three most common trades in rural areas. Under the circumstances the planter could charge what the traffic would bear, which might, in the eyes of the small farmer, be a high price indeed. The result then was a demand for skilled labor that could not be fulfilled within the slave system, and yet few whites cared to engage in mechanical work. The small farmer, however, was willing to deal with white or free black craftsmen who moved into the community.[4]

Throughout the plantation South a few white craftsmen did set up shop in villages and county seats. Many of these artisans were born abroad or in the North, where they had served apprenticeships before migrating to the South. They came because wages were higher than in the North; when he had work, a mechanic could earn $2 or $3 a day rather than the $1 or $1.50 common in the rural North. And town lots, which were ample enough for a garden that provided much of a family's food, were sold at prices below those in the North. Furthermore, there was less competition in the South, where vast distances between settlements and the lack of a strong artisan tradition often produced a local monopoly. Lack of competition in turn meant that quality was less important to success than in the North. Finally, northern master craftsmen were already using huge sums of capital to acquire better tools and machinery that enabled them to drive weaker competitors out of business. In the South a poor craftsman could make a living through the support of loyal local customers remote from any large-scale capitalized competitors. There was one ironic twist to this state of affairs. Southern artisans seldom took apprentices. Few slaveholders wanted their slaves trained in the loose and open atmosphere of village shops, and local whites seldom entered craft apprenticeships. There is some evidence that whites found other work more lucrative. For example, one apprentice blacksmith gave up his trade to carry mail, then turned to overseeing, and within six years was a planter hoping "to by a negra." Another craftsman announced, "I have quit the Carpentern buisiness and gon into the ice speculation." A few months later he had taken a wealthy partner and pronounced the South "a fine Cuntry to make money." But perhaps the main reason for the lack of apprentices was the low population density that left most village craftsmen with more time than work. As small farmers sold out and moved west, leaving the land increasingly in the hands of planters with their own slave craftsmen, village artisans faced dwindling prospects.[5]

One cannot discuss slavery and apprenticeship for long without considering the ways in which these two ancient institutions were related. One way concerned the concept of "master." God was master of the world; the father was master of his family; the teacher was master of his pupils; the skilled craftsman was master of his apprentices; and the planter was master of his slaves. "Master" was a term both familial and hierarchical. It functioned as a descriptive label indicating power and authority, and it functioned as a means of establishing and maintaining psychological distance and deference. One always deferred to the master. A master ordered, commanded, decided. He—there were, of course, no female masters, the very notion being ludicrous—ruled; others obeyed. A master did not cajole or beg or ask or plead; he did not negotiate, mediate, or compromise. In his proper realm a master was supreme. He was a greater being, and he expected the obedience, reverence, respect, and deference of lesser beings. The father as master of the family was the original model. Religion borrowed the concept and extended it to the realm of the invisible, where the notion of God as master made the concept more splendid, more inspiring, and more awesome. Education applied the idea to learning, where the notion of teacher as master reinforced the concept of hierarchy. Then commerce borrowed the term and applied it to the world of work, where the notion of craftsman as master included both customary familial relations and more exotic economic ones. The master's exploitation of the labor of his apprentices was a by-product of the relationship. Slavery carried the concept to the realm of race, where the notion of planter as master not only established a hierarchy of familial paternalism and work organization but also made the slave into a child and thereby legitimated white supremacy. In traditional society a "master" was to be worshiped (in heaven), reverenced (in the family), obeyed (in the school and shop), and feared (on the plantation). By the 1850s traditional views were waning. To evangelicals, God was less a tyrannical "master" than a merciful "father"; the family was increasingly under the control of the mother, who claimed it as her "sphere"; in the school, too, the master was giving way to the school ma'am; in the shop, the boss now had employees. Only on the plantation did the slave still have his "master." It was a sign of how antiquated an institution slavery had become.

Although apprenticeship and slavery were parallel institutions, they served quite different functions. Slavery was both a system of economic exploitation and a means of social control guaranteeing white supremacy. Because race was a permanent condition, the institution of slavery froze master and slave into those positions for life. And because slavery was permanent, the slave was always at a disadvantage. He could neither remind his master what it had been like to be a slave nor appeal to him for any special consideration based on his own prospects. An apprentice, on the other hand, grew up—in theory—to become master of a craft, just as a son grew up to become a master of his own family. It was the absence of this reciprocal interest between master and slave that encouraged both to use their roles to further personal interest without caring how that interest affected the other party. In contrast, while apprenticeship was a system of partial economic exploitation as well as a means of social control for youths, it was also a system of education by which valuable knowledge was transmitted from generation to generation. The apprentice's interest in his master was enhanced by the belief that he would someday be a master, and the apprentice tolerated economic exploitation and irksome regulation of his conduct because of his expectation. His inconvenience was merely temporary. And the master could recall his own apprenticeship and thereby make allowances for the youth's behavior. Indeed, the apprentice might someday become a fellow master craftsman, and it was to the advantage of the master to cultivate a relationship that was potentially quite valuable. Both Benjamin Franklin and Isaiah Thomas had advanced themselves through cultivating their former apprentices. As an institution, then, apprenticeship lacked the qualities that made slavery so harsh. That was precisely why some abolitionists saw apprenticeship as an appropriate way station from slavery to complete freedom.[6]

Since slavery dealt with race and apprenticeship with the molding of youths, there were no intrinsic conflicts between the two institutions; rather, they existed side by side and even overlapped. There were, however, practical conflicts between slavery and free craftsmanship. In the nineteenth century free skilled workers, whether white or black, were paid wages, and those wages were determined by the labor market. A free craftsman hoped that his skill was sufficiently rare for him to receive high wages and that he could earn enough not only to survive but also to save money to open a shop or buy a farm and retire in comfort. Slave craftsmen, on the other hand, were not paid wages; rather, their owners were paid for their services, and out of this money the slave was provided with a meager allowance of food, clothing, and shelter. According to some calculations, a slave could be kept for $69 a year, about one-third the amount needed to furnish a free mechanic with the living standard to which he had become accustomed. In other words, the owner of a slave could underbid the free craftsman in the labor market, take care of the slave, and still make a profit. Southern white craftsmen reacted to this fact by advocating a racial segregation of work. Whites sought to reserve highly skilled jobs for themselves while leaving blacks unskilled work. Blacks were conceded entry into some of the rougher trades, such as blacksmithing, and blocked from entering the more sophisticated, fashionable, or lucrative trades. In 1829, for example, Georgia made it illegal for free blacks to become typesetters; twenty-five years later Savannah banned slave butchers. Both free blacks and slaves were restricted from many occupations.[7]

As every craftsman knew, an increase in the number of apprentices foreshadowed a future increase in craftsmen that would put downward pressure on wages. Except in boom times, journeymen favored restrictions designed to limit the number of apprentices. Naturally, artisans in both North and South opposed the taking of free black apprentices. Not only did these apprentices threaten to glut the future market for journeymen, but the very existence of black apprentices threatened artisans with loss of status. Craftsmen held this view not simply because they were racist—although they were, as was the rest of American society—but also because racism implied a system of racial-caste status. The whiter an occupation, the higher its status. In no section of the country were there black lawyers or doctors; there were many black dockworkers, draymen, and hotel waiters. The white mechanic wanted to maintain his distance from these unskilled groups and to stand closer to the wealthier and more powerful all-white occupational groups in society. It was probably status consciousness expressed as racism that explains why young Frederick Douglass could not get a job as a journeyman ship caulker in the North after he had escaped from slavery.[8]

Artisan opposition to apprenticeships for blacks also extended to slaves. But artisan opposition rubbed against the interest of the slaveholder, who wanted his slave to learn a trade that would increase his economic value. Whether kept at home or hired out, a slave artisan was valuable to his owner. Owners were wise enough to recognize that a slave artisan had to be cultivated in order to get the most out of him, and so many artisans were indulged. J. H. Hammond lamented, "Whenever a slave is made a mechanic, he is more than half freed." Slaves recognized that learning a craft could bring such benefits and thus sought the opportunity. By the 1850s a majority of slaves in southern cities probably were hired out, and many of them were allowed either to choose their own employers or to work on their own time in return for giving the owner a weekly payment. While such practices enabled a few slaves to work enough overtime to buy their freedom, they did not always benefit the owner. One slave, reported Diana Davis, "collected his last weeks wages and has absented himself since and I am fearful he may get off in some vessel and we shall finly loose him." A few years later Mrs. Davis's father-in-law had numerous difficulties hiring out his slaves in New Orleans while he remained on his plantation. At one point his agent wrote, "I think you had better Come down yourself and see about the boys for I dont believe they will get along well without your being here." After the owner found a new agent, he had fewer problems, but that agent quit, and the owner's next agent allowed the slaves to work their own time. When a number of them became delinquent with their weekly payments, the agent threatened to have them whipped.[9]

Although masters and slaves favored apprenticeships for slaves, white artisans did not. They resisted teaching skills to slaves, sometimes refused to work in the same shop with any hired slaves (leaving a careful loophole for a personal slave belonging to a master craftsman), and proposed laws restricting black access to artisan jobs. White craftsmen who lacked the capital to buy a slave resented competing with those few wealthy master craftsmen who were able to profit from the labor of a black they owned. In addition, they saw black mechanics as fierce competitors. "The Black Mechanics enjoy as complete a Monopoly," complained a group of Charleston white artisans, "as if it were secured to them by Law." They complained that wealthy Charlestonians allowed their slaves to decide whom to hire, and the slaves naturally perferred to hire black workmen. Although South Carolina passed laws prohibiting slaves from hiring their own time, slaveholders ignored prohibitions that worked against their own interest. Such laws could not be enforced, because slave craftsmen were vital to the economy, and these economically important slaves attained a degree of independence. In states like South Carolina, where manumission was difficult, it was as close to freedom as a slave could get. In 1858, when South Carolina white mechanics petitioned the legislature for stronger laws against black mechanics, the slaveholding legislators conceded that slaves who hired their own time undermined slavery but refused to pass any laws. "We are accustomed to black labor and it would create a revolution to drive it away," wrote the legislators. Such pronouncements did not assuage the fears of white mechanics, who simply resisted training any slave craftsmen. As a result of this reluctance, many slaves were apprenticed to slaves or free blacks, and slave artisans were concentrated in such crafts as blacksmithing or carpentry, which were commonly practiced on plantations.[10]

There was one other peculiarity about slave apprentices. Normally, they were not indented. Since a slave was not a legal person, he was not able to indent himself; whether he could be bound by his owner depended upon local custom, but in time that custom faded. Slaves therefore either served informal apprenticeships, which was the case on plantations, or were apprenticed through a legal agreement between the owner of the slave and the master craftsman in whose shop the craft would be learned. For example, in 1804 West Burgess bound "as an apprentice a Black boy named Billy unto the said Phillip Alts to the Black Smith trade for the term of two years." This agreement, like others of its type, did not provide the slave with an education or any of the other benefits that the law required in apprenticeship indentures. Commonly, the owner was paid for the slave's services, even in the first year of the apprenticeship. The exact legal status of such an apprentice was murky. For example, in 1791 a South Carolina slave was apprenticed to a hairdresser who went bankrupt. When one creditor tried to attach the apprentice as part of the hairdresser's property, the slave's owner resisted, and the court refused to allow the action on the grounds that an apprenticeship did not transfer the ownership of a slave. Without this ruling, few slaveholders would have apprenticed slaves, out of fear of attachment and seizure for a bankrupt master craftsman's debts. Yet the owner's rights and obligations were not absolute, as another South Carolina case from 1853 shows. A slaveholder had hired out two slaves to learn blacksmithing, and they had been treated as apprentices. Both ran away, were captured, and were lodged in the workhouse. Neither the owner nor the master smith would pay their expenses, although the smith did indicate that he would take them back into his shop. Perhaps that was a fatal mistake, for the court held that the blacksmith would have to pay the workhouse bill. This decision surely did not encourage master craftsmen to sign formal agreements accepting slaves as apprentices; that point, in fact, may have been exactly what the court intended.[11]

In the 1840s new industrial practices exacerbated relations between white and black slave artisans. Slaveholders hired out their slaves to highly capitalized, large-scale concerns such as Richmond's Tredegar Iron Works. In 1847, when the white ironworkers employed in that mill were ordered to train slaves in their craft, they refused. For several years blacks and whites had worked side by side in the mill, so the issue was not one of associating with another race. Rather, the highly paid iron-workers perceived that they were being asked to train cheap slaves who would become their own replacements. The unsuccessful strike by the white ironworkers did in fact lead to that result, and in the 1850s the mill was increasingly operated with skilled slave labor. As slaves learned the craft, some were promoted to positions of responsibility within the mill, and newly arrived slaves were routinely trained by other slaves. By mid-century the success of industrial slavery had alarmed southern white craftsmen, who perceived a threat to their own livelihoods. In 1849 white mechanics in the industrial city of Petersburg, Virginia, opposed teaching blacks any skilled craft and pledged themselves not to work for any em-ployer who hired black labor, unless a master craftsman was teaching his own slave a craft. Two years later Georgia mechanics meeting in Atlanta argued that black mechanics both degraded occupations so that whites would not enter them and posed a threat to social order. "Mechanical pursuits," said the convention, "elevate the Negro's mind and quicken his intellect, leading to a desire to read and write, the gratification of which is often obtained in a clandestine manner, by which he is furnished with facilities for making money, and led into depravity and dissipation, thereby making him restless and unhappy, and an unsafe associate for the dutiful and contented negroes of the state, of a lower grade of condi-tion." Absent from this line of argument was any attack upon black abili-ties. On the contrary, the threat was competition. In 1857 in Wilmington, North Carolina, white artisans burned a building framed by black car-penters and left behind a placard stating that only whites should be hired as craftsmen.[12]

Growing tensions may obscure the fact that craftsmanship among slaves was never common. It is true that there were frequent newspaper advertisements for black apprentices early in the century, but the total number of such advertisements, relative to the population, was quite small, and many of the notices were clearly directed toward free blacks rather than slaves. Evidence from North Carolina suggests that after 1830 poor free blacks indented by the courts were less likely to become craftsmen and more likely to be sent to farms to learn husbandry. This shift, also evident from the abrupt decline of newspaper advertising for black apprentices around 1830, may have been the result of a labor market glutted with white craftsmen. A similar shift away from crafts might also have taken place for slaves, although there is no direct evidence. Free black apprenticeship may have declined because slave skills increased. One can imagine that in the competition between free blacks and slaves for the same positions, the power of slaveholders would have determined the outcome in favor of their own interest. It may be that in the early nineteenth century few slaves were artisans (many, after all, were recent arrivals from Africa) and that free blacks had a greater opportunity to acquire skills. But as planters who needed craftsmen became more sophisticated in their operations, as the price of slaves rose, making artisanship more valuable to planters, and as later generations of slaves became more acculturated, slave artisans gradually took over from free blacks. In 1848 a Charleston city census showed large numbers of black artisans, both slave and free; they were concentrated in certain crafts, where skills were passed from black to black. There were more slave carpenters, for example, than either free black or white carpenters. However, one should not overestimate the importance of artisanship within the black community in the South as a whole. A study of 1851 personal-property records for two Virginia counties showed that only one-fifth to one-third of the adult free black males were craftsmen, and an analysis of Freedmen's Bureau records for four Virginia counties suggests that at most one-twelfth of the adult male slaves were craftsmen.[13]

Glimpses into slave artisan culture are few and far between. Certainly, the slave who left behind a written record of his apprenticeship was exceptional. Yet the experiences of even the exceptional slave can tell us something about what it was like for a slave to be an apprentice. One such slave was James Lindsey Smith. Born on a Virginia plantation, Lindsey as a boy suffered an accident that left him partially lame and useless as a field hand. He was hired out to an oysterer as a cook, worked as a houseboy, and finally was apprenticed by his owner to a master shoemaker. After four years, Lindsey's owner removed him from that shop and set him up in a shop of his own. The youth ran the shop for one year, until his jealous owner, suspicious that Lindsey was withholding part of his earnings, hired him out to a master shoemaker. This episode shows the extent to which a slave artisan was always at the mercy or whim of his owner. The new shop was five miles from the home of Lindsey's owner, and once a week the owner came to collect the slave's earnings. If Smith earned a great deal of money, he kept some of it back. Once he saved $15, bought cloth, and had a suit made. He already owned a watch and chain, and now young Smith made quite an impression on Sundays. The first time Smith wore the new suit, a man told his owner that he was better dressed than the owner. Fortunately, the owner had a sense of humor. After three years, Smith persuaded his owner to let him choose a new master craftsman, and he worked in that shop for a year. Then he ran away to the North, where he became a shoemaker and Methodist minister.[14]

Much more can be learned about the apprenticeship of Frederick Douglass. The slave son of an unidentified white man and a slave mother, Fred was raised on an eastern Maryland plantation by his slave grandmother, a somewhat independent woman who enjoyed a privileged status. When the boy was eight, he was sent to Baltimore to become a house servant to his owner's relatives. When Fred showed an eagerness for learning, the mistress of the household taught the boy to read the Bible, an accomplishment that made her husband furious. As a slave, Fred received no formal education, but he met free blacks on the streets of Baltimore, learned much while working at a shipyard, heard about Methodism and abolition, and acquired the money to buy his first book. When Fred was fifteen, his owner died, and the youth became the property of another Maryland planter, who removed him from Baltimore to his plantation. After Fred was caught trying to hold a Sabbath school, he was hired out for a year to a small-scale farmer with a big reputation for breaking obstinate slaves. Fred endured, and the following year he was hired out to a more benign planter. By this time the youth was planning an escape to the North, but he was caught, and his owner, concluding that Fred was a consistently disruptive influence on his docile plantation slaves, sent the youth to Baltimore.[15]

Family connections led Fred to be hired as an apprentice to a Fell's Point shipbuilder. The youth was told that he would be taught the trade of caulking. In the Baltimore shipyards caulking was a black skill that paid less than ship carpentry, which was reserved for whites. Fred, instructed to do whatever the journeymen ship carpenters told him to do, soon found himself ordered about by seventy-five journeymen. His life as an informal apprentice lasted about eight months, until racial conflict amid the depressed economy of 1837 swirled around Fred and the shipyard. White mechanics in Baltimore had long complained bitterly about competition from slave labor that drove down the wages of free labor. The apprentice Fred, owned by the brother of the shipyard's foreman, was visible proof. Yet slaveholders had exploited racist feelings among white mechanics to create an animosity that was even greater toward free blacks than toward slaves. The argument was made that only slavery could prevent the white mechanic from falling to the level of the slave

NEW BEDFORD SHIP CAULKERS

through competition with free black labor. In the mid-thirties white and black ship carpenters had worked side by side in four Baltimore shipyards without incident, but the depression of the late thirties had brought demands for the removal of black craftsmen. The shipyard where Fred worked was threatened with a strike if all free black craftsmen were not dismissed. Technically, as a slave and as an apprentice, Fred was not part of the dispute, but in fact the other apprentices in the yard, all white, considered working with him to be degrading. Talk began to be heard about "the niggers" taking over and how they "ought to be killed." The apprentices went to Fred and asked him to leave; he refused. They cursed him, and there were several fights. Finally, Fred was jumped by four apprentices, felled by a blow from a spike, pounded, and stomped in the face. Fifty whites, including many journeymen ship carpenters, witnessed the spectacle and did nothing. Some yelled, "Kill him! kill him! kill the damn nigger! knock his brains out! he struck a white person!"[16]

The incident left Fred not only bloody but shaken. When he reported it to his owner, he was removed from the shipyard. His owner tried to have the assailants arrested, but the local justice of the peace would not issue a warrant, because no white witnesses would testify to the assault. Meanwhile, Fred had time to ponder the hatred of the white mechanics. If he ever struck a white man, he would be lynched, but whites were free to strike Fred. Once he had been driving a bolt with a white apprentice named Ned Hayes. The bolt bent, and Ned swore and blamed Fred's hammering. Fred denied the charge and blamed Ned, whereupon Ned grabbed an adze and charged Fred, who parried the blows with a maul. Such anger might sooner or later have led to Fred's death, and the youth soon concluded that it would be best if he left Baltimore and moved North. After his wounds healed, Fred's owner found him work in another Baltimore shipyard. In a year he finished his apprenticeship as a caulker, and, with an improving economy, he was able to earn wages as high as those of any journeyman caulker in town. During a busy season he brought home $6 or $7 a week and sometimes as much as $9 a week. All of the money was turned over to Fred's owner, who gave the youth only a small allowance for incidentals. Soon Fred was allowed to find his own jobs and make his own oral contracts, and he concluded that he should be able to keep his own wages, too. When Fred asked his owner for permission to hire his own time at a fixed weekly rate, the owner at first refused, but after Fred demonstrated through a lazy week with little work that he had no intention of working without some incentive, the owner yielded. Fred worked on his own and paid his owner $3 a week for the privilege. But the youth feared being sold, and at age twenty he borrowed a set of seaman's free papers and ran away to the North.[17]

The decay of apprenticeship as a robust and viable institution for the transfer of knowledge from generation to generation during the nineteenth century meant that apprenticeship could no longer serve black Americans as a way station on the road from slavery to freedom. In 1780, when Pennsylvania had passed a gradual-emancipation law, it had tried to protect the property interest of slaveholders. Not only did the law free no existing slaves, but the owner of a slave was entitled to the services of any of the children of a slave born after 1780 until the age of twenty-eight if male, or twenty-one if female. This measure implicitly recognized that part of the value of a female slave was in the prospective offspring. At a time when parental authority was all but absolute and when, in the absence of parental control, a child was routinely bound to a master as an apprentice or servant until the age of twenty-one if male, or eighteen if female, the Pennsylvania gradual-emancipation law placed children of slaves in a condition that was little different, except for the longer term of service. Although abolitionists objected to the longer term of service, the legislature saw the additional years as a necessary compensation to a slaveholder whose slave's value was based in part on prospective off-spring. When New York adopted a gradual-emancipation law in 1799, it followed the Pennsylvania model, and New Jersy's 1804 law adhered to the same general plan. So long as apprenticeship was an established institution, the concept of binding the free children of slaves could be used as a device that broke the chain of slavery while providing some compensation to slaveholders for the loss of slave offspring.[18]

There are many reasons why New Jersey was the last state to adopt a plan for gradual emancipation. One important reason was surely the decline of both parental authority and apprenticeship, which made it impossible in the mid-nineteenth century to use bound service as part of a scheme for gradual emancipation. The erosion of apprenticeship among whites meant that the binding of the freeborn children of slaves would no longer place black and white on the same legal footing. Indeed, as time went on, it became clear that bound service for blacks could be used as a means to preserve a racial caste system as a disguised form of slavery. In Texas during the late 1820s southern planters who brought slaves with them from the American South had to get around the reality that the Republic of Mexico had abolished slavery. The Texans discovered that their technically free blacks could legally be turned into apprentices under lifetime contracts. This form of apprenticeship was strictly a legal technicality, and as soon as the proslavery Texans won their independence in 1836 they abandoned apprenticeship for the more familiar American institution of slavery. Meanwhile, in 1833 the British Parliament, after years of debate, had abolished slavery throughout the British Empire. As a concession to the West Indian interests, a system of apprenticeship was established in the British West Indies as a transitional phase. In 1838 an outraged Parliament, observing that apprenticeship had been abused to keep the ex-slaves in total subservience, coerced the colonial assemblies into abolishing apprenticeship. Perhaps nothing signaled the deterioration of the institution of apprenticeship so well as its use as a means to disguise slavery. In 1846 the New Jersey legislature abolished slavery in that state for slaves born before 1804 by declaring the remaining seven hundred slaves with an average age of fifty-five to be lifetime apprentices. No one really believed that New Jersey's action constituted the abolition of slavery, and in 1860 the census counted eighteen aged slaves in that state.[19]

After 1830, when apprentices were regularly paid cash wages, it was no longer possible for slavery to pass through apprenticeship on its way to oblivion. Yet the gradual-emancipation laws of the turn of the century should not be overlooked. It is no accident that Maryland was the one state with a sizable percentage of blacks where numerous manumissions took place; after 1800 nearly half the blacks in Maryland were free. Maryland was also a state with a highly developed institution of apprenticeship, and its 1793 apprentice law, for example, was the earliest to require the registration of indentures. This vigorous apprentice law encouraged manumissions, because it provided for an alternative form of social control for young blacks that both reassured anxious white opinion by maintaining white supremacy and dealt in a concrete way with the real problems of adjustment to a market economy that former slaves had. One cannot help wondering whether, had apprenticeship remained a viable institution through the first half of the century, something like the Maryland manumission movement might not have developed throughout the Upper South. In any event, it is a certainty that after 1830, when apprenticeship waned perceptibly, the absence of apprenticeship as a possible way station from slavery to emancipation left abolitionists in an awkward position. To abolish slavery outright was to suggest the sudden and abrupt removal of an age-old institution widely held to be necessary to maintain racial harmony and social control. On the other hand, the failure of an often fraudulently imposed system of apprenticeship following emancipation in the British West Indies in 1833 discredited that idea. The more apprenticeship declined, the more slavery was defended.[20]

Outside the South, one of the most important lingering traditions was paternal authority. Despite the more assertive style of youths, antebellum fathers still believed themselves to be in charge of their families. In those days, recalled James M. Bailey, boys ignored calls from their mothers to come home, but one word from a father brought the boy running. In another case eight-year-old William Taylor Baker ran away from home and "apprenticed" himself to a carpenter. However, a short time after he began to work William saw his father coming after him with a leather strap, and the boy quickly left the carpenter and headed for home by a back road. In traditional culture a father exacted much more than obedience; he also controlled the destiny of his sons. He determined how much education, if any, the sons would receive, and he often dictated the occupations they would follow. Huckleberry Finn was well aware of the power of his father to dictate his fate. Frequently, a father demanded that his sons follow his own occupation, even when it was doubtful that a particular son was suited. For example, Samuel Bowles, the son of a Springfield, Massachusetts, printer had his hopes for a college education dashed and was forced to take over the family business. The mechanically inept Sam became a brilliant editor, but, to his own humiliation and the disgust of the workmen in the shop, he never learned to set type. Another case involves William James Stillman of Schenectady, New York. His father, a machinist, insisted that all six sons serve apprenticeships in the family shop. Three did so, but then the oldest developed a business connection that made it possible for the three youngest to be sent to college at no cost. Although the father's plan to make all his sons machinists was overturned by opportunity, by the mother's aspirations for her sons, and by the intervention of the oldest brothers, it is instructive that the younger sons were not consulted in reaching a family decision concerning their careers. In this instance, while paternal authority had evolved into familial authority, the youth remained subordinate. In others, as we shall see, paternal authority was more pronounced.[21]

John Milton Gregory, the son of a farmer-tanner in upstate New York, early was put to the family trade. But the boy was sickly, and an older brother, Lewis, persuaded a reluctant father to send John to school to become a schoolmaster. As soon as John left the tannery, his health improved, and at thirteen he was withdrawn from school and put back in the tannery. He was kept there two years, until Lewis again interceded by employing John as his assistant teaching a country school. Alternating between schools and the tannery, the youth again suffered failing health, and Lewis wrote another brother, James, "Pa talks of sending him to school for he cant work." At seventeen John asked his father for permission to become a store clerk. "Pa," wrote the youth, "there is a chance for me to go into a store in Poughkeepsie now if you are willing. It is a dry goods store in main streete. I think it would agree with my present state of health better than tanning but you are the best judge of that. If you conclude to let me stay you can send what clothes I need if not you can write." Although John's father gave permission, Lewis again intervened and procured another teaching job for his brother. Throughout these years the father would from time to time assert his right to John's labor until the son was twenty-one, and Lewis always shielded his brother from these old-fashioned claims. In a letter to his father, Lewis bluntly wrote, "Respecting John I would just say that his health is about as usual and I think he would be of little more service to you at home. He has the offer of the school in the village at a fair price for the summer season and I think for one that he had better take it. . . . John according to his present appearance will not be able to earn a living by labor and I think that if he clothes himself and gets his profession without your assistance he does extremely well. Teaching school seems to agree with him very well." In this case a reluctant father finally gave up his claim to the labor of his son primarily because he was forced to recognize that the son's labor was practically worthless.[22]

John Gregory, however, was the exception and not the rule. The view in most artisan households was that a father was entitled to the services of his son until he reached twenty-one. While such a requirement benefited a father, it effectively prohibited many sons of artisans from obtaining the kind of education and training necessary to enter business or one of the professions. John's brother James had left the tannery without permission before turning twenty-one, and the elder Gregory was furious. Later the father wrote that errant son a letter on the subject of filial duty. "I had made up my mind after Receiving your first letter not to answer it," he wrote, "nor to manifest to any person that I had a son James in this world and have felt that all that I could say or do for you would be worse than Last for I considered the Spirit you manifested in going from me at such a Critical time with me as to the affairs of this life & the few days I had to Expect your Service before you could have gone as a Man & not as a Runaway Boy I say I expected that spirit would lead you to Texas or some other Distant place far from home. But it would seem that the Lord had watched over us both for good that the seperation has been for his glory. . . ." He then offered his son forgiveness and the privilege of returning home for a visit.[23]

Another farmer-tanner whose family life was run on traditional, authoritarian, and paternalistic principles was John Brown. Family members, apprentices, and journeymen who lived in the household attended daily worship services that were a visible manifestation of the regularity, order, and authority that this serious, stern father exerted. Brown's rigid child-rearing practices were not without a price, and years later one of Brown's sons told his father, "The trouble is, you want your boys to be brave as tigers, and still afraid of you." Sometimes it was difficult to know exactly what Brown intended. Once, after the eldest son, John, Jr., had neglected his work in the tannery for quite some time, an exasperated father had informed his son that an account book of his shortcomings would be kept in order to render punishment at the proper time. Entries read:

> **John, Jr.,**
>
> | | |
> |---|---|
> | For disobeying mother | 8 lashes |
> | For unfaithfulness at work | 3 lashes |
> | For telling a lie | 8 lashes |

From time to time the elder Brown showed John the book. Then one Sunday the father decided it was time to settle accounts. The two walked to the tannery. "We went into the upper or finishing room," recalled the son, "and after a long and tearful talk over my faults, he again showed me my account, which exhibited a fearful footing up of *debits*. I had no credits or off-sets, and was of course bankrupt. I then paid about *one-third* of the debt, reckoned in strokes from a nicely-prepared blue-beech switch, laid on 'masterly.' Then, to my utter astonishment, father stripped off his shirt, and seating himself on a block, gave me the whip and bade me 'lay it on' to his bare back. I dared not refuse to obey, but at first I did not strike hard. 'Harder!' he said, 'harder, harder!' until he *received the balance of the account.* Small drops of blood showed on his back where the tip end of the tingling beech cut through."[24]

Paternal authority usually did not take such a bizarre form. Lewis W. Brewster, an apprentice to his father, the publisher and printer of the *Portsmouth Journal,* found his craft boring and dreamed of travel as a tramping journeyman. At eighteen he began to keep a diary. "I should like to go away to work a year or so to learn more of my trade than I have yet had a chance to," he wrote, "and to see more of the world than I now do. I have never been entirely contented with Portsmouth since all my companions have gone away. I hope to be somewhere else before a great while. I *must* learn my whole trade if possible, and something else besides." The youth knew only too well the limitations to learning the craft in a small country printing office. All had become dull routine. "I cannot bear to jog on in this dull Portsmouth life," he wrote, "and find no time to do any thing but distribute, set, press; distribute, set, press and no time to study." He concluded that he did not need any more knowledge of the mechanics of the trade, because he planned to become an editor. And to that end he thought it proper to travel, to see the world, and to live off his own resources for a year or so. It was a kind of self-education that he sought. He observed, "Many is the young man who has with no donation from a father, or any body else *worked* his way to the best scholarship of a good class of collegians." Concluding that travel should precede any further schooling, Lewis decided to seek his father's permission for his plan to tramp around the country. Although he wanted desperately to talk to his father about his plans, it was a week before Lewis screwed up his courage to remark in an offhand way that he might want to leave Portsmouth; to Lewis's consternation, his father did not reply, and when the son mentioned the idea again the following day, the father merely advised him to go back to school before undertaking any travels. It was several days before Lewis concluded that his father had no strong objection to his leaving Portsmouth; then he began to plan his travels in some detail.[25]

Meanwhile, Lewis continued to take on new tasks in his father's printing office. As he began to do job work, he concluded that the practice would enable him to get a position in a Boston job printing office. "I wish to become as well acquainted with my trade as possible before starting from home," he wrote in his journal, "well enough, at least, to fit me to fill a situation with credit to myself in any office. I think I could get along very well now, but the more I know the better. I shall not expect to find so good a situation as I now have, that is, for easy life, in all my travelling about,—but I cannot learn the world and live an easy life at the same time." A few days later Lewis's father, by now convinced that his son was serious about leaving the shop, had a long talk with him. He wanted Lewis to go back to school and wait until he was twenty years old before leaving home to tramp. The father feared that tramping would lead to "unsteady habits" and that if he did not return to school now, he would lose the inclination to do so as he got older. Lewis did not take kindly to this parental advice, and in his journal he stated that he was still determined to leave. A letter from a tramping friend endorsing Lewis's plan to leave only fired the youth's convictions. Still, he would not disobey his father. Although the son decided to try to persuade his father of the wisdom of his scheme, he feared a veto. There was one slender hope. "If I could get my mother on my side," wrote Lewis, "I should soon be far away." While the Brewster family was ostensibly paternal in character, mid-nineteenth-century female influence was clearly at work. It seems doubtful that Lewis ever got permission or defied his father to tramp; he became his father's partner and spent the rest of his life in Portsmouth.[26]

In the end it was the family rather than the father that exerted the most potent influence upon apprentices. When Samuel Langhorne Clemens was twelve, his father died and left a widow with five children, only one over twenty-one. Although the eldest son, Orion, sent some money from St. Louis, where he was a journeyman printer at $10 a week, to the family in Hannibal, and although Mrs. Clemens took in boarders, the family's resources were stretched too thin. Thus, when a new weekly-newspaper office was established in Hannibal, Mrs. Clemens pulled Sam out of school and apprenticed him to the *Journal*. Sam found printing rather boring, but he enjoyed the people he lived and worked with at the shop. The boy became friends with an eighteen-year-old apprentice named Wales Macormick. The two apprentices, in traditional fashion, slept in the printing office, and they took their meals in the master's kitchen, where they were surrounded by the black slave cook and the cook's good-looking mulatto daughter. Wales pestered this girl so much that the apprentices were finally sent to eat in the dining room, where they ate with the family and a journeyman printer named Pet MacMurray. The hungry boys, however, discovered that the food in the dining room was no more plentiful than it had been in the kitchen. When the master's wife sweetened the coffee, she first dipped the sugar spoon in the coffee cup. Thus, a heaping spoonful of sugar came out of the sugar bowl but remained stuck to the spoon. In desperation the boys raided the cellar for potatoes and onions, which Wales cooked late at night over the office stove.[27]

To a small-town boy like Sam, the adventures of the tramping journeyman Pet MacMurray sounded fascinating. For a time Sam resolved to be just like Pet, and the journeyman had a pronounced effect upon the youth. One of the virtues of old-fashioned apprenticeship was the way in which it provided eager youths with easy role models. Two years passed, Sam learned to set type and pull a press, and Sam's older brother Orion left St. Louis to come to Hannibal to set up a small weekly newspaper. Orion borrowed $500 to take over a printing office, and he brought Sam and a younger brother, Henry, into the shop to assist. The eleven-year-old Henry set type, but his work was very poor, and Sam spent much of his time correcting his brother's dirty copy. Sam believed that his older brother treated him unfairly by working him too hard, and on one occasion he ran away. Years later, in a letter to his friend and fellow author William Dean Howells, Sam noted that running away had turned out to be a big disappointment. Although Orion later realized that he had overworked Sam, such exploitation was in fact necessary to keep the office afloat. Even with Orion, Sam, and Henry working late nights, they could generate barely enough income to meet the overhead, and every year Orion had to beg or borrow the $50 that was the annual interest payment on the loan he had taken out to acquire the office; that $50 was more cash than the office saw during the entire year. As Sam's confidence in his ability as a printer grew, Orion's control of the shop became more and more oppressive. Finally, Sam resolved to leave and strike out on his own, like the tramping Pet MacMurray. But Sam knew his brother well enough to know that a straightforward departure would be resisted. So he arranged a visit to his sister Pamela in St. Louis, and then once in St. Louis he got a job as a journeyman, saved some money to travel, and tramped to the East.[28]

In the summer of 1853 the eighteen-year-old Sam Clemens visited New York, where he found work as a journeyman and went to the Crystal Palace world's fair. He earned $4 a week, but most of the money went for his board bill. He told his sister that he had kept his promise to his mother neither to drink nor to play cards and that he spent his evenings at the mechanics library, with its more than 4,000 books. Although he wrote that New York was an "abominable place," he kept postponing his departure. He was nearly mesmerized by the city's charms; one evening, for example, he went to the theater and was entranced by the legendary Edwin Forrest. Amid all the glitter of the big city, how was the boy from Hannibal faring? He offered his sister reassurances. "For if you have a brother nearly eighteen years of age who is not able to take care of himself a few miles from home," he wrote, "such a brother is not worth one's thoughts." Although Sam had come from the world of traditional artisans, it did not take him long to assume the assertive style of city youths. He assured her that he could "take care of *No. 1*." He added, "I am not afraid, however. I shall ask favors from no one, and endeavor to be (and shall be) as 'independent as a wood-sawyer's clerk.' "[29]

Later that month Sam drifted down to Philadelphia, where he wrote his brother Orion expressing concern about the news that Orion had sold the Hannibal newspaper. Sam said that he wanted to send some money home to his mother but was uncertain whether Mrs. Clemens was still in Hannibal. Sam could easily realize that it was his departure from Hannibal that had forced Orion to sell the office. Perhaps that was why no one in the family would write him letters. In any event, he liked Philadelphia better than New York, and he preferred being paid in minted gold rather than in wildcat bank notes that had been heavily discounted. At the *Inquirer* office, where Sam subbed, he was dismayed to find that he was one of the slowest typesetters. Despite this discouraging discovery, Sam claimed that he liked being away from Hannibal in a large and exciting city. Not everything about Philadelphia, however, met with Sam's approval, and he disliked particularly the large number of immigrants. Many were at work even in the printing offices; he estimated that half the *North American* printers were foreign-born. By December he was homesick for Missouri, but he had just spent his savings on clothes, and it would take him time to save enough money to travel.[30]

It was months later when Sam made his way back to St. Louis, visited his sister, and then went on to Muscatine, Iowa, where Orion had taken a small printing office. Orion was unable (or unwilling) to hire Sam, and young Clemens went to St. Louis and worked as a journeyman. Then Orion gave up the Muscatine office, married a woman from Keokuk, Iowa, and settled in that town, where he opened a job printing office. Sam quit his job in St. Louis and went to work for Orion, who offered high pay, but like Orion's other promises, the extravagance of his language was contradicted by the poverty of his circumstances. For a time Sam was put in charge of printing the first Keokuk city directory, in which he indulged in a joke by listing himself as an "antiquarian." Sam basically solicited job work, but he found that his calculations about how long it would take to complete a job were constantly being upset by Orion's orders to the staff. His brother Henry and another typesetter were either very lazy or very slow, and the impatient Sam became exasperated. His brother's career was going nowhere, his own career was going nowhere, and in a flight of fancy reminiscent of the gold rush years Sam Clemens decided to go to South America and strike it rich in the Amazon.

Confiding his secret plans to his mother, he was advised not to tell Orion, who would be irate at Sam's impractical dreams, and so Sam told Orion only that he wished to go to New York to work. The youth found a $50 bill in the street, and he made his way to Cincinnati, where he worked as a journeyman for several months. He took all his savings—$100—and boarded a steamboat bound for New Orleans, where he planned to sail for Brazil. But on board the boat he fell to talking with the pilot, Horace Bixby, and decided to become a river pilot. The work was challenging, adventurous, and somewhat dangerous, but its greatest appeal to the journeyman printer Sam Clemens was a combination of autonomy and high wages. The pilot was, in many respects, master of the vessel; he was no flunky journeyman under orders. And a pilot made from $100 to $500 a month, a journeyman printer only $40 a month. Sam Clemens never set type again.[31]

What is surprising is not that Sam Clemens left printing but that a sense of family obligation had kept him at the trade for so long. Lewis Brewster, Will Howells, and Sam Bowles had been bound by family obligation to the trade of their fathers, and even John Gregory had avoided any action that could be construed as an affront to the family, its interests, or its ideals. In all these cases it was family ties that had kept the artisan tradition of apprenticeship intact, and to the extent that apprenticeship was an institution that operated within the family, it survived so long as small-scale family businesses could be passed from generation to generation. Although family businesses continued to survive and even prosper, especially in rural areas, they formed a dwindling proportion of an overall economy increasingly dominated by large-scale enterprises. Such large businesses could give youths jobs, but they could not offer any expectation of economic independence, and to the extent that fathers had become wageworkers in factories or mills, sons had little reason to expect that they would transcend the paternal model. Apprenticeship, then, had become a mere shadow of its former self, which cast ghostlike reminders of former glory across a world now largely composed of the new, hard industrial age.

Civil War

In 1846, when the United States went to war against Mexico, apprentices, observed Herman Melville, were "running off to the wars by scores." Fifteen years later, when the Civil War broke out, apprentices in both North and South again rushed to enlist. In Galveston, Texas, the thirteen-year-old apprentice printer Albert R. Parsons told his master that he wanted to join Robert E. Lee in Virginia. The employer told the boy to forget the idea, since the war would be over in sixty days. "I will," boasted the master, "hold in my hat all the blood that's shed in this war." That boast only made Albert determined to enlist before it was too late, so he ran away to join an older brother's artillery company. In New York another apprentice printer, eighteen-year-old Edmund F. Hartshorn, was sufficiently outraged by South Carolina's attack on the American flag at Fort Sumter that he overcame his own southern birth and family ties to heed Lincoln's call for 75,000 volunteers. The enlistment of youths like Hartshorn left many vacancies in the printing industry, and among those who gained a job was fifteen-year-old Charles H. Taylor. In 1861 that youth quit school to work in a series of Boston printing offices. Once he dropped two galleys of type on the stairs, and he was certain that he would be fired, but amid the war's labor shortages, he was merely ordered to pick up and sort the types. Within a year Charles was setting type, working the press, and hauling newspapers to the train station for $3 a week—double his original wages. In 1862, just past his sixteenth birthday, Charles enlisted in the army. It was his second attempt, and he had to persuade his father to sign a statement that he was eighteen years old. Some apprentices got around the minimum-age requirement by inserting slips of paper marked "18" in their shoes and then swearing before the recruitment officers that they were "over 18."[1]

Another volunteer was George Westinghouse, Jr. Born in 1846, he was the son of a Schenectady machinist and inventor. George and his older brothers all worked in the shop, but George often quarreled and sometimes daydreamed. After a couple of years, the father confronted his wayward son with his idleness and contrasted it with the enterprise shown by the shop's journeymen. George explained that whereas the men were paid for their work, he had been given no incentives. So George got paid. In 1860 George began at fifty cents a day; a year later his pay was raised to seventy-five cents a day, and then to $1.12. Meanwhile, the war had broken out, and his older brothers John and Albert had declared that they wanted to enlist. The elder Westinghouse counseled patience and advised against it, and the two sons yielded to their father's wishes. Noting what had happened, George decided to avoid a parental prohibition by running away to enlist. One day the youth made his way to the railroad station carrying a carpetbag. That morning George's mother, wanting him for some errand, had observed that his schoolbooks were at home, and she learned from a neighbor that the youth had been seen walking toward the station. George's father rushed to the station, ordered the conductor to halt the train, which was about to depart, and found his son. "George," he said, "I guess you'd better come back home!" At dinner the father told his son that he could enlist if the war continued. In 1862 brother Albert joined the army, and a year later John got a navy commission. In September 1863 the seventeen-year-old George enlisted. One-third of the Union army's soldiers were under the age of twenty-one, and one-quarter were artisans. Among American-born apprentice artisans an overwhelming majority—perhaps 90 percent—participated in the Civil War.[2]

To apprentices the war had an almost irresistible charm. The records of the Baldwin Locomotive Works in Philadelphia speak clearly to this point. Before the war, the firm had used a standard indenture form for its apprentices. It promised them medical benefits, training in a specific craft, $2.25 to $3.25 a week for five years, and a bonus of $130 upon completion of the apprenticeship. After the war began, the company altered its indentures. In August 1861 the firm reserved "the right (in case of disorderly conduct or violation of any rules of the shop) of withholding such sum or sums from the above-named wages as they may think proper, and also, of discharging the said [apprentice] entirely from their service." Indentures that allowed the employer to discharge the employee at will were a far cry from the apprenticeship of an earlier day. The pressures of war were taking their toll on what remained of the institution. As the war continued, the pressures increased. By August 1863 so many Baldwin apprentices had enlisted that the firm was in disarray, and a complete listing was made of all youths taken as apprentices since 1857. The five apprentices taken in 1857 had finished their apprenticeships in normal fashion, but this was not true of later apprentices. Of eighty-eight apprentices taken from 1858 through 1862, only three had completed their terms. And of the remaining eighty-five only forty-eight continued to be employed by the firm. One had died, three had run away, five had left with permission, seven had been discharged, and twenty-four had enlisted. Not only had the firm lost more than a quarter of its apprentices to the army, but the wartime boom among machinists had encouraged apprentices to run away or be dismissed in order to obtain high-paid journeyman's jobs at other firms.[3]

It is difficult to reconstruct the atmosphere that compelled so many youths to rush to adventure and glory at the risk of destruction. The cynic might observe that the working conditions in the Baldwin Works were such that even the rigors of the army promised to be an improvement. But trading the life of an industrial operative for that of an army private cannot be explained simply as the exchange of one difficult and lowly place for another. What drove youths into the army, in addition to enlistment bonuses, was not so much the desire to escape from industrial life as the prospect of transcending it. One could cease to be a boy and become a man. One could risk one's life, prove bravery and courage, and rise above the common herd that one belonged to as an apprentice in the machine age. One could become somebody. Even in the old days, during the Revolutionary War, apprentices had clamored to enlist. All the old reasons remained, and they were now joined by new ones. An apprentice saw at the end of his training a lifetime of working for a company as an employee. Joining the army was a way to escape thinking about that prospect. In the army he might test his mettle as a man outside the industrial system, and he might win a battlefield commission and become an officer, a gentleman, and a hero. But even if he did not, he would have the satisfaction of having participated in a cause larger than himself. Craft consciousness, in other words, was displaced by patriotism, and the apprentices, journeymen, and masters who had marched together in ranks arranged by craft at the celebration of the adoption of the Constitution now marched in a different order. Apprentices and journeymen from all crafts mingled to form ranks arranged by military regiment. The modern nation had triumphed over the artisan tradition.[4]

Patriotism rallied youths in a world gone awry. Stripped of the dignity of craftsmanship, conscious of the limits of journeyman status, dehumanized by industrial processes, and devoid of a master's fatherly cares, apprentices increasingly lived in a world in which their livelihoods mattered less and less except in the strictest sense of employment. Yet the age-old need of youths for pride of craft, for aspirations of autonomy, and for familial feelings had to be met. Competence, self-control, destiny, and camaraderie could be obtained through a patriotism expressed in military service in time of national peril. In both North and South, apprentices rallied to the flag just as artisan ancestors might have rallied to the defense of the guild. The country became the larger cause that absorbed all those energies traditionally expressed through an institution now moribund and dead. And the country's cause absorbed those energies through the discipline of the machine age. Apprentices trained in firms like the Baldwin Works made a new kind of soldier. The new soldier instinctively thought of himself as a part of a vast war machine, a cog in a wheel within a wheel. "The mechanic," George R. Russell observed, "makes a good soldier. The transition from the hammer to the musket is not unnatural, and sinews which have hardened in unremitting toil care little for the fatigues of the field." But there was more: "Men, accustomed to system and regularity, fall easily into the discipline and privations of military life." The artisan accepted the discipline of an industrial system that would have appalled and frightened his Revolutionary War ancestors, and he became a part of the modern mass machinery of war. Charles Taylor recalled that the war had given him increased self-confidence, and George Westinghouse said that it had given him self-discipline and "a spirit of readiness to carry out the instruction of superiors." Here then was the end of old-style apprenticeship and the emergence of the modern nation, the transformation of the youthful craftsman into the industrial worker, and the crystallization of a psychology that, for better or worse, would dominate the next century.[5]

The recruitment of apprentices into the army and swollen production to meet military needs left much of the American economy crying for labor. At the same time, the war reduced immigration from Europe. The result was a wartime labor shortage and soaring wages. In 1864 the Manchester, New Hampshire, *Dollar Weekly Mirror* commented, "We have never known such a demand for laborers of all kinds in this city as now . . . those that never worked a day in the mills, find steady employment, at an advance of from 25 to 35 percent above former prices." Employers hired anyone they could, including boys too young to join the army. Artisans watched the cost of living rise, noticed the handsome profits of employers, and began to organize labor unions to increase their own wages. During the war machinists, under the leadership of William H. Sylvis, were able to establish a strong national union, and printers were not far behind. In each case one of the principal goals of the union was to limit the number of apprentices, and thus the number of future journeymen. During the war the unions tried new strategies to keep the increased number of apprentices under their control. In 1861 Troy, New York, iron molders admitted apprentices to membership, and the following year the national printers union recommended that apprentices be allowed to participate in local unions. Labor leaders recognized that wartime labor shortages dictated an increase in apprentices to meet production demands, but they were determined to control this unpredictable and unskilled labor force at the end of the war, when large numbers of soldiering artisans would be looking for work. While skilled workmen who remained on the job prospered, the large numbers of apprentices meant that few youths were being trained properly, and, besides, youths tended to quit apprenticeships early either to join the army or to take journeyman's positions before they had learned a complete craft.[6]

The war accelerated the decline of apprenticeship. One woman, desperately trying to place her grandson, lamented that it was "a hard matter to get anyone to take on an apprentice at anything. They do not take them as they used to do. . . ." In 1863 the editor of *Fincher's Trades' Review,* a labor newspaper, complained that American apprentices emerged as "mere botches" because of short terms, lack of shop discipline, parental pressure for youths to quit apprenticeships to take jobs, and employers who taught their apprentices only part of a trade. Jonathan C. Fincher contrasted the situation with that of a quarter century earlier, when apprenticeship had encompassed both practical and moral training. All of that had been swept away. What remained, said Fincher, was increased "vice and rowdyism," as masters lost control of youths. "The question how to reform juvenile delinquency," he wrote, "is bound up in the support and increase of regular apprenticeship." Yet Fincher admitted that the large-scale factory precluded the possibility of a youth's living in the household of his employer. A year later, Fincher warned, "There is a lack of interest in the welfare of apprentices which must eventually lead to serious results." If youths were not trained properly in either work or morals, society would suffer from both incompetent craftsmanship and increased crime. "The sole ambition of every master," lamented Fincher, "seems to be to get as much work out of his apprentices as he can, with the least possible cost." The master controlled his apprentice only during the working day. The rest of the time the youth ran at large with whatever company he wanted, and he boarded wherever he pleased. At the end of the week the youth took his wages to his parents but held back "more spending money than he ought to have control of." The result was premature independence and a flirtation with moral ruin.[7]

During the war employers used apprentices as strikebreakers, and when orders for military goods began to fall off toward the end of the war, journeymen were sometimes laid off while apprentices were kept on. But the most remarkable development during the war was the use of indentures as a device to obtain and hold youths to unskilled factory labor. Employers created indentures that merely provided for employment, without promising any education or training in a skilled craft. Labor leaders compared such contracts to southern slavery, and in 1863 a Pennsylvania trial-court judge agreed with this view. An apprentice agreement, stressed the judge, had to be a contract for mutual benefit. When indentures provided that an employer would pay a youth for unspecified labor whenever the employer happened to be operating and left the youth to fend for himself when ill or unemployed, there was no mutual benefit. Such a document was simply too one-sided. This "new-fashioned indenture," said Jonathan Fincher, "was framed entirely for the benefit of the master." Despite the Pennsylvania court ruling, employers continued to use such indentures. In an industrial system inexorably moving toward a concentration of capital and a devaluation of skills, that result could hardly be surprising. But publicity about the "bogus indenture" must have caused both youths and parents to have second thoughts about signing any indentures. If one was going to be a factory drudge, it was better not to be indented. And so, amid wartime chaos in which bogus apprenticeship often could not be distinguished from the genuine article, the entire apprentice system faltered.[8]

In 1862 Joel Chandler Harris became an apprentice printer for *The Countryman*, an unusual newspaper published on a large-scale plantation in rural Georgia. He was not indented. The teenage Joel quickly learned to set type and to pull the old handpress, and he also became enamored of the woods, the plantation hat works, the library in his master's house, and Uncle George Terrell, the slave who became the model for Uncle Remus. Despite rural tranquillity, the youth could not help noticing the war; the departure of local recruits from the Eatonton railroad station had brought tears to Joel's eyes. In a composition book he wrote, "The past is like a dream of cloudless skies. While the future looms up before us, a reality, a startling reality." The war could drive him to fury, as when he planned a play concerning Gen. Benjamin Butler's capture of New Orleans, to be entitled "Butler the Beast." On another occasion Joel wrote a mock letter to President Lincoln promising to "draw his blood with a lead pill the first time he sets his peepers on him." The anger sometimes subsided into humor. In 1863 he slipped a riddle into the paper that asked, "Why do the Yankees delay their attack upon the chief Rebel port?" The answer was, "Because they find a Charles*ton* too heavy for their gunboats to *carry*." As the war dragged on, acquaintances and friends departed for the front, and all too often they were never seen again. Of Edward S. Davis's death he wrote, "And he is one among the thousand slain, for whose murder the Yankees will have to answer at the great day of Judgment." A letter from a friend brought more depressing news. "You ask me about the boys of those good old days," wrote the correspondent. "There has been sad changes since then. I suppose, however, you are posted as to the deaths among the boys. Eli Aubry & Jim Johnson were killed in the late fights at Spottsylvania C.H. Old Siddon you can't kill. Always foremost in the fight—he has passed through over a dozen fights unscathed. I don't know where Gordon Whiting can be. He was nearly dead from consumption the last I heard of him."[9]

As the war ground on, Joel noticed inflation, shortages, and the pressures of conscription. There is some evidence that Joel falsified his age to make it easier for him to sit out the war. In any event, his master had to certify that each member of the seven-man printing office was exempt; beside Joel's name was the notation that the youth was "frail and feeble." He was also called a compositor, an occupation specifically exempted from military service by Confederate law. When the Confederate congress considered removing the exemption, Joel wrote an essay bitterly accusing the government of seeking to destroy a free press and turn printing into a craft for blacks. From time to time Joel toyed with the idea of leaving *The Countryman* for a journeyman's position elsewhere. When young Harris made inquiries to W. F. Williams, his friend in Columbus replied, "You say you want work down here. I should be delighted if you would come, as I am bored to death with the society with which I am compelled to associate. The boys in the office are clever (in the American sense of the word) enough but with a few exceptions stupid wooden heads." However, at the time there were no vacancies. Williams suggested that Harris try Macon, but he warned, "You will have to work, work all the time, day and night, and you would soon get tired of it." Toward the end of the war, as Sherman pressed closer to Middle Georgia, Joel went to Eatonton for a visit. He found the town strange—under martial law, plagued with smallpox, and filled with wounded soldiers and refugees from North Georgia. When he met a veteran who had rushed eagerly to war three years earlier, Joel was shocked by the man's worn looks. In November the Yankees came and stripped the plantation of stock and food. Joel kept a German soldier from carrying off hats from the plantation hat works, and the irritated soldier retaliated by trying to burn the shop. To Joel's amusement, the soldier was stopped by an officer. Joel experienced the invasion as a wild dream, and all was soon changed. Gone was the Confederacy, slavery, and *The Countryman,* and with the paper went Joel's job.[10]

At the end of the war two million soldiers returned home to look for work, and they were joined by others who had been employed in wartime industries. Labor leaders, aware of the glutted labor market, advocated policies to reduce the glut. They favored western homesteading, the establishment of an eight-hour working day, and a reform of apprenticeship. Strong unions, like those of the iron molders and the printers, demanded and got the right to control the proportion of apprentices that would be admitted into any shop. But labor leaders also recognized that, if apprenticeship was to survive, changes were needed in state laws. While the effort failed in New York, Pennsylvania, and Illinois, some changes were made in Massachusetts. There a legislative committee appointed to investigate the situation reported that indenturing had fallen into general disuse. The reason, the committee thought, was that the 1794 Apprentice Law gave employers little reason to sign indentures. The old law emphasized the capture of runaway apprentices, whereas modern employers did not particularly care to have absconding youths returned. In most trades the proportion of skilled workmen had declined, and in some trades all the journeymen were foreigners, because no Americans learned the craft. In any event, in 1865 the legislature repealed the legal sanctions pertaining to runaways. This modification of the law left masters without any legal recourse against runaway apprentices, and Massachusetts in effect removed any reason for employers to want to sign indentures. After the war several state courts discouraged indentures in another way by overturning Revolutionary War precedents and ruling that an apprentice who enlisted in the military dissolved his apprenticeship, voided the indentures, and was entitled to receive bounty money without interference from his master. These rulings, which favored public needs over the private rights of the master, discouraged indentures, since a master ran the risk that, in the event of war, his apprentice might enlist without any compensation to the master.[11]

A changing psychology also played a role in what was happening. In 1860 Henry Ashworth visited Washington, D.C. One morning the English traveler was stopped in front of his hotel by an American boy, who politely asked if Ashworth would like a morning newspaper. Ashworth said yes, and the boy disappeared and quickly returned with a paper. The Englishman handed the boy a nickel for the two-cent newspaper, and the boy started away, until Ashworth called him back to demand his change. The boy said that he charged three cents for delivery, and when Ashworth protested, the boy said, "Here's the money, and if you think my charge too much, you can give me back the paper, and fetch one yourself." It is not easy to contemplate such a boy as an apprentice bowing and scraping before his master, weeding the garden, and chopping firewood on command. That youth heard not the call of Ben Franklin but the cry of Horatio Alger. And there were many like him. "The opportu-

YOUNG AMERICA ON HIS DIGNITY
OLD AMERICA—Another impertinent word and I'll box your ears!
YOUNG AMERICA—Lay your hand upon me, Sir, and I abandon your roof forever.

nities for a young man in New England to make his own way in the world, from eighteen years upwards," said the Massachusetts Board of State Charities, "are so great that few can resist the temptation of them." By the time Terence V. Powderly became an apprentice machinist in the late 1860s, it was all that that youth could do to restrain himself from publicly ridiculing the bosses in the shop. Instead, young Powderly expressed his contempt in his diary, where he wrote such lines as "had another blow up with old Dixon. Told him to give me my time but he didn't" or "old man Dixon very mad." He thought the bosses "all jackasses," and upon completion of his apprenticeship he did not celebrate but merely noted "three years ago today went to work." Three days later he was laid off. The master had become the boss, craftsmanship had become work, and a youth's mind was preoccupied with wages and unemployment—two words an old-time apprentice had never heard.[12]

In 1865 a reporter described how modern apprenticeship was conducted. An employer might say, "William, how would you like to let your Harry come here to learn his trade? You know he must have one."

The father replied, "Well, Mr. B., I know Harry must learn a trade, and would like him to get a good place. How do you take apprentices, and what wages do you give them?"

"Well, we take them on easy terms. We do not wish to have your boy bound by law just take his promise to stay."

"Yes, Mr. B., but there's no security of his staying or of your giving him his trade."

"O! yes, there is. We keep the boy's first year's wages back, and he will be pretty sure to stay and be a good boy, for if he goes away before his time is up or is a bad boy, he forfeits his 'back money.' "

"Oh! What do you give a boy a week?"

"$3."

"And you can turn him off whenever he offends you?"

"Well no—yes—that is if he is a bad boy we can; but you know he can go, too, whenever he wishes."

"Yes, and lose his wages; but suppose I were to die before he is free— $3 will not clothe him and pay his board; or suppose he were to take sick—you stop his wages—what is to keep the boy?"

"Well, William, you are rather particular. I must say you know that if he is a good boy we would not see him want."

"No, Mr. B., I know nothing of the kind. I only have your word for it, and that would soon be forgotten if anything should happen." The father went on to object that without indentures the youth would have no legal recourse if he were not taught the trade, that nothing would prevent the youth from being laid off in slack times, and that the employer might use trickery to retain the held-back wages. Yet such apprenticeships, said the reporter, were now commonplace.[13]

The postwar years brought further signs of the entrenchment of the new industrial system. While traditional apprenticeship continued to thrive in the building trades, it gave way to exploited and unskilled child labor throughout manufacturing. As early as 1865 one artisan told the Massachusetts legislature, "I have a son; and sooner than see him a mechanic, to suffer as I have; to toil worse than a slave, and with a low and degraded social standard, I would see him in his grave." That same year another artisan ridiculed the proposed changes in Massachusetts law governing apprentices by asking, "Is it possible that the mechanics of New England . . . can think of no better remedy . . . than to . . . exhume the decomposed carcass of a system as odious (as far as it goes) as slavery itself, and totally unAmerican in its character?" As one might guess, the author of that remark had had a very unsatisfactory, exploited apprenticeship. He disparaged the attempt "to reinstate a system which has long since disappeared from the surface of society, simply because it belongs not to American civilization." But other mechanics disagreed. With all its imperfections, asserted one artisan, apprenticeship was preferable to "the utter chaos that now reigns throughout all mechanical business." In every civilized society there was "subordination of the young to laws of order, enacted by the wise and good for their instruction and government." The writer saw a connection between rising chaos and the declining status of artisans. On that point there was widespread agreement. In testimony before the Massachusetts legislature, a machinist said, "Under the present arrangement boys are not as likely to go to trades as formerly. The disposition of parents at the present day is to put their boys into stores, as it is more respectable."[14]

In the decade after the war apprenticeship all but disappeared. Observers noted its "virtual abandonment," called it "nearly if not quite obsolete," and declared it "next to impossible to get a boy a situation to learn a trade." Instead, boys were hired as unskilled laborers—a policy that alarmed labor leaders. In 1866 a Baltimore labor congress called the entry of youths into trades without regulation "suicidal," and a year later a Chicago labor meeting reached similar conclusions. Young Americans were also aware of what was happening; one apprentice blacksmith wrote, "All i can here is hard times and worse acoming." In 1869 the Massachusetts Charitable Mechanics Association surveyed its members on the subject of apprenticeship. Of fifty-two master craftsmen who answered the association's questionnaire, forty-six had served apprenticeships. Although these masters had served an average five years, only six of them had been indented. They were from that in-between generation during which indenting ceased while apprenticeship lingered, and their situation contrasted with the experience of the next generation. That apprenticeship was in decline was clear from the fact that of these fifty-two master craftsmen only twenty-seven currently employed apprentices. While eleven employers had had good experiences with apprentices, seven reported mixed experiences, and nineteen were negative, calling apprentices "trouble," "no advantage," or "more plague than profit." The lack of apprenticeships led to shortages of skilled labor in some trades and to surpluses of unskilled labor. In many poor families sons were sent to work in factories at early ages and were unable to obtain apprenticeships; in other cases youths considered prospects better in the mercantile world than in crafts. Entire fields were devoid of apprentices. Tailoring, for example, had been abandoned, and most tailors were foreign-born. By the 1880s in Massachusetts the ratio of apprentices to journeymen in the building trades had fallen to one to fifty—below the ratio set by labor unions and far below the ratio needed for replacement. Immigrants and the sons of immigrants increasingly filled the ranks of skilled craftsmen, and by the turn of the century they were to dominate many crafts in many locales.[15]

In the end old-fashioned apprenticeship was swept away by a wave of change that engulfed traditional society and its artisan culture through the power of concentrated capital, the genius of mechanical innovation, and the ideology of individualism and self-help. Gone was the intricate and carefully balanced social fabric that had both comforted and constricted youths as they learned to become adults at work and in the family. Gone was a support network of custom and the master's rules that governed the lives of the young. Gone were the old rules for learning how to grow up. In the place of apprenticeship with its semibondage was a mixture of new attitudes and new institutions. Youths were encouraged to think for themselves, to push ahead on their own at their own pace, to become entrepreneurs, and to rise, like Horatio Alger's characters, to moral and financial success. To help them get ahead, the American public school created a more wide-ranging, creative, and flexible system for the education of the young than apprenticeship ever had offered. And American religious values of the mid and late nineteenth century reinforced the notion of personal responsibility for one's life. Yet the price paid for these changes was high. Many youths could not live up to the more demanding personal responsibility that the new system dictated, and when they failed, the society was so fluid and shapeless that they could find no support to grasp. For some the end of apprenticeship meant an education and success in business or the professions; for others it meant a life sentence at low wages in a factory; and for still others it meant becoming a street urchin and drifting into crime, drugs, and an early death. The decline of social order alarmed many, but no one could put the humpty-dumpty of apprenticeship together again. And so today we retain the legacy of disgruntled youths and perplexing delinquency. We are left with a present that does not work and a past that is lost. What we have gained is freedom, but the cost was high.

STATISTICAL APPENDIX

TABLE 1. Frederick County, Maryland, Indentures, 1795–1864

Years	White Males 15<20	Average Number Bound per Year	%WM of Those Bound	Average Number WM Bound per Year	Average Number WM Bound per 5-Yr Term	%WM 15<20 Bound	%WM 15<20 Bound if 30% Labor Is Non-Ag.
1795–1804	1411e	58	90	52	260	18.4	61.5
1805–1814	1563e	77	92	71	355	22.7	75.7
1815–1824	1839e	57	68	39	195	10.6	35.3
1825–1834	1998	42	79	33	165	8.3	27.5
1835–1844	1605	30	64	19	95	5.9	19.7
1845–1854	1826	17	53	9	45	2.5	8.2
1855–1864	2180	14	29	4	20	.9	3.1

e = estimated

SOURCES: U.S. Census, 1830, *Fifth Census* (Wash., 1832), 8–9, 82–83; U.S. Census, 1840, *Compendium of the Enumeration of the Inhabitants and Statistics of the United States* (Wash., 1841), 28–31; U.S. Census, 1850, *The Seventh Census of the United States: 1850* (Wash., 1853), 218–20; U.S. Census, 1860, *Population of the United States in 1860* (Wash., 1864), 210–17; Apprentice Indentures, Register of Wills, Frederick County, Maryland, 1794–1874, 8 MS vols., Maryland Hall of Records.

TABLE 2. Disposition of White Males Apprenticed from the New York House of Refuge, in Percentages

Years	Farms	Crafts	Sea	Merchants	Military	N
1832–1837*	41	36	23	0	0	522
1838–1842	67	29	3	1	0	486
1843–1847	61	27	12	0	0	684
1848–1852	50	39	9	3	0	1004
1853–1857	62	33	2	4	0	1086
1858–1860	60	30	2	8	0	717
1861–1862	42	12	1	3	43	401

* no data for 1836
SOURCES: Society for the Reformation of Juvenile Delinquents, *Annual Reports*, 1833–1836, 1838–1863.

TABLE 3. Educational Level of Admittees to New York House of Refuge, in Percentages

	1838	1851
Did not know alphabet	13	15
Could spell and read two-letter words	32	24
Could read easy lessons	32	44
Could read in books generally	19	9
Could read well	3	7
Knew no arithmetic	97	75
Started with subtraction	3	4
Started with multiplication	0	7
Started with division	0	6
Knew advanced arithmetic	0	7
N	116	327

SOURCES: Society for the Reformation of Juvenile Delinquents, *Fourteenth Annual Report* (1839), 18; *Twenty-Seventh Annual Report* (1852), 13.

✌ NOTES ✌

Abbreviations

AAS	American Antiquarian Society, Worcester, Massachusetts
AHR	*American Historical Review*
APS	American Philosophical Society
DH	*Delaware History*
HML	Hagley Museum and Library, Wilmington, Delaware
HSD	Historical Society of Delaware
HSP	Historical Society of Pennsylvania
JEH	*Journal of Economic History*
LC	Library of Congress
LCP	Library Company of Philadelphia
LH	*Labor History*
LSU	Louisiana State University
MESDA	Museum of Early Southern Decorative Arts, Winston-Salem, North Carolina
MHS	Massachusetts Historical Society
NCSA	North Carolina State Archives
NHHS	New Hampshire Historical Society, Concord
N-YHS	New-York Historical Society
NYPL	New York Public Library
PMHB	*Pennsylvania Magazine of History and Biography*
S-CHS	South-Carolina Historical Society, Charleston
SCL	South Caroliniana Library, Columbia
SHC	Southern Historical Collection, University of North Carolina, Chapel Hill
WMQ	*William and Mary Quarterly*, 3d series

Preface

1. See Mary Adams's correspondence negotiating an apprenticeship in tailoring, in Jo Anne Preston, ed., " 'To Learn Me the Whole of the Trade': Conflict between a Female Apprentice and a Merchant Tailor in Ante-Bellum New England," *LH*, 24 (1983), 259–73.

2. Phinehas S. Bradley Diary, 1813–1816, Manuscript Collection, Yale Univ.

3. Lawrence W. Towner, "A Good Master Well Served: A Social History of Servitude in Massachusetts, 1620–1750" (Ph.D. thesis, Northwestern Univ., 1955). Towner's work was continued in "The Indentures of Boston's Poor Apprentices: 1734–1805," Colonial Soc. of Mass., *Publications*, 43 (1966), 417–68. Ian M. G.

Quimby, "Apprenticeship in Colonial Philadelphia" (M.A. thesis, Univ. of Delaware, 1963). David T. Ruddel, "Apprenticeship in Early Nineteenth Century Quebec, 1793–1815" (M.A. thesis, Univ. of Laval, 1969), translated into French and published in Jean P. Hardy and David T. Ruddel, *Les apprentis artisans à Québec, 1660–1815* (Montreal, 1977). See Prologue, n. 7.

Prologue

1. Throughout this chapter material on Franklin has been drawn from his autobiography. For a chronology of Franklin's early life see Benjamin Franklin, *Papers,* ed. Leonard W. Labaree (New Haven, 1959–ㅤ), 1:lxxxvii–lxxxviii. The standard biography is Carl Van Doren, *Benjamin Franklin* (N.Y., 1938). I also have profited from David Levin, "The Autobiography of Benjamin Franklin," *Yale Rev.,* 53 (1963), 258–75; Henry P. Rosemont, "Benjamin Franklin and the Philadelphia Typographical Strikers of 1786," *LH,* 22 (1981), 398–429; John W. Ward, "Who Was Benjamin Franklin?" *Am. Scholar,* 32 (1963), 541–53; introd. to Clarence W. Miller, *Benjamin Franklin's Philadelphia Printing, 1728–1766* (Phila., 1974).

2. A concise statement is in Lawrence A. Cremin, *American Education: The Colonial Experience, 1607–1783* (N.Y., 1970), 121–22. On England see Olive J. Dunlop, *English Apprenticeship and Child Labour* (London, 1912); Margaret G. Davies, *The Enforcement of English Apprenticeship* (Cambridge, Mass., 1956); Harold Perkin, *The Origins of Modern English Society* (London, 1969), 188–89; E. P. Thompson, *The Making of the English Working Class* (N.Y., 1964); C. R. Dobson, *Masters and Journeymen* (London, 1980); P. E. Razzle and R. W. Wainwright, eds., *The Victorian Working Class* (London, 1973), 123–24, 140, 157; David Vincent, *Bread, Knowledge and Freedom* (London, 1981). On France see Sarah C. Maza, *Servants and Masters in Eighteenth-Century France* (Princeton, 1983); Robert Darnton, *The Business of Enlightenment* (Cambridge, Mass., 1979), 177–245; William H. Sewell, Jr., *Work and Revolution in France* (Cambridge, Eng., 1980); Craig J. Calhoun, "Industrialization and Social Radicalism," *Theory and Society,* 12 (1983), 485–504; Craig J. Calhoun, "The Radicalism of Tradition," *Am. J. Sociology,* 88 (1983), 886–914. On Germany see Mack Walker, *German Home Towns* (Ithaca, 1971), 73–107, 433–51. On poor law apprentices in America see below, n. 7.

3. American case law followed English precedents. See Richard B. Morris, ed., *Select Cases of the Mayor's Court of New York City, 1674–1784* (Wash., 1935), 9, 28–31, 182–89. There are some astute observations in William E. Nelson, *Americanization of the Common Law* (Cambridge, Mass., 1975), 51. See also Thomas C. Cochran, *Frontiers of Change* (N.Y., 1981), 9–10, 12; Richard B. Morris, *Government and Labor in Early America* (N.Y., 1946). On workmanship see Harold E. Davis, *The Fledgling Province* (Chapel Hill, 1976), 95–99, 109 (quote); Peter C. Marzio, "Carpentry in the Southern Colonies during the Eighteenth Century with Emphasis on Maryland and Virginia," *Winterthur Portfolio,* 7 (1972), 240–41.

4. Gary B. Nash, *The Urban Crucible* (Cambridge, Mass., 1979), 13–20, 59–63, 104, 114, 117–18, 120–22, 124. See also Billy G. Smith, "Struggles of the 'Lower Sort': The Lives of Philadelphia's Laboring People, 1750 to 1800" (Ph.D.

thesis, UCLA, 1981), 73–143, 147, 172, 174, 194; Allan Kulikoff, "The Progress of Inequality in Revolutionary Boston," *WMQ*, 28 (1971), 375–412; Jackson T. Main, *The Social Structure of Revolutionary America* (Princeton, 1965), 79–82.

5. In general see Carl Bridenbaugh, *The Colonial Craftsman* (N.Y., 1950); Nash, *Urban Crucible*, 16–17. (tailors) Main, *Social Structure*, 275; (shoemakers) John R. Commons, "American Shoemakers, 1648–1895," *Q. J. Econ.*, 24 (1910), 39–83; Blanche E. Hazard, *The Organization of the Boot and Shoe Industry in Massachusetts before 1875* (Cambridge, Mass., 1921); John P. Hall, "The Gentle Craft: A Narrative of Yankee Shoemakers" (Ph.D. thesis, Columbia Univ., 1953). A good biographical sketch is in Alfred F. Young, "George Robert Twelves Hewes (1742–1840)," *WMQ*, 38 (1981), 561–623; (carpenters) Main, *Social Structure*, 76n, 77; William Whitteker, "Memorandum . . . ," *West Va. Hist.*, 1 (1940), 207–11; (blacksmiths) Main, *Social Structure*, 275; (silversmiths) Martha G. Fales, *Early American Silver*, rev. ed. (N.Y., 1973; orig., 1970), 131, 210; Peter Bohan and Philip Hammerslough, *Early Connecticut Silver, 1700–1840* (Middletown, 1970), 3, 5; E. Milby Burton, *South Carolina Silversmiths, 1690–1860* (Charleston, 1942), 183; Deborah D. Waters, " 'The Workmanship of an American Artist': Philadelphia's Precious Metals Trades and Craftsmen, 1788–1832" (Ph.D. thesis, Univ. of Delaware, 1981), 12–14; Hermann F. Clarke, *John Coney, Silversmith, 1655–1722* (Boston, 1932); C. Donald Dallas, *The Spirit of Paul Revere* (Princeton, 1944); Esther Forbes, *Paul Revere and the World He Lived In* (Boston, 1942).

6. The conclusion about fees is based on a comparison of American and English indentures and biographical accounts. See Burton, *South Carolina Silversmiths*, 183. A succinct statement about printing is in Stephen W. Botein, "Reluctant Partisans: The Role of Printers in Eighteenth-Century American Politics" (Ph.D. thesis, Harvard Univ., 1970), 253–54. More generally see Hellmut Lehmann-Haupt, ed., *The Book in America*, 2d ed. (N.Y., 1951; orig., 1939); William L. Joyce et al., eds., *Printing and Society in Early America* (Worcester, 1983).

7. Once an apprenticeship was completed, indentures had no value. Hence, few indentures have survived. Boston indentures, pertaining only to poor-law apprentices, were the basis of Towner's dissertation and of W. Graham Millar, "The Poor Apprentices of Boston: Indentures of Poor Children Bound Out Apprentice by the Overseers of the Poor of Boston, 1734–1776" (M.A. thesis, College of William and Mary, 1958). Philadelphia indentures for 1771–1773, many of which pertain to indentured servants, have been published in Pennsylvania-German Society, *Proceedings*, 16 (1907). Others are in manuscript at the Philadelphia Archives. They have been studied by Ian Quimby. New York City indentures for 1695–1707 and 1718–1727 have been published in N-YHS, *Collections*, 18 (1885), 565–622, and 42 (1910), 111–99. Others are loose at the Society. No more than a handful of indentures have been located for other early American jurisdictions. See Preface, n. 3.

8. Franklin's indentures have disappeared; my account is based on Franklin's autobiography and standard provisions in colonial indentures.

9. The best study of indentured servants is David W. Galenson, *White Servitude in Colonial America* (N.Y., 1981). On slaves see Marcus W. Jernegan, *Laboring and Dependent Classes in Colonial America, 1607–1783* (Chicago, 1931), 7–16; Richard Walsh, *Charleston's Sons of Liberty* (Columbia, S.C., 1959), 24–25; and this book, Chapter 9.

10. In general see Samuel McKee, Jr., *Labor in Colonial New York, 1664–1776* (N.Y., 1935), 27; Whitteker, "Memorandum," 207–11; Robert B. St. George, "Fathers, Sons, and Identity: Woodworking Artisans in Southeastern New England, 1620–1700," in *The Craftsman in Early America*, ed. Ian M. G. Quimby (N.Y., 1984), 102, 112–13, 121, 124. (Lanes) Samuel Lane, *A Journal for the Years 1739–1803*, ed. Charles L. Hanson (Concord, N.H., 1937), 1–2; contracts dated Dec. 29, 1746; May 15, 1755; June 10, 1777; Joshua Lane to Samuel Lane, Mar. 22, 1797; and genealogy, all in Lane Family Papers, NHHS; (Dunlaps) Charles S. Parsons, "The Dunlaps of New Hampshire and Their Furniture," in *Country Cabinetwork and Simple City Furniture*, ed. John D. Morse (Charlottesville, 1970), 109–50. See also Bernard Farber, *Guardians of Virtue* (N.Y., 1972), 96–105. (Dominys) Charles F. Hummel, *With Hammer in Hand* (Charlottesville, 1968). In Germantown, Pa., for the period 1771–1773, Stephanie G. Wolf, *Urban Village* (Princeton, 1976), 311, found only 10 apprentices to skilled crafts out of 9,000 in all of Philadelphia County.

11. John Fitch, *Autobiography*, ed. Frank D. Prager (Phila., 1976), 37 (quote), 38 (quote). For other colonial rural apprentices see Charles C. Sellers, *Charles Willson Peale* (Phila., 1947), 1:2, 23–24, 33, 35–44; Thomas B. Hazard, *Nailer Tom's Diary*, ed. Caroline Hazard (Boston, 1930).

12. Fitch, *Autobiography*, 41 (quote), 42 (quote).

13. A complete description of a printing shop is in Thomas F. Adams, *Typographia* (Phila., 1837), pt. 2. See also Lehmann-Haupt, *Book*, 25–26, 29; Milton W. Hamilton, *The Country Printer* (N.Y., 1936), 45; Thomas MacKellar, *The American Printer* (Phila., 1885; orig., 1866), 122. The minimum weight for a printer is in James S. Wamsley, *The Crafts of Williamsburg* (Williamsburg, 1982), 5.

14. MacKellar, *American Printer*, 121; Rollo G. Silver, *The American Printer, 1787–1825* (Charlottesville, 1967), 3; Hamilton, *Country Printer*, 32; Colin H. Bloy, *A History of Printing Ink, Balls and Rollers, 1440–1850* (London, 1967), 7–8.

15. On James Franklin's legal troubles see *New-England Courant*, Feb. 11, 1723, reprinted in Franklin, *Papers*, 1:47–50.

16. The prospect of printers in America was modest compared with that of printers in England. See Stephen W. Botein, " 'Meer Mechanics' and an Open Press," *Perspectives in Am. Hist.*, 9 (1975), 141.

17. Benjamin Franklin, *The Autobiography and Other Writings*, ed. L. Jesse Lemisch (N.Y., 1961), 34 (quote). Editions are listed in the Evans and Shaw-Shoemaker bibliographies. The autobiography was published separately twenty-nine times and in Franklin's works twenty-six times.

Chapter 1: Chaos

1. Stephen Allen, "The Memoirs of Stephen Allen (1767–1852)" (typescript), 37, N-YHS; Jerry L. Surratt, *Gottlieb Schober of Salem* (Macon, 1983), 22–23. See also McKee, *Labor*, 175; Morris, *Government and Labor*, 291–94; Charles G. Steffen, *The Mechanics of Baltimore* (Urbana, 1984), 53–80.

2. Francis Baylies, *Eulogy on the Hon. Benjamin Russell* (Boston, 1845), 7–8 (quote at 8). For another account of the episode see Joseph T. Buckingham, *Specimens of Newspaper Literature* (Boston, 1850), 2:3.

3. Baylies, *Russell*, 8–9.

4. Ibid., 9–12; Samuel L. Boardman, *Peter Edes* (Bangor, Maine, 1901), 15–16. On Edes's later career see Joseph Griffin, ed., *History of the Press of Maine* (Brunswick, Maine, 1872), 87–88.

5. Baylies, *Russell*, 12 (quote); Buckingham, *Specimens*, 2:5; Isaiah Thomas, "Diary . . . 1805–1828," ed. Benjamin T. Hill, AAS, *Transactions and Collections*, 9 (1909), 90n–91n.

6. Annie R. Marble, *From 'Prentice to Patron* (N.Y., 1935), esp. 97; Ebenezer S. Thomas, *Reminiscences of the Last Sixty Years* (Hartford, Conn., 1840), 2: 16–17. In general see Clifford K. Shipton, *Isaiah Thomas* (Rochester, 1948); Isaiah Thomas, *Three Autobiographical Fragments* (Worcester, 1962).

7. Thomas, *Three Fragments*, 7–13, 16, 18–20, 26 (quote at 18); Shipton, *Thomas*, 2–19; Marble, *Thomas*, 7–40, 50, 52–53, 85, 93; E. S. Thomas, *Reminiscences*, 2:16; Benjamin F. Thomas, *Memoir of Isaiah Thomas . . .* (Boston, 1874), 35; Baylies, *Russell*, 62 n. 1. See also Botein, "Meer Mechanics," esp. 131–56; John C. Oswald, *A History of Printing* (N.Y., 1928), 354.

8. Marble, *Thomas*, 94, 103, 136; Buckingham, *Specimens*, 2:5. The high quality of Thomas's work is best seen in an inspection of his imprints at the AAS.

9. John R. Bartlett, ed., *Records of the Colony of Rhode Island . . .* (Providence, 1862), 7:319; Worthington C. Ford, ed., *Journals of the Continental Congress, 1774–1789* (Wash., 1906), 4:103–4; 7:369; John Adams to Abigail Adams, Apr. 8–11, 1777, in L. H. Butterfield, ed., *Adams Family Correspondence* (Cambridge, Mass., 1963), 2:204. See also William W. Hening, ed., *The Statutes at Large* (Richmond, 1819–1823), 10:335–36; "Pa. War Office, May 5, 1777," *Pa. Packet, or the Gen. Advertiser,* May 6, 1777; Richard Smith Diary, Jan. 26, 27, 29, 30, 31, Feb. 14, 1776; Thomas Burke to Richard Caswell, Apr. 15, 1777, both in Paul H. Smith, ed., *Letters of Delegates to Congress, 1774–1789* (Wash., 1976), 3:157, 161, 167, 172, 175, 257; 6:581.

10. Ebenezer Fox, *The Adventures of Ebenezer Fox* (Boston, 1847), 45–49, 55 (quote at 47).

11. Ibid., 56, 58 (quote), 232n.

12. Salem Board Minutes, Feb. 6, 1782, in Adelaide L. Fries et al., eds., *Records of the Moravians in North Carolina* (Raleigh, 1922–1969), 4:1801; Allen, "Memoirs," 23.

13. Buckingham, *Specimens*, 2:6.

14. Ibid., 2:9; Thomas, "Diary," 9:91n; Baylies, *Russell,* 13. See also Benjamin Russell to Isaiah Thomas, Sept. 29, 1780, Richmond Collection, MHS.

15. Main, *Social Structure*, 66–67, 79–82, 186, 191, 193, 228 (quote); McKee, *Labor,* 16–17; Kulikoff, "Progress," 405–6; Eric Foner, *Tom Paine and Revolutionary America* (N.Y., 1976); Charles S. Olton, *Artisans for Independence* (Syracuse, 1975). See also Jonathan Plummer, *Something New* (Montpelier, Vt., 1808), 3–9; John P. Marquand, *Lord Timothy Dexter of Newburyport, Massts.* (N.Y., 1925); Samuel L. Knapp, *Life of Lord Timothy Dexter* (Boston, 1858); Roger S. Boardman, *Roger Sherman* (Phila., 1938); Forbes, *Revere;* Dallas, *Revere;* Noah Brooks, *Henry Knox* (N.Y., 1900); North Callahan, *Henry Knox* (N.Y., 1958); Francis S. Drake, *Life and Correspondence of Henry Knox* (Boston, 1873); Theodore Thayer, *Nathanael Greene* (N.Y., 1960); Francis V. Greene, *General Greene* (N.Y., 1898); William Johnson, *Sketches of the Life and Correspondence of Nathanael Greene* (Charleston, 1822); William G. Simms, *The*

Life of Nathanael Greene (N.Y., 1849). On naming see Richard Holmes, *Communities in Transition* (Ann Arbor, 1980), 176.

16. Devereux Jarrett, "Autobiography," *WMQ*, 9 (1952), 361; Robert Coram, "Political Inquiries" (1791), in *Essays on Education in the Early Republic*, ed. Frederick Rudolph (Cambridge, Mass., 1965), 139. See also Nathanael Emmons, *A Discourse, Delivered November 3, 1790* (Providence, 1790), esp. 19, 27; David Daggett, *An Oration, Pronounced in the Brick Meeting-House . . .* (New Haven, 1787); Josiah Bridge, *A Sermon Preached before His Excellency John Hancock, Esq. Governor* (Boston, 1789), 38. More generally see Edwin G. Burrows and Michael Wallace, "The American Revolution," *Perspectives in Am. Hist.*, 6 (1972), 287–89; Winthrop D. Jordan, "Familial Politics: Thomas Paine and the Killing of the King, 1776," *J. Am. Hist.*, 60 (1973), 294–308.

17. On the 1780s see Merrill Jensen, *The New Nation* (N.Y., 1950), 289–98. A newer, more sophisticated view is in Cochran, *Frontiers*, 38–44. On the shortage of apprentices in the 1790s see Waters, "Workmanship," 134. On Belknap's negotiations see Jeremy Belknap to Ebenezer Hazard, June 10, July 14, Sept. 1, 20, 29, Oct. 4, 12, 27, 31, Nov. 7, 1783, "Belknap Papers," MHS, *Collections*, 5th ser., 2 (1877), 215, 230–32, 244–46, 250, 257, 259, 262, 269–73; replies, Sept. 24, Oct. 8, 15, 1783, ibid., 256, 260–61, 266; John Eliot to JB, Sept. 18, 1783, "BP," 6th ser., 4 (1891), 263. On Bache's apprenticeship see Bernard Faÿ, *The Two Franklins* (Boston, 1933), esp. 62–65; Luther S. Livingston, *Franklin and His Press at Passy* (N.Y., 1914), 72–75, 109, 175; Benjamin Franklin Bache Diaries, 1782–1785, Bache Family Papers, APS. The quote is from Benjamin Franklin to Richard Bache, Nov. 11, 1784, BF, *Writings*, ed. Albert H. Smyth (N.Y., 1907), 9:279. See also BF, *Papers*, 1:lxiii; BF to Mary Hewson, Jan. 12, 1777; to Richard Bache, June 2, 1779; to Sarah Bache, June 3, 1779; to William Strahan, Dec. 4, 1781, BF, *Writings*, 7:10, 345–46, 348; 8:336; BFB to Richard Bache, Nov. 11, 1784; to Sarah Bache, Feb. 9, 1785, both in Bache Family Papers, APS.

18. (general) Howard B. Rock, *Artisans of the New Republic* (N.Y., 1979); Steffen, *Mechanics;* Sean Wilentz, "Artisan Republican Festivals and the Rise of Class Conflict in New York City, 1788–1837," in *Working-Class America*, ed. Michael H. Frisch and Daniel J. Walkowitz (Urbana, 1983), 41–45; (clocks) Levi Hutchins, *The Autobiography . . .* (Cambridge, Mass., 1865); John W. Willard, *A History of Simon Willard, Inventor and Clockmaker* (Boston, 1911); (silver) Waters, "Workmanship," 13, 31, 125, 134, 140; Burton, *South Carolina Silversmiths*, 210; Vivian S. Gerstell, *Silversmiths of Lancaster, Pennsylvania, 1730–1850* (Lancaster, 1972), 8, 45–55, 57, 97–100; (building) Henry Wansey, *The Journal of an Excursion to the United States of North America* (Salisbury, Eng., 1796), 226–27; Grant Thorburn, *Forty Years' Residence in America* (London, 1834), 30–35; Smith, "Struggles," 229–234; Brooke Hindle, ed., *Material Culture of the Wooden Age* (Tarrytown, N.Y., 1981); (Phyfe) Charles O. Cornelius, *Furniture Masterpieces of Duncan Phyfe, 1768–1854* (Garden City, N.Y., 1923); Nancy V. McClelland, *Duncan Phyfe and the English Regency, 1795–1830* (N.Y., 1939); Kendall H. Bassett, "The Apprenticeship of William Brown, Jr., to Duncan Phyfe," *Chronicle of the Early American Industries Association*, 29 (1976), 61; (shoemakers) Johannes Schweizer, "Account of a Journey to North America . . ." (1823), in *The Old Land and the New*, ed. Robert H. Billigmeier and Fred A. Picard (Minneapolis, 1965), 121–22; Billy G. Smith,

"The Material Lives of Laboring Philadelphians, 1750 to 1800," *WMQ*, 38 (1981), 195–98; (tailors) ibid., 199–200.

19. Publishing statistics compiled from Evans's bibliography. (IT) Thomas, "Diary," 9:15n, 19n, 32n–33n, 90, 166n, 175n–176n; 10:124, 315; Shipton, *Thomas*, 49, 67; Buckingham, *Specimens*, 2:10–13; Baylies, *Russell*, 14; (LW) William E. Channing, *A Tribute to the Memory of the Rev. Noah Worcester, D.D.* (Boston, 1837), 12–13; Henry Ware, Jr., *Memoirs of the Rev. Noah Worcester, D.D.* (Boston, 1844), 1–13; Samuel M. Worcester, *The Life and Labors of Rev. Samuel Worcester, D.D.* (Boston, 1852), 1:57, 65–67, 85–89; E. S. Thomas, *Reminiscences*, 2:13; (DC) Shipton, *Thomas*, 61, 68; Isaiah Thomas Letterbook, 1823–1826, p. 134, IT Papers, AAS; Buckingham, *Specimens*, 2:174–75, 180–81, 196; Thomas, "Diary," 9:7n, 8n, 406.

20. Thomas Indenture, June 4, 1756, IT Papers, AAS, is reprinted in Thomas, *Three Fragments*, frontispiece. Haswell Indenture, July 23, 1771, Apprentices Indentures, AAS. On Haswell's later career see John Spargo, "Early Vermont Printers and Printing," Vt. Hist. Soc., *Proc.*, n.s. 10 (1942), 223. James Reed Hutchins Indenture, June 18, 1785, IT Papers, AAS.

21. Stephen Sewall to IT, July 26, 1791; Joseph Reynolds to IT, Aug. 31, 1792; Archibald McElroy to IT, Sept. 1, 1792; Alexander Thomas, Jr., to IT, Feb. 18, 1792, all in IT Papers, AAS; E. S. Thomas, *Reminiscences*, 2:13.

22. Albigance Waldo to Elisha H. Waldo, Apr. 19, 1786; Samuel Prentice to AW, Sept. 8, 1785; IT to AW, Aug. 20, 1787, all in Waldo Family Papers, AAS. A brief biographical sketch of AW is in his published diary, *PMHB*, 21 (1897), 299.

23. EHW to AW, May 11, 178[6?], Dec. 10, 17, 1786, WF Papers, AAS. The date on the first letter is partly obliterated.

24. (quotes) EHW to AW, Apr. 29, Oct. 21, 1787; Jan. 11, 1789; Mar. 2, 1790; (clothes) Apr. 17, 1788; note of AW to IT in AW to EHW, Apr. 16, 1786; (time) EHW to AW, Aug. 19, 1792, all in WF Papers, AAS. On Waldo's shop see EHW to IT, Jan. 10, Mar. 30, Apr. 8, Oct. 1, 3, 7, 8, 26, Nov. 6, 10, Dec. 6, 20, 1794, IT Papers, AAS.

25. Leonard Worcester to Noah Worcester, Sept. 18, 1787, quoted in Buckingham, *Specimens*, 1:342–44. See also Worcester, *Samuel Worcester*, 1:86; Ware, *Noah Worcester*, 3; Shipton, *Thomas*, 49; LW to IT [1796?], IT Papers, AAS. David Chambers to Joseph Gaston Chambers, Jan. 8, 1795; Feb. 9, Apr. 23 (quote), 1796; replies, Feb. 8, 1795; Apr. 28, 1796; BFB to JGC, Sept. 14, 1796 (quote), all in DC Papers, AAS. A biographical sketch is in the collection. On failures see William McCulloch to IT, Sept. 1, 1812, IT Papers, AAS; "Belknap Papers," 5th ser., 3 (1877), 277n; Shipton, *Thomas*, 49. Also useful is Botein, "Reluctant Partisans," 253.

26. Donald R. Adams, Jr., "Wage Rates in the Early National Period," *JEH*, 28 (1968), 404–26; Donald R. Adams, Jr., "Some Evidence on English and American Wage Rates, 1790–1830," *JEH*, 30 (1970), 499–520; William A. Sullivan, *The Industrial Worker in Pennsylvania, 1800–1840* (Harrisburg, 1955), 79; Steffen, *Mechanics*, 47–48; Paulus Henkel to "Most Beloved Co-Worker," Jan. 8, 1810; to Fredrich Smith, Feb. 10, 1810; Ambrosius Henkel to "Dear Brother," Mar. 4, 1810, all in Henkel Family Papers, Special Collections, College of William and Mary; Rita S. Gottesman, "The Arts and Crafts in New York, 1726–

1804," N-YHS, *Coll.*, 69 (1938); 81 (1954); 82 (1965); Towner, "Indentures," 426. See also the letter by "A Friend," Phila. *Fed. Gaz.*, Apr. 27, 1793, p. 3.

27. In general see Adams, "Wage Rates"; Adams, "Some Evidence"; Murray N. Rothbard, *The Panic of 1819* (N.Y., 1962); foreign-trade data are in the American State Papers; compare the census of manufactures for 1810 with that for 1820. The concept of fluctuation is stressed in Paul A. David, "The Growth of Real Product in the United States before 1840," *JEH*, 27 (1967), 151–97, esp. 155, 184, 187–88. On differential prosperity for different crafts see Sullivan, *Industrial Worker,* 79, and the creative study by Thomas Smith, "Reconstructing Occupational Structures: The Case of the Ambiguous Artisans," *Hist. Methods Newsletter,* 8 (1975), 140–41. Smith shows that master printers were better off than other master craftsmen but that journeymen printers were only equal to other journeymen. Henry C. Wright, *Human Life* (Boston, 1849), 152; Hiram Hill Autobiography and Diary, no pagination, Rhode Island Historical Society; for a sketch of Hill see Gary J. Kornblith, "From Artisans to Businessmen: Master Mechanics in New England, 1789–1850" (Ph.D. thesis, Princeton Univ., 1983), 423–52; Mary W. F. Tileston, *Caleb and Mary Wilder Foote* (Boston, 1918), 321–22.

28. Allen, "Memoirs," 15–21.

Chapter 2: The Master's Authority

1. British Tar Company, *Account of, and Directions for Using the Different Kinds of Coal Tar and Varnish . . .* (N.Y., 1788). See also David Townsend, *Principles and Observations Applied to the Manufacture and Inspection of Pot and Pearl Ashes* (Boston, 1793).

2. John Hargrove, *The Weavers Draft Book and Clothiers Assistant* (Balt., 1792), 2; Asa Ellis, Jr., *The Country Dyer's Assistant* (Brookfield, Mass., 1798); William Morse, *Mechanical Arts, in Thirty-Two Receipts* (Hartford, 1795); Oliver Evans, *The Young Mill-Wright & Miller's Guide* (Phila., 1795); (engraving) *Valuable Secrets in Arts, Trades, &c.* (N.Y., 1809), iii; Batty Langley, *The Builder's Jewell,* 1st U.S. ed. (Charlestown, Mass., 1800).

3. Amanda Jones, *Rules and Directions for Cutting Men's Clothes,* improved ed. (Middlebury, Vt., 1822), 1; *The London and Paris Union Rule: or, The Tailor's Assistant* (Boston, 1826); Joseph Watts, *The Tailor's Instructer* (Hallowell, Maine, 1828), 2; J. Bronson and R. Bronson, *Early American Weaving and Dyeing,* ed. Rita J. Adrosko (N.Y., 1977; orig., 1817), v, 3–4; William Tucker, *The Family Dyer and Scourer* (Phila., ca. 1830), vi–vii; Cornelius Molony, *The Practical Dyer* (Boston, 1833). See also Morse and Lathrop, *The Country Dyer* (n.p., 1808); James Queen and William Lapsley, *The Taylors' Instructor* (Phila., 1809); Cornelius S. Van Winkle, *The Printers' Guide* (N.Y., 1818).

4. Alexander Anderson, *Autobiography of an Early American Wood Engraver* (N.Y., 1968), no pagination. The thirteen-page manuscript is in the NYPL. Helen M. Knubel, "Alexander Anderson and Early American Book Illustration," *Princeton Univ. Library Chronicle,* 1 (1940), 10, 17–18; Benson J. Lossing, "Revolutionary Memoirs," undated newspaper clipping, Rare Books, LC; undated newspaper clipping obituary, Misc. Clippings Folder, AA Papers, NYPL. Additional material is in AA, "Diary" (1795), *Old New York,* 1 (1889), 46ff; AA

Diary, 1798–1799, AA Papers, N-YHS; family letters, AA Papers, NYPL and N-YHS.

5. Simon Newcomb, *The Reminiscences of an Astronomer* (Boston, 1903), 33–34.

6. Charles W. Janson, *The Stranger in America, 1793–1806* (N.Y., 1935; orig., 1807), 304; Fox, *Adventures,* 17–18. On revolutionary ideology see Bernard Bailyn, *The Ideological Origins of the American Revolution* (Cambridge, Mass., 1967); Jay Fliegelman, *Prodigals and Pilgrims* (N.Y., 1982); Mary B. Norton, *Liberty's Daughters* (Boston, 1980).

7. Grenville Mellen, *An Address Delivered before the Maine Charitable Mechanic Association* (Portland, 1821), 9; Louis W. Flanders, *Simeon Ide* (Rutland, Vt., 1931), 28–30 (letters at 28–29, 30). See also Simeon Ide, *A Biography of William B. Ide* (Oakland, 1944; orig., 1880). On evidence for a shift in child rearing see John Bristed, *America and Her Resources* (London, 1818), 459–60; Philip J. Greven, *The Protestant Temperament* (N.Y., 1977); Bernard Wishy, *The Child and the Republic* (Phila., 1968); Jacqueline R. Reinier, "Attitudes toward and Practices of Child-Rearing: Philadelphia, 1790 to 1830" (Ph.D. thesis, Univ. of California, Berkeley, 1977); documents published in Robert H. Bremner, ed., *Children and Youth in America* (Cambridge, Mass., 1970), vol. 1; Joseph F. Kett, "Adolescence and Youth in Nineteenth-Century America," *J. Interdisciplinary Hist.,* 2 (1971), 283–98; Joseph F. Kett, "Growing Up in Rural New England, 1800–1840," in *Anonymous Americans,* ed. Tamara K. Hareven (Englewood Cliffs, 1971), 1–16; Robert Sunley, "Early Nineteenth-Century American Literature on Child Rearing," in *Childhood in Contemporary Cultures,* ed. Margaret Mead and Martha Wolfenstein (Chicago, 1955), 150–67.

8. Simeon Baldwin, *An Oration Pronounced before the Citizens of New-Haven, July 4th, 1788* (New Haven, 1788), 13; *A Parent's Advice for His Family* (New London, 1792), 18; William Arthur, *Family Religion Recommended* (Phila., 1794), 13. See also Jonathan M. Sewall, *An Oration, Delivered at Portsmouth, New-Hampshire, on the Fourth of July, 1788 . . .* (Portsmouth, 1788), 8–10; Samuel Stillman, *An Oration, Delivered July 4th, 1789 . . .* (Boston, 1789), 25–27; *A Serious Address to Godfathers and Godmothers* (Windsor, Vt., 1794), 16; John Ely, *A Regiment to Consist of One Thousand Boys* (Phila., 1800), broadside; Alden Bradford, *An Oration, Pronounced at Wiscasset, on the Fourth of July, 1804 . . .* (Wiscasset, Maine, 1804).

9. Thomas Baldwin, *A Brief Account of the Late Revivals of Religion . . .* (Boston, 1799), 5 (quote), 7–9, 14 (quote); Thaddeus M. Harris, *A Discourse, Addressed to the Religious Society of Young Men in Dorchester . . .* (Charlestown, Mass., 1799); Nathan Perkins, *A Half Century Sermon* (Hartford, Conn., 1822), 23. See also Elisha Cushman, *A Sermon, Delivered before the Legislature . . .* (New Haven, 1820), 5, 15; Thomas Snell, *Signs of the Times* (Brookfield, Mass., 1824). The Second Great Awakening awaits definitive treatment. See John B. Boles, *The Great Revival, 1787–1805* (Lexington, Ky., 1972); Charles I. Foster, *An Errand of Mercy* (Chapel Hill, 1960); Donald G. Mathews, *Religion in the Old South* (Chicago, 1977); Lyman Beecher, *Autobiography,* ed. Barbara M. Cross (Cambridge, Mass., 1961; orig., 1864), introd.; the various collected documents edited by W. W. Sweet.

10. Martin Tullar, *A Concise System of Family Duty* (Windsor, Vt., 1802), 90; Luther Gleson, *The Duty of Parents and Children* (Sag Harbor, N.Y., 1805).

See also John Willard, *The Pious Education of Children* (Middletown, Conn., 1801); Asa Messer, *An Oration, Delivered at Providence . . .* (Providence, 1803); *Moral Education. By a Disciple of the Old School Philosophy* (New Haven, 1804); Benjamin Trumbull, *An Address on the Subjects of Prayer and Family Religion* (New Haven, 1804); Thomas Worcester, *Two Sermons, on the Government and Religious Education of Children* (Concord, N.H., 1804); Baptists, Tennessee, Concord Association, *Minutes* (Nashville, 1812), 5–8; Jonathan Ward, *Parental and Filial Obligation Illustrated and Enforced* (Augusta, Maine, 1814), 3.

11. William Enfield, *Prayers for the Use of Families* (Phila., 1788; reissued, Boston, 1802); Ebenezer Thayer, *Family Worship* (Newburyport, 1799); Tullar, *Concise System.*

12. Thomas, *Three Fragments,* 19. See William Marshall, *A Catechism for Youth . . .* (Phila., 1784); Joseph Priestley, *Extracts from Doctor Priestley's Catechism* (Salem, Mass., 1785); Presbyterian Church in the U.S.A., Presbytery of New Castle, Del., *An Address from the Presbytery of New-Castle to the Congregations under Their Care* (Wilmington, 1785), 33–39; Congregational Churches in Massachusetts, Berkshire Association, *A Plan for the More Effectual Religious Instruction of Children and Youth* (Goshen, N.Y., 1801), 3–4; Congregational Churches in Massachusetts, Westminster Association, *An Address, by the Ministers of the Westminster Association . . .* (Charlestown, Mass., 1801), 3–5, 7, 23–26; Congregational Churches in New Hampshire, Piscataqua Association, *A Prayer Book, for the Use of Families* (Portsmouth, 1802), iii–vi, x, xii.

13. (tracts) See, e.g., Samuel Spring, *Three Sermons to Little Children* (Boston, 1783; reissued, N.Y., 1790). Isaiah Thomas published many of these children's booklets, e.g., *The House That Jack Built* (Worcester, 1786). Anna Barbauld was the leading author. A good collection is at the AAS. (Sunday schools) An unusually graphic instruction manual is *A Visit to a Sabbath School* (Boston, 1820). A good example of the literature is *Richard and James* (Boston, 1820). See also James Hardie, *A Short Account of the City of Philadelphia* (Phila., 1794), 20–21.

14. James Barton Longacre to Robert Armstrong, Dec. 11, 1816, JBL Papers, LCP. JBL Papers contain miscellaneous letters; biographical sketch, Box 1, folder 1; "Autobiographical Notes," Box 3, folder 9; long quotes from letters and a diary in Andrew Longacre's detailed biography, Box 3, folder 10. For apprentice converts see Heman Bangs, *The Autobiography and Journal* (N.Y., 1872); E. P. Swift, *Memoir of the Rev. Joseph W. Barr,* new ed. (Phila., 1854); Nathaniel Bouton, *Autobiography* (N.Y., 1879); William Morgan, "William Morgan's Autobiography and Diary," ed. Harold B. Hancock, *DH,* 19 (1980), 39–52, 106–26; Ray Potter, *Memoirs of the Life and Religious Experience* (Providence, 1829); Eleazer Sherman, *The Narrative of . . .* (Providence, 1830); Nathaniel Stacy, *Memoirs of the Life . . .* (Columbus, Pa., 1850).

15. Wright, *Life,* 19–24, 64–65, 91, 124–27, 133–34, 138–39, 141, 150–58, 165 (quote at 150); Lewis Perry, *Childhood, Marriage, and Reform: Henry Clarke Wright, 1797–1870* (Chicago, 1980), 72–80, 100–101, 258.

16. Bangs, *Autobiography,* 6–13 (quote at 7); Paul E. Johnson, *A Shopkeeper's Millennium* (N.Y., 1978), 95–135. On Methodism see Sean Wilentz, *Chants Democratic* (N.Y., 1984), 77–86; Steffen, *Mechanics,* 253–75.

17. John Prentiss, "Autobiography," quotes at 39, 40, JP Papers, AAS. Four

MS memoirs are bound in one volume; a family genealogy is at the front. For another case see Salem Board Minutes, Nov. 7, 1793, in Fries, *Moravians*, 6:2482–83.

18. Millard Fillmore, "Autobiography," Buffalo Hist. Soc., *Publications*, 10 (1907), 6–8 (quote at 7).

19. Jeremy Belknap to Ebenezer Hazard, Apr. 29, May 18, 1787, "Belknap Papers," 2:473, 478–79 (quotes at 479, 478–79); June 23, July 14, 1787, JB Papers, MHS; July 29, Aug. 16, 1787, "BP," 2:483, 486; replies, May 5, 1787, "BP," 2:476; June 23, 1787, JB Papers, MHS; Aug. 2, 1787, "BP," 2:483–84. In general see Jane Marcou, *Life of Jeremy Belknap, D.D.* (N.Y., 1847), esp. 120–21, 139; "Jeremy Belknap," *Dictionary of American Biography*, 2:147; "Belknap Papers," MHS, *Coll.*, 5th ser., 2–3; 6th ser., 4; Belknap Papers at MHS and NHHS.

20. On this second apprenticeship see Jeremy Belknap Travel Diary, Sept. 20, 1785, JB Papers, MHS; EH to JB, Apr. 15, 1786, "BP," 2:435; JB to EH, July 14, 1787, JB Papers, MHS; Jeremy Belknap to Joseph Belknap, Sept. 29, 1787; Sept. 10, 1788; Aug. 18, 1789; July 30, Oct. 6, Nov. 27, 1790; replies, Mar. 2, Aug. 30 (quotes), 1789; Nov. 14, 1790, all in JB Papers, NHHS.

21. Samuel Mather, *A Serious Letter to the Young People of Boston* (Boston, 1783), 5; Joseph Huntington, *God Ruling the Nations for the Most Glorious End* (Hartford, 1784), 26, 27; Jeremy Belknap, *An Election Sermon . . .* (Portsmouth, 1785), 16. See also Samuel Wales, *The Dangers of Our National Prosperity* (Hartford, 1785); Samuel Haven, *An Election Sermon . . .* (Portsmouth, 1786); Henry T. Channing, *God Admonishing His People of Their Present Duty* (New London, 1787); Joseph Lyman, *A Sermon, Preached before His Excellency James Bowdoin, Esq. Governour* (Boston, 1787); Baldwin, *Oration;* Aaron Bascom, *A Sermon, Preached at the Execution of Abiel Converse . . .* (Northampton, Mass., 1788); Aaron Kinne, *A New-Year's Gift, Presented Especially to the Young People . . .* (New London, 1788); *The Present State of America* (Phila., 1789); Salem Board Minutes, Mar. 24, 1803, in Fries, *Moravians*, 6:2740; Henry Orne, *An Oration, Pronounced at Boston, 4th July, 1820 . . .* (Boston, 1820), 11.

22. Matthew Clarkson, *An Address to the Citizens of Philadelphia, Respecting the Better Government of Youth* (Phila., 1795), quotes at 11, 12–13. See also *A Friendly Address to the Inhabitants of the Town of Providence* (Providence, 1794), broadside; Hardie, *Short Account*, 20–21; Bradford, *Oration*, 13–14.

23. William Otter, Sr., *History of My Own Times* (Emmitsburg, Md., 1835), 68–81.

24. Ibid., 81–89, 98, 101–8 (quotes at 81, 108).

25. Ibid., 109–11 (conversation paraphrased and quote marks added). *To cornish* means to do fancy curved work such as coved ceilings.

26. Ibid., 111–14.

27. Robert Bailey, *The Life and Adventures of . . .* (Richmond, 1822), 17–33; Burton A. Konkle, *The Life of Chief Justice Ellis Lewis, 1798–1871* (Phila., 1907), 33–35 (quote at 35).

28. Konkle, *Lewis,* 35–41 (*Oracle* advertisement, 35; Ellis Lewis to Eli Lewis, Sept. 17, 1816, 38).

29. Solomon F. Smith, *Theatrical Management in the West and South for Thirty Years* (N.Y., 1868), 9–22.

30. *Richmond and Manchester Advertiser*, Jan. 13, 27, 30 (quote), 1796, in

William McKim file; *Charleston Courier,* Jan. 28, Feb. 1 (quote), 4, 1806, in John Mushett file; *Charleston Times,* July 31, Aug. 2 (quote), 1809, in James Marsh file; ibid., Sept. 11, 14, 27 (quote), 1813, in Daniel Henderson file; Washington *National Intelligencer,* June 6, 1815, in William Worthington file; *Norfolk Herald,* Nov. 6, 15, 20 (quote), 1811; Aug. 21, Sept. 6, 8, 1815, in John Jarvis file—all in the Index of Early Southern Artists and Artisans, MESDA. MESDA has an on-line index and card file containing biographical information for more than 46,000 southern craftsmen active before 1820.

31. Albany, N.Y., *Laws and Ordinances* (Albany, 1791), 79–80, 91–95, 107 (quote at 79); Georgetown, D.C., *Ordinances* . . . (Georgetown, 1811), 62–63; Newburyport, Mass., *Bye-Laws* . . . (Newburyport, 1797), broadside; New York (City), Common Council, *Minutes . . . 1784–1831* (N.Y., 1917), 2:560. See also Boston, *The By-Laws and Orders* . . . (Boston, 1801), 8–9, 51–52.

32. Based on an examination of state session laws and codes. Laws were passed by N.H., 1792; Mass., 1794; R.I., 1798; Conn., 1784; N.Y., 1788; N.J., 1798; Pa., 1799; Del., 1797; Md., 1793; Va., 1785, 1792; S.C., 1783; Ky., 1797.

33. Petition, 1808, in N.Y. Common Council, *Minutes,* 5:193; Black v. Hardenbrook, 1802, in New York (City). Mayor's Court, *Judicial Opinions, Delivered in the Mayor's Court* . . . (N.Y., 1803), 23–24; Petition, 1818, in N.Y. Common Council, *Minutes,* 10:75, 91–92 (quote). For a contrary decision on medical care see Percival & Johnson v. Neville, S.C., 1819, in 1 Nott & McCord 452.

34. On court bias see numerous cases in Philadelphia Mayor's Court Docket, 1789–1792, Philadelphia Municipal Archives; Robert Edging Petition to Frederick Co. Md. Court, Mar. 28, 1794; Isaac Martz Petition to same court, Nov. 17, 1794, both in Paul H. Downing Coach and Carriage Papers, Colonial Williamsburg, Inc.; Paddock v. Higgins, Conn., 1795; Hewit v. Morgan, 1796; Clement v. Wheeler, 1796, all in 2 Root 316, 363, 466. Benjamin Johnson case, 1811, is in John Bosher file, Index of Early Southern Artists and Artisans, MESDA. Shippen Opinion, Jan. 27, 1793, in Shippen Folder, Misc. Coll., HSP. On the Massachusetts case parallel to Shippen's see Day v. Everett, 1810, in 7 Mass. Rep. 145. Compare *Conductor Generalis* (N.Y., 1711); (N.Y., 1749); (Phila., 1792).

35. Lewis v. Wildman, Conn., 1803, in 1 Day 153 (quote at 154); Blunt v. Melcher, 1806, in 2 Mass. Rep. 228 (quote at 230). See also Woodruff v. Corry, 1809, in 3 N.J. Law 540.

36. People v. William P. Connelly, 1820, in Barent Gardenier, *The New-York Reporter* . . . (N.Y., 1820), 12–13 (quote at 12). For a master acquitted of assaulting his apprentice see People v. Robert Matthews and George Matthews, 1820, ibid., 52. For a similar stand upholding a violent master see Mitchell v. Armitage, La., 1821, in 10 Martin's Rep. o.s. 38.

37. Gardenier, *New-York Reporter,* 12–13 (quote at 13).

38. People v. Philips, N.Y., 1823, in 1 Wheeler's Crim. Cases 155. See also People v. Sniffen, N.Y., 1823, ibid., 502. The statistical conclusion is based on an examination of cases, mostly appellate, in state law reports.

39. Cyrus P. Bradley, *Biography of Isaac Hill* (Concord, N.H., 1835), esp. 10–17; Hill quoted in Silver, *American Printer,* 2. For another example of mutual respect see Jonathan Roberts Memoirs, p. 80, HSP. My analysis of Frederick County, Md., is based on published census data and the Frederick County Indentures, Maryland Hall of Records. See Statistical Appendix, Table 1. In Baltimore the indenture/population ratio declined 25 percent in the years 1801–

1815. See Steffen, *Mechanics*, 4, 29. Information on Sir John Barnard, *A Present for an Apprentice,* was compiled from the Evans and Shaw-Shoemaker bibliographies.

40. On child rearing see Edward S. Abdy, *Journal of a Residence and Tour in the United States of North America* (London, 1835), 1:70–73; Bristed, *America,* 459–60; Basil Hall, *Travels in North America* (Edinburgh, 1829), 2:170–72; Isaac Holmes, *An Account of the United States of America* (London, 1823), 382; Harriet Martineau, *Society in America* (N.Y., 1837), 2:268–73; Alexis de Tocqueville, *Journey to America,* ed. J. P. Mayer (New Haven, 1959), 57, 255–56; Alexis de Tocqueville, *Democracy in America,* ed. Phillips Bradley (N.Y., 1945), 2:202–8; Francis Trollope, *Domestic Manners of the Americans,* ed. Donald Smalley (N.Y., 1949; orig., 1832), 67, 122–24, 213, 379.

Chapter 3: A Cash Wage

1. (optimism) Zachariah Allen, *The Science of Mechanics* (Providence, 1829); Zachariah Allen, *Sketches of the State of the Useful Arts . . .* (Hartford, 1835); Charles Babbage, *On the Economy of Machinery and Manufactures* (Phila., 1832); Edward S. Bellamy, *Domestic Manufactures, the Source of Real Independence* (N.Y., 1821); (seamstresses) Mathew Carey, *Miscellaneous Essays . . .* (Phila., 1830), esp. 147n, 194; (Clay) Henry Clay, *Speech in Support of an American System* (Lexington, Ky., 1824); Caleb Cushing, *Summary of the Practical Principles of Political Economy* (Cambridge, Mass., 1826); Harrisburg Convention, 1827, *General Convention, of Agriculturists and Manufacturers, and Others Friendly to the Encouragement and Support of the Domestic Industry of the United States* (Baltimore, 1827?); (democratic ideology) Drew McCoy, *The Elusive Republic* (Chapel Hill, 1980); (popular views) Joseph L. Tillinghast, *Address Delivered before the Rhode-Island Society for the Encouragement of Domestic Industry* (Providence, 1827); Thomas R. Mercein, "Address," in New-York Mechanic and Scientific Institution, *Charter, Constitution, and By-Laws* (N.Y., 1822). Two provocative, speculative recent studies are David G. Pugh, *Sons of Liberty* (Westport, 1983); James N. Kenworthy, "Selfishness or Individualism? The Emotional Lives of Antebellum Americans" (Ph.D. thesis, Univ. of Michigan, 1979).

2. James J. Strang, *The Diary,* ed. Mark A. Strang (E. Lansing, 1961), Mar. 21, May 27, 1832, pp. 17 (quote), 19 (quote). See also Milo M. Quaife, *The Kingdom of Saint James* (New Haven, 1930). Christopher Colt to Samuel Colt, Feb. 24, 1834 (quote); H. L. Ellsworth to CC, Feb. 20, 1832, both in SC Papers, Connecticut Historical Society. See also Henry Barnard, *Armsmear* (N.Y., 1866), esp. 144–56.

3. Crockett is quoted in Brown Thurston Journal, June 15, 1834, AAS. The classic study of the market remains George R. Taylor, *The Transportation Revolution, 1815–1860* (N.Y., 1951). See also Cochran, *Frontiers,* 78–100. (distilling) W. J. Rorabaugh, *The Alcoholic Republic* (N.Y., 1979), 84–88; (tanning) Lucius F. Ellsworth, *Craft to National Industry in the Nineteenth Century* (N.Y., 1975); (shoes) Commons, "American Shoemakers"; Hazard, *Boot and Shoe,* esp. ix, 25, 86, 95, 143; Hall, "Gentle Craft," esp. 140–41, 146–48, 150, 243, 247, 249; Jesse W. Hatch, "The Old-Time Shoemaker and Shoemaking," Rochester Hist.

Soc., *Publication Fund Series,* 5 (1926), 79–95. For a shoemaker's diary, 1817–1832, see Joseph Lye, "Diary," Lynn Hist. Soc., *Register,* 19 (1915), 41–53. See also Robert W. Lovett, "Augustus Roundy's Cincinnati Sojourn, 1838–1845," Hist. and Phil. Soc. of Ohio, *Bulletin,* 19 (1961), 254–64. (Lynn) Alonzo Lewis, *The History of Lynn,* 2d ed. (Boston, 1844); Alan Dawley, *Class and Community* (Cambridge, Mass., 1976); Paul G. Faler, *Mechanics and Manufacturers in the Early Industrial Revolution* (Albany, N.Y., 1981).

4. Cargill Family Papers, AAS; Anna R. English, *In Memoriam James Edward English* (New Haven? 1891), 11–15; New Haven Colony Hist. Soc., New Haven, *Proceedings* (New Haven, 1893), 47–48; William G. Brownlow, *Sketches of the Rise, Progress, and Decline of Secession* (Phila., 1862), 17; E. Merton Coulter, *William G. Brownlow* (Chapel Hill, 1937), 4; Herbert A. Kellar, ed., *Solon Robinson* (Indianapolis, 1936), 3–41; Calvin Goodspeed Autobiography in CG Journal, pp. 122–45, NHHS; Alonzo B. Cornell, *Biography of Ezra Cornell* (N.Y., 1884), 41–49, 57; Philip Dorf, *The Builder: A Biography of Ezra Cornell* (N.Y., 1952), 10–18. For other success stories see Kornblith, "From Artisans to Businessmen."

5. George W. Swartz, *Autobiography of an American Mechanic* (Phila., 1895), 3–24 (quote at 23n); William M. Thayer, *The Bobbin Boy* (Boston, 1860); Joseph P. Dwinnell, "Extracts from the Diary . . . 1837–1838," Danvers Hist. Soc., *Hist. Coll.,* 26 (1938), 23–41. See also "Communication from the Governor . . . ," New York (State), Assembly, *Documents . . . Sixty-Second Session, 1839* (Albany, 1839), vol. 5, doc. 275, pp. 77–79; A. Hall, "Brick Making," New York (State), Senate, *Documents . . . Sixty-Eighth Session, 1845* (Albany, 1845), vol. 3, doc. 85, pp. 457–63.

6. A cogent summary is in Robert B. Zevin, *The Growth of Manufacturing in Early Nineteenth Century New England* (N.Y., 1975), pt. 1, pp. 1–16. A definitive biography of Slater is needed. See E. H. Cameron, *Samuel Slater* (n.p., 1960), 11–26; George S. White, *Memoir of Samuel Slater,* 2d ed. (Phila., 1836; orig., 1835), 31–42. (R.I. area mills) There is an excellent dissertation by Gary B. Kulik, "The Beginnings of the Industrial Revolution in America: Pawtucket, Rhode Island, 1672–1829" (Ph.D. thesis, Brown Univ., 1980), esp. 229–35; James L. Conrad, Jr., "The Evolution of Industrial Capitalism in Rhode Island, 1790–1830: Almy, the Browns, and the Slaters" (Ph.D. thesis, Univ. of Connecticut, 1973), esp. 73, 101–4; Jonathan Prude, *The Coming of Industrial Order* (N.Y., 1983). See also Brendan F. Gilbane, "Pawtucket Village Mechanics—Iron, Ingenuity, and the Cotton Revolution," *Rhode Island Hist.,* 34 (1975), 3–11. (Delaware Valley) Anthony F. C. Wallace, *Rockdale* (N.Y., 1978); Philip Scranton, *Proprietary Capitalism* (N.Y., 1983); (Boston area) Caroline F. Ware, *The Early New England Cotton Manufacture* (Boston, 1931); Thomas Dublin, *Women at Work* (N.Y., 1979).

7. (weaving) *A Letter, on the Present State of the Labouring Classes in America* (Bury, Eng., 1827), 4–9; Conrad, "Evolution," 333–34; Richard A. McLeod, "The Philadelphia Artisan 1828–1850" (Ph.D. thesis, Univ. of Missouri, 1971), 82–106, 151–52, 160; David Montgomery, "The Shuttle and the Cross: Weavers and Artisans in the Kensington Riots of 1844," *J. Social Hist.,* 5 (1972), 411–46. On the more devastating English situation see Neil J. Smelser, *Social Change in the Industrial Revolution* (Chicago, 1959). (bewitching) John Fritz, *The Autobiography* . . . (N.Y., 1912), 25; Barnard, *Armsmear,* 257; (placement) Wilmington *Am. Watchman,* May 25, 1811, clipping; James Givin to Messrs.

E. I. DuPont, June 10, 1823; William Young to E. I. DuPont, June 28, 1823, all in Elutheria B. DuPont Collection, HML; A. McKim to Peter Bodue, Apr. 28, 1812, DuPont Allied Businesses, Longwood Manuscripts, HML; David Alcorn to Thomas Moore, Nov. 5, 1817, TM Papers, Duke Univ.; The Philadelphia Society for the Promotion of National Industry, *Addresses* (Phila., 1819); (Peale) BFP to Charles Linnaeus Peale, Dec. 14, 1814. See also Charles W. Peale to BFP, Nov. 18, Dec? 19, 1813; July 31 (2 letters), Oct. 23, Dec. 23, 30, 1814; Rembrandt Peale to BFP, Mar. 7, July 25, 1814. All letters as well as biographical material are in the published microfiche of the Peale Family Papers, APS. A family genealogy is in Charles W. Peale, *The Selected Papers . . .* , ed. Lillian B. Miller (New Haven, 1983–   ), 1:xlv–lviii. The 1820 census is quoted in Scranton, *Proprietary Capitalism*, 105–6.

8. George Escol Sellers, "Memoirs," bk. 3, pp. 7, 18–19, 32–34; bk. 1, pp. 15–16; "Autobiography," pt. 3, pp. 10–12, all in Peale-Sellers Collection, APS. For a biographical sketch as well as an edited version of the memoirs see Eugene S. Ferguson, ed., Smithsonian Institution, *Bulletin*, 238 (1965).

9. Sellers, "Memoirs," bk. 1, p. 16; bk. 3, pp. 41, 43, 47–48, 50.

10. John Pintard to Eliza Noel Pintard Davidson, May 18, 26, June 8, 17 (quote), 1830; Dec. 22, 1832, in JP, "Letters . . . ," N-YHS, *Coll.*, 72 (1941), 146–47, 149, 151, 156 (quote); 73 (1941), 113. TCS was JP's nephew. John Morton Poole to Joseph Bancroft, Sept. 19, 1830, JMP Papers, HSD. A biographical sketch is in one family folder in this collection.

11. JMP to JB, Aug. 6, 1832 (quote); Oct. 1, 1833 (quote); Feb. 12, 1837; to Sarah, Mar. 8, 22, 1835; to Samuel S. Poole, July 24, Nov. 30, 1836 (quote), JMP Papers, HSD.

12. Thomas R. Navin, *The Whitin Machine Works since 1831* (Cambridge, Mass., 1950), esp. 33; George S. Gibb, *The Saco-Lowell Shops* (Cambridge, Mass., 1950), 89 (quote), 749 n. 49.

13. George S. Gibb, *The Whitesmiths of Taunton* (Cambridge, Mass., 1946), esp. 4–8, 34, 36–41, 48–50, 66, 69–70, 87, 89, 145–46.

14. Felicia J. Deyrup, "Arms Makers of the Connecticut Valley," *Smith College Studies in History*, 33 (1948), esp. 47, 49, 96–100. Although Merritt R. Smith, *Harpers Ferry Armory and the New Technology* (Ithaca, 1977), is more analytical, it depends upon poorer sources. On early arms makers see Jeannette Mirsky and Allan Nevins, *The World of Eli Whitney* (N.Y., 1952); S. N. D. North and Ralph H. North, *Simeon North* (Concord, N.H., 1913). For the struggles and collapse of a small-scale armorer see A. Stanton to Adam Caruth, Mar. 7, 1821; John S. Cogdell to AC, Apr. 10, 1821; Thomas Bridgman to AC, June 28, 1821; other business letters, 1803–1821, AC Papers, SCL.

15. Deyrup, "Arms," 101–6, 110, 117–20, 123.

16. Ibid., 37, 100, 107, 160–61. See also Smith, *Armory*, 62–65, 240. On an early Harpers Ferry apprentice see Daniel Johnson Claim, Mar. 26, 1830, in U.S. Congress, *American State Papers* (Wash., 1860), Class V (Military Affairs), 4:364–65. On the W. Troy, N.Y., arsenal see the *Harbinger*, 5 (1847), 127.

17. Two important articles on barter are Michael Merrill, "Cash Is Good to Eat: Self-Sufficiency and Exchange in the Rural Economy of the United States," *Radical Hist. Rev.*, 3 (1977), 42–71; Christopher Clark, "Household Economy, Market Exchange and the Rise of Capitalism in the Connecticut Valley, 1800–1860," *J. Social Hist.*, 13 (1979), 169–89. The account books at Harvard's Baker Business Library give ample evidence of the barter economy. The lure of cash

wages is shown in both Wallace, *Rockdale*, and Dublin, *Women at Work*. See also Ebenezer H. Stedman, *Bluegrass Craftsman*, ed. Frances L. S. Dugan and Jacqueline P. Bull (Lexington, Ky., 1959), 14, 22. The history of banking is traced in Bray Hammond, *Banks and Politics in America* (Princeton, 1957). See also McLeod, "Philadelphia Artisans," 123, 155–56. An excellent case study is Cynthia Shelton, "Labor and Capital in the Early Period of Manufacturing: The Failure of John Nicholson's Manufacturing Complex, 1793–1797," *PMHB*, 106 (1982), 341–64. On the Whiskey Rebellion see Leland D. Baldwin, *Whiskey Rebels* (Pittsburgh, 1939).

18. McLeod, "Philadelphia Artisans," 55; Aufseher Collegium, Salem, Nov. 25, Dec. 23, 1833, in Fries, *Moravians*, 8:4092, 4093; *The Andrus Bindery* (Hartford, 1940), 23, 32–33.

19. Indenture, Diamond Ingalls to Nathan Moore, Apr. 30, 1822; David Ingalls Certificate, Mar. 14, 1827; Agreement, Diamond Ingalls and NM, Mar. 22, 1827; Receipt, NM to Diamond Ingalls, Jan. 5, 1828, all in Moore Family Papers, NHHS; Richard N. Current, *Pine Logs and Politics* (Madison, Wis., 1950), 12–13; Fillmore, "Autobiography," 8–13. See also Ivory Chamberlain, *Biography of Millard Fillmore* (Buffalo, 1856); Robert J. Rayback, *Millard Fillmore* (Buffalo, 1959); MF to Z. Cheney, June 26, 1820, MF Papers, Buffalo and Erie Co. Hist. Soc.; N. and I. P. Fillmore to MF, June 29, 1820, MF Papers, State Univ. of N.Y. College at Oswego (both on film).

20. (KC) The basic source remains KC's autobiography, which is available in an excellent annotated edition in Harvey L. Carter, *'Dear Old Kit': The Historical Christopher Carson* (Norman, 1968), 37–150 (early life, 38–39). The runaway notice is reprinted at 39n. See also chronology, 217; Edwin L. Sabin, *Kit Carson Days* (N.Y., 1935), 1:12–13. (AJ) Indenture, Feb. 18, 1822, reprinted in Andrew Johnson, *Papers*, ed. Leroy P. Graf and Ralph W. Haskins (Knoxville, 1967–ʌ), 1:3. The apprenticeship may have begun several years earlier. Ibid., n. 2. The runaway notice is ibid., 3–4. See also Robert V. P. Steele, *The First President Johnson* (N.Y., 1968), 11–23; Lloyd P. Stryker, *Andrew Johnson* (N.Y., 1929), 2–6; Frank Moore's sketch in Andrew Johnson, *Speeches* (Boston, 1866), v–viii.

21. Edward Jenner Carpenter Journal, Mar. 6, Apr. 8, 22, May 4, 12, Aug. 3, Sept. 4, 5, 17, Nov. 16, 19 (quote), Dec. 27, 1844, AAS.

22. *The British Mechanic's and Labourer's Hand Book . . .* (London, 1840), 60–61 (quote at 61); William E. Channing, *Lectures on the Elevation of the Labouring Portion of the Community* (Boston, 1840), 10–11, 62; Charles H. Haswell's reminiscences quoted in John B. Jentz, "Artisans, Evangelicals, and the City: A Social History of Abolition and Labor Reform in Jacksonian New York" (Ph.D. thesis, CUNY, 1977), 238–39. For an early satire on dandies see Robert Waln, *The Hermit in America on a Visit to Philadelphia* (Phila., 1819), 85–98.

23. (Mary Thomas) Marble, *Thomas*, 150–51; Shipton, *Thomas*, 40–41; E. S. Thomas, *Reminiscences*, 2:13–18; (Sophia Williams) John C. Williams, *An Oneida County Printer, William Williams* (N.Y., 1906), 48, 56–57, 138, 143–44; Frederick W. Williams, *The Life and Letters of Samuel Wells Williams, Ll.D.* (N.Y., 1889), 6–11; (DC) David Clapp, *Journal . . .* (n.p., 1904), 1, 4–5, 8–10.

24. Johnson, *Shopkeeper's Millennium*, 43–47. See Gear v. Conrow, 1846, 2 Pa. Rep. 402.

25. David Carroll Account Book, no pagination, MS. 200, Maryland Historical

Society Library. For two other apprentices' expenditures see Dwinnell, "Diary," 23–41; Thomas H. Savery Copy Books, 1854–1858; Diaries, 1855–1859, Savery Papers, HML.

26. (Dyott) Thomas W. Dyott, *An Exposition of the System of Moral and Mental Labor, Established at the Glass Factory of Dyottville* (Phila., 1833), 54, 69n; Dyottville Apprentices' Library Company, *Preamble and Constitution* (Phila., 1834); McLeod, "Philadelphia Artisans," 70, 118, 120–21; (factories) *Pennsylvania Senate Journal (1837/8)* (Harrisburg, 1837–38), 1:322–27; 2:278–359; *Pennsylvania Senate Journal (1838/9)* (Harrisburg, 1838–39), 1:428, 436, 473, 482, 527, 831; "Report of the Select Committee . . . ," New York (State), Assembly, *Documents . . . Fifty-Fifth Session, 1832* (Albany, 1832), vol. 4, doc. 308; New Hampshire, House of Representatives, *Journal* (Concord, N.H., 1847), 475–78; Thomas Man, *Picture of a Factory Village* (Providence, 1833), 143–44; Henry Barnard, *Legal Provision Respecting the Education and Employment of Children in Factories, &c.* (Hartford, 1842), esp. 12.

Chapter 4: The Crisis in Printing

1. Van Winkle, *Printers' Guide*, 83–192; Adams, *Typographia*, 310–21; Bloy, *History*, 53–54; Hamilton, *Country Printer*, 32–33, 242. (rollers) Charles T. Congdon, *Reminiscences of a Journalist* (Boston, 1880), 10; James R. Newhall, *The Legacy of an Octogenarian* (Lynn, Mass., 1897), 35, 44–46.

2. *Scenes of American Wealth and Industry in Produce, Manufactures, Trade, the Fisheries, &c. &c.* (Boston, 1833), 35–36; Lehmann-Haupt, *Book*, 77–79; Griffin, *History*, 24–25; Silver, *American Printer*, vii; Sigfrid H. Steinberg, *Five Hundred Years of Printing* (N.Y., 1959; orig., 1955), 201; Theodore L. DeVinne, *Printing in the Nineteenth Century* (N.Y., 1924), 7–9. (BT) Brown Thurston Journal, 1834–1850, 1893, AAS. The end of the journal contains unpaginated reminiscences written in 1893. See also entry for June 15, 1834. A family genealogy is in BT, *Thurston Genealogies* (Portland, Maine, 1880), 89–92, 102, 171–72. BT also wrote *Improvements in the Art of Printing during the Last 100 Years* (Portland, Maine, 1877).

3. Ethelbert Stewart, *A Documentary History of the Early Organizations of Printers* (Indianapolis, 1907; orig., 1905), 77; George E. Barnett, *The Printers* (Cambridge, Mass., 1909), 163–64, 283; Lehmann-Haupt, *Book*, 96–98; Hamilton, *Country Printer*, 42–45; Frederick Follett, *History of the Press of Western New-York* (Rochester, 1847), 62; George A. Stevens, *New York Typographical Union No. 6* (Albany, 1912), 106–7, 214–16. For another case see Joseph S. Wall to Caleb Wall, Feb. 4, 1839; to Caleb and Sarah Wall, Mar. 10, 1839, Wall Family Papers, AAS.

4. (separation) Griffin, *History*, 27–28; Sidney Babcock Agreement with Thomas Babcock, Aug. 2, 1825, Babcock Papers, AAS. Such newspaper owners as Elijah Fletcher, James Gordon Bennett, and George D. Prentice were not printers, and neither were the editors N. P. Willis, Elizur Wright, John Wentworth, and Henry J. Raymond. (art) Imprints prove the point, as do the wide array of types and other items in typographer's sales brochures. In general see MacKellar, *American Printer*. (drink) Hamilton, *Country Printer*, 242; Silver, *American Printer*, 9.

5. Horace Greeley, *Recollections of a Busy Life* (N.Y., 1868), 35–61 (quote at 55); James Parton, *The Life of Horace Greeley* (N.Y., 1855), 84–85 (quote). (Other historians have accused Parton of taking liberties, but the dialogue is plausible.)

6. Parton, *Greeley*, 86.

7. Ibid., 87. A shorter account is in Greeley, *Recollections,* 62.

8. Terms, 1826, Box 3, HG Papers, LC. Although Vermont was one of the few states without an apprenticeship statute, the courts recognized apprenticeship. See Conant v. Raymond, 1827, in 2 Aiken 243; Squires v. Whipple, 1829, in 2 Vt. 111.

9. Greeley, *Recollections,* 62–63 (quote at 63); Parton, *Greeley,* 88–90; William H. Hale, *Horace Greeley* (N.Y., 1950), 18.

10. Parton, *Greeley,* 91–92, 94–96, 103, 106; Greeley, *Recollections,* 75–76. HG to Obadiah A. Bowe, Nov. 19, 1829, HG Papers, LC; Thurlow Weed, *Autobiography,* ed. Harriet A. Weed (Boston, 1883), 22–24. For another case see Salem Board Minutes, May 29, 1826, in Fries, *Moravians,* 8:3774.

11. Parton, *Greeley,* 108–12 (quotes at 112); Greeley, *Recollections,* 80.

12. HG to OAB, Feb. 13, 1831, HG Papers, NYPL. See also Parton, *Greeley,* 112–16.

13. HG to OAB, Feb. 13, 1831, HG Papers, NYPL; Mar. 11, 1831, HG Papers, LC.

14. HG to OAB, Apr. 3, 1831, HG Papers, LC.

15. Ibid. (quotes); Greeley, *Recollections,* 81–82; Parton, *Greeley,* 117.

16. Greeley, *Recollections,* 84–85 (quotes at 84); *N.Y. Commercial Advertiser,* Nov. 30, 1872, clipping in Greeley Scraps, bound MS volume, HG Papers, NYPL.

17. HG to OAB, Nov. 20, 1831 (quotes), HG Papers, LC; Greeley, *Recollections,* 85–86.

18. Greeley, *Recollections,* 86–96, 104; Hale, *Greeley,* 17, 25; Don C. Seitz, *Horace Greeley* (Indianapolis, 1926), 4.

19. Eugene Exman, *The Brothers Harper* (N.Y., 1965), 1–10, 13; J. Henry Harper, *I Remember* (N.Y., 1934), 10; J. C. Derby, *Fifty Years among Authors, Books and Publishers* (N.Y., 1884), 88–100; Thurlow W. Barnes, *Memoir of Thurlow Weed* (Boston, 1884), 5 (quote); Weed, *Autobiography,* 57. There are no biographies. See also Eugene Exman, *The House of Harper* (N.Y., 1967).

20. Derby, *Fifty Years,* 94; Exman, *Brothers Harper,* 13, 17, 20, 22, 24, 36, 92, 121, 173–74; (women) Stewart, *Documentary History,* 30n; Barnett, *Printers,* 310.

21. (m. and j.) Lansingburgh and Troy, United Society of House-Carpenters and Joiners, *Lansingburgh, 19th June, 1790. Rules and Regulations* (n.p., 1790), broadside; Carlisle, Pa., Carpenter's Society, *Constitution . . .* (Carlisle, Pa., 1795); Hampshire Co., Mass., Joiners and Cabinetmakers, *At a General Meeting of the House Joiners and Cabinet-Makers . . .* (Northampton, Mass, 1796), broadside; Providence Association of Mechanics and Manufacturers, *The Charter, Article of Agreement, Bye-Laws, Rules and Regulations* (Providence, 1798); Boston, Carpenters, *The Rules of Work . . .* (Cambridge, Mass., 1800); Albany Mechanic's Society, *Charter of Incorporation* (Albany, 1803); Beverly, Mass., Housewrights, *The Rules of Work . . .* (Salem, Mass., 1805); Providence Association of Mechanics and Manufacturers, *The Charter, Article of Agreement, By-Laws, Rules and Regulations* (Providence, 1808); (m. only) Philadelphia, Carpenters, *Articles of the Carpenters Company of Philadelphia* (Phila., 1786); Philadelphia, Cordwainers, *A List of the Prices of Boots and Shoes, &c.* (Phila.,

1790), broadside; Newport Association of Mechanics and Manufacturers, *The Charter, Constitution and Bye-Laws* (Newport, 1792); Philadelphia, Printers, *The Constitution of the Company of Printers of Philadelphia* (Phila., 1794); Boston, Mechanics, *Constitution of the Associated Mechanics of the Town of Boston* (Boston, 1795); *Associated Mechanics and Manufacturers, of the Commonwealth of Massachusetts* (Boston, 1800); Baltimore, Brickmakers, *Rules. To Be Observed by the Hands Employed in the Brick-Making Business* (Balt., 1802), broadside; Associated Housewright Society of Boston Records, 1804–1837, in the Massachusetts Charitable Mechanic Association Records, MHS; (j. only) Philadelphia, Cabinet and Chairmakers, *The Journeymen Cabinet and Chair-Makers Philadelphia Book of Prices*, 2d ed. (Phila., 1795); Thomas Ringwood, *An Address, Delivered before the Franklin Typographical Association of New-York . . .* (N.Y., 1802); New York (City), Shipwrights, *Constitution of the New-York Journeymen Shipwrights Society . . .* (N.Y., 1804); New York Journeymen Cordwainers' Constitution is in *Trial of the Journeymen Cordwainers of the City of New-York* (N.Y., 1810); (secrecy) Union Association of Journeymen Hatters of the City of Cincinnati, *Constitution and By-Laws* (Cincin., 1827), 11; Carpenters Company of the City and County of Philadelphia, *An Act to Incorporate* (Phila., 1840), 14; New York (City), Company of Master Builders, *House Carpenters' Book of Prices* (N.Y., 1802); Stewart, *Documentary History*, 12. For an early strike see Rosemont, "Benjamin Franklin," 398–429. (apprentices) Associated Mechanics and Manufacturers of the State of New-Hampshire, *Constitution* (Portsmouth, 1802); Newburyport Mechanic Association, *The Constitution* (Newburyport, 1807). See also Steffen, *Mechanics,* 102–20. (trials) Thomas Lloyd, *The Trial of the Boot & Shoemakers of Philadelphia* (Phila., 1806); *Trial of the Journeymen Cordwainers;* (Balt., 1809) Steffen, *Mechanics,* 210.

22. (tariffs) National Institution for the Promotion of Industry, *An Address to the People of the United States* (N.Y., 1820). Among the advocates were Mathew Carey, in numerous pamphlets, and Hezekiah Niles, in *Niles' Weekly Register.* (antibank) Daniel Raymond, *Thoughts on Political Economy* (Balt., 1820); William Leggett, *A Collection of the Political Writings . . .* (N.Y., 1840), 1:102–4. The Jacksonian press agreed. (reform) Frances Wright, "To the Intelligent among the Working Classes," in *Popular Tracts. No. 3,* ed. Robert D. Owen (N.Y., 1830), 3–6. See also Jentz, "Artisans"; McLeod, "Philadelphia Artisans," 74–78. (labor theory of value) National Institution, *Address,* 1; William Hilliard, *An Address Delivered before the Massachusetts Charitable Mechanic Association . . .* (Cambridge, Mass., 1827), 9. A good summary is in Maurice F. Neufeld, "Realms of Thought and Organized Labor in the Age of Jackson," *LH,* 10 (1969), 5–43. (labor) e.g., Union Association of Journeymen Hatters, *Constitution;* Pennsylvania Society of Journeymen Cabinet-Makers, *Constitution* (Phila., 1829); William Heighton, *An Address, Delivered before the Mechanics and Working Classes Generally* (Phila., 1827); William Heighton, *An Address to the Members of Trade Societies* (Phila., 1827). See also Edward Pessen, *Most Uncommon Jacksonians* (Albany, 1967).

23. See, e.g., Samuel Whitcomb, Jr., *An Address before the Working-Men's Society of Dedham . . .* (Dedham, Mass., 1831), 3–6; A. P. Peabody, "Address on Taxation," in Middlesex County Lyceum, *Publications* (Charlestown, Mass.? ca. 1833), 5–48; Robert Rantoul, Jr., "An Address to the Workingmen of the United States of America," ibid., 49–103; Frederick Robinson, *An Oration De-*

livered before the Trades Union of Boston and Vicinity . . . (Boston, 1834); Ely Moore, *Address Delivered before the General Trades' Union of the City of New-York* . . . (N.Y., 1833); Boston Mechanics, Committee, *Proceedings of the Government and Citizens of Philadelphia, on the Reduction of the Hours of Labor, and Increase of Wages* (Boston, 1835). For a more theoretical view see Theodore Sedgwick, *Public and Private Economy* (N.Y., 1836); James W. Alexander, *The Working-Man* (Phila., 1839). See also Abdy, *Journal*, 1:30–34.

24. "Chips," reminiscences, *Fincher's Trades' Review*, Feb. 10, 1866, p. 83; *British Mechanic's Hand Book*, 17–18; Stewart, *Documentary History*, 42–70; Stevens, *New York*, 106–8, 155–59. See also McLeod, "Philadelphia Artisans," 59–64.

25. Aufseher Collegium, Salem, Feb. 20, Mar. 5, 19, 1832; Mar. 1, May 13, 1833, in Fries, *Moravians*, 8:4028–29, 4073, 4077 (quoting last two items); *Andrus Bindery*, 20; Concord, N.H. Mechanics' Association, *Report* (Concord, N.H., 1830), 1–8.

26. Alexander, *Working-Man*, 114–19; Channing, *Lectures*, 1–38; Boston Mechanics' Institution, *First Annual Report* (Boston, 1828); *Third Annual Report* (Boston, 1830); James L. Homer, *An Address Delivered before the Massachusetts Charitable Mechanic Association* . . . (Boston, 1836), 16.

27. Baltimore Typographical Society, *Constitution and By-Laws* (Balt., 1832), 8–9; Typographical Association of New-York, *Constitution and By-laws* (N.Y., 1833), 4 (quote). See also Stevens, *New York*, 106–8.

28. (DG) A brief biographical sketch is in Fletcher M. Green, "Duff Green, Militant Journalist of the Old School," *AHR*, 52 (1947), 247–56. See also Kenneth L. Smith, "Duff Green and the *United States' Telegraph*, 1826–1837" (Ph.D. thesis, College of William and Mary, 1981), 13–35. (CTS) George G. Seibold, *Historical Sketch of Columbia Typographical Union Number One Hundred and One* (Wash., 1915), 4–16. Additional information is in the pamphlets cited below.

29. Columbia Typographical Society, Washington, D.C., *Protest of the Columbia Typographical Society* (Wash., 1834), 4–5, 7, 19–20. This valuable pamphlet summarizes DG's original proposal and reprints his "Prospectus of the Washington Institute," Mar. 1, 1834, pp. 18–21. Additional material, including quotations on both sides, is in CTS, *Reply of the Columbia Typographical Society to the Strictures of Gen. Duff Green* (Wash., 1834). See also F. B. Emerson to DG, Apr. 1, 1834; John Manners to DG, Sept. 25, 1834; DG to W. W. Sands, May 15, 1834, all in DG Papers, SHC (film).

30. CTS, *Protest*, 4–7 (quote at 5).

31. Ibid., 7–9 (quotes at 7, 9).

32. Ibid., 9–11 (quotes at 10, 11).

33. "Prospectus," ibid., 18–21 (quotes at 19).

34. CTS to DG, Apr. 3, 1834, ibid., 14–15 (quote at 15); DG to CTS, Apr. 7, 1834, ibid., 15–16 (quote at 16); CTS to DG, Apr. 17, 1834, ibid., 16–18. See also CTS, *Reply*; Seibold, *Historical Sketch*, 14–15; Green, "DG," 262–63; Smith, "DG," 253–54, 257.

35. Convention recommendations are in International Typographical Union of North America, *General Laws* (Wash., 1838), 1–3. Although the original report has vanished, a reprint is available: National Typographical Convention, *Proceedings* . . . (Indianapolis? 1896? orig., 1836), 1–16. Stewart, *Documentary History*, 51–58, 128–34.

36. (Harpers) Exman, *Brothers Harper,* 93; Exman, *House of Harper,* 22; (N.O.) Stewart, *Documentary History,* 70, 116.

Chapter 5: Personal Relations

1. Exman, *Brothers Harper,* 1–2 (quote); Wright, *Life,* 124–26; Perry, *Wright,* 79.

2. Clapp, *Journal,* May 13, 1822, p. 1. (This 1822–1824 diary, published in 1904, only rarely duplicates an 1820–1824 MS Diary, AAS.) A biographical sketch is in William B. Trask, "Memoir of David Clapp," *New-England Hist. and Gen. Reg.,* 48 (1894), 145–56. See also the family genealogy in Ebenezer Clapp, *The Clapp Memorial* (Boston, 1876), 246–52; David Clapp, Jr., Account Book, 1827–1835, MHS.

3. Christopher Colt to Samuel Colt, Mar. 30, 1832, quoted in Barnard, *Armsmear,* 142. See also SC Papers, Connecticut Historical Society; Neal Dow, *The Reminiscences . . .* (Portland, Maine, 1898), 56–57; Allen Richmond, *The First Twenty Years of My Life* (Phila., 1859), 177, 183, 185, 203; Sidney D. Bumpas Autobiography, p. 5, SHC; William S. Robinson, *"Warrington" Pen-Portraits,* ed. Mrs. W. S. Robinson (Boston, 1877), 10–11, 14 (quote at 10); Charles W. Peale to Benjamin F. Peale, Nov. 18, 1813, BFP Papers in Peale Family Papers, APS (microfiche); Joseph S. Wall to Caleb S. Wall, July 1835, Wall Family Papers, AAS; Francis Brinley, *Life of William T. Porter* (N.Y., 1860), 31; Alexander J. Davis to Hetty Jackson, Oct. 8, 1820, AJD Papers, Avery Architectural and Fine Arts Library, Columbia Univ. See also John Donoghue, *Alexander Jackson Davis* (N.Y., 1982).

4. John Morton Poole to his sister Sarah, Mar. 8, 1835, JMP Papers, HSD.

5. Joel Munsell, Jr., Diaries, 1828–1834, four MS volumes, N-YHS. Vol. 1, pp. 1–59, contains an autobiography for 1808–1828 (quotes at 18). On his early life see 9–16. See also John J. Latting, *A Memorial Sketch of Joel Munsell* (N.Y., 1880); George R. Howell, *Biographical Sketch of Joel Munsell* (Boston, 1880); David S. Edelstein, *Joel Munsell* (N.Y., 1950). A genealogy is in Howell, 14. Munsell gives a charming account of his birthplace in *Reminiscences of Men and Things in Northfield . . .* (Albany, 1876).

6. Wendell P. Garrison and Francis J. Garrison, *William Lloyd Garrison* (Boston, 1894), 1:12–35. A chronology is in William L. Garrison, *Letters,* ed. Walter M. Merrill (Cambridge, Mass., 1971–), 1:xxvi–xxvii. See also Archibald H. Grimke, *William Lloyd Garrison* (N.Y., 1891); John J. Chapman, *William Lloyd Garrison* (N.Y., 1913); Walter M. Merrill, *Against Wind and Tide* (Cambridge, Mass., 1963).

7. Garrison and Garrison, *Garrison,* 1:35–40, 42–44, 48–50 (FG to WLG, July 1, 1822, quoted at 44; WLG to FG, May 26, 1823, excerpt quoted at 50). The latter letter is reprinted in full in Garrison, *Letters,* 1:10–13.

8. Garrison and Garrison, *Garrison,* 1:51–54 (FG to WLG, June 3, 1823, quote at 51). The full letter to Allen is in Garrison, *Letters,* 1:14–15.

9. Garrison and Garrison, *Garrison,* 1:35–37; Wright, *Life,* 134–35; Frazee Autobiography quoted in Jentz, "Artisans," 124; Parton, *Greeley,* 91–96.

10. Newcomb, *Reminiscences,* 29–30; Horace Greeley to Obadiah A. Bowe, Feb. 13, 1831, HG Papers, NYPL; Wright, *Life,* 133, 138–39; F. W. Williams,

S. W. Williams, 6–10; Samuel I. Prime, *Memoirs of the Rev. Nicholas Murray, D.D.* (N.Y., 1863), 17–19, 32–37, 52–55; John Gage, "Selections from the Autobiography . . . ," *Vineland Hist. Mag.,* 9 (1924), 180.

11. Clapp, *Journal,* 1, 4, 10–11 (quotes at 10, 11).

12. Ibid., 11–13.

13. WLG to Frank W. Miller, Apr. 30, 1870, in Garrison and Garrison, *Garrison,* 1:40–41 (quotes at 41); George G. Foster to Rufus W. Griswold, Sept. 30, 1834, RWG Correspondence, Boston Public Library. This letter is published in Joy Bayless, *Rufus Wilmot Griswold* (Nashville, 1943), 10. See also George R. Taylor, "Gaslight Foster: A New York 'Journeyman Journalist' at Mid-Century," *N.Y. Hist.,* 58 (1977), 297–312.

14. Leonard A. Swann, Jr., *John Roach: Maritime Entrepreneur* (Annapolis, 1965), 8; Wright, *Life,* 128–29; Clapp, *Journal,* 2–3 (quote at 3). See also *Andrus Bindery,* 23, 34–35, 39.

15. Clapp, *Journal,* 3–10, 14–19 (quote at 4); Trask, "Clapp," 151–53.

16. Edward Jenner Carpenter Journal, Mar. 30, Apr. 27, May 26, July 7, 9, 10 (quote), 16, 20, 21, Aug. 19, 21, Oct. 5, 24, Dec. 22, 1844; Apr. 6 (quote), 25 (quote), 1845, AAS. See also J. K. Moore to EJC, May 21, 1848, Misc. MSS, AAS.

17. Clapp, *Journal,* 2; Munsell Diaries, vol. 1, pp. 20–21 (quote at 21), N-YHS.

18. Clapp, *Journal,* 1–10 (quotes at 1, 3).

19. Lydia M. Child, *Isaac T. Hopper: A True Life* (Boston, 1853), 28–31 (quotes at 30).

20. Wright, *Life,* 135–36; Exman, *Brothers Harper,* 2 (quote).

21. Munsell Diaries, vol. 1, pp. 27–35 (quote at 29), N-YHS.

22. Thomas McKeller to Charles Patrick Daly, Apr. 30 (quote), June 23 (quote), Aug. 22, Sept. 12, 1833 (quote); Jan. 25, 1834; Allen McKeachnie to CPD, May 8, 1835 (quote), all in CPD Papers, NYPL Annex.

23. Marcus M. Pomeroy, *Journey of Life* (N.Y., 1890), 72; Carpenter Journal, Apr. 29, 1844, AAS; Munsell Diaries, vol. 1, pp. 22–25 (quote at 23), N-YHS.

24. John Rogers, Jr., to Ellen Rogers, Aug. 5, 23, 1848 (quotes), JR Letters, JR Papers, N-YHS. See also Lewis G. Matson to Washington Gladden, Mar. 17, 1855, WG Papers, Ohio Historical Society.

25. Strang, *Diary,* 12; James Horton to Almy & Brown, Nov. 25, 1799, quoted in Kulik, "Industrial Revolution," 235; Richard H. Abbott, *Cobbler in Congress . . . Henry Wilson* (Lexington, Ky., 1972), 1–6; Ernest McKay, *Henry Wilson* (Port Washington, N.Y., 1971), 6–12; Stedman, *Bluegrass Craftsman,* 42 (quote), 51.

26. Nathaniel P. Willis to George J. Pumpelly, Oct. 2, 1825, NPW Papers, Rare Book and Manuscript Library, Columbia Univ.

Chapter 6: The Limits of Reform

1. The traditional view, articulated by Horace Mann and other reformers, has been challenged by Michael B. Katz, *The Irony of Early School Reform* (Cambridge, Mass., 1968); David Nasaw, *Schooled to Order* (N.Y., 1979). A more balanced view is in Lawrence A. Cremin, *American Education,* 2 vols. (N.Y., 1970–1980). See also Carl F. Kaestle, *Pillars of the Republic* (N.Y., 1983).

2. (early) Benjamin Rush, *A Plan for the Establishment of Public Schools and*

the Diffusion of Knowledge in Pennsylvania (Phila., 1786); Enos Hitchcock, *A Discourse on Education* . . . (Providence, 1785), 9; Boston, School Committee, *Recommendations to the Schoolmasters* (Boston, 1789), broadside; Samuel H. Smith, *Remarks on Education* (Phila., 1798), 9–10; (Conn.) Heman Humphrey, *An Address Delivered at the Opening of the Convention of Teachers* (Hartford, 1831); (N.Y.) William O. Bourne, *History of the Public School Society of the City of New York* (N.Y., 1870), 86–87; (S.) Joseph Caldwell, *Letters on Popular Education* (Hillsborough, N.C., 1832); William Hooper, *A Lecture on the Imperfections of Our Primary Schools* (Newbern, N.C., 1832); Walter R. Johnson, *A Concise View of the General State of Education in the United States* (Phila.? ca. 1832), 4; Abdy, *Journal*, 2:253–56; (shortages) Warren Burton, *The District School As It Was* (Boston, 1833); William A. Alcott, *A Historical Description of the First Public School in Hartford, Conn.* (Hartford, 1832); James Strong, *An Address on the Necessity of Education and the Arts in a Republican Government* (Burlington, Vt., 1827), 12; (JL) Joseph Lancaster, *Improvements in Education* (N.Y., 1804); DeWitt Clinton, *An Address, to the Benefactors and Friends of the Free School Society of New-York* (N.Y., 1810), 12; Joseph Lancaster, *The Lancasterian System of Education* (Balt., 1821); High School Society of New-York, *Report of a Committee, Appointed by the High School Society of New-York* (N.Y., 1824), 5–6; Solyman Brown, *A Comparative View of the Systems of Pestalozzi and Lancaster* (N.Y., 1825); Henry K. Oliver, *A Lecture on the Advantages and Defects of the Monitorial System* (Boston, 1831); B. Hall, *Travels*, 1:26–27; Thomas Hamilton, *Men and Manners in America* (Edinburgh, 1834), 1:83–85.

3. (RH) Susan Hale, *Life and Letters of Thomas Gold Appleton* (N.Y., 1885), 23–61; (P.) *Hints to Parents* (Salem, Mass., 1825); (BA) Dorothy McCuskey, *Bronson Alcott: Teacher* (N.Y., 1940), esp. 25–26, 29; F. B. Sanborn and William T. Harris, *A. Bronson Alcott: His Life and Philosophy* (Boston, 1893), esp. 1:73–90; (seeping) e.g., George B. Emerson, *Reminiscences of an Old Teacher* (Boston, 1878); (books) *The New-England Primer, Improved* (Hartford, 1820), quotes at 11. Contrast with editions of Boston, 1784; Middletown, 1786; Cincin., 1829; N.Y., 1829. Franklin Co., Mass., *The Franklin Primer*, 2d ed. (Greenfield, 1826); 9th ed. (1830). "Ape" is in 9th ed., p. 8. See also McCuskey, *Alcott*, 27; (buildings) Essex County Teachers' Association, *A Report on School Houses* (Newburyport, 1833); Baltimore, Commissioners of Public Schools, *Twelfth Annual Report* (Balt., 1841), 1; (infant schools) Infant School Society of Philadelphia, *First Annual Report* (Phila., 1828); Infant School Society of the Northern Liberties and Kensington, *1–3, 5 Annual Reports* (Phila., 1829–1831, 1833); Charles Wheeler, *Address on Behalf of the Infant School Society of the Northern Liberties and Kensington* (Phila., 1835); Bourne, *History*, 115.

4. (early) Benjamin Rush, *Thoughts upon the Amusements and Punishments Which Are Proper for Schools* (Phila., 1790), 3–6. See also Boston, School Committee, *Recommendations*, broadside; Joseph Priestley, *Miscellaneous Observations Relating to Education* . . . (New London, Conn., 1796), 34–36; Enos Weed, *The Educational Directory* (N.Y.? 1803?), 18; (experiments) Hale, *Appleton*, 31; Emerson, *Reminiscences*, 25, 53; (cons.) Hubbard Winslow, *On the Dangerous Tendency to Innovations and Extremes in Education* (Boston, 1835), esp. 18; Samuel Nott, Jr., *Sermons for Children* (N.Y., 1828), 1:62–71 (quote at 66); (reform) Horace Mann, *Lectures on Education* (Boston, 1845), 45–47, 204–5, 303–38.

5. Contrast David B. Warden, *A Sermon on the Advantages of Education* (Kingston, N.Y., 1802), 5, with John Morton Poole to his sister Sarah, Mar. 8, 1835, JMP Papers, HSD; Joel Munsell, Jr., Diaries, vol. 1, p. 11, N-YHS. Children of artisans, however, were never indulged to the degree children of planters were. See Jan Lewis, *The Pursuit of Happiness* (N.Y., 1983), esp. 106–30; Jane T. Censer, *North Carolina Planters and Their Children, 1800–1860* (Baton Rouge, 1984), 40–41, 48–54.

6. (new view) Dorothea Dix, *Conversations on Common Things* (Boston, 1826), 3; Mann, *Lectures*, 17, 174; McCuskey, *Alcott*, 23; *Brief Hints to Parents, on the Subject of Education* (N.Y., 1821); Mrs. Louisa G. Hoare, *Hints for the Improvement of Early Education and Nursery Discipline* (Keene, N.H., 1826); Convers Francis, *Errors in Education* (Hingham, Mass., 1828); *Thoughts on Domestic Education* . . . (Boston, 1829); *Hints to Parents;* (corp. pun.) *Rules for the Good Government and Discipline of the Scholars in the Different Schools* . . . (Phila., 1795), broadside; Winslow, *Dangerous Tendency;* (anti) William A. Alcott, *A Word to Teachers* (Boston, 1833), esp. xiv; Hoare, *Hints*, 68–71; (rote) William Woodbridge, *Plain and Concise View of the System of Education* (Middletown, Conn., 1799); Mann, *Lectures*, 41, 277; Burton, *District School*, 136; (anti) Weed, *Educational Directory*, 14; John Griscom, *A Discourse, on the Importance of Character and Education* (N.Y., 1823), esp. 22; Theodore Sedgwick, *Hints to My Countrymen* (N.Y., 1826); Strong, *Address*, 13.

7. American Tract Society, *Second Annual Report* (N.Y., 1827), 24; George W. Blagden, *The Effects of Education upon a Country Village* (Boston, 1828); (Pa.) Emerson Davis, *The Half Century* (Boston, 1851), 50–72, esp. 64; (N.Y.) Bourne, *History*, esp. 136–38, 153–54, 190, 355–56; High School Society, *Report;* Abdy, *Journal*, 1:9. See also Carl F. Kaestle, *The Evolution of an Urban School System* (Cambridge, Mass., 1973); (Balt.) Baltimore, Commissioners of Public Schools, *1–30 Annual Reports* (Balt., 1830–1859). The enrollments are from *6 AR*, 3; *12 AR*, 4. On high schools see *12 AR*, 2–5. See also Tina H. Sheller, "The Origins of Public Education in Baltimore, 1825–1829," *Hist. Ed. Q.*, 22 (1982), 23–42; (Boston) Boston School Committee, *The Report of the Annual Examination of the Public Schools* . . . (Boston, 1850), 44–46; B. Hall, *Travels*, 2:164–71. See also Stanley K. Schultz, *The Culture Factory* (N.Y., 1973). In general see Kaestle, *Pillars*, 120–21.

8. On child labor in factories see "Petition," Massachusetts, House of Representatives, *Documents* (Boston, 1842), doc. 4.

9. Baltimore, Commissioners of Public Schools, *12 Annual Report* (1841), 3; *21 AR* (1850), 15. These reports give occupations of the fathers of graduates. See, e.g., *23 AR* (1852), 58.

10. Thomas Coke and Francis Asbury, *An Address to the Annual Subscribers for the Support of Cokesbury-College* . . . (N.Y., 1787); Baptist Education Society of the State of New York, *Fifteenth Annual Meeting* (Utica, 1832), 4–9; *Eighteenth Annual Meeting* (Utica, 1835), 10, 14; anon. Baptist minister, speech, 1835, in Furman Univ., MS vol., SCL; Oneida Institute, *Proceedings of a Meeting Held at the Masonic Hall on the Subject of Manual Labor in Connexion with Literary Institutions, June 15, 1831* (Jamaica, N.Y., 1831); *Third Report of the Trustees* (Utica, 1831); Chittenango, N.Y., Polytechny, *Charter* (Chittenango, N.Y., 1829); Shrewsbury, Monmouth Co., N.J., Polytechnic Institute, *Constitution and By-Laws* (N.Y., 1829); Society for Promoting Manual Labor in Literary Institutions, *First Annual Report* (N.Y., 1833); Frances Wright,

"Sketch of the Plan of National Education," in *Popular Tracts. No. 3,* ed. Robert D. Owen (N.Y., 1830), 7–10.

11. (NPB) Thayer, *Bobbin Boy,* 209; (EB) William H. Lee, *Reminiscences of the Early Life of Elihu Burritt* (N.Y., 1881), 4–8 (quote at 8); Merle Curti, *The Learned Blacksmith* (N.Y., 1937), 2–4; Peter Tolis, *Elihu Burritt* (Hamden, Conn., 1968), 7–20. An autobiography is in EB, *Ten-Minute Talks on All Sorts of Topics* (Boston, 1874), 9–68 (9–15 on early life).

12. On mechanics' institutions see Jentz, "Artisans," 93–94; Steven J. Ross, "Workers on the Edge: Work, Leisure, and Politics in Industrializing Cincinnati, 1830–1890" (Ph.D. thesis, Princeton Univ., 1980), 46–47; Sheller, "Public Education," 30–31; Franklin Institute of the State of Pennsylvania for the Promotion of the Mechanic Arts, *First Annual Report* (Phila., 1825); FI, *Address of the Committee on Premiums and Exhibitions . . .* (Phila., 1832), esp. 4. See the FI, *Journal,* 1826– . See also Bruce Sinclair, *Philadelphia's Philosopher Mechanics* (Balt., 1974). The apprentice library movement warrants a monograph. On individual cities see: (Boston) Mechanic Apprentices' Library Association, Boston, *Catalogue of Books . . .* (Boston, 1820); Theodore Lyman, Jr., "Address" (1820), 1–4, MS in the MALA Records in the Massachusetts Charitable Mechanic Association Records, MHS. A concise description of the founding is in Rollo G. Silver, "The Boston Lads Were Undaunted," *Library J.,* July 1949, pp. 995–97. (Portland) Mellen, *Address;* (Salem) Salem Mechanic Library, *Rules and By-Laws* (Salem, 1821); (Providence) Walter R. Danforth, *An Oration Delivered before the Providence Association of Mechanics and Manufacturers April 8, 1822* (Providence, 1822); (Albany) Solomon Southwick, *Address, Delivered by Appointment, in the Episcopal Church, at the Opening of the Apprentices' Library . . .* (Albany, 1821), 7; (N.Y.) Apprentices' Library, *Catalogue* (N.Y., 1820); Thomas R. Mercein, *An Address, Delivered on the Opening of the Apprentices' Library . . .* (N.Y., 1820), 3–12; Mordecai M. Noah, *An Address Delivered before the General Society of Mechanics and Tradesmen . . .* (N.Y., 1822); John Pintard to Eliza Noel Pintard Davidson, Feb. 26, Nov. 25, 27, 1820; Nov. 24, 1821, in JP, "Letters," N-YHS, *Coll.,* 70 (1940), 271, 348, 349–50; 71 (1940), 109. MSS are at GSMT. (Phila.) Apprentices' Library Company of Philadelphia Constitution (1820), MS; Minutes, 1820–1857, MS vol.; Minutes of the Board of Managers, 1820–1833, MS vol., all in ALCP Collection, HSP; Mathew Carey statement on "Apprentices' Library" in "Correspondence on Internal Improvements," MS volume, p. 122, Carey MSS, LCP; John F. Lewis, *History of the Apprentices' Library of Philadelphia, 1820–1920* (Phila., 1924), 1–2, 23, 25, 53, 57; (Balt.) Sheller, "Public Education," 30; *New England Farmer,* 2 (1824), 367; (Wash.) *Am. J. Education,* 3 (1828), 635–36; (Charleston) Petition, ca. 1824, Joseph Johnson to S.C. House of Representatives, South Carolina State Archives; Samuel H. Dickson, *Address, Delivered at the Opening of the New Edifice of the Charleston Apprentices' Library Society* (Charleston, 1841), 10–12; *The Rambler,* Oct. 16, 1843, p. 26; ALS, *Constitution* (Charleston, 1841). Smaller cities also had libraries. Burlington Apprentices' Library Company, *A Catalogue . . .* (Burlington, N.J., 1824); Apprentices Library Association of Carlisle Minutes, 1831–1839, MS vol., HSP; *Savannah Georgian,* Feb. 10, 1829. On Canada see Patrick Keane, "Library Policies and Early Canadian Adult Education," *Humanities Association Rev.,* 29 (1978), 1–20.

13. John Sergeant, *An Address, Delivered at the Request of the Managers of the Apprentices' Library Company of Philadelphia* (Phila., 1832), 34–35; (Bos-

ton) MALA Records, 1832–1834, MS vol. 4 (esp. Mar. 1, 1833 meeting), in MCMA Records, MHS; MALA, *Catalogue* (1820); MALA, *Catalogue of Books* . . . (Boston, 1838); (Phila.) undated clipping, *Military Mag.*, in clipping folder box; Minutes of the Annual Meetings, 1820–1857, MS vol.; Mar. 13, Apr. 14, 1830; May 21, 1831, entries in Minutes of Committee of Attendance, 1830–1837, MS vol., all in ALCP Records, HSP; Lewis, *History*, 57, 61 (Tyson quoted at 60); Joseph Harrison to J. B. Lippincott, Oct. 12, 1863, JH Letterbooks, HSP (transcription courtesy of Charles Royster).

14. (early history) Frederick W. Lincoln, Jr., *An Address, Delivered before the Mechanic Apprentices' Library Association* (Boston, 1844), 11–13 (quotes at 12, 13); (Wightman) MALA Records, 1832–1834, MS vol. 4, Nov. 13, 1832 meeting, MCMA Records, MHS; (minutes) the above vol. and Records, 1834–1835, MS vol. 5, in the same collection; (militancy) John Smith, *An Address, Delivered before the Associated Mechanics & Manufacturers of the State of New-Hampshire* (Portsmouth, 1831); Sergeant, *Address;* William B. Sprague, *A Discourse, Delivered on Sabbath Evening, March 17, 1833* . . . (Albany, 1833). In general see Walter Hugins, *Jacksonian Democracy and the Working Class* (Stanford, 1960). (women) Karen J. Blair, *The Clubwoman as Feminist* (N.Y., 1980). A similar pattern can be seen for Charleston's free blacks. Edmund L. Drago and Susan M. Bowler, "Black Intellectual Life in Antebellum Charleston" (Paper, Organization of American Historians, Los Angeles, Apr. 7, 1984). (FWL) *In Memoriam: Frederick Walter Lincoln* (Boston, 1899), 11, 41.

15. MALA Records, vol. 4, Jan. 15, Mar. 12, 26, Oct. 29, Nov. 26, 1833; Jan. 28, 1834; vol. 5, Jan. 27, Feb. 24, 1835; FP presidential address, Sept. 3, 1833, in vol. 4, both in MCMA Records, MHS. For other debates see Carlisle Apprentices Library Association Minutes, 1831–1839, MS vol., HSP.

16. (local studies) Johnson, *Millennium*, esp. 48–55; Ross, "Workers," esp. 28, 30, 31, 35, 37, 45, 259, 261; Jentz, "Artisans," esp. 5, 13, 16, 21, 28, 256; Michael B. Katz, *The People of Hamilton, Canada West* (Cambridge, Mass., 1975), esp. 287, 305–7; (orphans) Boston, Overseers of the Poor, *The Overseers of the Poor of the City of Boston, to Their Constituents* (Boston, 1823), 19; Guardians for the Relief and Employment of the Poor of Philadelphia, &c., *Report of a Committee* . . . (Phila., 1834), 7; (cities) Joseph Tuckerman, *Mr Tuckerman's First Semiannual Report of the Fourth Year of His Service as a Minister at Large* . . . (Boston, 1830), 7–9, 17–19; Society for the Prevention of Pauperism in the City of New-York, *Second Annual Report* (N.Y., 1820), 17, 19; *Fifth Annual Report* (N.Y., 1821), 25, 27–28; (streets) Joseph Tuckerman, *Mr Tuckerman's Second Semiannual Report of the Fourth Year* . . . (Boston, 1830), 33; JT, *Mr Tuckerman's Seventh Semiannual Report* . . . (Boston, 1831), 7; SPPCNY, *4 AR* (N.Y., 1821), 31–32; *6 AR* (N.Y., 1823), 5–6; SPPCNY, *Report of a Committee Appointed . . . Juvenile Delinquents* (N.Y., 1823), 7, 9–11; SPPCNY, *Report of a Committee Appointed . . . Juvenile Delinquents* (N.Y., 1824), 16–17; Elias Cornelius, *The Moral and Religious Improvement of the Poor* (Salem, Mass., 1824), 7–8; *An Appeal to the Mechanic Interest of the City of New-York, in Relation to Apprentices* (N.Y., 1826), 5; Frederick T. Gray, *An Address Delivered at the Odeon before the Society for the Prevention of Pauperism* (Boston, 1839), 13. In general see Daniel T. McColgan, *Joseph Tuckerman* (Wash., 1940); Joseph M. Hawes, *Children in Urban Society* (N.Y., 1971); Robert S. Pickett, *House of Refuge* (Syracuse, 1969).

17. Boston Society for the Moral and Religious Instruction of the Poor,

Seventh Annual Report (Boston, 1823), 32; *14 AR* (Boston, 1831), 25; Boston, Common Council, Standing Committee on the Subject of the House of Reformation for Juvenile Offenders, *Report* (Boston, 1832), 5–6; Tuckerman, *7 Semiannual Report*, 12–25; *8 Semiannual Report* (Boston, 1831), 13, 16; SPPCNY, *6 AR*, 4, 7–8; SPPCNY, *Report . . . Juvenile Delinquents* (1824), 9.

18. (drink) Tuckerman, *7 Semiannual Report*, 16–17; *8 Semiannual Report*, 23–25; SPPCNY, *Report . . . Juvenile Delinquents* (1823), 7; SPPCNY, *Report . . . Juvenile Delinquents* (1824), 7; (ignorance) BSMRIP, *First Annual Report* (Boston, 1817), 4; *4 AR* (Boston, 1820), 2–3; *8 AR* (Boston, 1824), 4; Boston Asylum for Indigent Boys, *Account* (Boston, 1831), 5–6; Joseph Tuckerman, *A Word to Fathers and Mothers* (Boston, 1828), 1–4; JT, *First Semiannual Report of the Third Year . . .* (Boston, 1829), 13; *8 Semiannual Report*, 4–5, 11–12; SPPCNY, *2 AR*, 5; *6 AR*, 5; SPPCNY, *Report . . . Juvenile Delinquents* (1823), 18; (parents) Tuckerman, *7 Semiannual Report*, 19–26; SPPCNY, *6 AR*, 8–10; SPPCNY, *Report on the Penitentiary System in the United States* (N.Y., 1822), 60; SPPCNY, *Report . . . Juvenile Delinquents* (1823), 2, 23, 26; SPPCNY, *Report . . . Juvenile Delinquents* (1824), 7, 21–29; (begging) Brooklyn Association for Improving the Condition of the Poor, *Seventh Annual Report* (Brooklyn, 1850), 7–8; New-York City Tract Society, *Eleventh Annual Report* (N.Y., 1837), 20–24.

19. Boston, Common Council, Standing Committee, *Report,* 17–24; SPPCNY, *Report . . . Penitentiary,* 60; SPPCNY, *Report . . . Juvenile Delinquents* (1823), 23; Society for the Reformation of Juvenile Delinquents in the City of New-York, *Documents Relative to the House of Refuge . . .* (N.Y., 1832), esp. 21–22; SRJD, *Second Annual Report* (N.Y., 1827), 80; *3 AR* (N.Y., 1828), 124–25; *4 AR* (N.Y., 1829), 180–81. See also House of Refuge, Philadelphia, *2–5 Annual Reports* (Phila., 1830–1833); B. Hall, *Travels,* 1:24–26; Hamilton, *Men and Manners,* 1:276–77.

20. SRJD, *Annual Reports* (1833–1836, 1838–1863). See Statistical Appendix, Table 2. (HW) McKay, *Wilson,* 6–10; (HHS) Clifford M. Drury, *Henry Harmon Spalding* (Caldwell, Idaho, 1936), 17–25. Davidson County Apprentice Bonds, 1824–1918, at the NCSA, show that orphans were not promised a trade; orphan apprenticeship was really a form of guardianship. See also Stanley R. Keyser, "The Apprenticeship System in North Carolina to 1840" (M.A. thesis, Duke Univ., 1950).

21. (lit.) Jean R. Kirkpatrick, "The Temperance Movement and Temperance Fiction, 1820–1860" (Ph.D. thesis, Univ. of Pennsylvania, 1970). See also Anne S. MacLeod, *A Moral Tale* (Hamden, Conn., 1975); (city life) Boston Asylum and Farm School for Indigent Boys, *Report* (Boston, 1845); Tuckerman, *7 Semiannual Report,* 16–17; William Howe, *An Address Delivered at the Berry Street Church* (Boston, 1840), 8–20.

22. John B. Gough, *Autobiography and Personal Recollections* (Springfield, Mass., 1869), 19–83 (quote at 74); Carlos Martyn, *John B. Gough* (N.Y., 1893), 17–69. On his early life see an anti-Gough pamphlet, *Goffiana* (Boston, 1846), 5–8. David Mannering, the upstate farmer, disputed Gough's claims, 12. Another attack is in Jesse Pound, *The Echo of Truth to the Voice of Slander* (N.Y., 1845), 4–13.

240 / NOTES

Chapter 7: The Machine Age

1. David, "Growth," 184. For a more pessimistic assessment see David M. Gordon et al., *Segmented Work, Divided Workers* (N.Y., 1982), 9, 49–50. (inequality) Ross, "Workers," 45, 121–22, 257–62, 276–77, 283–88; Kathleen N. Conzen, *Immigrant Milwaukee, 1836–1860* (Cambridge, Mass., 1976), 75, 78; Edward Pessen, "The Egalitarian Myth and the American Social Reality," *AHR,* 76 (1971), esp. 1021–25; John H. Cordulack, "The Artisan Confronts the Machine Age: Bureau County, Illinois, 1850–1880" (Ph.D. thesis, Univ. of Illinois, Urbana, 1975), 71, 149, 183–86; Katz, *Hamilton,* 52–53, 71–73, 77, 82; Paul B. Hensley, "An Eighteenth-Century World Not Quite Lost: The Social and Economic Structure of a Northern New York Town, 1810–1880" (Ph.D. thesis, College of William and Mary, 1979), 114–20; Bruce Laurie, *Working People of Philadelphia, 1800–1850* (Phila., 1980), 21; (quotes) John Hoffman to William H. Garland, Jan. 27, 1839; WHG to Harriet Garland, June 13, 1841; John W. Evans to WHG, Aug. 6, 1847, all in WHG Papers, #2982, SHC. (crafts) On shoemakers see Chapter 3, n. 3; weavers, Chapter 3, n. 7; silversmiths: Fales, *Silver;* Henry N. Flynt and Martha G. Fales, *The Heritage Foundation Collection of Silver* (Old Deerfield, Mass., 1968); Burton, *South Carolina Silver,* xvii; George B. Cutten, *The Silversmiths of Virginia* (Richmond, 1952), xxiv; George B. Cutten and Minnie W. Cutten, *The Silversmiths of Utica* (Hamilton, N.Y., 1936), 14–15; Gerstell, *Silversmiths,* 8; Ruthanna Hindes, "Delaware Silversmiths, 1728–1880," *DH,* 19 (1981), 127; potters: Susan H. Myers, "The Business of Potting, 1780–1840," in *The Craftsman in Early America,* ed. Ian M. G. Quimby (N.Y., 1984), esp. 194, 226–27.

2. (EJC) Edward Jenner Carpenter Journal, Aug. 24–26, Nov. 2, 1844; Apr. 20, 29, 1845; June 11 (quote), 25, July 23, 1844 (quote); Feb. 24, 26, 1845; Mar. 27, Apr. 19, 23 (quote), May 3, Apr. 14, 1844; Apr. 19, June 2, 9, 10 (quote), 1845; Apr. 22, 1844; June 17, 1845; Brattleboro, Vt., *Sun Reporter,* May 22, 1892, clipping, all in EJC Journal, AAS; EJC, "Journal of a Cabinet Makers Apprentice," ed. Winifred C. Gates, *Chronicle of the Early American Industries Association,* 15 (1962), 23, 35. (furn. industry) An excellent account is Jane E. Sikes, *The Furniture Makers of Cincinnati, 1790 to 1849* (Cincin., 1976), esp. 45–49. See also Ross, "Workers," 161–68; Sharon Darling, *Chicago Furniture* (N.Y., 1984), 6–35, esp. 20; Wilentz, *Chants Democratic,* 127–28; Clare Vincent and Polly A. Earl essays in *Technological Innovation and the Decorative Arts,* ed. Ian M. G. Quimby and Polly A. Earl (Charlottesville, 1974), 207–34, 307–29; Kathleen M. Catalano, "Cabinetmaking in Philadelphia, 1820–1840," *Winterthur Portfolio,* 13 (1979), 81–138; Harold B. Hancock, "Furniture Craftsmen in Delaware Records," ibid., 9 (1974), 175–212; Harold B. Hancock, "Delaware Furnituremaking, 1850–1870: Transition to the Machine Age," *DH,* 17 (1977), 252–57.

3. The classic study remains Oscar Handlin, *Boston's Immigrants* (Cambridge, Mass., 1941). See also Rowland T. Berthoff, *British Immigrants in Industrial America* (Cambridge, Mass., 1953); Conzen, *Immigrant Milwaukee,* 73, 77, 233; Douglas V. Shaw, *The Making of an Immigrant City* (N.Y., 1976), 18, 21, 34–35; Robert Ernst, *Immigrant Life in New York City, 1825–1863* (N.Y., 1949), 214–17; Laurie, *Working People,* 30; JoEllen Vinyard, *The Irish on the Urban Frontier* (N.Y., 1976), 7–8, 40, 61–62, 73, 365; Wilentz, *Chants Democratic,* 117,

406; Keil and Levine essays in *German Workers in Industrial Chicago, 1850–1910*, ed. Hartmut Keil and John B. Jentz (DeKalb, Ill., 1983), 21, 23, 164–65; Ross, "Workers," 37; Laurence A. Glasco, "Ethnicity and Social Structure: Irish, Germans and Native-Born of Buffalo, N.Y., 1850–1860" (Ph.D. thesis, SUNY, Buffalo, 1973), 17, 18, 31, 93, 96–97, 101, 139; Carol G. Pernicone, "The 'Bloody Ould Sixth': A Social Analysis of a New York City Working-Class Community in the Mid-Nineteenth Century" (Ph.D. thesis, Univ. of Rochester, 1973), 34, 36, 53–64, 104–21; McLeod, "Philadelphia Artisan," 82–106; Cordulack, "Artisan," 113–15. (Boston) Robert F. Waterston, *An Address on Pauperism* (Boston, 1844), 14, 17; John T. Sargent, *An Address on Pauperism* (Boston, 1846), 4–5; Boston Society for the Prevention of Pauperism, *Twenty-First Annual Report* (Boston, 1856), 17–30. See also New-York City Tract Society, *Seventeenth Annual Report* (N.Y., 1844), 50.

4. New York Association for Improving the Condition of the Poor, *Twelfth Annual Report* (N.Y., 1855), 18; BSPP, 22 *AR* (1857), 12. See also *N.Y. Times*, Apr. 5, 1853, pp. 4, 6; Jan. 24, 1857; Pernicone, "Bloody Ould Sixth," 90–99.

5. "Cordwainer's Song," *Awl*, Aug. 7, 1844, quoted in Philip S. Foner, *American Labor Songs of the Nineteenth Century* (Urbana, 1975), 66. See also *N.Y. Tribune*, May 27, 1851, p. 7; Mar. 4, 1854, pp. 6–7.

6. George A. Custer, *My Life on the Plains*, ed. M. M. Quaife (Chicago, 1952), xxiv–xxv; Zadock Pratt, *Address Delivered Tuesday Evening, January 16th, 1849, before the Mechanics' Institute* (N.Y., 1849), 8 (quote); "Those Dirty Mechanics," *Voice of Industry*, Feb. 18, 1848, quoted in Foner, *Songs*, 57; John P. Kennedy, *Address Delivered before the Maryland Institute for the Promotion of the Mechanic Arts* . . . (Balt., 1851), 26 (quote), 28 (quote). See also James T. Austin, *An Address, Delivered before the Massachusetts Charitable Mechanic Association* (Boston, 1839), 11; Robert M. Patterson, *Address Delivered at the Close of the Thirteenth Exhibition of American Manufactures* . . . (Phila., 1843), 7; Frederic W. Lincoln, Jr., *An Address Delivered before the Massachusetts Charitable Mechanic Association* . . . (Boston, 1845), 28; Joseph H. Buckingham, *An Address Delivered before the Massachusetts Charitable Mechanic Association* (Boston, 1851), 22; George R. Russell, *An Address before the Massachusetts Charitable Mechanic Association* (Boston, 1853), 32.

7. "Song," *Awl*, July 24, 1844, quoted in Foner, *Songs*, 64–65 (quote at 64); Johnson, *Millennium*, 42. See also Henry B. Fearon, *Sketches of America* (London, 1818), 81.

8. Lincoln, *Address* (1845), 30–31; Salem Aufseher Collegium Minutes, Nov. 16, 1846, in Fries, *Moravians*, 9:4911; Contract, Ephraim Barker and W. S. and I. G. Wetmore, Apr. 1, 1840, Connecticut State Library; six Bonds, 1854–1859, Talbott & Brother Papers, Virginia Historical Society. See also Phila. *Public Ledger*, July 23, 1840, p. 2; Aug. 6, 1841, p. 2; *Poughkeepsie Casket*, 3 (1839), 13–14.

9. Elihu Geer draft letter to Mr. Ely, May 21, 1844, crossed out, Aug. 15, 1844, written above, and in the left margin, July 15, 1844, Samuel Nelson Dickinson Letters, AAS.

10. William Z. Morton to William Blount Rodman, Dec. 6, 1845, WBR Papers, East Carolina Univ. WBR legal files show that WZM was from North Carolina.

11. Edward Jenner Carpenter Journal, Mar. 27 (quote), May 2, 26, June 2, 1844 (quote); Feb. 18, 1845 (quote), AAS.

12. Henry C. Brokmeyer, *A Mechanic's Diary* (Wash., 1910), 7–8. See also Jared B. Graham, *Handset Reminiscences* (Salt Lake City, 1915), 50–52.

13. Nathaniel A. Ware, *Notes on Political Economy* (N.Y., 1844), 30–33, 201 (quote at 32); Job R. Tyson, *Letters, on the Resources and Commerce of Philadelphia* (Phila., 1852), 43; Charles L. Brace, *The Dangerous Classes of New York* (N.Y., 1872), 33, 37–38 (quote at 37).

14. Fritz, *Autobiography*, 32–36 (quote at 35). On the rise of machinists see Cochran, *Frontiers*, 101–15; John W. Lozier, "Taunton and Mason: Cotton Machinery and Locomotive Manufacture in Taunton, Massachusetts, 1811–1861" (Ph.D. thesis, Ohio State Univ., 1978), esp. 1–11; Thomas Murphy to Emily Cook, Nov. 14, 1852, Cook Family Papers, East Carolina Univ.; Robert S. Woodbury, *Studies in the History of Machine Tools* (Cambridge, Mass., 1972).

15. (THS) Thomas H. Savery Copy Book, 1854–1856, entry for Nov. 19, 1854, Savery Papers, Acc. 285, HML. (JR) John Rogers, Jr., Autobiography, 7–8, in JR Papers, N-YHS; David H. Wallace, *John Rogers* (Middletown, Conn., 1967), 27–30; JR to John Rogers, Sr., July 16, 19 (time schedule), 1850; to Sarah Rogers, July 28, 1850 (quotes), JR Letters, in JR Papers, N-YHS.

16. (WHS) James C. Sylvis, *The Life, Speeches, Labors and Essays of William H. Sylvis* (Phila., 1872), 24–26; Jonathan Grossman, *William Sylvis* (N.Y., 1945), 19–21; (WT) William Turner to William H. Garland, Sept. 7, 1845, WHG Papers, #2982, SHC; (railroads) Albert Fishlow, *American Railroads and the Transformation of the Ante-Bellum Economy* (Cambridge, Mass., 1965), 101–4, 132–56. On locomotives see Malcolm C. Clark, "The Birth of an Enterprise: Baldwin Locomotive, 1831–1842," *PMHB*, 90 (1966), 423–44; Lozier, "Taunton and Mason," 396–498. (technology) John Fritz, "The Development of Iron Manufacture in the United States . . . ," in Franklin Institute, Philadelphia, *Commemorative Exercises at the Celebration of the Seventy-Fifth Anniversary* (Phila., 1900), 99–105, 118–19, 121; David J. Jeremy, *The Transatlantic Industrial Revolution* (Cambridge, Mass., 1981). Two excellent studies of small-scale ironworks are Joseph E. Walker, *Hopewell Village* (Phila., 1966); on Meramec, Mo., James D. Norris, *Frontier Iron* (Madison, Wis., 1964).

17. Brokmeyer, *Diary*, 7–11 (quotes at 9, 9, 10).

18. Ibid., 20, 23, 32–34, 65 (quotes at 32).

19. Fritz, "Iron Manufacture," 99–102, 118–19, 121; Convention of Iron Workers, *Proceedings* (Albany, 1849), esp. 17, 20n, 33, 47–48, 55; John L. Hayes, *Memorial of the Iron Manufacturers of New England* (Phila., 1850), 35–36; Edwin T. Freedley, *Philadelphia and Its Manufactures* (Phila., 1859), 290–310. (RC) Alfred H. Lewis, *Richard Croker* (N.Y., 1901), 36, 39–40; Theodore L. Stoddard, *Master of Manhattan . . . Richard Croker* (N.Y., 1931), 29–30; (WHS) Sylvis, *Sylvis*, 26; Grossman, *Sylvis*, 20–21. An excellent description of a foundry is in J. R. Chapin, "Among the Nail-Makers," *Harper's New Monthly Mag.*, 21 (1860), 155–64. On stove molders see Joseph A. Barford, "Reminiscences . . . ," *International Molders' and Foundry Workers' Journal*, 94 (July 1958), 8–11 (orig. in *Iron Molders' J.*, Mar. 1902); Brian Greenberg, "Worker and Community: The Social Structure of a Nineteenth-Century American City, Albany, New York, 1850–1884" (Ph.D. thesis, Princeton Univ., 1980), 19–21, 47–54; Daniel J. Walkowitz, *Worker City, Company Town* (Urbana, 1978).

20. Sylvis, *Sylvis*, 30–34 and passim. See also Edgar B. Cale, *The Organization of Labor in Philadelphia, 1850–1870* (Phila., 1940), 10, 18–23; Walkowitz,

Worker City; David Montgomery, *Beyond Equality* (N.Y., 1967). The richest
sources are the labor newspapers of the 1860s, e.g., *Fincher's Trades' Review,*
Boston *Daily Evening Voice,* Chicago *Workingman's Advocate.*

21. Advertisement for presses is in Samuel Nelson Dickinson Letters, AAS;
Nathan C. Geer to Elihu Geer, Mar. 5, 19, 1847; Jan. 11, 1849 (misdated 1848);
July 1849; July 22, Aug. 27, Sept. 11, 25, Dec. 2, 1850; Sept. 27, 1852; to Messrs.
Cohner & Son, July 22, 1850; Sophia C. Geer to EG, July 27, 1846; *Scale of
Prices* (Peoria, 1859), broadside; all in NCG Collection of Letters, Newberry
Library, Chicago; C. C. P. Moody to EG, June 10, 1847; S. N. Dickinson to EG,
July 10, 1848, both in SND Letters, AAS; William H. Lyon, *Pioneer Editors
in Missouri, 1808–1860* (Columbia, Mo., 1965), 105; Horatio King affidavit,
Sept. 21, 1847, HK Papers, Duke Univ. See also W. C. Felch to Melzar Gardner,
Jan. 1, 1842, MG Papers, Duke Univ.

22. Isaac Munroe to Hoe & Co., Jan. 2, 1850; W. W. and L. A. Pratt to Hoe &
Co., Jan. 30, 1850, both in Hoe & Co. Records, AAS; R. Hoe & Co., *Catalog*
(N.Y., 1854), frontispiece, 10, 12 (quote), 20; *Catalog* (N.Y., 1860), 26, 50; *Cata-
logue* (N.Y., 1867), 11, all at NL; Edward Everett to J. O. Sargent, Dec. 24,
1859, JOS Papers, MHS; Van Winkle, *Printers' Guide,* 154–92; Thomas Lynch,
The Printer's Manual (Cincin., 1859), 149–73 (quote at 149).

23. Exman, *Brothers Harper,* 348–49; Jacob Abbott, *The Harper Establishment* (N.Y., 1855), 32, 40–49, 67, 71, 88, 96–102 (quote at 40).

24. Ibid., 119, 122.

25. J. Denio and TW quoted in Follett, *History,* 62, 67; Griffin, *History,* 27–
28 (quote), 80. Compare imprints in the Shaw-Shoemaker bibliography for 1801–
1829 with those in Orville Roorbach's later book catalogs; William Gregg,
Essays on Domestic Industry (Graniteville, S.C., 1941; orig., 1845), 50–51.

26. International Typographical Union of North America, Union No. 33,
Providence, *Printers and Printing in Providence, 1762–1907* (Providence, 1907),
28, 31. See also ibid., 189; William Welles, "A Journeyman Printer," *Littell's
Living Age,* 8 (1846), 626–27; Stewart, *Documentary History,* 59n; (bids) Ohio,
Senate Journal, 1848–9 (Columbus, 1849), appendix, 56–158; "Remonstrance
. . . ," in Massachusetts, House of Representatives, *Documents* (Boston, 1849),
doc. 44, pp. 2–3 (quote at 2); Stewart, *Documentary History,* 77; Stevens, *New
York,* 210–11.

27. ITUNA, Providence, *Printers,* 190; Stevens, *New York,* 210, 213, 214;
Stewart, *Documentary History,* 77, 78; Phila. *Public Ledger,* July 30, 1849, p. 3;
N.Y. Tribune, May 22, 1850, pp. 1–2; *Albany Eve. J.,* Sept. 14, 1850, quoted in
Greenberg, "Worker," 42–45. For three cases see apprentice Thomas J. Whitman to his parents, Feb., Mar. 14, 27, Apr. 23, 1848, in Walt Whitman, *Correspondence,* ed. Edwin H. Miller (N.Y., 1961), 1:27–36; William T. Sherman
to apprentice Lampson P. Sherman, June 30, 1844, William A. Whitaker Papers, SHC; journeyman Edward Eastman to Mrs. Sarah Jackson, Jan. 20, 1846;
to Mrs. Charles Houston, June 18, 1846; to Phinehas Eastman, July 18, 1846;
Mrs. Martha Ryan to PE, Dec. 27, 1846, all in EE Collection, LSU.

28. Stewart, *Documentary History,* 77, 78, 80; Ohio, *Senate Journal, 1848–9,*
156–58; Stevens, *New York,* 214; Barnett, *Printers,* 167; *N.Y. Tribune,* May 22,
1850, pp. 1–2; Phila. *Public Ledger,* Sept. 2, 1850, p. 2.

29. John McVicar, *Origin and Progress of the Typographical Union* (Lansing,
Mich., 1891), 4–12; Barnett, *Printers,* 167–68, 170; Stewart, *Documentary History,*
85, 86, 136; Stevens, *New York,* 570–71; ITUNA, *Proceedings . . . 1852* (Cincin.,

1852), 9. See also Robert C. Smith, "National Typographical Union," *Printers' News Letter*, 2 (July 1858), 4; Samuel Slawson, "A Brief History of the National Typographical Union," in ITUNA, *Proceedings . . . 1858* (N.Y., 1858), 32–40. The *Proceedings, 1852–1859*, contain a wealth of material and have been published on film by the State Historical Society of Wisconsin.

30. (economy) Seibold, *Historical Sketch*, 16–17. See also ITUNA, Providence, *Printers*, 34; David H. Hunter letter, Nov. 14, 1857; George L. Russell letter, Sept. 13, 1857, both in ITUNA, Union No. 21, San Francisco, Minutes, 1853–1859, MS vol., Bancroft Library, Univ. of California, Berkeley; (women) ITUNA, *Proceedings . . . 1854* (n.p., 1854), 4 (quote). See also Stevens, *New York*, 422–25; Barnett, *Printers*, 311–12; (foremen) ITUNA, *Proceedings . . . 1857* (New Orleans, 1857), 45. See also McVicar, *Typographical Union*, 12; (Baton Rouge) ITUNA, *Proceedings . . . 1860* (Boston, 1860), 42–44; John McGrath, "An Old Time Strike," newspaper clipping, ca. 1915, in JM Scrapbook, p. 8, LSU. See also ITUNA, Union No. 46, Sacramento, Minutes, 1859–1882, MS vol., 16, 73, 78, 84, Bancroft Library, Univ. of California, Berkeley; (Charleston) Charleston Typographical Union No. 43, Minute Book, 1859–1862, Oct. 1 (quote), 3, 6, Dec. 29, 1860, SCL. A good summary is in Yates Snowden, "Notes on Labor Organizations in South Carolina, 1742–1861," Univ. of South Carolina, *Bulletin*, 38, pt. 4 (1914), 30–34. One local had no discussion of apprentices. See ITUNA, No. 54, Raleigh, Records, 1854–1871, Duke Univ. (film). The best local records I have located are New Orleans Typographical Union, No. 17, Records, Univ. of New Orleans.

31. On tramps see Graham, *Reminiscences*, 50–52, 57–60, 69–74, 83; Welles, "Journeyman Printer," 626–27.

Chapter 8: A Way Out?

1. J. W. Alexander, "Young Men of Cities Urged to the Work of Mental Improvement," in *The Young Man*, ed. W. W. Everts et al. (Lowell, Mass., 1852), 91–92.

2. For an imaginative use of these books see Wishy, *Child;* Joseph F. Kett, *Rites of Passage* (N.Y., 1977), 86–108; Graham J. Barker-Benfield, *The Horrors of the Half-Known Life* (N.Y., 1976). For an apprentice reader see Carpenter Journal, Feb. 16, 1845, AAS.

3. For traditional views see *A Father's Gift to His Son* (N.Y., 1821); John A. James, *The Family Monitor* (Boston, 1829). William A. Alcott, *The Young Man's Guide*, 11th ed. (Boston, 1837), 47–53, 158–60, 170–71, 174, 176, 183, 192, 208, 242 (quote at 50); John Todd, *The Young Man*, 3d ed. (Northampton, Mass., 1846), 153–56; T. S. Arthur, *Advice to Young Men on Their Duties and Conduct in Life* (Boston, 1850; orig., 1847), 64, 73–74, 86–87, 139, 142; *The Duties of Employers and Employed Considered with Reference to Principals and Their Clerks or Apprentices* (N.Y., 1849), 21–25.

4. John C. Rudd, *A Series of Discourses Addressed to Young Men . . .* (Auburn, 1830), 42–43.

5. Todd, *Young Man*, 120; Arthur, *Advice*, 152–54, 158, 177; Alcott, *Guide*, 103–8, 139–40; William Hague, "The Duties of Employers and the Employed," in *Young Man*, ed. Everts, 174. See also Solomon Southwick, *Five Lessons for Young Men* (Albany, 1837), 172–73.

6. Arthur, *Advice*, 52–61. See also William G. Eliot, Jr., *Lectures to Young Men* (Boston, 1854), 33–34, 39–58.

7. Rudd, *Series*, 21, 39–40 (quotes at 21, 40); Joel Hawes, *Lectures to Young Men, on the Formation of Character, &c.*, 4th ed. (Hartford, 1830; orig., 1828), 35–37; Daniel C. Eddy, *The Young Man's Friend* (Boston, 1856), 22–24 (quote at 24); Todd, *Young Man*, 68; Arthur, *Advice*, 134 (quote), 131 (quote).

8. Eliot, *Lectures*, quotes at 8, 30–31; William Thomson, *A Tradesman's Travels in the United States and Canada, in the Years 1840, 41, & 42* (Edinburgh, 1842), 46–47; James D. Burn, *Three Years among the Working-Classes in the United States during the War* (London, 1865), 24, 69–72. See also George Santayana in Pugh, *Sons*, 87.

9. Hawes, *Lectures*, 44; Edwin H. Chapin, *Duties of Young Men* (Boston, 1849), 87, 90 (quote); Todd, *Young Man*, 20, 31–32; Rudd, *Series*, 10–12 (quote at 10); Chapin, *Duties*, 59. See also Arthur, *Advice*, 19–21.

10. Here I have been influenced by C. Wright Mills. For a concise discussion of reform see Ronald G. Walters, *American Reformers, 1815–1860* (N.Y., 1978). A cryptic but shrewd comment is offered by Katz, *Hamilton*, 307.

11. Apprentices' Library Company of Philadelphia, *Annual Report* (Phila., 1843), 5–6; ALCP, *Annual Report* (Phila., 1845), 3; *Evening Schools and District Libraries* (Phila., 1850), 5–9 (quotes at 7). A copy of the latter pamphlet is in ALCP Papers, HSP. See also Phila. *Public Ledger*, Jan. 28, 1850, p. 3.

12. *Evening Schools*, 9–21 (quotes at 10, 10, 11, 20n).

13. Samuel S. Spear, *An Address Delivered before the Mechanic Apprentices' Library Association* (Boston, 1855), 5–20 (quote at 19). A copy is in MALA Records, MHS. Other quotes are from Gleason's poem appended to this address at 23, 24, 27. The quest for respectability has been discussed by E. P. Thompson, "Time, Work, Discipline, and Industrial Capitalism," *Past and Present*, no. 38 (1967), 56–97; Bruce Laurie, " 'Nothing on Compulsion': Life Styles of Philadelphia Artisans, 1820–1850," *LH*, 15 (1974), 337–66; Paul Faler, "Cultural Aspects of the Industrial Revolution: Lynn, Massachusetts, Shoemakers and Industrial Morality, 1826–1860," ibid., 367–94. A vast literature developed to support the concept of success. For an assessment see Rex Burns, *Success in America* (Amherst, 1976).

14. Traditional culture needs much study. See Wilentz, "Artisan Republican Festivals," 37–77; Laurie, *Working People*, 53–66.

15. The interpretation is my own. See Michael Feldberg, *The Philadelphia Riots of 1844* (Westport, 1975). On the Bowery Boys see Jentz, "Artisans," 238–39. Two apprentice gang leaders who rose to prominence were David Broderick and Richard Croker. See David A. Williams, *David C. Broderick* (San Marino, 1969); James O'Meara, *Broderick and Gwin* (San Francisco, 1881); Jeremiah Lynch, *A Senator of the Fifties* (San Francisco, 1911); Stoddard, *Croker*; Lewis, *Croker*.

16. Frank H. Schell, "Old Volunteer Fire Laddies" MS, esp. chap. 1, p. 2, chap. 2, p. 3, HSP; John J. Sturtevant, "Recollections of a Resident of New York City from 1835 to 1905" MS, 29–30, NYPL; Bruce Laurie, "Fire Companies and Gangs in Southwark: The 1840s," in *The Peoples of Philadelphia*, ed. Allen F. Davis and Mark H. Haller (Phila., 1973), 71–87, esp. 71; Andrew H. Neilly, "The Violent Volunteers: A History of the Volunteer Fire Department of Philadelphia, 1736–1871" (Ph.D. thesis, Univ. of Pennsylvania, 1959), esp. 36–37, 72–73.

17. A study of the militia is badly needed. See S. B. Cloudman, "Recollections of the Old Time Militia and the Annual General Muster," Maine Hist. Soc., *Coll.*, 3d ser., 2 (1906), 331–41; John Morton Poole to Joseph Bancroft, Sept. 19, 1830 (quote), JMP Papers, HSD; Carpenter Journal, Mar. 22, Apr. 8, 12, 14, May 27, 29, June 15, 29, July 4, 27, 1844, AAS; Lewis Brewster Diary, Sept. 12, 15, 16, 19, 21, 22, 1848, NHHS; John Rogers, Jr., to Laura Rogers, Sept. 22, 1850, JR Letters in JR Papers, N-YHS. See Steffen, *Mechanics*, 53, 62.

18. Susan G. Davis, " 'Making Night Hideous': Christmas Revelry and Public Order in Nineteenth-Century Philadelphia," *Am. Q.*, 34 (1982), 185–99. This sort of ritual was well established in Europe. See Natalie Z. Davis, "The Reasons of Misrule: Youth Groups and Charivaris in Sixteenth-Century France," *Past and Present*, no. 50 (1971), 41–75.

19. Feldberg, *Philadelphia Riots;* Laurie, *Working People,* 169–72; Wilentz, *Chants Democratic,* 315–24; Ira M. Leonard, "The Rise and Fall of the American Republican Party in New York City, 1843–1845," *N.Y. Hist. Soc. Q.,* 50 (1966), 151–92. For more detail see Ira M. Leonard, "New York City Politics, 1841–1844: Nativism and Reform" (Ph.D. thesis, New York Univ., 1965); Herbert I. London, "The Nativist Movement in the American Republican Party in New York City during the Period 1843–1847" (Ph.D. thesis, New York Univ., 1966). On Cincinnati see Ross, "Workers," 345–46. For background see Ray A. Billington's dated *The Protestant Crusade, 1800–1860* (N.Y., 1938).

20. Michael F. Holt, "The Antimasonic and Know Nothing Parties," in *History of U.S. Political Parties,* ed. Arthur M. Schlesinger, Jr. (N.Y., 1973), 1:593–620; MFH, "The Politics of Impatience: The Origins of Know Nothingism," *J. Am. Hist.,* 60 (1973), 309–31; Dale Baum, "Know-Nothingism and the Republican Majority in Massachusetts," ibid., 64 (1978), 959–86; Stephen E. Maizlish, "The Meaning of Nativism and the Crisis of the Union," in *Essays on American Antebellum Politics, 1840–1860,* ed. SEM and John J. Kushma (College Station, 1982), 166–98; William E. Gienapp, "The Origins of the Republican Party" (Ph.D. thesis, Univ. of California, Berkeley, 1980); Dale Baum, *The Civil War Party System* (Chapel Hill, 1984). On New Orleans see Clement Eaton, *The Growth of Southern Civilization* (N.Y., 1961), 166. For an insightful comment on how economic growth destabilizes politics see Mancur Olson, Jr., "Rapid Growth as a Destabilizing Force," *JEH,* 23 (1963), 529–52. I am grateful to Donald Horowitz for this reference.

21. U.S. Census, 1850, *Statistical View of the United States* (Wash., 1854), 394; U.S. Census, 1850, *The Seventh Census of the United States: 1850* (Wash., 1853), xlii, 976.

22. Edwin Corle, *John Studebaker* (N.Y., 1948), 37–77; Florence M. Christman, ed., *One Man's Gold* (N.Y., 1930), xi–xiii, 11–13, 19, 57–58, 68, 109, 185, 225–26 (quotes at 19, 68).

23. Henry George, Jr., *The Life of Henry George* (Toronto, 1900), 1–19, 41–48 (quotes at 47, 47–48). A good chronology is in Edward J. Rose, *Henry George* (N.Y., 1968), 15–17.

24. George, *George,* 48–49.

25. Ibid., 49–52 (quotes at 49, 50–51).

26. Ibid., 68, 71, 72, 83–86, 95–96 (quotes at 72, 95).

27. Ibid., 96–97, 99, 104–5, 107–8, 118, 123, 135 (quote at 118).

Chapter 9: Lingering Traditions

1. (WDH) William D. Howells, *A Boy's Town* (N.Y., 1918; orig., 1890), esp. 189–90, 238–39; WDH, *The Country Printer* (n.p., 1896), 3–7, 12–15, 23, 29–32; WDH, *Years of My Youth* (Bloomington, Ind., 1975; orig., 1916), 15–16, 20, 23–24, 31–36, 38, 59–60, 70–78; WDH, *My Year in a Log Cabin* (N.Y., 1902; orig., 1893), 1–49; Edwin H. Cady, *The Road to Realism . . . William Dean Howells* (Syracuse, 1956), 11–32, 35, 37–38, 42–43. See also WDH, *Selected Letters*, ed. George Arms et al. (Boston, 1979–   ), 1:8–17. A genealogy is in WDH, *Years*, 259–63; (BP) Pomeroy, *Journey*, 10–11, 54–58. See also Ruth A. Tucker, "M. M. 'Brick' Pomeroy: Forgotten Man of the Nineteenth Century" (Ph.D. thesis, Northern Illinois Univ., 1979). (AR) Arthur W. Richards, *Progress of Life and Thought* (Des Moines, 1892), 32–35. In general see Clarence H. Danhof, *Change in Agriculture* (Cambridge, Mass., 1969), 1–26; Cordulack, "Artisan," esp. 5, 8–9, 11, 24, 48, 50–53, 66, 71, 76, 78–87, 146–62, 183; Jerusha W. Clark, "Childhood Reminiscences of Princeton," Ill. State Hist. Soc., *Journal*, 49 (1956), 95–106; Hensley, "New York Town," esp. 114–16, 118, 120; Merle Curti, *The Making of an American Community* (Stanford, 1959), esp. 61–63, 232–34, 254, 258; Don H. Doyle, *The Social Order of a Frontier Community* (Urbana, 1978), esp. 99–101, 261–62; Gordon W. Kirk, Jr., *The Promise of American Life* (Phila., 1978), 36.

2. For examples of the farmer-craftsman tradition see William Bartell Diary, 1823–1835, SCL; Emsley Burgess Diary, 1845–1847, EB Diary and Papers, SHC; Joel Shofner to Michael Shoffner, July 22, 1855, MS Papers, SHC; Henry Anderson bill to William Adams, 1840, WA Papers, Duke Univ.; Steven Hahn, *The Roots of Southern Populism* (N.Y., 1983), esp. 21–22, 29, 71, 189, 295. For examples of slave craftsmen on plantations see Arney R. Childs, ed., *Planters and Business Men* (Columbia, S.C., 1957), 54–55, 58–62, 66; Frances A. Kemble, *Journal of a Residence on a Georgian Plantation in 1838–1839*, ed. John A. Scott (N.Y., 1961; orig., 1863), 62–66, 117, 233–34; Frederick L. Olmsted, *The Cotton Kingdom*, ed. Arthur M. Schlesinger (N.Y., 1953; orig., 1861), 186–87; Rachel S. O'Connor to Mary Moore, May 23, 1842, in RSO, *Mistress of Evergreen Plantation*, ed. Allie B. W. Webb (Albany, 1983), 236.

3. On the value of slave craftsmen see John H. Franklin, *From Slavery to Freedom*, 3d ed. (N.Y., 1967), 196; Henry Pelling, *American Labor* (Chicago, 1960), plate 2 (reproduces sales data); Leonard P. Stavisky, "The Negro Artisan in the South Atlantic States, 1800–1860: A Study of Status and Economic Opportunity with Special Reference to Charleston" (Ph.D. thesis, Columbia Univ., 1958), 118. This latter work contains a wealth of information. On craftsmen see Thomas P. Jones, *An Address on the Progress of Manufactures and Internal Improvement in the United States* (Phila., 1827), 13; Olmsted, *Cotton Kingdom*, 186; Raymond B. Pinchbeck, *The Virginia Negro Artisan and Tradesman* (Richmond, 1926), 47–52; Janet S. Hermann, *The Pursuit of a Dream* (N.Y., 1981), 14, 18. In general see Kenneth M. Stampp, *The Peculiar Institution* (N.Y., 1956), 37–38, 41, 59; James Oakes, *The Ruling Race* (N.Y., 1982), 59, 247; Eugene D. Genovese, *Roll, Jordan, Roll* (N.Y., 1974), 388–98; Leslie H. Owens, *This Species of Property* (N.Y., 1976), 177–81; John W. Blassingame, ed., *Slave Testimony* (Baton Rouge, 1977); George P. Rawick, ed., *The American Slave*, 41 vols. (Westport, 1972–1979), e.g., vol. 2, pt. 1, p. 173; vol. 4, pt. 1, p. 14; pt. 2, p. 256;

vol. 5, pt. 3, p. 259; vol. 8, pt. 1, p. 31. Donald M. Jacobs, ed., *Index to the American Slave* (Westport, 1981), lists more than a thousand entries under "work skills," 270–73. On this source see the comments of Paul D. Escott, *Slavery Remembered* (Chapel Hill, 1979), 16, 61–63, 93, 139.

4. A pioneer study was James C. Bonner, "Profile of a Late Ante-Bellum Community," *AHR*, 49 (1944), 671, 675–79. My examination of Jasper County, Ga., confirms this study. See also Raymond, *Thoughts*, 440–41; Tocqueville, *Journey*, 72; Luther P. Jackson, *Free Negro Labor and Property Holding in Virginia, 1830–1860* (N.Y., 1969; orig., 1942), 80. For a penetrating analysis of the entire slave society and its economic structure see Gavin Wright, *The Political Economy of the Cotton South* (N.Y., 1978).

5. Bonner, "Profile," 663–80; Eugene D. Genovese, *The Political Economy of Slavery* (N.Y., 1965), 165, 177n, 227; Genovese, *Roll*, 405; Herbert G. Gutman, *Slavery and the Numbers Game* (Urbana, 1975), 50. See also Bertram Wyatt-Brown, *Southern Honor* (N.Y., 1982), 189–90. (wages) Thomson, *Travels*, 16; Charleston Typographical Union No. 43, Minute Book, 1859–1862, p. 50 (June 30, 1860), SCL. On northern capital see John Morton Poole to Samuel S. Poole, July 24, 1836, JMP Papers, HSD. (other work) Jefferson McKinney to Jeptha McKinney, Dec. 26, 1841; Apr. 29, Oct. 10, 1842; Feb. 17, 1843; Jan. 26, 1844; Jan. 8, 1846; Apr. 1, Nov. 2, 1848 (quote), Jeptha McKinney Papers, LSU; Charles Green to Mrs. Henrietta Green, Dec. 18, 1834; Mar. 29, 1835; to George Green, Mar. 27, 1836 (quote); to Mrs. HG, June 19, July 31, 1836 (quote), CG Papers, LSU. See also Oakes, *Race*, 59–60; William Little Papers, NCSA; Lucas Family Papers, S-CHS. (depop.) W. E. B. DuBois, "The Negro Landholder in Georgia," U.S. Dept. of Labor, *Bulletin*, 35 (Wash., 1901), 651–61.

6. Among the abolitionists was Lydia Child (Martin Duberman, "The Northern Response to Slavery," in *The Antislavery Vanguard*, ed. Martin Duberman (Princeton, 1965), 404n). The idea was suggested as late as 1862 in a letter to the *N.Y. Times*. See Philip S. Foner and Ronald L. Lewis, eds., *The Black Worker* (Phila., 1978), 1:31.

7. Jones, *Address*, 12n, 13; Kemble, *Journal*, 105; Robert Mills, *Statistics of South Carolina* (Charleston, 1826), 427; Leon F. Litwack, *North of Slavery* (Chicago, 1961), 156; Franklin, *From Slavery*, 219, 222–23; Claudia D. Goldin, *Urban Slavery in the American South, 1820–1860* (Chicago, 1976), 29; Stampp, *Peculiar Institution*, 427; Richard C. Wade, *Slavery in the Cities* (N.Y., 1964), 273–75; Robert S. Starobin, *Industrial Slavery in the Old South* (N.Y., 1970), 159, 211–12, 296–97; Ira Berlin, *Slaves without Masters* (N.Y., 1974), 230–31. On the complexities of the urban South see Ira Berlin and Herbert G. Gutman, "Natives and Immigrants, Free Men and Slaves," *AHR*, 88 (1983), 1175–1200.

8. Litwack, *North*, 155–61; Foner and Lewis, *Black Worker*, 1:63, 134–35, 254–56. See also Ethan A. Andrews, *Slavery and the Domestic Slave-Trade in the United States* (Boston, 1836), 162; Daniel A. Payne, *Recollections of Seventy Years* (Nashville, 1888), 11–18; Stephen F. Miller Memoir, pp. 51–52, East Carolina Univ.; James Boon Papers, NCSA.

9. In general see Franklin, *From Slavery*, 196; Foner and Lewis, *Black Worker*, 1:107. JHH is quoted in Genovese, *Roll*, 393. (overwork) Blassingame, *Slave Testimony*, 47–48, 250–54, 269, 391, 490; (hiring out) Goldin, *Urban Slavery*, 36, 74–75; Diana Davis to George L. C. Davis, May 16, 1833 (quote); P. N. Carroll to GLCD, Nov. 29, 1839 (quote); John B. Murison to GLCD, Aug. 27, Sept. 13, 26, 29, 1842; D. R. Carroll to GLCD, Nov. 5, 1845, all in GLCD Papers, Tulane

Univ. See also Jane D. Wright to John Dewees, Sept. 8, 1859, JD and Family Papers, LSU.

10. A Charleston Craftsman's Day Book, 1827–1830, S-CHS; Unidentified Carpenter's Day Book, 1853–1854, Georgia Historical Society; (slaveholder competition) James Kirker Inventory, 1852, MacKenzie Family Papers, SCL; Blassingame, *Slave Testimony*, 621, 743–45; Rawick, *American Slave*, vol. 6, pt. 2, p. 131. (slave competition) Charleston Mechanics Petition to S.C. Senate, 1811 (misdated, after 1822; quote), South Carolina State Archives. See also Columbia Mechanics Petition to S.C. House of Rep., ca. 1818; to S.C. Senate, 1819; S.C. House Judiciary Committee Report, 1818; SCHJCR, 1819; S.C. Senate Judiciary Committee Report, 1819, all MSS in SCSA. (independence) Stavisky, "Negro Artisan," 91–95, 179; (1858) S.C. House Committee on Colored Population Report, 1858, SCSA.

11. West Burgess Agreement, LSU; Helen T. Catterall, ed., *Judicial Cases Concerning American Slavery and the Negro* (Wash., 1926–1937), 2:197, 201, 210–11, 274, 407, 427, 436, 456.

12. Kathleen Bruce, *Virginia Iron Manufacture in the Slave Era* (N.Y., 1931), esp. 223–54; Charles B. Dew, *Ironmaker to the Confederacy* (New Haven, 1966), 22–26; *Charleston Mercury*, Mar. 30, 1846; Oct. 3, 1848; Mar. 3, May 24, 1849; May 14, 1850; May 21, 1851; Savannah *Daily Morning News*, Aug. 24, 1852; Thomson, *Travels*, 113; John Wilkes to Charles Wilkes, Jan. 29, May 31, Aug. 3, 1856, Wilkes Family Papers, Dalton Collection, Duke Univ.; Foner and Lewis, *Black Worker*, 1:86; Olmsted, *Cotton Kingdom*, 371, 371n; L. F. W. Andrews, *An Address Delivered before the Georgia State Convention of Mechanics . . .* (Macon, 1851), 31 (quote); Eaton, *Southern Civilization*, 167. In general see Starobin, *Industrial Slavery;* Fred Siegel, "Artisans and Immigrants in the Politics of Late Antebellum Georgia," *Civil War Hist.*, 27 (1981), 221–30; Fred Bateman and Thomas Weiss, *A Deplorable Scarcity* (Chapel Hill, 1981), 17, 53, 158.

13. Foner and Lewis, *Black Worker*, 1:5–14; Cumberland County, North Carolina, Apprentice Records, NCSA. I am indebted to Harry L. Watson for bringing these records to my attention. Franklin, *From Slavery*, 196, 223; Jackson, *Free Negro*, 78, 82; Herbert Gutman and Richard Sutch, "Sambo Makes Good, or Were Slaves Imbued with the Protestant Work Ethic?" in *Reckoning with Slavery*, ed. Paul A. David et al. (N.Y., 1976), 74–79, 87; Gutman, *Slavery*, 52, 62–77, 81–82; Genovese, *Roll*, 389–90; Stavisky, "Negro Artisan," 113–16; Wade, *Slavery*, 30, 32.

14. James L. Smith, *Autobiography* (Norwich, Conn., 1881), 1–40. See also William Hayden, *Narrative . . .* (Cincin., 1846), 13–30; Noah Davis, *A Narrative of the Life . . .* (Balt., 1859), 9–19; James P. Beckwourth, *The Life and Adventures*, ed. Delmont R. Oswald (Lincoln, 1972; orig., 1856), esp. 13, 18–20, 539n–541n; Elinor Wilson, *Jim Beckwourth* (Norman, 1972), 4, 17–21, 27–29.

15. Frederick Douglass, *Life and Times . . .* (N.Y., 1962; orig., 1892), 113–33, 175; Nathan I. Huggins, *Slave and Citizen* (Boston, 1980), 3–11; Dickson J. Preston, *Young Frederick Douglass* (Balt., 1980), 7–19, 31, 65. Preston was able to prove an 1818 birthdate.

16. Douglass, *Life*, 175–82 (quotes at 181, 182). See also Preston, *Douglass*, 142–44; Huggins, *Slave*, 11–12; Steffen, *Mechanics*, 27, 41–42.

17. Douglass, *Life*, 182–85, 187–88; Preston, *Douglass*, 145; Huggins, *Slave*, 12–14.

18. Arthur Zilversmit, *The First Emancipation* (Chicago, 1967), 192–99, 202–14.

19. In general see Berlin, *Slaves,* 226; (Texas) Frederick Douglass, *Papers,* ed. John W. Blassingame (New Haven, 1979–), 1:121n; (BWI) Franklin, *From Slavery,* 347; the standard sources are Izhak Gross, "Parliament and the Abolition of Negro Apprenticeship, 1835–1838," *Eng. Hist. Rev.,* 96 (1981), 560–76; William L. Burn, *Emancipation and Apprenticeship in the British West Indies* (London, 1937); William A. Green, *British Slave Emancipation* (Oxford, Eng., 1976), 129–61; (NJ) Zilversmit, *Emancipation,* 215–22. After the Civil War a number of southern states sought to use apprenticeship to supplant slavery; these attempts failed. See Comas v. Reddish, 1866, 35 Ga. Rep. 236; Adams v. Adams, 1867, 36 Ga. Rep. 236; in re Turner, D.C., 1867, 1 Abb. U.S. 84.

20. Edward O. Hinkley, *The Testamentary Law and the Law of Inheritance and Apprentices in Maryland* (Balt., 1878). For an abolitionist view see Charles Stuart to Theodore Weld, June 8, 1839, in Theodore D. Weld et al., *Letters,* ed. Gilbert H. Barnes and Dwight L. Dumond (N.Y., 1934), 2:766–72.

21. James M. Bailey, *Life in Danbury* (Boston, 1873), 82; Charles H. Baker, *Life and Character of William Taylor Baker* (N.Y., 1908), 18–28; George S. Merriam, *The Life and Times of Samuel Bowles* (N.Y., 1885), 15–17, 20–24; William J. Stillman, *The Autobiography of a Journalist* (Boston, 1901), 1:2–6, 12–28, 33, 40–43, 47, 51–52, 61–62.

22. Allene Gregory, *John Milton Gregory* (Chicago, 1923), 1–14; Harry A. Kersey, Jr., *John Milton Gregory and the University of Illinois* (Urbana, 1968), 2–3; Lewis Gregory to James Gregory, May 23, 1839, JMG Papers, Archives, Univ. of Illinois (misattributed to LG to Dorcas Gregory in the authorized biography); JMG to Joseph Gregory, June 12, 1839, JMG Papers, UI (an inaccurate transcription is in the authorized biography); LG to Joseph Gregory, Mar. 7, 1841, in Gregory, *Gregory,* 14–15. On changes in the tanning trade see Ellsworth, *Craft to National Industry;* William Edwards, *Memoirs* (Wash., 1897).

23. Joseph Gregory to James Gregory, Dec. 4, 1840, JMG Papers, UI.

24. John Brown to Henry L. Stearns, July 15, 1857, in Franklin B. Sanborn, *The Life and Letters of John Brown* (Boston, 1891), 17; Stephen B. Oates, *To Purge This Land with Blood,* 14–15; James Foreman to James Redpath, Dec. 28, 1859; Ruth B. Thompson reminiscences, Salmon Brown reminiscences, all in Louis Ruchames, ed., *A John Brown Reader* (London, 1959), 163–65, 178, 186; Watson Brown quoted in Oswald G. Villard, *John Brown, 1800–1859* (Boston, 1910), 20 (quote); John Brown, Jr., account in Ruchames, *Brown,* 174–75 (quotes at 175).

25. Lewis Brewster Diary, quotes at Sept. 13, Oct. 3 (twice), 1848, NHHS. See Lewis W. Brewster, *Elder William Brewster and the Brewster Family of Portsmouth, New Hampshire* (Portsmouth, 1908), 11–17.

26. LB Diary, quotes at Oct. 18, 21, 25, 1848, NHHS.

27. Mark Twain, *The Autobiography of Mark Twain,* ed. Charles Neider (N.Y., 1959), 87–93; Albert B. Paine, *Mark Twain* (N.Y., 1912), 1:75–80; Justin Kaplan, *Mark Twain and His World* (N.Y., 1974), 12–15, 25; Edgar L. Masters, *Mark Twain: A Portrait* (N.Y., 1938), 21–23; SLC MSS, Oct. 2, 1906; July 7, 1908, in Mark Twain, *Mark Twain in Eruption,* ed. Bernard De Voto (N.Y., 1940), 388, 303–4; Mark Twain, "The Turning-Point of My Life," in *What Is Man?* (N.Y., 1917), 131–32. A genealogy is in Henry N. Smith and William M. Gibson, eds., *Mark Twain–Howells Letters* (Cambridge, Mass., 1960), 2:921.

28. Twain, *Autobiography,* 93–94; Paine, *Twain,* 1:84–93; SLC to William D. Howells, Oct. 3, 1902, in Smith and Gibson, *Twain–Howells Letters,* 2:746. On

Orion Clemens see OC autobiographical fragment, pp. 696–705, Mark Twain Papers, Bancroft Library, Univ. of California, Berkeley. Travel appealed to many apprentices. See Thomas H. Savery Copy Book, 1854–1856, entry for Mar. 6, 1855, Savery Papers, HML; Bayard Taylor, *Life and Letters,* ed. Marie Hansen-Taylor and Horace E. Scudder (Boston, 1884), 1:32–41; BT, *At Home and Abroad. First Series* (N.Y., 1860), 3–22; BT, *Unpublished Letters,* ed. John R. Schultz (San Marino, 1937), 5–6; Russell H. Conwell, *The Life, Travels, and Literary Career of Bayard Taylor* (Boston, 1881), 34–35, 38–40; Richmond C. Beatty, *Bayard Taylor* (Norman, 1936), 29–30; Albert H. Smyth, *Bayard Taylor* (Boston, 1896), 35–36.

29. SLC to Pamela Moffett, Oct. Saturday 1853, in Mark Twain, *The Selected Letters of Mark Twain,* ed. Charles Neider (N.Y., 1982), 13–14 (quotes at 13, 14); to same, summer 1853, ibid., 11–12; Twain, *Autobiography,* 94–95; Paine, *Twain,* 1:96. See also SLC to Jane L. Clemens, Aug. 24, 31, 1853, in MT, *Mark Twain's Collected Letters,* ed. Lin Salamo et al. (Berkeley, forthcoming), vol. 1, galleys.

30. SLC to Orion Clemens, Oct. 26, 1853, MT, *Selected Letters,* 14–17; to same, Nov. 28, 1853, ibid., 17–18; to Pamela Moffett, Dec. 5, 1853, in MT, *Mark Twain's Letters,* ed. Albert B. Paine (N.Y., 1917), 1:30–31; Twain, *Autobiography,* 95; Paine, *Twain,* 1:97–101.

31. SLC to Annie E. Taylor, May 25, 1856, MT, *Collected Letters,* vol. 1, galleys; to Mrs. Clemens and Pamela Moffett, June 10, 1856, MT, *Letters,* 1:32–33; to Henry Clemens, Aug. 5, 1856, MT, *Selected Letters,* 18–19; Twain, *Autobiography,* 95; Paine, *Twain,* 1:102–11; Kaplan, *Twain,* 30.

Epilogue

1. Herman Melville, *Letters,* ed. Merrell R. Davis and William H. Gilman (New Haven, 1960), 29; Lucy E. Parsons, *Life of Albert R. Parsons* (Chicago, 1903; orig., 1889), 1–3, 12–14 (quote at 14); Edmund F. Hartshorn, *Experiences of a Boy* (Newark, N.J., 1910), 25; James Morgan, *Charles H. Taylor* (n.p., 1923), 13–19.

2. Henry C. Prout, *A Life of George Westinghouse* (N.Y., 1922), 1–7; Francis E. Leupp, *George Westinghouse* (Boston, 1919), 14–30 (quote at 27). In general see Benjamin A. Gould, *Investigations in the Military and Anthropological Statistics of American Soldiers* (N.Y., 1869), 35, 38, 60, 64; James M. McPherson, *Ordeal by Fire* (N.Y., 1982), 359. Using these sources plus archival records, I have calculated enlistments by both age and occupation. See W. J. Rorabaugh, "Who Fought in the Union Army? An Estimate and a Hypothesis" (unpub., 1984). See also Earl J. Hess, "The 12th Missouri Infantry: A Socio-Military Profile of a Union Regiment," *Mo. Hist. Rev.,* 76 (1981), 53–77. On the South see Charleston *News and Courier,* Mar. 25, 1953, clipping in Charleston Typographical Society, Minutes and Misc. Papers, S-CHS; "Sketches of Camp Life during the Civil War from Charleston to Gettysburg" (1885), p. 13, in Mechanics' Union of Charleston Papers, SCL.

3. Apprentice Book, 1858–1861, vol. 1; quote from 1861–1868, vol. 2; the 1863 list is pasted in the front of vol. 2, Baldwin Locomotive Works Papers, HSP.

4. On bonuses see Cain v. Snyder, 1865, 6 Phila. Rep. 24; Kelly v. Sprout, 1867, 97 Mass. Rep. 169. In general I have been influenced by Karl Polanyi, *The Great Transformation* (Boston, 1957; orig., 1944).

5. Russell, *Address*, 11; Morgan, *Taylor*, 25; Prout, *Westinghouse*, 5. See also John C. Simonds and John T. McEnnis, *The Story of Manual Labor in All Lands and Ages* (Chicago, 1887), 445–48.

6. Quoted in James P. Hanlan, *The Working Population of Manchester, New Hampshire, 1840–1886* (Ann Arbor, 1981), 60; Walkowitz, *Worker City*, 88–92; McVicar, *Origin*, 28–32; International Typographical Union of North America, *Report of Proceedings of the Xth, XIth, and XIIth Annual Sessions . . .* (Detroit, 1864), 15, 23, 68. See also John R. Commons et al., *History of Labour in the United States* (N.Y., 1918–1935), 2:81–83, 82n; Greenberg, "Worker," 70–74; Cale, *Organization*, 50–51.

7. Mrs. M. J. Roop to her children, Feb. 20, 1863, quoted in Harold B. Hancock, "The Indenture System in Delaware, 1681–1921," *DH*, 16 (1974), 59; *Fincher's Trades' Rev.*, July 18, 1863, p. 26; Nov. 14, 1863, p. 95; Sept. 24, 1864, p. 66.

8. (strikes) *FTR*, June 6, 1863, p. 2; Apr. 2, 1864, p. 71; Chicago *Workingman's Advocate*, Mar. 25, 1865; Walkowitz, *Worker City*, 90; (law) Commonwealth v. Bowen, 1863, 5 Phila. Rep. 220. For comment see *FTR*, Nov. 7, 1863, p. 90 (2 articles); Nov. 14, 1863, p. 95 (quote); Jan. 9, 1864, p. 23 (quote); July 9, 1864, p. 22.

9. Julia C. Harris, *The Life and Letters of Joel Chandler Harris* (Boston, 1918), 23–24; Joel C. Harris, *On the Plantation* (N.Y., 1892), 12–27, 48–55; Paul M. Cousins, *Joel Chandler Harris* (Baton Rouge, 1968), 14–16, 29–44; JCH Boyhood Composition Book, pp. 55–56, 74 (quote), 87 (quote), JCH Papers, Emory Univ.; the mock letter, quoted in Harris, *Harris*, 46, is at EU; *The Countryman*, Apr. 14, 1863, quoted in Robert B. Bickley, Jr., *Joel Chandler Harris* (Boston, 1978), 21. An incomplete file is in the JCH Papers, EU; JCH Boyhood Composition Book, p. 73; 'Smickey' [?] to JCH, July 20, 1864, box on early life, JCH Papers, EU.

10. The master is quoted in Cousins, *Harris*, 59. For doubts about JCH's claimed 1848 birthdate see W. J. Rorabaugh, "When Was Joel Chandler Harris Born? Some New Evidence," *Southern Literary Journal*, 17 (1984), 92–95. See also W. F. Williams to JCH, Oct. 15 [1861–1864], box on early life, JCH Papers, EU; Harris, *On the Plantation*, 122–25. On conscription see Savannah Typographical Society to Gov. Joseph E. Brown, Feb. 22, 1862, JEB Papers, Georgia Historical Society; JCH Boyhood Composition Book, p. 123; WFW to JCH, Feb. 25, 1864 (quote), box on early life, JCH Papers, EU; Harris, *On the Plantation*, 162–63, 168, 224–30. See also Harris, *Harris*, 49–54.

11. Throughout this chapter I owe much to David Montgomery's path-breaking *Beyond Equality*. Terence V. Powderly, *Thirty Years of Labor* (Columbus, Ohio, 1890), 43–44, 59–61, 65, 67; Commons, *History*, 2:81–84; "Our Working Classes," series, *N.Y. Times*, Feb. 22, 1869, p. 2; Feb. 24, 1869, p. 2; Mar. 5, 1869, p. 12; Mar. 17, 1869, p. 12; Mar. 24, 1869, p. 1; *Fincher's Trades' Rev.*, Dec. 5, 1863, p. 3; May 28, 1864, p. 102; Oct. 22, 1864, p. 82; June 3, 1865, p. 4; Wendell Phillips, *Remarks of Wendell Phillips, at the Mass Meeting of Workingmen in Faneuil Hall, Nov. 2, 1865* (Boston, 1865), 7–10; Walkowitz, *Worker City*, 95–97; Barnett, *Printers*, 168–69; Harry C. Bates, *Bricklayers' Century of Craftsmanship* (Wash., 1955), 1, 3, 17–25; Robert A. Christie, *Empire in Wood* (Ithaca, 1956), 24–27. On Massachusetts see Boston *Daily Eve. Voice*, Jan. 12, 1865, p. 2; Mar. 30, 1865, p. 1; Apr. 1, 1865, p. 1; "The Joint Special Committee . . . in Regard to the Present Defective Apprentice System . . . ," in Mas-

sachusetts, House of Representatives, *Documents* (Boston, 1865), doc. 256, pp. 1–11; "The Joint Special Committee . . . Propriety of Reducing the Hours of Labor . . . ," ibid., doc. 259, pp. 2–5; Massachusetts, *The General Statutes* . . . , 2d ed. (Boston, 1873; orig., 1860), 549–51. See also *FTR*, Dec. 3, 1864, p. 2; Feb. 18, 1865, p. 46; May 13, 1865, p. 94; Commons, *History*, 2:83. The courts broke new ground during the War of 1812. For an early trial court record see Ludwell Lee Oath, Oct. 20, 1812; Thomas Hill Petition to Judges of the Superior Courts of Law, Oct. 27, 1812; Justice of the Peace Hugh Holmes, Writ of Habeas Corpus, Nov. 6, 1812, Mar. 19, 1813; HH to Judge White, Mar. 26, 1813, all in Thomas Hill Court Papers, Colonial Williamsburg, Inc. (film). The governing case was Commonwealth v. Barker, Pa., 1813, 5 Binney 423. See Turner v. Smithers, 1867, 8 Del. Rep. 430; Kelly v. Sprout, 1867, 97 Mass. Rep. 169; Johnson v. Dodd, 1874, 56 N.Y. Rep. 76; Judson v. Worden, 1867, 39 Vt. Rep. 382.

12. Henry Ashworth, *A Tour in the United States, Cuba, and Canada* (London, 1861), 31 (quote); Burn, *Three Years*, 69–70; S.B. letter, *Fincher's Trades' Rev.*, Feb. 6, 1864, p. 39; Massachusetts, House, *Documents* (1865), doc. 256, p. 3; Terence V. Powderly Diaries, quotes at Feb. 25, July 6, 9, Aug. 1, 1869, in TVP Papers, Catholic Univ. of America (film).

13. *Fincher's Trades' Rev.*, June 17, 1865, p. 22.

14. Quoted in Massachusetts, House, *Documents* (1865), doc. 259, p. 4; *Boston Daily Eve. Voice*, 1865: E.D.L. letter, Mar. 21, p. 1; B.G.C. letter, Mar. 25, p. 1; A.S. Hadley testimony, Mar. 30, p. 1. Other letters are Mar. 30, p. 2; Apr. 6, p. 1; Apr. 10, p. 1; Apr. 26, p. 1; May 2, p. 1; May 13, p. 1; May 18, p. 1. See also artisan testimony in "Statements and Experiences of Working-Men," Massachusetts, Bureau of Statistics of Labor, [*Second Annual*] *Report* (Boston, 1871), 570–621.

15. *Argus*, May 27, 1867, quoted in Greenberg, "Worker," 87; Thomas Bigham, 1873, quoted in Irwin Yellowitz, *Industrialization and the American Labor Movement, 1850–1900* (Port Washington, N.Y., 1977), 100; *Albany Eve. J.*, Mar. 22, 1866, quoted in Greenberg, "Worker," 86; Committee Report to Baltimore Congress, Aug. 1866, in John R. Commons et al., eds., *A Documentary History of American Industrial Society* (Cleveland, 1909–1911), 9:154–55 (quote at 155); National Labor Congress, Chicago, 1867, ibid., 9:192; Stanley Koch to his mother, Feb. 8, 1868, Christian D. Koch and Family Papers, LSU; Massachusetts Charitable Mechanic Association, *Report of the Committee . . . on the Subject of the Relations of Apprentices to Their Employers* (Boston, 1869), 5–6 (quote at 5); James S. Whitney, "Apprenticeship—and a Boy's Prospect of a Livelihood," *Penn Monthly*, 3 (1872), 197–202; Ohio, Bureau of Labor Statistics, *First Annual Report* (Columbus, 1877), 197, 218; *Second Annual Report* (Columbus, 1878), 301–7; E. W. Bemis, "Relation of Trades-Unions to Apprentices," *J. Social Science*, 28 (1891), 108–25; Commons, *History*, 2:316n; Michael B. Katz et al., *The Social Organization of Early Industrial Capitalism* (Cambridge, Mass., 1982), 186–90; Gibb, *Whitesmiths*, 281; Laurence A. Glasco, "The Life Cycles and Household Structure of American Ethnic Groups . . . Buffalo, New York, 1855," in *Family and Kin in Urban Communities, 1700–1930*, ed. Tamara K. Hareven (N.Y., 1977), 123–32; Clyde Griffen and Sally Griffen, *Natives and Newcomers* (Cambridge, Mass., 1978), 142, 182, 201–2; Hancock, "Indenture System," 59; Mary P. Ryan, *Cradle of the Middle Class* (N.Y., 1981), 167–79; Shaw, *Immigrant City*, 21, 34.

✑ INDEX ✑

Abbott, Jacob, 150–51
Adams, Mrs. Thomas, 42
Adams, Thomas; printer, 42
Adams steam press, 86
advice books, 158–63; early rising, 159; entertainment, 159, 161; education, 159, 160–61; liquor, 159, 160; runaways, 159–60; setting up shop, 160; bookkeeping, 161; morals, 161–62; traditions lost, 162; ideology, 162–63; religion, 163
agriculture, *see* farms; planters; rural life
Aitken, Robert; printer, 25, 29, 43
Albany, N.Y., 25, 50, 121–22, 154
alcohol, *see* liquor
Alcott, Bronson, 114–15
Alcott, William A., 159, 160
Alger, Horatio, 130, 174, 205, 209
Allen, Ephraim W.; publisher, 100–101
Allen, Stephen (1767–1852); apprentice sailmaker to James Leonard, New York; mayor, 16, 22, 31, 42
Alts, Phillip; blacksmith, 183
American Antiquarian Society, 121
American party, *see* Know-Nothings
American Republican party, 169–70
Amoskeag textile mill, 141
Anderson, Alexander (1775–1870); self-taught engraver, New York, 35
Andrews, Ebenezer T.; apprentice printer to Isaiah Thomas; partner with Thomas, Boston, 26
apprentice libraries, 121–24, 164–66, 195; apprentice control, 122
apprentices: limited numbers, 4–5, 95–96, 181, 201–2; freedom dues, 8, 26–27, 128, 172, 199; beatings, 11, 43, 45, 50, 53–54, 93, 103, 192–93; work habits, 11, 76, 97–98, 104, 136, 159;

labor conflict, 16, 89, 90, 152–54, 172, 174, 183–88, 202; military, 18, 20–23, 168–69, 198–201, 205; character, 42–48, 106, 121, 136, 141, 195–97; entertainment, 46–48, 79, 106, 110, 122, 130, 159, 161, 173; carries pass, 49; recordkeeping, 73–74; initiation, 80, 104–5, 144; holidays, 101, 136, 169, 170, 193–94; reading, 102, 121–24, 173, 203; beds, 99, 103–4, 106; poetry, 104, 106; pranks, 105, 108–9; dismissed, 107, 130, 137–38, 200, 206; death, 203–4
apprenticeship: terms, 3–4; fees, 6, 8; trials, 6, 28, 79; juvenile delinquents, 127–28; termination, 171; slaves, 177, 178, 180–81, 188–89; education, 180; Civil War, 202; laws, 205; new style, 207; statistics, 208; *see* indentures
armories, 65–67
Arthur, T. S., 160, 161
Arthur, William, 37
artisans, *see* crafts
Ashtabula, Ohio, *Sentinel*, 176
Ashworth, Henry, 205
Atlanta, Ga., 184
attitudes: Revolution, 24; apprentices, 28–29; planters, 178; Civil War, 203–4; youths, 205–6
Aubry, Eli, 204
authority, 42–43, 116–17, 136; *see* fathers; master craftsmen
Awl, 134, 135

Babbitt, Isaac; jeweler, 65
Bache, Benjamin Franklin (1769–98); Franklin's grandson; apprentice printer to François-Ambroise Didot, Paris; printer, Philadelphia, 25, 29
Bacon, Judge, 134

Bailey, James M. (1841–94); apprentice sawmiller, Danbury, Conn.; editor, Danbury, 190

Bailey, Robert (b. 1773); apprentice in four trades; gambler, 48

Baker, William Taylor (1841–1903); "apprentice" carpenter; businessman, Chicago, 190

baking, 46–48

Baldwin, Simeon, 37

Baldwin Locomotive Works, 199–201

Baltimore: trial, 87; printing, 90, 100–101; education, 114, 117, 119; apprentice library, 121; labor, 131, 208; printers union, 154, 155; shipyards, 186–88

Baltimore rule; limits apprentices, 154

Bangs, Heman (1790–1869); apprentice blacksmith to his brother John; Methodist minister, 42

Bangs, John; blacksmith, 42

bankruptcies, 26, 60, 62, 65, 78, 80, 81, 96, 105, 121, 142, 149, 183

banks, 30–31, 68, 87

Banks, Nathaniel P. (1816–94); apprentice textile machinist; politician, 60–61, 120

Baptists: manual labor schools, 120

barter, 9, 10, 68, 128, 195

Bartholf, John G.; chairmaker, 53–54

Bartholomew, Truman, 103

Bartholomew family, 103

Barton, Charles, 65

Baton Rouge, La., 155

begging, 126

Belknap, Rev. Jeremy, 43–44

Belknap, Joseph (1769–1800); apprentice printer to Robert Aitken, Philadelphia, and to William Mycall, Newburyport, Mass.; printer, Boston, 25, 29, 31, 43

Billy, slave apprentice blacksmith, 183

blacks, 139, 167, 169, 178, 181–88, 190, 204; see slaves

blacksmithing, 6, 42, 67, 120–21, 140, 176, 177, 178, 179, 181, 183

Blanchard, Thomas, 66

Bliss, Amos, 78–79

board, 8, 20, 65, 72–73, 80, 90, 98, 99, 102–4, 106, 107, 109, 129, 132, 174, 194–95, 202

boardinghouses, 73, 102–3, 129–30, 141

Bogart, Joseph O.; master, 51–52

bookbinding, 27, 69, 86, 89–90, 129

bookkeeping, 161, 172

books, 40–41, 114, 120, 122, 150–51, 164, 186, 195, 203; craft manuals, 33–36; novels, 122, 161; advice manuals, 158–63; see apprentice libraries

boss: new word, 135

Bosson, John; barber and wigmaker, 21

Boston: colonial, 3–7, 14–15; Revolution, 16–21; Centinel, 26; printing, 26, 42, 152, 153, 193, 198; poor boys, 30; religion, 38; textiles, 61; board, 98; education, 117; apprentice library, 121–24, 165–66; unemployment, 133

Boston Mechanic Apprentices' Library Association, 165

Boston Overseers of the Poor, 19, 26, 30

Bowe, Obadiah A.; journeyman printer, 82–83

Bowles, Samuel (1826–78); apprentice printer to his father, Springfield, Mass.; publisher, 190, 197

Brace, Rev. Charles Loring, 139–40

Brackenridge, H. H.; Modern Chivalry, 122

Brewster, Lewis W. (b. 1830); apprentice printer to his father, Portsmouth, N.H.; publisher, 193–94, 197

brickmaking, 60–61

Bright, David G.; hatter, 30, 31, 108

Bright, Mrs. David G., 102

Britannia ware, 65

British West Indies, 189, 190

Brokmeyer, Henry C. (1828–1906); German-born apprentice currier, New York; apprentice iron molder; politician, St. Louis, 138–39, 142, 144, 145, 146

Bronson and Bronson, 34

Brown, John, Jr.; apprentice tanner to his father, Ohio, 192–93

Brown, John, Sr., 192–93

Brownlow, William G. (1805–77); apprentice carpenter; Methodist minister, 60

building trades, *see* brickmaking; carpentry; masonry

Burgess, West, 183

Burritt, Elihu (1810–79); apprentice blacksmith to Samuel Booth, New Britain, Conn.; lecturer, 120–21

business cycles, *see* economics

butchers, slaves barred, 181

Butler, Gen. Benjamin, 203

cabinetmaking, *see* furnituremaking

Calhoun, John C., 91

California gold rush, 171–75

Cambridge, Mass., 17, 18

Canada, 26, 174

candlemaking, 3, 6

Cape Horn, 171

capital, 59, 61, 62, 64, 65, 68, 77, 142, 144, 146, 149, 203; lacking, 10, 29, 81–83, 85, 93–94, 132, 151, 160–61, 171, 175, 178, 179, 195; to set up, 29, 86; California gold, 171–75

Cargill, John Milton (1806?–1890); apprentice cabinetmaker to John Carpenter, Uxbridge, Mass.; cabinetmaker, Providence, 60

Carlisle, David, Jr.; apprentice printer to Isaiah Thomas, Worcester, Mass.; printer, Walpole, N.H., 26

Carpenter, Edward Jenner (1825–1900); apprentice cabinetmaker to Isaac Miles and Joel Lyons, Greenfield, Mass.; businessman, Brattleboro, Vt., 71, 106, 132, 137, 138

carpentry, 6, 10, 34, 48, 60–61, 67, 178, 179, 183–85, 190

Carrier, Ralph; apprentice tailor, Greenfield, Mass., 137

Carroll, David (b. ca. 1811); apprentice textile machinist to Daniel Sack, Howard County, Md.; mill supervisor, 73–74

Carson, Christopher (1809–1868); apprentice saddler to David Workman, Franklin, Mo.; explorer, 70

Carter, Master; schoolmaster, 17

Catholics, 102, 167, 169, 170

Cattaraugus County, N.Y., 81

Chambers, David (1780–1864); apprentice printer to Benjamin Franklin Bache, Philadelphia; politician, Ohio, 29, 31

Channing, Rev. William E., 72

Chapin, Rev. Edwin H., 162–63

charity agencies, 126

Charleston, S.C.: printing, 26, 27, 155; apprentice library, 121; anti-steam law, 151; *Evening News*, 155; race, 182; census, 185; joke, 203

Cheney, Benjamin; farmer-clockmaker, 10–11

Cheney, Timothy; clockmaker, 11

Chicago: furniture, 132; newspapers, 149; labor, 208

child labor, 74, 86, 92, 94, 131–33, 176, 205, 207, 208; shoes, 59–60; textiles, 61; printing, 77, 90–91, 149, 154

child rearing, 116–17, 157

children, 55–56, 124, 126

Chittenango Polytechny, 120

Christman, Enos (1828–1912); apprentice printer to Henry S. Evans, West Chester, Pa.; printer, 171–72

Christmas Eve, 169

Cincinnati: printing, 26, 197; wealth, 131; furniture, 132, 176; printers union, 154, 155

city life, 84, 98, 109, 110, 114, 124–30, 132–33, 166–71, 182, 195–96, 205; *see individual cities*

Civil War, 162, 174–75, 198–205

Clapp, David, Jr. (1806–93); apprentice printer to John Cotton, Jr., Boston; printer, Boston, 72, 73, 98, 103–8

Clarkson, Matthew; city recorder, 44–46

classes, socioeconomic, 3, 5–6, 23–24, 72, 103, 119, 121, 123, 124, 131, 134, 158, 166, 168, 177–78, 181–82; status, 103, 106, 181–82

Clay, Henry, 57, 87

Clemens, Henry; apprentice printer, Hannibal, Mo., 195, 196

Clemens, Mrs. Jane Lampton, 194, 196, 197

Clemens, Orion; printer, 194–97
Clemens, Samuel Langhorne (1835–
    1910); apprentice printer to the
    Hannibal, Mo., *Courier;* author,
    194–97
clockmaking, 10–11, 25
clothdressing, 69–70
clothes, 10, 11, 28–29, 48, 66–67, 69–73,
    78–79, 83, 109, 119, 129, 185–86, 196
Cochituate Gossiping Club, 111
Colden, Cadwallader; mayor, 54
Colt, Christopher; factory owner, 98
Colt, Samuel (1814–62); apprentice
    machinist in his father's factory,
    Ware, Mass.; inventor, 58
Columbia Typographical Society, 91–
    95
Columbus, Ga., 204
Concord, Mass., 17
Concord, N.H., 90
Conductor Generalis, 52
Connecticut: court case, 52–53; schools,
    114
Connelly, William P.; apprentice
    chairmaker to John G. Bartholf,
    New York, 53
conscription: Revolution, 22–23; Civil
    War, 204; *see* military
Coram, Robert, 24
Cornell, Ezra (1807–1874); apprentice
    carpenter, upstate N.Y.; mill agent,
    60
corporal punishment, 115–16, 192–93;
    see apprentices: beatings
Cortlandville, N.Y., 82, 83
cotton, *see* textiles
Cotton, John, Jr.; printer, 105–6
Cotton, John, Sr.; manufacturer,
    103–6
The Countryman, 203–4
court cases, *see* laws
Cowan, Bill; apprentice printer to
    Thomas Adams, Boston, 42–43
crafts: traditions, 4, 33–36, 157, 162,
    166, 176–79, 200, 209; status, 6, 8–9,
    124; rural, 9–11, 177–79; secrets, 33–
    36; pride, 133–34, 138, 140–41, 144,
    173, 208; race, 139, 178–79, 181–88;
    setting up, 149, 160; immigrants, 209

craftsmanship, 120, 178, 202
crime, 45, 50–52, 124–28, 139, 202;
    petty, 108; *see* juvenile delinquents
Crocker, Charles; author, 105
Crockett, David, 58
Croker, Richard (1843–1922); Irish-
    born apprentice machinist, New
    York; politician, 145
Crossman, William W.; jeweler, 65
culture: craft pride, 133–34; respecta-
    bility, 165–66; traditions, 166–67;
    fire companies, 167–68; militia, 168–
    69; politics, 169–71; *see* education
Currans, Timothy; plasterer, 47
currying, 138–39, 142
Custer, Gen. George Armstrong, 134
cutlery, 6

dandies, 71–72
Davis, Alexander Jackson (1803–92);
    apprentice printer, Alexandria, Va.;
    architect, New York, 99
Davis, Diana, 182
Davis, Edward S., 203–4
death, 27, 203–4
debates, 80, 102, 123, 173
Declaration of Independence, 22
Delaware, 63, 64
Democrats, 170
Detroit, Mich., 153
Dexter, Timothy; breechesmaker and
    speculator, 23
Didot, François-Ambroise; printer, 25
disputes: age of apprentice, 50
distilling, 58
Dixon, Mr.; machinist, 206
Dominy family; farmer-craftsmen, 10
Don Quixote, 122
Dorchester, Mass., 38, 104
Douglass, Frederick (1818–95); appren-
    tice ship caulker, Baltimore; black
    leader, 182, 186–88
Dow, Neal (1804–97); apprentice
    tanner to his father, Portland, Me.;
    politician, 98
draft, *see* conscription
drink, *see* liquor
Dunlap family; farmer-furniture-
    makers, 9–10

Duties of Employers and Employed,
135
Dwinnell, Joseph P. (1820–39); apprentice brickmaker to Matthew Hooper, Marblehead, Mass., 61
dyeing, 34
Dyott, Thomas; glass manufacturer, 74

East Poultney, Vt., 78–81
Eatonton, Ga., 203, 204
economics, 3, 5–6, 29–31, 87, 103, 144, 204; changes, 24–26, 57–61, 65, 80–81, 118, 119, 124, 127, 130, 162; depressions, 25, 64, 87–88, 96, 119, 121, 131, 146, 154; booms, 60–61, 64, 89, 142, 201–2; labor theory of value, 88; modernization, 128; cash wages, 136–37; statistics, 142, 146, 149; advice books, 158–63; slavery, 177–78, 180–81; *see* classes; wage rates; wages; wealth
Eddy, Rev. Daniel C., 161
Edes, Peter (1756–1840); apprentice printer to his father, Boston; printer, Maine, 17–18
editing, 77–78, 85
education, 3, 17, 24, 27, 46–47, 67, 78, 90, 92, 99, 129, 144, 157, 159, 172, 180, 190–93, 198; indentures, 7–8; financed by crafts, 60; manual labor schools, 92, 119–20; college, 98, 190–91; public schools, 113–19; Lancasterian, 114; corporal punishment, 115–16; high schools, 117–19; discipline, 120, 141, 164; apprentice libraries, 121–24; technological, 122; for poor, 124, 126; recommended, 160–61; for youths, 163–66; evening schools, 164–65; slaves, 183, 186; statistics, 212
Eliot, Rev. William G., Jr., 162
emancipation, *see* slaves
embargo of 1808, 30
encyclopedias, 33, 35
England: Poor Law, 4; Statute of Artificers, 4; guilds, 4–5; printing, 7; commerce, 25; textiles, 61, 64; tools, 62; immigrants, 64, 142; authors, 86; emancipation, 189; travelers, 205

English, James E. (1812–90); apprentice carpenter, New Haven, Conn.; businessman, 60
engraving, 34, 35, 41
enlistments, *see* military
entertainment, 58, 80, 90, 132, 173; *see* apprentices
entrepreneurs, 137, 209
equality, 162
Erie, Pa., 81–83; *Gazette,* 81
Eureka Typographical Union, 174
evangelicalism, 38–42; *see* religion
Evans, Oliver (1755–1819); apprentice wheelwright, Pa.; inventor, 34
evening schools, 164–65
Everett, Edward, 121, 150
Evergreen Plantation, 177

factories, 65, 67–68, 74, 100, 119, 132, 171, 176, 184, 200, 202, 207; *see* machinery; manufactures
families: quarrels, 46; traditions, 157, 179–80; businesses, 176, 191, 194–97; *see* relations
family government, 37–40, 45
Fanny Hill, 112
farmer-craftsmen, 9–11, 72, 99, 140–41, 177, 191, 192; *see* rural life
farms, 78, 81, 83, 127–28, 129, 168, 178; poor boys, 19, 30; labor, 68; apprentices, 127
fathers: paternalism, 64–65; authority, 83, 103, 116, 125, 136, 139, 179–80, 190–94; rights to labor of minor children, 83, 126, 191–92; advice to children, 98–99, 158; *see* relations
Fell's Point, 186
females, *see* women
fights, 46, 64, 107–8, 187, 188; playful, 173
Fillmore, Millard (1800–1874); apprentice clothdresser, upstate N.Y.; politician, 43, 69–70, 171
Fincher, Jonathan C.; labor leader, 202, 203
Fincher's Trades' Review, 202
Finn, Huckleberry, 190
fires: at Harpers, 150; fire companies, 167–68

Fisher, George, 33

Fisher, John; apprentice printer, Boston, 105, 107

Fitch, John (1744–98); apprentice clockmaker to Benjamin Cheney, Conn.; apprentice brass founder to Timothy Cheney; inventor, 10–11, 42

Fluck, Fred; apprentice printer, Erie, Pa., 82

Folsom, Henry; apprentice hatter to David G. Bright, upstate N.Y., 108

food, 10–11, 14, 15, 17, 18, 20, 42–43, 53, 54, 99, 107, 108, 109, 129, 194–95

Foote, Caleb (1803–94); apprentice printer to Thomas C. Cushing, Salem, Mass.; publisher, 31

Fort Sumter, S.C., 198

Foster, George G.; printer, 104

foundries, see ironworking

Fowle, Zechariah; printer, 19

Fowles, Mr.; printer, 105

Fox, Ebenezer (1763–1843); apprentice barber and wigmaker to John Bosson, Boston; barber, 21–22, 36

France, 25

Franklin, Benjamin (1706–90); apprentice printer to his brother James, Boston; publisher, Philadelphia, 3–9, 11–12, 14–15, 25, 26, 31, 48, 151, 159–60, 167, 180, 205; autobiography, 15, 27, 55, 158

Franklin, James; printer, 7, 8, 14–15

Franklin, Josiah; candlemaker, 3

Franklin Institute, 121

Franklin Post, 99–100

Franz; apprentice printer, Greenfield, Mass., 107, 110

Frazee, John (1790–1852); apprentice bricklayer to William Lawrence, N.J.; sculptor, 102

Frederick County, Md., 55, 211

Freedmen's Bureau, 185

freedom, see liberty

freedom dues, see apprentices

Freeman, James; laborer in print shop, 107

Freeman, Joel, 53

Fritz, John (1822–1913); apprentice

machinist, rural Pa.; businessman, 62, 140–41, 145

funerals, 129, 141

furnituremaking, 9, 25, 53–54, 67, 100, 131, 132, 176

Gage, John (1802–90); apprentice iron molder, upstate N.Y.; businessman, 102

Gallipolis, Ohio, 176

Galveston, Tex., 198

gangs, 45, 125–26, 166–67, 169

Garrison, Elizabeth, 101

Garrison, Fanny; nurse, 100–101

Garrison, James; apprentice shoemaker; seaman, 100

Garrison, William Lloyd (1805–79); apprentice printer to Ephraim W. Allen, Newburyport, Mass.; reformer, 100–101, 104

Geer, Elihu; printer, 136–37, 139

Geer, Nathan; publisher, 149

General Society of Mechanics and Tradesmen, 121

George, Henry (1839–97); apprentice printer, Philadelphia; reformer, 172–75

Georgetown, Md., 50

Georgia, 184, 203–4

Germany: immigrants, 63, 132–33, 138, 204

Girard College, 139

girls, see women

glassmaking, 74

Gleason, Herbert; apprentice, Boston, 166

Glenham Company, 64

Gleson, Luther, 39

godparents, 38

gold rush: California, 171–75; fantasy, 196

Goodspeed, Calvin (b. 1806); apprentice brickmaker to his father, Litchfield, N.H.; mill construction foreman, Lowell, 60–61

Gough, John B. (1817–86); English-born apprentice bookbinder to Methodist Book Concern, New York; temperance lecturer, 129–30

Gough, Mary; servant, 129–30

Gough, Mrs., 129

Grant, Mr., 137

Great Britain, *see* England; Scotland; Wales

Greeley, Horace (1811–72); apprentice printer, East Poultney, Vt.; editor, New York, 78–85, 98, 102, 105, 128, 154, 175, 176

Green, Duff; publisher, 77–78, 91–95

Greene, Nathaniel (1742–86); apprentice blacksmith to his father, R.I.; general, 23

Greenfield, Mass., 99–100, 132, 137–38

Gregory, James, 192

Gregory, John Milton (1822–98); apprentice tanner to his father, upstate N.Y.; educator, 191, 197

Gregory, Lewis, 191

Griffin, Joseph (b. 1798); apprentice printer to Flagg & Gould, Andover, Mass.; printer, Maine, 151

Griswold, Rufus Wilmot (1815–57); apprentice printer; author, 104

guilds, 4–5, 65, 87

gunsmithing, 66–67

Habersham, James, 5

hairdressing, 21, 183

Hale, David; editor, 84

Hall, Edward; apprentice printer, Boston, 103–4

Hamilton, Alexander, 25, 68

Hammond, J. H., 182

Hannibal, Mo., 194–95, 196; *Journal*, 194

Hargrove, John; weaver, 33

Harper, Fletcher, 86

Harper, James (1795–1869); apprentice printer to Paul & Thomas, New York; publisher, New York, 85–87, 97, 109, 175

Harper, John; apprentice printer, New York; publisher, 86

Harper, Mrs., 102

Harper Bros., 91, 96; steam plant, 150–51

Harpers Ferry, Va., 65, 67

Harris, Joel Chandler (1848?–1908);

apprentice printer to Joseph Addison Turner, Turnwold Plantation, Ga.; author, 203–4

Harris, Rev. Thaddeus M., 38

Harrisburg, Pa., 48

Harrison, Ebenezer, 173

Harrison, Joseph, 122

Hartford, Conn., 38, 69, 89, 136–37

Hartshorn, Edmund F. (b. 1843); apprentice printer to C. C. Mead, New York; journeyman, 198

Harvard College, 17, 18

Haswell, Anthony (1756–1816); English-born apprentice printer to Isaiah Thomas, Boston; printer, Vermont, 26–27

hatmaking, 41, 108, 203, 204

Haverhill, Mass., 100

Hawes, Joel, 161, 162

Hayes, Ned; apprentice ship caulker, Baltimore, 188

health, 35, 51, 85, 90, 92, 93, 101, 105, 129–30, 136, 173, 191, 199, 204; strength for printing, 13

Heighton, William, 88

Henkel, Andrew; printer, 30

hierarchy, 36–40, 158, 179–80

Hill, Hiram (1803–76); apprentice carpenter to John H. Greene, Providence, R.I.; lumber dealer, 31

Hill, Isaac (1788–1851); apprentice printer to Joseph Cushing, Amherst, N.H.; politician, 55

Hoe & Co., press manufacturers, 149

holidays, *see* apprentices

Homer, James L.; master mechanic, 90

Hopper, Isaac T. (1771–1852); apprentice tailor to an uncle, Philadelphia; gentleman farmer, Long Island, N.Y., 108

Horner, Bill, 173

housing, *see* board

Howe, James, 85

Howell Iron Works, 104

Howells, William Dean (1837–1920); apprentice printer to his father, Ohio; author, 176, 195, 197

Hunter, John W.; printer, 81–82

Huntington, Joseph, 44

Hutchins, James Reed; apprentice printer to Isaiah Thomas, Worcester, Mass., 27

Ide, Simeon (1794–1889); apprentice printer, rural New England; printer, Vermont, 37
ideology, 36–38, 87–88, 162–63; child rearing, 116–17; education, 120–21; planters, 177–78; youths, 205–6
illegitimacy, 128
Illinois, 205
immigrants, 74, 84, 124, 132–33, 138, 201; from Scotland, 25; from Germany, 63, 117, 204; from England, 129, 142; from Ireland, 132–33, 144; nativists oppose, 140, 167, 169–71; from Wales, 142; to California, 171; printers, 196; craftsmen, 208–9
income, see wages
indentured servants, 9
indentures, 10, 11, 18, 26–27, 51, 52, 53, 64, 70, 74, 79–80, 89–90, 99, 100, 138, 190, 199; described, 7; terms, 26–27, 28, 31, 46; decline, 55, 135, 136; end, 70, 153, 203, 205, 207; girls, 111; by courts, 128; health, 136; printed forms end, 136; printers union, 155; slaves, 178, 183–84; compared to slavery, 203; statistics, 211
independence, 73–75, 82–83, 94, 99, 116, 130, 139–40, 158, 183, 196, 197, 202, 205
India, 172
Ingalls, Diamond; apprentice farmer, N.H., 69
initiation, see apprentices
Ireland: immigration, 132–33, 144; opposed, 169, 170
ironworking, 65, 131, 136, 142–46, 184; molding, 104–5, 142–46; pattern molders, 144, 145; puddling, 145; at Harper Bros., 150; union, 201, 202, 205; see machinists

Jackson, Andrew, 91
Jake; iron molder, 144
Janson, Charles, 36
Jarrett, Rev. Devereux, 24

Jeffreys, Jo, 173, 174
Jersey City, N.J., Daily Sentinel and Advertiser, 149
Jews, 169
Johnson, Andrew (1808–75); apprentice tailor to James J. Selby, Raleigh, N.C.; politician, Tenn., 70, 139
Johnson, Benjamin; apprentice, Richmond, Va., 52
Johnson, Bill; apprentice tailor to James J. Selby, Raleigh, N.C.; farmer, Tenn., 70
Johnson, Jim, 204
Jones, Amanda; tailoress, 34
Jones, Bill, 173
journalism, 101
journeymen: definition, 8; lack capital, 29; wander, 63; union secrecy, 87; decline, 131, 134–35
juvenile delinquents, 126–28, 130, 139–40, 165, 202, 209; statistics, 211–12

Kennedy, John Pendleton, 135
Keokuk, Iowa, 196
King, Horatio; printer, 149
King, Kenwith; plasterer, 46–48
Know-Nothings, 165, 170–71
Knox, Henry; bookseller, 23
Kuglar, Mathias; papermaker, 111–12

labor: skilled, 5, 77, 131, 138–41, 146, 170; unskilled, 29–30, 131–33, 145, 181, 203, 207; skills devalued, 59–60, 66–67, 133–35, 145, 149, 157, 203; semiskilled, 66–67, 76; ideology, 87–88, 94, 201; trials, 87; shortages, 89, 198, 200–202; degraded, 93–94, 139; statistics, 150
labor theory of value, 88
labor unions, 87–90, 140, 141, 144, 154, 184, 201–2, 205, 208; printing, 30, 90–96, 154–56, 174, 205; iron, 145–46, 205; apprentices, 154–56, 164, 201–2
Lancaster, Joseph, 114
Lane, John; apprentice baker, New York; journeyman, Philadelphia, 46–47

Lane, Samuel (1718–1806); apprentice farmer-craftsman, Stratham, N.H., 9

Lane family; farmers-tanners-shoe-makers, N.H., 9

Langley, Batty, 34

language, 170; "juvenile delinquents," 126; changes, 135; "master," 179–80; slaves called "apprentices," 189

Laurens County, S.C., 70

Lawrence Literary Society, 173

laws: 45–46, 50–55, 203, 205, 207–8; Statute of Artificers, 4; Poor Law, 4; father's right to labor of minor children, 10, 191–92; trials, 22, 52–55; common law, 52; court-ordered apprentices, 128; enticement, 137; conspiracies, 155; blacks, 182–83, 188; *see* conscription

lectures, 121, 123, 135, 159, 164

Lee, Robert E., 198

Lee, Roswell, 67

Leonard, James; sailmaker, 22

Levin, Lewis, 169–70

Lewis, Ellis (1798–1871); apprentice printer to John Wyeth, Harrisburg, Pa.; politician, 48–49

Lexington, Mass., 17

liberty, 36–37, 139, 162–63, 209

libraries, *see* apprentice libraries

Lincoln, Abraham, 174, 198, 203

Lincoln, Frederic W. (1817–98); apprentice instrument maker to Gedney King, Boston; mayor, 123, 135–36

liquor, 10, 104–5, 126, 128, 130, 144, 156, 159, 160, 164–66, 168–69, 173

Litchfield, Me., 38

Long Island, N.Y., 10

Longacre, James Barton (1794–1869); apprentice engraver to George Murray, Philadelphia; engraver, 41

Louisville, Ky., 49

Lowell, Mass., 60, 61, 64–65

Lyceums, *see* lectures

Lyman, Theodore, Jr., 121

Lynch, Thomas; printing manual, 150

Lynn, Mass., 59–60, 100, 134, 135

McElroy, Archibald, 27

machine tending, 66–67, 77, 131–33, 140, 158, 170

machinery, 91, 131, 134, 140; shoes, 59–60; lure of, 61–62; violent opposition, 64; armories, 66–67; stocking machines, 66; printing, 146, 149–51; *see* factories; manufactures

machinists, 62–65, 99, 120, 140–41, 190–91, 199–200, 206; scale drawings, 62; safety, 62; welds, 63; large shop, 141; *see* ironworking

McKellar, Thomas; apprentice, New York; journeyman, Philadelphia, 110

MacMurray, Pet; printer, 194–95

Macon, Ga., 204

Macormick, Wales; apprentice printer, Hannibal, Mo., 194–95

Maine, 151

Manchester, N.H., *Dollar Weekly Mirror*, 201

manhood, 136, 158, 200

Mann, Horace, 116

manufactures, 68; clerks, 118; increases, 124; printing, 150–51; slaves, 184; child labor, 207; *see* factories; machinery

market economy, 58–61, 89–90, 118, 139

marriage, 8, 110–12, 175

Maryland, 73, 186, 189–90

masonry, 48

Massachusetts, 113, 152, 205, 207–8; court case, 53

Massachusetts Board of State Charities, 206

Massachusetts Charitable Mechanic Association, 90, 135–36, 208

Massachusetts Spy, 20

master craftsman: defined, 8; wife, 10–11; death, 27; authority erodes, 44–45, 50–55, 73–75, 136; absentee, 105; concept, 179–80; *see* relations

Masters Association, Concord, N.H., 90

Mather, Samuel, 44

Matteawan, N.Y., 63–64

mechanics, *see* crafts

mechanics' fairs, lectures, institutes, etc., 90, 121; *see* lectures

medicine, *see* health
Mellen, Grenville, 36
Melville, Herman, 198
Mercein, Thomas R.; baker, 121
merchants, 5, 68, 131, 134; clerks, 118, 158, 161, 172, 191, 208; South, 179
metal working, *see* ironworking; machinists
Methodist Book Concern, 129, 130
Methodists, 85, 129, 169, 174, 186; manual labor schools, 119–20
Mexico, 189, 198
middle colonies, 9
Middlesex Mechanics Association, 65
Mike; iron molder, 144
Miles and Lyons; cabinetmakers, 132
military: Revolution, 16, 17, 20–23; navy, 21–22; hero, 134; Civil War, 198–201, 204, 205; conscription, 22–23, 204
militia, 168–69
Miller, John; publisher, 152
Miller, Tobias H.; printer, 104
milling, 34, 48
Mills, Thomas, 46–48
Missouri, 70
Mogeme, Henrie; machinist, 63
Molony, Cornelius, 34
money, *see* wages
Moody, Paul, 64–65
Moore, Jo; apprentice, Greenfield, Mass., 106
morals, 115, 202; advice books, 158–63
Moravians, 22, 69, 89, 136
Morton, William Z.; apprentice to Mr. Safford, Portland, Me., 137
mummery, 169
Munsell, Joel (1808–80); apprentice printer to *Franklin Post,* Greenfield, Mass.; publisher, Albany, N.Y., 99–100, 107, 110, 116
Muscatine, Iowa, 196
music, 106, 173
Mycall, William; printer, 44

naming patterns, 24
Nantucket, Mass., 77
Napier steam press, 86
Nashville, Tenn., 49

National Typographical Union, 155
nativism, 167, 169–71
Nelson, Samuel; printer, 81–82
New Bedford, Mass., 187
New England: colonial rural, 9–11; revivals, 38; education, 114, 117; primers, 115; ministers, 158; youths, 205–6
New-England Courant, 14
New Hampshire, 9–10, 43, 78
New Jersey, 51, 189
New Orleans: printers union, 96; unemployment, 131; slaves, 182; play, 203
New York (city): colonial, 5, 7, 14; Revolution, 16, 31; furniture, 25, 132; runaways, 30; plastering, 46–48; printing, 48–49, 77, 91, 151, 153–54, 195–96; rowdies, 50–51; Common Council, 51–52; Mayor's Court, 53–54; dandies, 71; Greeley, 83–85; *Journal of Commerce,* 84; *Morning Post,* 85; *Tribune,* 85, 175; Harper Bros., 85–87, 109, 150–51; trial, 87; girls, 110; education, 114, 117, 126; apprentice library, 121; Five Points, 126; Gough, 129–30; immigrants dominate crafts, 133; currying, 138–39; reform, 139–40; Hoe Co., 149; printers union, 154; politics, 169; enlistment, 198
New York House of Refuge, 127; statistics, 211–12
New York (state): laws, 51, 205; tanning, 58–59, 191; education, 117; farms, 129; printing, 152; emancipation, 189
New Yorker, 85
Newburyport, Mass., 44, 50; *Herald,* 100–101
Newcomb, Simon (1835–1909); apprentice botanic physician to Dr. Foshay, Moncton, New Brunswick; astronomer, 35, 102
newspapers, 14, 20, 152, 153, 203–4; exchange, 81; publishing, 146, 149; boys, 205
North, Simeon (b. 1765); apprentice pistolmaker; armorer, 65

North Carolina, 184–85
Northbridge, Mass., 64
Northfield, Mass., 99–100
Nott, Samuel, Jr., 115
Nova Scotia, 19, 35

O'Connor, Rachel, 177
Ohio, 152, 176
One Thousand Valuable Secrets, 33
Oneida Institute, 120
Oregon, 128, 172
orphans, 46, 91–95, 120, 128, 139
Otter, William (b. 1799); English-born
    apprentice plasterer to Kenwith
    King, New York; journeyman, Pa.,
    46–48
overtime, 73–74, 85–86, 93, 136
Owen, John, 173
Owen, Robert, 87

panic of 1819, 30–31, 87, 121
A Parent's Advice for His Family, 37
Parsons, Albert R. (1848–87); appren-
    tice printer to Willard Richardson,
    Galveston, Tex.; labor leader, 198
Parsons, Francis; apprentice, Boston,
    123
paternalism, *see* fathers
patriotism, 170, 175, 200–201; *see*
    military
pay, *see* wages
Peale, Benjamin Franklin (1795–1870);
    apprentice textile machinist, Wil-
    mington, Del.; millowner, 62, 63,
    98–99
Peale, Charles Linneaus (1794–1832);
    apprentice printer to Fry &
    Kammerer, Philadelphia, 98–99
Peale, Charles Willson (1741–1827);
    apprentice saddler to Nathan
    Waters, Annapolis; artist, 98–99
Pearce, B. W.; apprentice printer,
    Providence, 152
Peck, Mr.; printer, 105
Pennsylvania: farms, 68, 81; education,
    117; iron, 140, 142; emancipation,
    188–89; court case, 203; laws, 205
Peoria, Ill., *Daily Transcript*, 149
Perkins, Rev. Nathan, 38

Pestalozzi, Johann, 114, 116
Petersburg, Va., 184
pewter, 65
Philadelphia: colonial, 5, 7, 14–15;
    Revolution, 16; printing, 25, 29, 43,
    151, 172–75, 196; wages, 26, 69;
    wealth, 26; religion, 41; rowdiness,
    44–46; runaways, 47–48; apprentice
    library, 55, 121–22; seamstresses, 57;
    textiles, 61; machine shops, 62–63,
    141, 199–200; glass works, 74; trial,
    87; girls, 110; Franklin Institute,
    121; orphans, 139; iron, 142; printers
    union, 154; evening schools, 164–65;
    fire companies, 167; gangs, 167;
    street Christmas, 169; politics, 169–
    70; *Inquirer*, 196; *North American*,
    196
Phyfe, Duncan (1768–1854); Scots-born
    apprentice cabinetmaker, Albany,
    N.Y.; furnituremaker, New York, 25
Pittsburgh, 154
planters, 77–78, 177–80, 182, 185, 186,
    203–4
plastering, 46–48
politics, 23–24, 36–38, 57, 101, 169–71
Pomeroy, Marcus M. ("Brick") (1833–
    96); apprentice blacksmith to his
    uncle, rural Pa.; apprentice printer
    to Thomas Messenger, Corning,
    N.Y.; journalist, 176
Poole, John Morton (1812–79);
    apprentice machinist, Matteawan,
    N.Y.; machine shop owner,
    Wilmington, Del., 63–64, 99, 116,
    169
poor boys, 3–4, 19, 26, 30, 91–95, 124–
    30, 133, 184–85
Poor Law, 4
Porter, William T., 85
Portland, Me., 121, 137, 149
Portsmouth, N.H., *Journal*, 193
potteries, 131
Poughkeepsie, N.Y., 191
poverty, 78, 124–30, 133
Powderly, Terence V. (1849–1924);
    apprentice machinist to Delaware
    and Hudson Canal Co., Carbondale,
    Pa.; labor leader, 206

Pratt, W. W. and L. A.; publishers, 149

Prentiss, John (1778–1873); apprentice
printer to Thomas Adams, Boston;
printer, 42–43

Presbyterians, 102

A Present for an Apprentice, 55

printing, 6–8, 18–20, 25–29, 37, 42,
48–49, 98–101, 105–6, 109, 130, 136–
37, 171–76, 190, 194–98, 203–4; typesetting, 11–13, 76, 84, 86, 146, 150,
172, 174, 196; apprentices, 13–14,
152–54; balls, 13, 76; presswork, 13,
76, 77, 82, 85–86, 105, 146–47;
capital lacking, 29, 152; unions, 30,
90–96, 154–56, 201–2, 205; crisis, 76–
96; ink rollers, 76; political ties, 77–
78, 82, 91–93; as an art, 78; drinking,
78; steam presses, 86, 146, 149, 150–
51; stereotyping, 86, 150; transformation to an industry, 146–54; press
manufacturing, 149; manuals, 150;
country shops, 151, 193–94; statistics,
153–54, 155; tramps, 154, 156, 193–
97; blacks, 181, 204; immigrants, 196

progress, 58, 174

Protestants, 167, 170

Providence, R.I., 64, 121; *Daily Advertiser,* 152; *Journal,* 152

publishing, 77–78, 152

puddling, 142–43; *see* ironworking

Putnam, Gen. Israel, 18

Quakers, 55, 98, 100, 122

quarrels, 11, 137, 138–39, 172, 188

race, *see* blacks; slaves

radicals, 87–88

Raleigh, N.C., 70

Reed, Henry, 65

Reed & Barton, 67

Rees, Dr., 33

reform, 123, 130, 139–40, 163–66, 205;
conservatives oppose, 115–16;
manual labor schools, 119–20;
juvenile delinquents, 126–28; statistics, 211–12; *see* education

Reinhart, Amelia, 173

relations: apprentice with master, 10–

11, 14, 20, 39, 42–43, 45–46, 52–55,
69, 70, 72–73, 80, 84, 100–104, 107,
109, 128, 135–39, 171, 176, 180, 202,
206; with father, 27–29, 37, 41, 69,
83, 161, 190–94, 199; with apprentices, 41, 79, 106–9, 161, 166, 171–73,
188; with master's wife, 42–43, 49,
72, 82, 102–3, 108, 194; with journeymen, 63, 104–6, 140, 144, 152, 186–
88, 195; strained, 89–90; with foreman, 90, 141, 172; with parents, 97–
101; with girls, 107, 109–12; with
guardian, 137; with family, 176, 191,
194–97; with slaveholders, 185–86;
with friends, 194; with mother, 194;
see families; fathers

religion, 38–42, 72, 97, 98, 101, 102,
115, 116, 119–20, 174, 192, 209;
ministers, 26, 158; books for children, 40–41; catechism, 40; family
devotion, 40; Sunday schools, 40–41,
186; evangelical, 41–42, 83, 163;
escorting a girl to church, 110;
missionaries, 128; denominations,
167, 169, 170, 186; masters, 179–80

republicanism, 36–38, 46, 87–88, 116–
17, 120; pride, 42–48, 55–56

respectability, 134, 165–66

responsibility, 74–75, 94, 99, 115, 122,
209; advice books, 158–63

Revere, Paul (1735–1818); apprentice
silversmith to his father, Boston;
silversmith, 23

revivals, 38, 42

Revolution, American, 16–24, 36, 58,
65, 114, 205

Reynolds, Joseph, 27

Rhode Island, 61

Richards, Arthur Wherry (b. 1832);
apprentice cabinetmaker to Solomon
Howard, Gallipolis, Ohio; cabinetmaker, Iowa, 176

Richmond, Va., 136, 184; court case,
52

Riddell, William, 67

riots, 50–51, 165

rituals, 39–40

Roach, John (1813–87); Irish-born
apprentice iron molder to Howell

Works, Monmouth Co., N.J.; ship-
builder, New York, 104–5
Robertson, James; currier, 138–39
Robinson, Solon (1803–1880); appren-
tice carpenter to his uncle, William
Bottom, Lisbon, Conn.; journalist,
60
Robinson, William S. (1818–76);
apprentice printer to G. F. Bemis,
Concord, Mass.; journalist, 98
Robinson Crusoe, 122
Rochester, N.Y., 73, 135
Rogers, John, Jr. (1829–1904); apprentice machinist to Amoskeag mill,
Manchester, N.H.; sculptor, 111, 141
romance, 107, 109–12, 134, 173
romanticism, 104
Round Hill school, 114, 115
rowdyism, 45, 100, 107, 202
Roxbury, Mass., 17
Rudd, Rev. John C., 159–60, 161, 162
runaways, 5, 14–15, 17–18, 19, 48–50,
70, 81, 89–92, 95, 100, 138, 139, 153,
159–60, 186, 195, 200, 205; enlist, 16,
20–23, 198, 199, 205; statistics, 30;
advertisements, 48–50, 70; penalties
increased, 51; unions oppose, 154;
slaves, 183–84
rural life, 9–10, 99–100, 109, 120, 128,
176; *see* farmer-craftsmen; farms
Rush, Benjamin, 114, 115
Russell, Benjamin (1761–1845);
apprentice printer to Isaiah Thomas,
Worcester, Mass.; publisher, Boston,
17–20, 22–23, 26
Russell, John; stonemason, 17–19
Rust, J. P.; tailor, 137

Saco-Lowell shops, 64–66
Sacramento, Calif., 175
saddling, 70, 71
Safford, Mr., 137
Saint Crispin, 134
St. Louis, Mo., 194, 195, 196; *Missouri
Republican,* 149
Salem, Mass., 23, 121
Salem, N.C., 16, 69, 89, 136
San Francisco, 172; *Evening Journal,*
174

Savannah, Ga., 5
Savery, Thomas H. (1837–1910);
apprentice machinist to Bancroft &
Sellers, Philadelphia; manufacturer,
Wilmington, Del., 141
sawmilling, 69
Sawyer, Philetus; sawmill worker, 69–
70
Schenectady, N.Y., 190, 199
schoolmasters, 17, 70, 191
schools, *see* education
Scotland: immigration, 25
Scott, Sir Walter; *Waverley,* 122
seamen, 3, 7, 172, 173, 188
Second Great Awakening, *see* religion
self-improvement, 160–61, 174, 205
Sellers, George Escol (1808–99);
apprentice machinist to his father,
Philadelphia; machine shop owner,
62–63
servants, 112, 130, 186; indentured, 9
Servoss, Thomas C.; apprentice machinist, Matteawan, N.Y.; textile
mill manager, 63
Sewall, Stephen, 27
Seward, William Henry, 117
Shaftsbury, Vt., 38
Sherman, Roger (1721–93); apprentice
shoemaker, Conn.; politician, 23
ship caulking, 182; slaves, 186–88
Shippen, Edward, 52
shoemaking, 6, 9, 26, 59–60, 100, 131,
134–35, 142, 178; trials, 87; slaves,
185–86
Shrewsbury Polytechnic Institute, 120
silversmithing, 6, 25, 131
skills, *see* labor
Slater, Samuel (1768–1835); apprentice
textile manufacturer, England;
manufacturer, R.I., 61
slaves, 9, 36, 49, 77–78, 123, 139, 177–
90, 194; emancipation, 188–90; *see*
blacks
Smith, Adam, 87
Smith, James Lindsey (b. ca. 1815);
slave apprentice shoemaker to John
Langsdon, Fairfield, Va.; shoemaker
and Methodist minister, Norwich,
Conn., 185–86

Smith, Seba; publisher, 149
Smith, Solomon F. (1801–69); apprentice printer to Elihu Stout, Vincennes, Ind.; actor, 49
Smith, William; iron molder, 102
Snow, Mrs., 41
social classes, *see* classes
social control, 180–81, 190
soldiers, *see* military
Sonora, Calif., *Herald*, 172
Sons of Temperance, 164
South, 177–79, 181–82; colonial, 9; planters, 68; education, 114
South America, 196
South Bend, Ind., 171
South Carolina, 182–83, 198
Southwick, Solomon; printer, 122
Spalding, Henry Harmon (1803–74); apprentice farmer to Andrew J. Broat, Steuben Co., N.Y.; missionary, Ore., 128
Spear, Samuel S.; apprentice, Boston, 165
Spirit of the Times, 85
Spottsylvania C.H., Va., 204
Springfield, Mass., 65–67, 190
Springfield Armory, 66
statistics: socioeconomic, 5, 181, 201; wages, 26, 29–31; poor boys, 30, 211–12; runaways, 30; apprentices, 208; indentures, 211
status, *see* classes
Statute of Artificers, 4
steam engines, 140–41; railroads, 142; puddling, 145; printing, 146, 149–51; banned in Charleston, 151
steamboat pilots, 197
Sterrett, Joseph M.; printer, 81–83
Sterrett, Mrs. Joseph M., 82, 102
Steuben County, N.Y., 128
Stillman, William James (b. 1828); apprentice machinist to his father, Schenectady, N.Y.; journalist, 190–91
Story, Francis V., 85
Stout, Elihu; printer, 49
Stout, Mrs. Elihu, 49
Stradivari, Antonio; violinmaker, 33
Strang, James Jesse; farm laborer, 58
street Christmas, 169

strikes, 89, 95, 135, 141, 146, 154, 184; apprentices, 16, 109; strikebreakers, 155, 172, 202
Stuart, Mrs., 64
Studebaker, John Mohler (1833–1917); apprentice wagonmaker to his brothers, South Bend, Ind.; wagon manufacturer, 171
success, *see* advice books
Sunday schools, *see* religion
Swartz, George W. (b. 1817); apprentice carpenter, near Buffalo, N.Y.; journeyman, 60
Sylvis, William H. (1828–1869); apprentice iron molder, rural Pa.; labor leader, 142, 144, 145, 146, 201

tailoring, 6, 26, 34, 70, 108, 137, 208
Talbott & Brother, ironworks, 136
tanning, 9, 48, 58–59, 142, 191–93
Taos, N.M., 70
tariffs, 57, 65, 87
Taunton, Mass., 65
Taylor, Charles H. (1846–1921); apprentice printer, Boston; publisher, 198, 201
technology: innovation, 33–36, 86, 144; transfer to U.S., 142
temperance, *see* liquor
Tennessee, 70
Terrell, Uncle George, 203
Texas, 189
textiles: mills, 60, 61–65, 69, 73, 140, 141
theaters, 49, 130, 159, 161, 195
Thomas, Alexander, Jr., 27
Thomas, Ebenezer Smith (1775–1845); apprentice printer to his uncle, Isaiah Thomas, Worcester, Mass.; printer, Charleston and Cincinnati, 26, 27
Thomas, Isaiah (1749–1831); apprentice printer to Zechariah Fowle, Boston; printer, Worcester, Mass., 18–20, 22–23, 26–29, 40, 121, 180
Thomas, Mrs. Isaiah, 72
Thurston, Brown (1814–1900); apprentice printer to John Allen, Lowell, Mass.; printer, Portland, Me., 77

Tocqueville, Alexis de, 55
Todd, John, 160, 161–62
traditions, 90, 124, 166–67, 176
travels, 193–94
Treadwell, Abraham; apprentice printer to John Cotton, Jr., Boston, 106, 107
Tredegar Iron Works, 184
trials, *see* laws
Troy, N.Y., 202
Tucker, William, 34
Tullar, Martin, 38–39
Turner, William; ironworker, 142
Twain, Mark, *see* Clemens, Samuel Langhorne
typesetting, *see* printing
Tyson, Job R., 122, 139

Uncle Remus, 203
unemployment, 25, 64, 77, 83–85, 91, 131–33, 138, 173–75, 204–6
U.S. Telegraph, 91, 95

Van Winkle, Cornelius; printing manual, 150
Vaux, Roberts, 122
Vermont, 78, 80, 81, 132
village life, 80, 99–100, 102, 110–11, 120, 132, 137–38
Vincennes, Ind., *Western Sun,* 49
violence, 64, 124–26, 169, 202
Virginia, 63, 185–86, 198
Voice of Industry, 134

wage rates, 64, 65, 69, 73, 81, 85, 91–92, 129, 136, 137, 142, 144, 145, 152, 155, 160, 161, 172, 174, 178, 181, 188, 194, 195, 197, 198, 199, 201
wages: journeymen, 8, 26, 146; apprentices, 14, 16, 20, 64–70, 198, 199, 207; master seizes, 21–22; cash, 25, 29–31, 47, 64–75, 79, 84, 92, 119, 129, 132, 136–37, 142, 174, 195, 196, 202; statistics, 26, 29–31, 131; piece rates, 66, 132; unpaid, 85, 105, 207; cuts, 133, 146; fines, 138–39; slaves, 181, 182, 185–86, 188; *see* economics; wealth
wagonmaking, 99, 140, 171

Waldo, Albigance; physician, 27–29
Waldo, Elisha H. (1773–1801); apprentice printer to Isaiah Thomas, Worcester, Mass.; printer, 27–29
Wales: immigrants, 142
Wall, Caleb Arnold (1820–98); apprentice printer to *Spy,* Worcester, Mass.; journeyman, Worcester, 99
Wall, Joseph Southwick (1817–42); apprentice printer, Worcester, Mass.; journeyman, 99
Walpole, N.H., 26
Walton, Charlie, 173
War of 1812, 30
Ware, Nathaniel, 139
Washington, George, 170
Washington, D.C.: Institute, 91–95; printers union, 154; wage rates, 155; newspaper boys, 205
Washingtonian, 37
Watts, Joseph, 34
Waukegan, Ill., 149
wealth: colonial Boston, 5–6; inequality increases, 124; per capita, 131; relative, 134; South, 181; rising, 201; *see* economics; wages
weaving, 33–34, 61, 131
Weed, Thurlow (1797–1882); apprentice printer to five different offices, upstate N.Y.; publisher, Albany, 81, 85–86, 151
West, John T.; publisher, 84–85
West Chester, Pa., *Record,* 171–72
Westinghouse, Albert, 199
Westinghouse, George, Jr. (1846–1914); apprentice machinist to his father, Schenectady, N.Y.; inventor, 199, 201
Westinghouse, John, 199
whaling, 77
Whigs, 82, 170
Whiskey Rebellion, 68
whites, in South, 178–83
Whitin Works, 64
Whiting, Gordon, 204
Whitney, Eli, 65
wigmaking, 21
Wilkes-Barre, Pa., 83
Williams, Mrs. William, 72, 102

Williams, W. F.; printer, 204

Willis, Nathaniel P. (1806–67); apprentice printer to his father, Boston; editor, 112

Wilmington, Del., 62

Wilmington, N.C., 184

Wilson, Henry (1812–75); apprentice farmer to William Knight, rural N.H.; apprentice shoemaker, Natick, Mass.; politician, 111, 127–28

women, 109–12, 123; seamstresses, 57; shoemaking, 59; textiles, 61; printing, 86, 150, 151, 154, 155; mocked, 169; influence, 194

Wood, William; apprentice machinist, Taunton, Mass., 65

Wood, William; merchant, 121

Woodstock, 28

Worcester, Leonard (1767–1846); apprentice printer to Isaiah Thomas, Worcester, Mass.; minister, 26, 29, 31

Worcester, Mass., 18–20, 22–23, 26–29, 121

work: hours, 63, 89, 141, 205; seasonal, 69, 83, 91, 129; terms, 69–70; job interviews, 81, 84; statistics, 153–54; race, 178, 181; skills, *see* labor

Wright, Frances, 87, 120

Wright, Henry Clarke (1797–1870); apprentice hatter to David G. Bright, Chenango Co., N.Y.; Congregational minister, 41, 97–98, 101–2, 108

Yarmouth, Me., 137

Yates, J. D., 34

Young, Sallie, 173

youths: father's right to labor, 10, 191–92; attitudes, 24, 50, 58, 205–6; advice books, 158–63; alienation, 170–71; lack respect, 53, 208